'Church planting has received a lot of attenti[on]
caused some people to think it is a new phe[nomenon]
many of the books on church planting ar[e]
biblical theology. John Valentine has written a timely book that offers a
biblical and theological foundation for church planting in today's complex
and challenging world. If you are looking for a fresh introduction to
church planting for today's world that is theologically sound, while at the
same time practical, this book is for you!'
Revd Dr Winfield Bevins, author of *Liturgical Mission*

'Anchored in biblical and theological truth, and reflections on John's
many years of practical experience, this book underpins the intertwined nature of mission and church planting while infusing a fuel
of encouragement and inspiration to the existing fire. A vital companion for the contemporary church leader and church planter. It is a
must-read.'
Revd Dr Girma Bishaw, Director and founder at Gratitude initiative,
City Catalyst for the London Project and part of the pastoral team at
Reality Church London

'I was privileged to attend the church planting course that John helped
lead in 2017, so I am delighted to see that he has set out here the funda-
mentals for those who are setting out on, reflecting on, or seeking to
understand the church-planting journey. Church planting is without a
doubt the most exciting and challenging thing I have been involved in,
and John brings theological depth and sound biblical knowledge to the
task, as well as being a sure and experienced guide. I wholeheartedly
commend this book.'
Fran Carabott, pioneer minister and leader of St Margaret's Community
Church plant in Southsea, Portsmouth

'I am delighted that John has written this full and robust theology of
church planting. It will give confidence to both trainers and practitioners
to continue this much-needed movement in the church.'
Archie Coates, vicar, Holy Trinity Brompton

'Church planting has been perceived as a missional strategy that prioritizes
numerical growth over theological rigour. Valentine responds to this
criticism with scholarly conviction and the passion of an experienced

practitioner. Through careful analysis and thorough research, he locates the impulse of church replication in the very warp and weft of the biblical narrative, not to mention some of the core concerns of Christian ecclesiology. This book will be an indispensable resource for any church planter or student of the discipline.'
Fr Justin Dodd, church planter and vicar of St Barnabas Ealing

'John Valentine's theological gifts and his personal experience as a church planter make him uniquely qualified to write this book. John knows what he is writing about.'
Nicky Gumbel, former vicar of Holy Trinity Brompton

'For centuries the church was so wedded to Christendom that church planting was rarely considered – and, if it was, it was often misunderstood or even seen as illegitimate. As John so wonderfully shows, this view has been largely turned over by a wonderful wave of new and varied new church-planting activity. This book gives us exactly what is now needed – a significant contribution to the theological underpinnings of this most biblical and missional expression of the gospel.'
Paul Harcourt, National Leader, New Wine England

'John Valentine has given us a wonderful gift! Church planting is all the rage these days, but few books anchor the practice within sound biblical theology. *Jesus, the Church and the Mission of God* offers us precisely that. Written in a highly accessible prose, Valentine situates church planting firmly within God's mission, with timely reflections for what this means for the church of Jesus Christ in our contemporary day. The book reads as if talking with John Valentine: kind, wise and filled with poignant insights. It's a must-read for anyone involved in church planting.'
Gregg Okesson, Provost, Asbury Theological Seminary, and author of *A Public Missiology: How Local Churches Witness to a Complex World* (2020)

'This book is that rare combination of theological, practical, thoughtful and challenging. It will make you think – and do! The author's passion for God, the church and for people shines through. Any prospective church planter – and their objectors – would do well to read, reflect and respond.'
Dave Richards, Rector at St Paul's and St George's Edinburgh

'John has provided us with a helpful and clear examination of some of the biblical and theological foundations for church planting. His biblical focus calls all constituencies to come back to the call of Christ in his word and to see where it leads. This is an important reference work for church planters, to equip our minds and hearts, even as we offer our hands in the service of Christ's kingdom.'
Revd Dr Jason Roach, founding pastor of The Bridge church Battersea and Director of Ministries at London City Mission

'*Jesus, the Church and the Mission of God: A biblical theology of church planting* is a robust exploration of church planting that can't be missed by anyone wanting to think deeply about the mission of God. John reminds us that church growth and planting isn't a side hobby of the Christian faith but a central and practical pursuit of the gospel. If we are to see the church move into a period when revitalization is happening and the church is growing, then church planting is going to be a major part of this work.

John Valentine gives us here a convincing theology and outworking that will help the church grapple with what is next. This book will become a central text for all those in seminary, training, dreaming of planting or wanting to understand the broad mission of God.'
The Revd Cris Rogers, church planter, urban theologian, chair of Spring Harvest and director of Making Disciples (wearemakingdisicples.com)

'John's gift to us in this book is valuable indeed. He is a scholar, a practitioner, a pray-er, and a man who cares deeply about people finding life in Jesus. There is so much in here: read it with a pen in hand!'
The Rt Revd Mark Tanner, Bishop of Chester, Chair of the Church of England's Ministry Council

'Church planting has become an inescapable and sometimes controversial part of the life of the church in recent decades. Yet it has often pursued pragmatic approaches rather than reflecting deeply on theological themes that might help strengthen, develop and direct the work of church planters. John Valentine's book is a big step in the right direction, towards a richer biblical and theological grounding for this vital aspect of the church's mission.'
Bishop Graham Tomlin, Director of the Centre for Cultural Witness, Lambeth Palace

'John Valentine has put us in his debt with this wide-ranging study of biblical and theological foundations and practices of church planting. Covering the Old Testament, the Gospels, Acts and the Pauline letters, his study combines thoughtful reading of Scripture with persistent attention to the implications of his findings for church planting in the Western world today.

He draws on good scholarship in his writing, providing depth to his discussions. In addition, his more theologically focused chapters on church, mission and God as Trinity provide coherence and reflective thinking about church planting in relation to mission and the nature of the Christian God. This is a book many will want to read. It moves well beyond the rather superficial "how to" nature of much previous writing on church planting to root this vital topic in the nature of God, mission and the church. Read it – it will do you and your church good!'

Steve Walton, Professor of New Testament and Senior Research Fellow, Trinity College, Bristol

JESUS, THE CHURCH AND THE MISSION OF GOD

John Valentine is the Dean of the Local Ministry Programme in the Anglican Diocese of Guildford, where he trains lay and ordained church leaders for mission and ministry. He is also a Gregory Associate with the Gregory Centre for Church Multiplication, London, where he trained church planters and their teams for a number of years. He was on staff at Holy Trinity Brompton, from where he planted St George's Church in Holborn, which went on to plant two other churches in London. John has a Doctor of Ministry in church planting from Asbury Theological Seminary. He is married to Catherine, and they have two teenage daughters. He loves reading (theology, biography, and contemporary British and American fiction) and pretty much any sport with a ball.

JESUS, THE CHURCH AND THE MISSION OF GOD

A biblical theology of church planting

John Valentine

APOLLOS

APOLLOS (an imprint of Inter-Varsity Press, England)
36 Causton Street, London SW1P 4ST, England
Email: ivp@ivpbooks.com
Website: www.ivpbooks.com

First published 2023

British Library Cataloguing-in-Publication Data
A catalogue record for this book is available from the British Library.

Paperback ISBN: 978–1–78974–427–9
eBook ISBN: 978–1–78974–428–6

Set in Minion Pro 11.5/15pt
Typeset in Great Britain by CRB Associates, Potterhanworth, Lincolnshire
Printed and bound in Great Britain by TJ Books Limited, Padstow, Cornwall

Produced on paper from sustainable sources

Inter-Varsity Press publishes Christian books that are true to the Bible and that communicate the gospel, develop discipleship and strengthen the church for its mission in the world.

IVP originated within the Inter-Varsity Fellowship, now the Universities and Colleges Christian Fellowship, a student movement connecting Christian Unions in universities and colleges throughout Great Britain, and a member movement of the International Fellowship of Evangelical Students. Website: www.uccf.org.uk. That historic association is maintained, and all senior IVP staff and committee members subscribe to the UCCF Basis of Faith.

For Winfield Bevins, my teacher in church planting, and Christian Selvaratnam, Graham Singh and Ric Thorpe, my fellow pilgrims, who are so much further ahead on this journey – friends and brothers all

Contents

Contents

Part II

IS THERE A THEOLOGY
OF CHURCH PLANTING?

Foreword

'Church planting' is not a term you will find in the Bible, but its practice and impact are riven into the pages of the New Testament. Its foundations are throughout the Scriptures.

Most church planters I know draw on the Scriptures intuitively as they go to new places to preach the gospel to new people, and find themselves starting new congregations and churches in new and renewed ways. They are primarily practitioners, and often break out of traditional ways of doing church. When this happens, leaders of older churches and centuries-old traditions often ask the question, 'What is the theology of all this?' Sometimes this question is a diversion, asked out of fear to throw a new church practice off into the long grass. But for most who ask this question it is a fundamental one, seeking to explore the foundations, and indeed assumptions, of practices that might well challenge or even enhance existing ways of doing church.

As church planting grows in practice across every denomination and tradition of the church, the need for a deeper look at its theology is becoming ever more important. Moving beyond intuitive church planting to deeply, theologically informed church planting can only give this extraordinary and exciting movement more depth and momentum. But who can do this vital task? It needs people who have planted churches in practice, who know what is involved, as well as people who know how to do the deeper reflective work, digging deep into the Scriptures and exploring the essential theological landscape.

I can't think of anyone better to do this than John Valentine, and I am delighted that he has stepped up to do this. I have known John for more than twenty years since our days on staff together at Holy Trinity Brompton (HTB). More recently, we have worked even more closely at the Gregory Centre for Church Multiplication in resourcing church planting in London, England and beyond.

John is an experienced practitioner. He planted in Holborn with a team from HTB, revitalizing a Church of England parish. From there he trained and sent two other church planters and teams to other parishes in London. As with most church leaders I know, it has not always been plain sailing. John is familiar with all the ups and downs of church planting on the ground.

He is an effective educator. Increasingly, his focus has become the theological formation of church planters. John hosted the Church Planting Course that we pioneered in the Diocese of London, which has become a national resource. He had a particular role helping church planters think theologically about what they were doing and why they were doing it.

John is also a thoughtful theologian. We both studied for doctorates in church planting at Asbury Theological Seminary. This was a wonderful experience, enabling us to dive deeply into theological waters in the context of a global cohort of church planters. Of the two of us, John was always the better theologian and his doctoral work focused on the theological training of church planters. This work has enabled him to speak into national conversations around issues of theology and church planting, theological education and how we can form church leaders for mission in our own contexts throughout this country.

It is for these reasons that I am so excited John has written this book. He handles Scripture with great care and precision. He positions church planting within its key theological landmarks. He shows how the Bible speaks with such power and clarity to church planting. It is an exhilarating read.

This book will be of great help to three groups of people. First, church-planting practitioners will find it helpful to know the secure biblical and theological ground on which they are building. It will give them confidence on the one hand and clarity on the other.

Second, it will be a great resource for those who teach and train church planters. For example, those in theological colleges will find it a staple for their reading lists in mission and evangelism modules, as well as those focused more specifically on church planting. More widely, all those who have input into the formation, training and support of church planters will find it fresh and clear. I hope it will play a major role in the increasing corpus of theological work currently being done in church planting.

Third, those who lead church-planting movements or who have senior positions within their networks or denominations will find the book helpful in giving a robust theological rationale for the vital place of church planting in their plans and strategies.

I commend this book to you, with the prayer that it will lead to an increase in church planting, to healthier and even more vibrant new churches in various contexts, and to the growth and impact of the church in the world.

Ric Thorpe, Bishop of Islington

Acknowledgments

This book came out of my doctoral studies at Asbury Theological Seminary, although the subject material is very different. It was in the research for that degree that the need for more in-depth biblical and theological work for church planters became apparent – for a confidence and health in church-planting practice, and for the credibility of the church-planting movement. I found myself drawn more and more to the depth and richness of the scriptural material, and its theological implications. I hope this book is a contribution to that continuing and deepening biblical and theological work.

That doctoral experience at Asbury was a joy, and deeply formational for me. I am grateful to all who made it possible – Winfield Bevins, Ellen Marmon, Gregg Okesson, and the phenomenal generosity of the seminary through the Beeson Foundation – and all with whom I was privileged to share on that doctoral journey, especially William Chaney, Christian Selvaratnam, Graham Singh, Tom Tanner and Ric Thorpe. It was a great joy. Latterly, it has been a privilege to host Asbury's Doctor of Ministry in church planting in the UK and Europe with the Gregory Centre; many thanks to the amazing cohort who are blazing the way in this country.

It was through the gracious invitation of Sandy Millar and Nicky Gumbel at Holy Trinity Brompton (HTB) that my own involvement in church planting, as a practitioner, began. Those two years at HTB were formational and inspirational for Catherine and me. We loved every minute! And it was a privilege to plant St George's, Holborn, with all our ups and downs, and, in turn, to give away planting leaders and teams into Islington and the City of London. Many thanks to Paul and Bonnie Zaphiriou and David Ingall, and to many other friends and colleagues with whom Catherine and I shared in the leadership of those exciting days.

Special thanks to all involved at the Gregory Centre for Church Multiplication (CCX). Under the generous and liberating leadership of

Ric Thorpe, it was exciting and rewarding to work with Andy Blacknell, Toria Gray and Sharon Whitmarsh on the Church Planting Course, and a privilege to work with many church planters and their teams over the years, in all kinds of contexts and from many different church traditions. The wider CCX team were unfailingly encouraging, and a joy to work with, especially Andrea Bleakley, Ros Hoare, H. Miller, John McGinley and Helen Shannon.

The writing of the book was a real journey of excitement and discovery. To spend hours deeply in the Scriptures was hard work, but a total joy. Many thanks to all those with whom I had stimulating and informative conversations, as well as opportunities to teach in dioceses and in theological colleges, especially Will Foulger and Philip Plyming at Cranmer Hall; Andrew and Sarah Dunlop and Paul Weston at Ridley Hall; Ed Olsworth-Peter, Hannah Steele, Graham Tomlin and Russell Winfield at St Mellitus College in London; and Michael Lloyd and Justyn Terry at Wycliffe Hall. Special thanks to Paul Bradbury, Chigor Chike, Simon Cuff, Paula Gooder, Tom Greggs, Jamie Hawkey, Hannah Steele, Ric Thorpe and Graham Tomlin for our stimulating ecclesiological conversations. Several scholars were kind enough to read chapters and sections of the book; I am grateful to Andy Byers, Mike Higton, Brian Hughes, Michael Moynagh and Steve Walton for their time, expertise and engagement – the mistakes remain my own.

The IVP team have been a pleasure to work with. Many thanks to Elizabeth Neep for our initial conversations, to Tom Creedy for his judicious and encouraging editing, and to Joy Tibbs and Mollie Barker for all their phenomenal work.

I have dedicated this book to Winfield Bevins, Christian Selvaratnam, Graham Singh and Ric Thorpe. Your friendship, example, encouragement and inspiration mean a great deal to me. Thank you for the challenge, stimulus and fun along the way.

Lastly, I want to record my thanks and love for my wife Catherine, and daughters Ellie and Rosie, who have, between them, lived church planting in word and deed along with me for over twenty years.

John Valentine

Abbreviations

ANTC	Abingdon New Testament Commentaries
BNTC	Black's New Testament Commentaries
BST	Bible Speaks Today
CMWE	Commission on World Mission and Evangelism
ESV	English Standard Version
ET	English translation
EvQ	*Evangelical Quarterly*
HTB	Holy Trinity Brompton
ICC	International Critical Commentary
JBL	*Journal of Biblical Literature*
LCC	Library of Christian Classics
MSG	*The Message*
NIBC	New International Bible Commentary
NICNT	New International Commentary on the New Testament
NIGTC	New International Greek Testament Commentary
NRSV	New Revised Standard Version
NTE	*New Testament for Everyone*
NTL	New Testament Library
REB	Revised English Bible
TNIV	Today's New International Version
TNTC	Tyndale New Testament Commentaries
WCC	World Council of Churches

Introduction

Church planting in England in recent years

Church planting in England (and beyond) has an increasingly high profile and is of growing importance to the strategies of churches, denominations and regional mission plans. Researcher David Goodhew wrote in 2012:

> Based on a range of studies, it is likely that over 5,000 new churches have been started in Britain in the 30 years since 1980 – probably significantly more . . . To put these numbers into some kind of scale, the number of new churches started since 1980 is substantially greater than the total number of Roman Catholic churches in England and equivalent to one third of all Church of England churches.[1]

George Lings traces the acceleration of church planting from 1967 to 1998, seeing at least 28,000 attending an Anglican church plant by 1998, 'equivalent to attendance across a fair sized diocese'.[2] Following the *Breaking New Ground* report from the Church of England in 1994, church planting had become a major element in Anglican thinking and practice.

This was accelerated by the publication of the groundbreaking *Mission-Shaped Church* in 2004, which had a seismic effect, certainly in the Church of England, and more widely afield too. By the time of the report, the then Archbishop of Canterbury, Rowan Williams, could write in his introduction that the Church of England was 'at a real watershed'.[3] *Mission-Shaped Church* tipped the Church of England firmly into the new territory of legitimizing church planting as mainstream to Anglican missionary

---

[1] Goodhew 2012: 7–8.
[2] Lings 2012: 168.
[3] Archbishops' Council of the Church of England 2004: v.

thinking and practice. The report followed Bob Hopkins in defining church planting as the discipline of 'creating new communities of Christian faith as part of the mission of God to express God's kingdom in every geographic and cultural context'.[4]

The report began with a clear-eyed look at the impact of consumerism on British society, seeing it as nothing less than a missionary call. Following the principle of the incarnation, the Anglican Church in the UK was to see itself as being with people wherever they were, both *where* (in terms of geography) and *how* (in their networks). After a summary of the recent history of church planting, it argued for a more contextually aware approach to planting in the future, seeing it as a dynamic process, consonant with the core Church of England value of being a church for the whole nation, and fitting for a context that was once more essentially missionary, not pastoral.

The heart of the report is a long chapter which looks at twelve different forms of new church, of which only one was described as a 'traditional church plant'. The emphasis was on stories and examples in practice. The methodology was deliberate: to promote a diversity of incarnational practice and to produce not so much a 'how to' book as a range of approaches, rooted in solid missional theology. The theology followed, arguing for the impact of the Trinity, the incarnation, the work of the Spirit, and eschatology, as these bear upon church planting and fresh expressions of church.[5] After two practical chapters, including a methodology for contextualizing planting and fresh expressions, training, and the place of bishops, the report closed with some specific recommendations. These revolved around strategies beyond the parochial, and measures concerning leadership and training.

The report has been summarized at some length because it has proved decisive and influential in making developments in church planting and fresh expressions of church possible, at least within the Church of England.

---

[4] Ibid. xi.

[5] The term 'Fresh Expressions of church' was first used in the *Mission-Shaped Church* report of 2004. The report defines the term as '[embracing] two realities: existing churches that are seeking to renew or redirect what they already have, and others who are intentionally sending out planting groups to discover what will emerge when the gospel is immersed in the mission context' (Archbishops' Council of the Church of England 2004: 34). See Croft 2008: ch. 1, for more discussion, and Lings 2012 for a useful historical overview.

It has introduced a whole new vocabulary, and, in some circles at least, it is proving a culture-changer. George Lings makes a list of 'what might change, for mission reasons':

- Church need not stay inside parish boundaries.
- Church need not only be congregational.
- Church need not be on Sunday.
- Church can happen outside dedicated buildings.
- Church need not be led by clergy.
- Church can be for segments of the population.
- Church is about more than public worship and attending it. Growing quality of community and serving others in mission are of equal priority.[6]

This list gives a sense of the seismic potential the report had to shift the ecclesial and missionary culture of the Church of England. The direction of travel has remained the same since 2004, and has accelerated. At a conference in June 2018, Bishop Ric Thorpe (the bishop with responsibility for church planting in the Diocese of London and increasingly with a national remit) said that in 2013 the dioceses of the Church of England pledged to plant 100 new churches, a figure which had increased to 2,472 in 2018. At the time of writing, several Anglican dioceses have stated aims to match the number of existing churches with new church plants or fresh expressions of church. There are now active plans to pray and work towards 10,000 new Anglican churches over the next ten years, hopefully stimulating similar numbers of church plants and fresh expressions of church in other denominations. In 2014, there were 6 Anglican so-called 'resource churches' (large churches with a specific remit to plant multiple churches across cities and regions) in England; by the end of 2016, there were 14; at 2020, there were 85; and there are hopes and plans to plant 200 by 2030. Church planting is deeply significant for the Church of England's missionary strategy in England and Wales. In 2018, the Anglican House of Bishops issued a statement, entitled 'Church Planting and the Mission of the Church', in which the bishops declared:

---

[6] Lings 2012: 174.

We welcome planting new churches as a way of sharing in the apostolic mission by bringing more people in England to faith in Christ and participation in the life of the Church. We will encourage it, and not seek to limit it, wherever the good practice in this statement is being followed.[7]

George Lings has written: 'church planting in the Church of England . . . is no whim or fad, nor mere human invention. It is, for me, a discernible movement of the Spirit in our day.'[8]

Why theology matters

I can speak from a certain amount of personal experience on this, too. I went as a curate to Holy Trinity Brompton (HTB). On my first day, I had lunch with the then vicar, Sandy Millar. Halfway through a very convivial meal, he asked me what I would like to do at HTB during my curacy. Fortunately, I had enough nous to ask him what he would like me to do. 'Well, John,' he said, 'as you are kind enough to ask: how about some church planting?' At the time, I had not really heard much about church planting – I had just read a rather fierce and discouraging book on the subject – but I was happy to say yes. And so began an adventure, which has lasted to this day, and a happy entrance into what I believe is the most fruitful and encouraging way of mission for the church in our times.

My wife Catherine and I had two years at HTB, just learning everything we could about church planting, and watching Sandy in action. Over those two years, we found a fantastic location, right in the heart of central London, surrounded by universities and colleges, legal London, some of London's most famous hospitals, with a rich artistic heritage and strong local culture. We were invited by the area bishop to plant a church there, taking a team from HTB and merging it with the small and faithful congregation that was already in place. My father had done his legal training in the area, and I have a love of English literature, so I was thrilled that

---

[7] House of Bishops 2018.
[8] Lings 2012: 162.

Dickens used to live opposite the Rectory, that Ted Hughes and Sylvia Plath were married in the church, and that the Bloomsbury Group had met just around the corner. It felt as though God had prepared us for this particular patch of London.

Several times, I heard Sandy quote C. Peter Wagner to the effect that church planting is 'the single most effective form of evangelism under heaven'. This was central to Sandy's 'why' when it comes to church planting. He is an evangelist, and church planting is simply the very best way of getting the job done.

I also heard Sandy say that, to launch anything new in the church, you need three things: a theology, a method and practice. Of the first, he would say that, sooner or later, the enemy would lodge the thought in your mind that you should not be doing whatever it is you are doing: 'What do you think you are doing? Who are you to be doing it? It won't work anyway.' The answer to that is theology. We need to know why, and root it in both personal calling and theological truth. That way we have an answer, and we have a motivation to give us perseverance in tough times. For the church planter, the answer to the 'why' question is a combination of personal vocation and a robust biblical and theological understanding of what we are about.

There is an urgency to bringing excellence and clarity to the task of the theological training of church planters. Craig Ott and Gene Wilson write that 'the theological reflection on and rationale for church planting has often been rather shallow'.[9] Stuart Murray argues:

> In some recent church planting literature, the scope and level of theological discussion and engagement with biblical teaching has been disappointing. Responding to the objection we are considering here requires advocates of church planting to move beyond selected proof texts and develop a hermeneutically responsible and theologically coherent framework for the practice they are advocating.[10]

There is striking unanimity from around the world about the challenging lack of theological training for church planters. From the UK field, George

---

9 Ott and Wilson 2011: 19.
10 Murray 1998: 33.

Lings and Stuart Murray report that the training of church planters 'is still inadequate and is perceived as one of the main reasons why church planting ventures fail . . . There is widespread discontent among pioneers in many denominations about the kind of training offered.'[11]

This is a recurring theme for Murray (one of the most experienced and incisive writers in the British field). He is interested in drawing out the point that this lack of theological training may not have significant short-term impact but there will almost certainly be damaging longer-term effects.[12] Murray also critiques current practice as being too oriented towards traditional academia and unintentionally excluding those whose background and previous educational experience are hurdles to such an ethos and approach.[13]

More widely in Europe, Stefan Paas draws out an ecumenical perspective when he reflects how church planters from a more catholic background will have difficulty with the language and limited perspective of much contemporary evangelical writing on church planting.[14] In the United States, there are similar concerns. Ed Stetzer writes: 'The greatest indicator of the inadequacy of our current missiology is its lack of theological depth.'[15] J. D. Payne summarizes more positively: *Church planters must be both outstanding theologians and outstanding missionaries.*[16]

Sometimes there can be a sense that church planting is a very modern phenomenon, starting only in around the 1980s. To some it is an American import, an imposition of an alien culture. To others it is sectarian. It does not sit easily with contemporary practices and understandings of church, threatening the parish system. How can something so disruptive be a part of the church's rationale and history? It even seems to rub against the grain of these things.

Or others may have a sense that church planting is effective, but there seems no justification for it beyond the fact that it works. That may be reason enough in some quarters, but it leaves people vulnerable to times of pressure and failure when things are palpably not working. Is church

---

[11] Lings and Murray 2012: 21.
[12] Murray 1998: 30.
[13] Ibid. 227.
[14] Paas 2016: 218.
[15] Stetzer 2006: 23, citing Hunsberger 1996: 5.
[16] Payne 2009: xxxi; emphasis original.

planting more than just a fad? Will we be on to the next thing in just a few years? Or is there actually a deeper and more powerful logic to it, something that yields principles as well as pragmatics, something that can give us the confidence to build for the long term, to shape the culture of how we do church, not just for our times and contexts but also for the long term? We need a robust biblical and theological rationale for what we are doing.

So, theology is crucial to effective church planting.

A theology of both church and mission

We can refine this further – that any theology of church planting must, of necessity, focus on the intersection of a theology of the church ('ecclesiology') and a theology of mission ('missiology'). To state the obvious, when it comes to church planting, we are thinking of the planting of *churches*; we thus need to know what a church is, if we are to plant one effectively. And by the same token, church planting is concerned with the launch of new churches as a way of best reaching out to those who are not yet Christians. This is *mission*, and so we will similarly need to know what we mean by this term. Steven Croft articulates the current challenge to the theological education of church planters. He writes: 'The key areas that need serious theological resourcing . . . are in the two areas of reflection on mission on the one hand and on the life of the church, and particularly the interface between the two.'[17]

It is not just that lack of theological clarity will weaken any churches planted by those trained without this depth of engagement with missiology and ecclesiology, but rather that the whole enterprise is called into question. If church planters see their activities as somehow separate from the person and mission of God, and if what they are planting are not actually churches and if their ministry is not actually mission, then any groupings gathered by these church planters will likely prove both highly questionable theologically and ineffective. The effect of being part of such work may well prove detrimental to those involved in it, and the wider mission of God will suffer.

---

[17] Croft 2009b: 14.

Thus, this book will attempt an interweaving of the biblical material about mission and about church. We will constantly try to hold the two in view. It is not always possible to do this simultaneously, but our double focus will guide us as we begin with familiar biblical texts and work towards a biblical theology of church planting.

Theology and practice: the structure of this book

The book is also concerned to occupy that middle ground between the best theological thinking and practical experience.[18] I entirely agree with those who have expressed concerns about the lack of theological depth in the contemporary church-planting movement, and while this book does not claim to be a comprehensive answer to that, I hope it is a step in the right direction. We will make our way in some detail through key biblical passages. It is here that we will find clarity of vision and strength of purpose in our church planting. The book also, however, attempts to locate our thinking right on the front line or at the coalface. This is a book for practitioners – or at least for good practice when it comes to church planting.

The book's subtitle is 'A biblical theology of church planting'. It really does not claim to be the last word on this, nor even the first, but it does want to argue that it is in the Scriptures that we find our clearest and most health-giving source of material for working towards church planting. And so the book is made up of two unequal halves, of which the first and longest is an exegesis of passages of the Bible that speak most clearly to the theology and practice of church planting. The order is canonical, even though it seems striking (at best) or perverse (at worst) to begin with the Old Testament and the Gospels, where evidence for church planting can appear tangential or inferential. The book is concerned to follow the work of God, though, as revealed in the holy Scriptures, building up a thorough biblical background to church planting before it becomes clear and explicit in Acts and the rest of the New Testament.

---

[18] See Tim Keller's (2012: 17–19) fascinating discussion of the work of Richard Lints about the need for deep biblical work and profound interaction with our culture, which he calls 'theological vision'.

The second part moves from biblical to systematic theology, engaging with contemporary thought and criticism of contemporary church planting, and putting the discussion about church planting in the frame of how we hold ecclesiology and missiology together, and how we can place church planting in the light of the Trinity. Some may find this section more demanding than the book's first half, but it is actually looking at the same material in a different register. It has been striking to me how the conclusions from the systematic theology section of the book map so closely onto those from the book's first exegetical half.

So, with no further ado, let's turn to the Bible to see what it says about church planting.

Part I
BIBLICAL MATERIAL

1

The Old Testament

It may seem strange to be looking at the Old Testament, as there are, obviously, no churches there. Nonetheless, there are fundamental principles to be discovered, which carry on into the New Testament, and not a few incidents and passages with a bearing on church planting.[1]

Abraham and the call to bless the world in community

By this point in the Bible story, we have had the creation of God's good world, the disaster of the fall of humankind and then the working out of the consequences of these events. We have the delineation of what life, birth, work, death, socialization, art and industry, and struggle are like in this world. This culminates at Babel (Gen. 11:1–9), which sees God scattering the peoples of the earth, separating them into distinct languages and cultures, so that they will not combine together to rebel against God. We have moved far away from the idyllic picture in the first two chapters of Genesis of human beings living at peace and with fruitfulness with one another and with God.

But God, being a God of grace, effectively restarts things, this time by working from within the creation. He does not write everything off (the flood of Genesis 6 – 8 will not be repeated), but instead works to bring a new start from inside that creation. The call comes to Abram, as Abraham was then known:

> Go from your country and your kindred and your father's house to
> the land that I will show you. I will make of you a great nation, and

---

[1] The phraseology of 'church planting' will be used, even in connection with Old Testament passages. This is clearly anachronistic, but I hope the reader will allow this.

I will bless you, and make your name great, so that you will be a blessing. I will bless those who bless you, and the one who curses you I will curse; and in you all the families of the earth shall be blessed.

(Gen. 12:1–3)[2]

This is a real turning point in the story, which we can trace through the use of the words 'bless' and 'curse'. It was when God made the heavens and the earth that we first heard of blessing: God blesses the living creatures (Gen. 1:22) and the human beings (1:28). In both instances, this is explained in terms of being fruitful and multiplying. Interestingly, God also blesses the sabbath day (2:3), this time with the sense of making it holy. All the more shocking, then, are the curses which come from God as a result of the fall: the serpent is cursed among all animals (3:14) and the ground is cursed because of the man (3:17). Creation is going into reverse, and the forces of life and multiplication are not eradicated, but made much harder. How all the more marvellous, therefore, to come across the language of blessing once again, and in such a concentrated form: five times 'bless' or 'blessing' is spoken by God in just two verses. And cursing is redefined as a reciprocal effect of cursing Abram and his family and nation. Fruitfulness, multiplication and holiness will once more revisit the earth, this time through Abram and his descendants.

What has all this to do with church and church planting? The New Testament does not hesitate to understand these statements about Abraham as looking forward to Christ, and, in him, to the church. For instance, in Galatians, Paul argues that 'the promises ... made to Abraham and to his offspring' apply to Christ (Gal. 3:16), and that those who have been baptized into Christ stand in him as recipients of these great promises: 'And if you belong to Christ, then you are Abraham's offspring, heirs according to the promise' (3:26–29). In Romans 4, he describes descendants of Abraham not in physical or ethnic terms but as 'those who share the faith of Abraham' (Rom. 4:16); this is how Abraham has become the 'father of many nations' (4:17). Paul probably had in his

---

[2] Unless otherwise stated, Scripture quotations are taken from the New Revised Standard Version (NRSV), Anglicized edition (1995).

mind's eye the churches of Rome to which he was writing, and the many nations, ethnicities and backgrounds represented in their gatherings, all descended from Abraham in the sense that they shared his faith in the God who could give life to the dead (4:17), and the various house churches and luminaries among the first Christians in Rome listed in Romans 16:1–16. Paul does the same thing when he declares that 'the God of peace will shortly crush Satan under your feet' (16:20). This echoes God's promise in Genesis 3 that the offspring of the woman will strike the head of the serpent (3:5). Now, Paul is applying that to the early churches in Rome.

So, what we have is a way of reading the Old Testament such that the promises made to Abraham (and, as we shall see, to other key Old Testament characters) are to be heard with New Testament ears as promises fulfilled by Jesus and lived out in the church.

With that paradigm in mind, we can say several things about the church from the great calling and declarations of blessing in Genesis 12. Bruce Waltke sees 'three expanding horizons': the call to Abraham to leave his home, lands, family and culture; the promise that God will make of him a great nation; and the promise of universal blessing.[3] We can reflect on the church from each horizon.

Church begins in vocation

Abram had to leave where he was, not just geographically but also in terms of his own culture, background and self-understanding.

At one level, this is true of all Christian conversion. It is also true of the genesis of churches. There is an element of separation in the establishing of any church; it is a different order of gathering from every other social activity within the culture in which it is planted. The challenge for any church is to negotiate what the points of similarity are to its society, and where it is dissimilar.

Calling is vital for the leaders and planters of churches. Recent American research on key competencies and characteristics of church planters[4] consistently puts calling at the head of the list. Missionary theologians Craig Ott and Gene Wilson comment:

---

[3] Waltke 2001: 203.
[4] Ridley 1988; J. A. Thompson 1995; 2007.

No amount of study, training, and experience can substitute for the call, leading, and power of the Holy Spirit in the lives of church planters. The assurance of God's appointment gives a tremendous amount of confidence and staying power . . . [C]andidates must give a genuine, settled, and enduring conviction (that is shared with their spouse, if married) of God's leading that is affirmed by their local church body.[5]

Neither church nor church planting, then, just arrives or just happens. There is something inherently dynamic in the life of churches. It is not that they have always been there, and are an absolute part of the scenery. Very obviously, someone somewhere will have started every church in every land. Each place of worship has a history and a genesis. The more we look into it, we will probably find that each church actually has several starts. It may be that a building was burned down and had to be rebuilt, or was bombed in times of war. It may be that the 'daughter church' has come to eclipse the 'mother church'. It may be that local geography has necessitated a relocation of missionary activity. Sadly, it may be that church splits have led to new churches. Or we might find that church buildings have been remodelled, extended, modernized. Churches are constantly restarting down their histories.

Church planters often have a personal sense of calling as well. I can think of two who knew that they would plant churches into particular buildings. They would drive past, and feel the call of God to plant churches into what, in both cases, are iconic and strategically placed buildings. Or others will have a call to a town or region, to rural or urban or suburban work, to particular people groups, ethnicities or social backgrounds. These may or may not reflect their own life histories.

Increasingly, church planters have a calling specifically to be church planters. For some, there is a journey, perhaps through more traditional models of church, the sense that they want to reach those who are not currently being reached by these churches, and a growing clarity that they want to be part of starting a new or revitalized church to reach new people. There is research to the effect that the more clearly there can be

---

[5] Ott and Wilson 2011: 308.

this sense of self-identifying as church planters, then the more effective the churches planted will be.[6]

Calling is clearly an important topic, one to which we shall return throughout. However, this is not a lonely pursuit.

Mission is fundamentally corporate

As we have seen, God's blessing will come through Abraham, his family and his descendants, who, famously, will be more numerous than the stars in the night sky (Gen. 15:5). What we have here is God's declaration of his methodology for the world: he will call individuals, yes, but the power of the blessing will come through peoples, groups, families, cohorts, tribes.

When we look down the story of the Bible, we see this pattern again and again.

- Genesis sees the birth of the twelve tribes of Israel stemming from the sons of Jacob. And it is no accident that Jesus will call twelve disciples to him, and appoint and name them apostles (e.g. Mark 3:14). Jesus affirms the story of Israel and the structure of how God will bless the peoples of the world, just as he also fulfils that very structure and remodels it around himself.
- In the eyes of God, it is Israel that is named God's son. The prophet Hosea retells the story of the exodus in precisely these terms:

> When Israel was a child, I loved him,
>   and out of Egypt I called my son.
> (Hos. 11:1)

The exodus was a national story: millions of people rescued from slavery, called to start a new corporate life, but summed up, in the eyes of God, as a single child and heir. Inheritance, in the culture of the day, would go to the firstborn son. But in the gracious way that God acts, the whole people are his heirs, his cherished offspring. The fantastic story of the birth of Israel is at once the tale of the son of God and the tale of a whole people.

---

6 E.g. Male 2013; Moynagh 2017.

- The prophets keep summoning the people of Israel to live up to this calling. This is why it is so important, in the times of the books of Kings and Chronicles, that the people worship their God and live in his ways, and are not led astray by their rulers to worship false gods and embrace the ways of injustice and wickedness. Here is where the relationship between the leader, as God's chosen king, and the people, goes drastically wrong. And the result is that the blessing of God cannot be experienced by the people, nor carried to those around them.
- Isaiah the prophet brings out this ambiguity in the key figure of the Servant. There are four so-called 'servant songs', in which the prophet describes a mysterious figure who is called by God to suffer for the world. Sometimes this figure is out-and-out called 'Israel' (e.g. Isa. 44:21; 49:3), and sometimes he has a mission to and through Israel (e.g. 49:5). The Servant's calling is to be 'a light to the nations' (42:6), the one in whom God will be glorified (49:3), to bring God's salvation to the ends of the earth (49:6). Whether as an individual or as the nation, the Servant has a calling to bring God's blessing and glory to the whole world.
- The New Testament ascribes this calling to the church. In the Acts of the Apostles, when Paul and Barnabas are preaching in Pisidian Antioch, they quote one of the servant songs (Isa. 49:6):

> For so the Lord has commanded us, saying,
>
> 'I have set you to be a light for the Gentiles,
>   so that you may bring salvation to the ends of the earth.'
> (Acts 13:47)

Note how Paul and Barnabas have no hesitation in saying that the prophecy is about 'us'. Further, the Greek 'you's are in the plural: in the eyes of the New Testament, the calling of the Servant is now the calling of the church. Emphatically, the pattern of the Old Testament – that blessing comes through groups, through God's people together – is reaffirmed and strengthened.

- It is, of course, in Jesus that the blessing of God comes most fully and definitively to the world. Well, doesn't this disprove the theory that

God wants to bless the world through groups of his people? No, for two reasons. First, Jesus is often shown to us in terms which fulfil how the Old Testament operated (he fulfils the law, he fulfils the temple and the sacrificial system etc.), and that includes the figure of the Servant from Isaiah. The most famous 'servant song' is in Isaiah 53, where we read that the Servant

> has borne our infirmities . . .
> was wounded for our transgressions,
>   crushed for our iniquities . . .
> All we like sheep have gone astray;
>   we have all turned to our own way,
> and the LORD has laid on him
>   the iniquity of us all.
> (53:4–6)

The New Testament repeatedly quotes and alludes to this famous prophecy, and declares that it was fulfilled in the death of Jesus on the cross (e.g. 1 Pet. 2:22–25; 3:18). Jesus Christ fulfils and fills out how the Old Testament operated. And so his 'leadership', if we may call it that, is couched in the same terms as that of other Old Testament figures, and is thus inescapably intertwined with the role and calling of God's people. Except, with Jesus, the model works perfectly, and is not undermined by the frailties and failures of the Old Testament leaders.

And second, the New Testament tells us that the mission of Jesus continues through his church. So, Acts begins by describing the Gospel of Luke as 'all that Jesus began to do and teach' (1:1 ESV, TNIV), implying that Acts is all that Jesus *continued* to do and teach through the ministry of the Holy Spirit through the church. And one of the central metaphors for the church in the New Testament is that it is 'the body of Christ' (e.g. Rom. 12:4–5; 1 Cor. 12:12–13, 27). We thus have the Old Testament pattern crystallized in the relationship between Jesus and his church. He is the source of the blessing, just as Abraham was in Genesis 12, but all the more fundamentally; and the people of Jesus, as they are constituted and held together in the church, share in that blessing and are carriers of it to the world around.

If we put this together, we find that the way God has chosen to work in the world is through people, and specifically people together, people as a group, people in relationship. He did not choose Abraham to be the way he would bring blessing to the world; he chose Abraham and his descendants. We must not read the story of the Bible as the narrative of great women and men, as if our goal is to be like them (or unlike them in their faults). Rather, we see them as they relate to Christ, and we see ourselves as the people called into the leadership of Christ. The power is in the people, not the individual, unless that individual is Jesus. Of course, our society is profoundly individualistic, and so will gravitate to the 'sole hero' model, and will struggle to grasp how a group is more potent than just one isolated person, however great that person may be. We only have to think of team sports, or orchestras and bands, to see how groups are still central to how human beings operate. Even when we think of great individuals, they were, of course, supported and complemented by the unseen work of others. A great actor needs others in the cast, as well as those who bring a production to the stage or screen. A brilliant surgeon needs a whole troop of others, both in and out of the operating theatre. And so on.

This is fundamental for church planters. What we plant is churches, and we do so in the full conviction that nothing is more beautiful than a church in the eyes of God, and nothing is more central to how he operates in the world, and nothing is more effective in displaying his glory.

Steven Croft is a significant figure in missional practice in the Church of England. He was principal of a theological college and then, between 2004 and 2008, the head of Fresh Expressions of Church for the Church of England and the Methodist Church. Of the work of training church planters and pioneers he has written: 'The key areas that need serious theological resourcing . . . are in the two areas of reflection on mission on the one hand and on the life of the church, and particularly the interface between the two.'[7] Further, his conclusion is that it is ecclesiology that is

---

[7] Croft 2009b: 14.

'significantly neglected in theological training'.[8] We need to take on board the profoundly corporate sense that mission has in the Bible. When we align ourselves with this, we put ourselves in touch with the spiritual and human dynamics that have activated the mission of God throughout the ages.

I did some research into the training of church planters. One of my key questions was: what are the obstacles to being trained as a church planter? As part of this, I interviewed a highly experienced church planter. He is head of a growing network of churches, largely based in London, but also in other British cities and in Europe. His answer was very thought-provoking, and has stayed with me:

> The biggest theological obstacle . . . is the tendency to undermine the definition of church in order to do more . . . [It] is cutting down the nature of the church theologically. So, basically, anything that you do, you can suddenly start to call the church . . . And actually, I don't think that's really going to help us.[9]

When we think about theology that gives strength, health and resilience to church planters, thinking clearly about the church is going to be key.

Mission is fundamentally corporate. Abraham's call teaches us that God wants to bless the world through his people together. This means that, when it comes to planting churches, the 'church' part is as central as the 'planting' part. A robust theology of church planting will hold together both church and mission, without watering down either.

Mission is blessing the world

The notion of blessing runs like a drumbeat throughout the calling of Abraham. He and his descendants are to reverse the effects of the fall, put the flood behind them and effectively restart creation – something altogether impossible, were it not for the Lord. The original blessing that God had put into the world is to be released again through Abraham and his family. The power to multiply, the impulse of life, the ability to carry

---

8 Croft 2008: 51.
9 Anonymous interview in Valentine 2020.

all the goodness of creation, the holiness of life – all these God lays before Abraham as the central feature of his mission.

The idea of blessing is one of the central themes of Genesis. You may remember how Jacob steals Esau's blessing, and how important it is that Jacob blesses all his sons. The people of God are to be carriers of blessing; it is what they do.

When it comes to Deuteronomy, the impact of God's covenant is embodied in the blessings of obedience and the curses of disobedience. 'If you will only obey the LORD your God, by diligently observing all his commandments . . . all these blessings shall come upon you and overtake you' (Deut. 28:1). There are blessings in fruitfulness, in family life, in business, in daily living, in battle. And the conclusion is a passionate invitation from Moses to walk the ways of blessing: 'I call heaven and earth to witness against you today that I have set before you life and death, blessings and curses. Choose life so that you and your descendants may live' (30:19). The people of God are to embody this life of blessing as they walk with God.

Blessing is the activity of God in the world as he renews his creation. A recurrent picture of this in the Old Testament is of water in the desert, making flowers bloom in places that looked dead. Isaiah draws together the themes of blessing, the Spirit of God and a transforming fruitfulness:

> I will pour water on the thirsty land,
>   and streams on the dry ground;
> I will pour my spirit upon your descendants,
>   and my blessing on your offspring.
> (Isa. 44:3)

Perhaps the most powerful image of this is in Ezekiel's vision of an ever-deepening river which flows from the place of sacrifice in the temple. The waters grow deeper the further they flow, not more shallow, as we might expect. The river flows into the desert, down into the Dead Sea: 'When it enters the sea, the sea of stagnant waters, the water will become fresh . . . and everything will live where the river goes' (Ezek. 47:8–9). Fish will flourish in the waters. Trees will grow on the riverbanks, and 'their fruit will be for food, and their leaves for healing' (47:12). It is a beautiful picture of creation restored and renewed, of life and healing. It is an image picked up in Revelation, and there it is interpreted as a vision of how creation will be when it is filled with the transforming presence of God: 'and the leaves of the tree are for the healing of the nations' (Rev. 22:2). Note that this wonderful future is of universal, global scope. This is not just a blessing for the people of God; it is the blessing from God for his whole world.

When it comes to the New Testament, how striking it is that Jesus describes life in the kingdom of God through the vocabulary and lens of blessing! The famous Beatitudes each begin with a pronouncement of blessing: 'Blessed are the poor in spirit, for theirs is the kingdom of heaven' (Matt. 5:3). This is a blessing that has undergone a shift in understanding, though: it is a reversal of what we might expect blessing to look like. There are blessings for those who mourn, for those who hunger and thirst for righteousness, for the persecuted. Luke's version of the Beatitudes is even more stark: the blessings are for the poor, the hungry, the weeping. This vision of blessing is far from the materialistic dreams of our age: it is the poor experiencing the transforming, life-giving action of God in Jesus.

In this light, perhaps it comes as no surprise that the language of blessing is prominent in the institution of the Lord's Supper: 'While [the disciples] were eating, [Jesus] took a loaf of bread, and after blessing it he broke it, gave it to them, and said, "Take; this is my body"' (Mark 14:22). Blessing is now followed by breaking. God's healing of creation is to be accomplished by the wounding of his Son. Blessing comes through blood, the death of Jesus.

And so it is that the language of blessing is increasingly linked to the gospel in the rest of the New Testament. Paul can say of his evangelistic work: 'I do it all for the sake of the gospel, so that I may share in its blessings' (1 Cor. 9:23). When he comes to reflect on the story of Abraham in Galatians, he says: 'Christ redeemed us . . . in order that in Christ Jesus the blessing of Abraham might come to the Gentiles, so that we might receive the promise of the Spirit through faith' (Gal. 3:13–14).

The Spirit who renewed creation in Isaiah, Ezekiel and Revelation is the fulfilment of the sacrificial death of Jesus on the cross; this is how the blessing promised to Abraham, all those centuries ago, comes in ever-widening, deepening circles to the whole world.

Ultimately, blessing will be turned back to God in praise. 'Blessed be the God and Father of our Lord Jesus Christ, who has blessed us in Christ with every spiritual blessing in the heavenly places,' begins the letter to the Ephesians (1:3). There has been blessing from God in Christ, and it is our response to bless him, in thankfulness and praise. In the vision of heaven in Revelation, the angels and the living creatures and the elders sing in praise to Jesus, the Lamb of God:

> Worthy is the Lamb that was slaughtered
> to receive power and wealth and wisdom and might
> and honour and glory and blessing!
> (Rev. 5:12)

The one through whom the blessing came is now the object of blessing from his grateful people. And so John hears

> every creature in heaven and on earth and under the earth and in the sea, and all that is in them, singing,
>
> > 'To the one seated on the throne and to the Lamb
> > be blessing and honour and glory and might
> > for ever and ever!'
> > (5:13)

It is a glorious virtuous circle of blessing, thankfulness, life and praise.

So, blessing is nothing less than the healing of God's world. It is focused on Jesus, and his sacrifice of himself for us, and leads to the outpouring of the healing, renewing Spirit. The end is to be caught up in this heavenly cycle of receiving and giving, turned into the language of praise. There is much more that can be said about blessing – this is just a partial snapshot – but already there is much here to move our hearts and to motivate our lives to action.

If church planting is the happy and fruitful marriage of church and mission, this is why we plant churches. Church plants see themselves as part of how God blesses his world, brings healing, renews life, leads all into an experience of his love through the cross of Christ lived out in the Spirit. Our church plants are a force for good in the world.

The exodus: the priestly kingdom

Our next pivotal moment is when the people of God are given the law. They have been led by God out of slavery in Egypt, but they have yet to establish themselves in the Promised Land. Three months into the journey,[10] they gather at the foot of Mount Sinai, and Moses prepares the people for what is about to happen. God briefs Moses like this:

> Thus you shall say to the house of Jacob, and tell the Israelites: You have seen what I did to the Egyptians, and how I bore you on eagles' wings and brought you to myself. Now therefore, if you obey my voice and keep my covenant, you shall be my treasured possession out of all the peoples. Indeed, the whole earth is mine, but you shall be for me a priestly kingdom and a holy nation. These are the words you shall speak to the Israelites.
> (Exod. 19:3–6)

This is deeply significant in the history of Israel; God lays out the covenant relationship into which the Israelites have entered by his grace, and in which he invites them to live. This is the vocation of the people of God, one that will be instantiated and further exemplified in Jesus Christ.[11] This, then, is the calling of all Christians and churches, and the calling of church plants.

Alec Motyer helpfully describes the main thoughts of our passage:

- what the Lord has done: the saving acts of the Lord (v. 4);
- what the Lord requires: our response of obedience (v. 5a);
- what the Lord promises: the blessings which obedience brings (vv. 5b–6a).[12]

May we take each in turn, viewed from how each theme applies to church planting.

---

10 Sarna 1996: 130.
11 I am grateful to Brian Hughes for this carefully chosen form of words.
12 Motyer 2005: 196.

Church plants are built on grace

It is striking that the first theme is what *God* has done. Any and every part of being a Christian starts with God, not with us. In a sense, we are always responding to divine initiatives, building our lives on his acts, what he has done, supremely the work of Christ.

So God begins by asking Moses to tell the Israelites first off that they should remember what he has done to Egypt, and (in a beautiful image) how he has carried them on eagles' wings and brought them to himself (19:4). Significantly, this verse is in the past tense.[13] It has already happened. The people of Israel were there; they saw it. It is done. God's rescue of them is what enables this whole new life to begin. They can become a nation because they are no longer captive to another nation. Their life is predicated on the freedom which God's rescue of them has brought.

The rest of the Bible will underscore this message. We do not save ourselves; we are saved by the gracious activity of God in Jesus Christ. Salvation is a free gift. Classically, in the words of Ephesians:

> For by grace you have been saved through faith, and this is not your own doing; it is the gift of God – not the result of works, so that no one may boast. For we are what he has made us, created in Christ Jesus for good works, which God prepared beforehand to be our way of life.
> (Eph. 2:8–10)

Motyer draws this out more clearly when he reflects further on the tenses of the verbs in Exodus 19:4–6; verse 4 is in the past tense, and verses 5 and 6 are in the future. We start with what God has already done, and he then invites us into what we might do together. And as Motyer comments: 'Nothing must ever be allowed to upset this order.'[14]

If you are a church planter, or considering whether God is calling you to plant churches, the chances are that you are highly motivated, energetic and possibly entrepreneurial. You are used to getting things done, finding

---

13 Ibid.
14 Ibid.

solutions, pushing through challenges and difficulties. All that is terrific, and may well be crucial as you lead or are involved in your church plant. It also carries within it a massive hidden danger: in Motyer's terms, you could easily upset the order of the tenses of these verses.

On the one hand, church planting is hard work. Churches do not plant themselves. Particularly if you are planting from scratch, you are having to build things yourself. Especially in the early days, the burden on the leaders is substantial. You will be doing everything from setting up the tech, to visiting the neighbours, to recruiting staff, to managing social media, to the actual core business of inviting people who are new to church to come along. There may not be any systems yet, you may be establishing the culture, there may not be any children's work (so guess who is doing that too), and so on. Starting up anything is demanding, and will take energy, long hours, dedication. It is also immensely exciting, and potentially all-consuming. It is all too easy to slip into the mindset that everything depends on you. We would never say it, of course, but we do not really need God; he is at best a sleeping partner, or someone to call in as and when we get out of our depth. And quite possibly, our energy and enthusiasm do indeed carry the day, at least for a while. We are living off the adrenalin, and loving it.

But on the other hand, this mindset is not right, and it is not good. There is, of course, sadly a whole literature now on the subject of pastors who overwork and crash and burn.[15] This does them no favours, nor the churches they plant and serve, nor the glory of God. Well-being, self-care, living well and wisely – these things are pushing their way to the top of the church planter's agenda, and often because they can be ignored no longer.

Church plants live out of covenant

The centre of the three points of what God commands Moses to say to the people of Israel concerns obedience. Having reminded them that it is he who has rescued them from Egypt, and before he gets on to the blessings that lie ahead, God introduces an 'if' clause: 'Now therefore, if you obey

---

15 E.g. Zack Eswine (2015), *The Imperfect Pastor: Discovering Joy in Our Limitations through a Daily Apprenticeship with Jesus*, Wheaton: Crossway; Diane Lanberg (2020), *Redeeming Power: Understanding Authority and Abuse in the Church*, Grand Rapids: Brazos; Marcus Honeysett (2022), *Powerful Leaders? When Church Leadership Goes Wrong and How to Prevent It*, London: Inter-Varsity Press.

my voice and keep my covenant . . .' (Exod. 19:5a). There is a condition to be fulfilled before the exciting and triumphant conclusion.

This condition does not relate to the rescue of God. That has already happened. Interestingly, the condition actually arises from this very rescue: 'Now *therefore* . . .' It is a logical consequence of having been rescued by God. Note, also, that God describes the covenant as '*my* covenant'; this is not a bipartisan agreement between equals, but is a relationship rooted in the character, purposes and initiative of God. What is under discussion is not *whether or not* the people are in this relationship with God (it is not a *qualification* issue), but rather *how* they are going to live now in the light of the fact that they are already in this relationship (it is a *quality-of-life* issue).

We must not evade the force of the condition, though. The blessings of this covenant come through obedience: 'if you obey my voice'. The key to flourishing within the covenant is in living faithfully within it.

A covenant is 'an unchangeable, divinely imposed legal agreement between God and [humanity] that stipulates the conditions of their relationship'.[16] The initiative and the invitation lie with God, as does the authority to set the terms of the relationship – this is not a negotiation! Covenants probably had their historical origin in the treaties between nations, and they carry over that sense of binding power; they are 'a solemn commitment guaranteeing promises or obligations undertaken by one or both covenanting parties'.[17] They have a promissory function, and also include a call to obedience. A covenant is a way of establishing a safe place in which parties can live together well, in healthy ways that make for mutual flourishing. God has established just such a covenant, and invites his people to step into it, to live in this way, to fulfil their promises and obligations, knowing that God has already fulfilled his, making an open future for their flourishing if they walk in the terms laid down by him in the covenant.

Fundamentally, the covenant is the way in which God binds himself to his people and they to him. They are inseparable. Their relationship is indissoluble, and the ties that bind them together in love and grace are

---

[16] Grudem 1994: 515.
[17] Williamson 2003: 139. Williamson is here describing covenants between human beings, but says that these shed light on divine–human covenants.

strong enough to withstand anything and everything which may come against them. It is most succinctly expressed in the phrase, 'I will be their God, and they shall be my people' (e.g. Exod. 6:6–7; Jer. 31:33; and frequently throughout the Old Testament).

Of course, Scripture speaks of a new covenant. It is prophesied by Jeremiah (31:31–34) and actualized by Jesus through his death on the cross. At the institution of the Lord's Supper, Jesus speaks of the cup as being 'the new covenant in my blood' (Luke 22:20). It is not completely new, in the sense of dismantling and making redundant the old; indeed Mark, in his account, has Jesus just say, 'This is my blood of the covenant, which is poured out for many' (14:24). There is a fundamental continuity in God's relating to the human race, and to his people in particular. But nonetheless, something shifts significantly.

If we take Jeremiah's prophecy as a baseline, then this shift is around forgiveness of sins and an inner ability to fulfil the obligations of the covenant:

> This is the covenant that I will make with the house of Israel after those days, says the LORD: I will put my law within them, and I will write it on their hearts; and I will be their God, and they shall be my people. No longer shall they teach one another, or say to each other, 'Know the LORD,' for they shall all know me, from the least of them to the greatest, says the LORD; for I will forgive their iniquity, and remember their sin no more.
> (Jer. 31:33–34)

This new covenant will be a deeper way of relating, such that there is heart knowledge of God made possible through the forgiveness of sins. The New Testament will speak in terms of the blood of Christ and the Holy Spirit making possible this new deep relating. The blood of the covenant is poured out 'for the forgiveness of sins' (Matt. 26:28). The Spirit does an inner and spiritual work in the heart, in place of an outward sign (Rom. 2:29),[18] while the ministry of the new covenant is about becoming a letter

---

[18] Although we should not forget that the Old Testament also speaks of the 'circumcision of the heart' (e.g. Deut. 10:12–17). Thanks to Brian Hughes for bringing this out in private correspondence.

of Christ, 'written not with ink but with the Spirit of the living God, not on tablets of stone but on tablets of human hearts' (2 Cor. 3:3). The new covenant is stepping into the realms of sanctification as well as justification: a means of being holy and living out the gospel, made possible by the Spirit of God.

How does this relate to a theology of planting churches?

It may seem redundant to say so, but the main business of the Christian, of churches and of church plants is to be 'God-people'. We are all about God. The fundamental identity is to be in relationship with God, a relationship which is secure and gives confidence and comfort, and which is demanding more than all else. Our chief joy, our primary raison d'être, that which we keep coming back to, the base from which we live and do all things, is that we stand in covenant relationship with the living God, through his grace. What we want people to see and know about us is that we are God-people and God's people. He has invited us into relationship with him, and made a way for this to be possible through the sacrifice of his Son on the cross and by the power of the Holy Spirit within us.

This means that church plants, along with all churches, are about God. They are not social gatherings, political associations, means of doing good, venues for entertainment; they are groups of people who define themselves solely by reference to God, who lives in their midst and with whom they are in living and dynamic relationship. Motyer has a lovely phrase when he says that the book of Exodus is 'the book of the presence of the Lord among his people'.[19] We can see an emblem of this in the burning bush from which God calls Moses (Exod. 3:1–6), and we can hear it when the LORD causes his presence to pass before Moses (33:17–23). We see it for certain as the fire breaks out on Mount Sinai in the giving of the law (19:16–19). The heart of the covenant is God making himself present among his people. And so the heart of church planting must be the same.

Worship, prayer, the word of God, the sacraments – all are central to church planting. They are never a means to an end; they are the end itself, because it is here that we meet God. This can be a strategic challenge for church plants that are starting with people who are a long way away from God; leaders may not want to 'scare the horses' by being too full-on in

---

[19] Motyer 2005: 195.

their worship too quickly with people for whom it may all be very new and alien. Nonetheless, church planting comes out of the heart of the God who has moved heaven and hell to be present with his people, and so we must reflect that same longing.

This does not mean that church planting must be a replication of traditional worship services in established churches. Far from it. It will probably be creative, looking for points of contact with unchurched people, ways in for them to experience God without perhaps being put off by what may be perceived as the dullness and irrelevance of traditional church worship. Whatever the form, though, the substance must, at its heart, be encounter with the God who lives among his people.

How then are church plants to order their lives in line with this covenant basis? To go back to Exodus 19, God is specific that, at root, it is about obedience to his word: 'if you obey my voice and keep my covenant . . .' (19:5a). Literally, this reads: 'if you listen attentively to my voice . . .'[20] The root of worship, of valuing and responding to God as he is present through the covenant, is to hear and obey what God says. In context, this means taking on board the Ten Commandments (Exod. 20:1–17) and the expanded Book of the Covenant (Exod. 20:22 – 23:33). More broadly, it means heeding the message of the Scriptures, and living out the gospel. It is what Paul will call, at the beginning and end of Romans, 'the obedience of faith' (Rom. 1:5; 16:26).

Church planting is a fundamentally covenantal activity. It draws its confidence and joy from the indissoluble bonds of the love of God in the blood of Christ. It aspires to live in the freedom of the Spirit's response to God's foundational covenant work. It lives to see the world coming into the church to experience this grace and love and life. And it draws its dynamism from listening carefully to the gospel word and responding with agility and creativity to what God is saying. I find it very striking that Paul can describe all those involved in his apostolic, missionary and church-planting work as 'ministers of a new covenant – not of the letter but of the Spirit' (2 Cor. 3:6 TNIV).

This means that attention to the word of God is integral to planting churches. How striking it is to hear Paul say that, when it comes to the

---

[20] Ibid. 200.

foundations of church, 'God has appointed . . . first apostles, second prophets, third teachers' (1 Cor. 12:28). Ephesians makes the same point: the church is 'built upon the foundation of the apostles and prophets, with Christ Jesus himself as the cornerstone' (2:20). We need to hear God's word applied in our contexts, in order that we may respond to it. We may use different language (intuition, learning, reflection, applied exegesis, emotional intelligence, for instance), but church planting has a sense of mobility built into it. It is constantly on the move, responding to what the Holy Spirit is saying. We make it our business to 'listen attentively' to the voice of the Lord. It is this, combined with a willing spirit, looking to respond to what the gospel commands us, which opens up the third strand of our Exodus 19 verses. Covenant obedience is the gateway to covenant blessings.

Church plants aim to see the world transformed

And so to the excitement of the blessings of the covenant. God has established the covenant through his rescue of his people, and he invites them into a way of life within it, shaped by an obedience to his word. If they live in this way, then they will find that three things happen: 'you shall be my treasured possession . . . you shall be for me a priestly kingdom and a holy nation' (Exod. 19:5b–6).

First of all, the beautiful knowledge that we are special to God. In the ancient world, everything belonged to the king, but there were some things that were special to him, his 'personal treasure', his 'jewel in the crown'.[21] Just so with God. 'The whole earth is mine' (19:5), but the people of the covenant hold a special place in his heart.

This is, of course, wonderfully true for each of us as individuals, but we must remember that this is a description of a *people*. The Bible thinks far more naturally of groups, tribes, nations, than it does of people on their own. In New Testament terms, we are talking here about just how much God loves churches. No matter how big or small, no matter what denomination, however new or old, regardless of their age make-up, the impressiveness or otherwise of those who make up their congregations, their fame or obscurity, their 'success' or 'failure', God loves

---

[21] Motyer 2005: 198, 199.

churches. Our church, our church plant, is precious, special, valued, treasured by God.

And these churches are 'a priestly kingdom'. This phrase occurs only here in the Old Testament (although Isa. 61:6 has parallel phrases[22]), but its ideas run throughout the Bible. Peter famously applies this language to the New Testament church: 'But you are a chosen race, a royal priesthood, a holy nation, God's own people, in order that you may proclaim the mighty acts of him who called you out of darkness into his marvellous light' (1 Pet. 2:9).

There is the sense of royalty – we are all in service of the king, and even take on something of the characteristics of the great king himself. There is a difference from the rest of the world; see how Peter begins with the adversative 'But you' to distinguish the churches from those who do not believe. Once more, we find the identity of God's people rooted in the covenant – we are 'God's own people'; that is covenant language.

But the dominant, driving thought is that of priesthood: churches are 'a *priestly* kingdom', a 'kingdom of priests' (Exod. 19:6 TNIV, ESV, MSG). The fundamental character and purpose of this people is priestly.

So, what is a priest? The priest was the mediator between God and humanity, between the Lord and his people. At this stage in Israel's history, there was no special priesthood. Rather, the calling was for the whole people of God to bring God's presence to the world. As Williamson puts it: 'The whole nation thus inherits the responsibility, formerly conferred on Abraham, of mediating God's blessing to the nations of the earth.'[23] We are back with God's call to Abraham in Genesis 12: it remains the calling of God's people down the ages. Peter draws this out when he alludes to our passage: the purpose of being 'a royal priesthood' is to 'proclaim the mighty acts' of God (1 Pet. 2:9). This is what priesthood is about.

And this is the reason why Israel has this special relationship with God. When God says that 'the whole earth is mine' (Exod. 19:5), he is not saying this as a kind of rejection of the rest of humanity in favour of his people, but rather he is explaining the reason why Israel is to be 'my treasured possession out of all the peoples': its priesthood is the calling to share the blessings of God with all those other nations. Israel is chosen to be the

---

[22] Williamson 2003: 150.
[23] Ibid.

means by which God mediates and spreads his blessings throughout the whole world and to all peoples, just as he had explained to Abraham all those years ago.[24]

But the people of Israel are not to be like the other peoples of the world, for they are a 'holy nation'. God uses the word for 'nation' when he could have used the more usual word for 'people'. This may be to draw out that they are just like other men and women in so many regards,[25] but it seems more likely that this is another conscious echo of God's call to Abraham in Genesis 12 to be a blessing to the 'nations'.[26] And to be effective carriers of God's blessings, God's people must be 'holy'. They are to be set apart for God, for his purposes; they are not to be distracted from their calling, but to live in ways conducive to it. This will mean living the Decalogue and obeying the voice of God. Here is the reason behind the constant refrain in both the Law and the Prophets to the people of Israel to be holy like their God, and in the New Testament that the church too should be holy. We are holy for the sake of God, whose we are, and for the sake of the world, to whom we are sent.

This is the calling of the covenant, indicated by the decisive 'Now therefore' of verse 5.[27] God has rescued his people, and so now they are to obey his voice, so that ('if . . . you shall . . . you shall . . .') they may be his treasured possession, a kingdom of priests and a holy nation. This is the calling of church plants too, as those who stand within the covenant of God for the sake of the world.

As Brevard Childs notes, 'the three terms [treasured possession, kingdom of priests, holy nation] . . . are to be interpreted in relation to one another'.[28] So, our church plants are treasured by God, not for themselves, but inasmuch as they are priestly, carrying God's blessing to the world, and it is this which makes them special to him. And they are set apart for God ('holy'), not in and for themselves, but inasmuch as they are dedicated to his purpose of loving and serving the world, and sharing his presence and mighty acts with all people. It is for these reasons that we gladly and

---

[24] Dumbrell 1988: 146, cited in Williamson 2003: 150. See also the careful discussion in Tomlin 2014.
[25] So Motyer 2005: 200.
[26] So Williamson 2003: 150.
[27] Childs 1974: 367.
[28] Ibid.

wholeheartedly obey the voice of God in the covenant, so that we may partner with him, sensing his pleasure and approbation, in sharing his blessing with the world. We discover our own sense of identity and purpose, as church plants, in precisely this: that we have a key and central role in expressing God's love for his world.

Maybe the biggest application of these verses to church plants is that the focus for every church plant is those outside the church. To live fruitfully and obediently within the covenant is to be diligent in seeing ourselves as working with God to bring his blessing to others. This is frequently the major impetus for the planting of new churches. We become conscious that our current churches, marvellous as they may be, are simply not reaching whole sections of our community, city or region. They are simply not set up for this. So, what is needed? A new church, with the specific remit of reaching new people in new ways, maybe in a new place. It is set up so that it can do this in the best way possible. It is visionary, exciting, demanding.

This is a primary task for the leaders of church plants – to make sure that the initial missionary vision stays central to the life of the church. This is not because of pragmatic and programmatic issues, but for robust theological reasons: to enjoy the blessings of the covenant, we need to obey God in living out his covenant for *the sake of the world*. This is God's purpose for his people, and it is the central purpose for all healthy church plants as well.

From gathering to synagogue to church

It seems a leap from Abraham and his descendants, and the people of Israel in their thousands, gathered at the foot of Mount Sinai ready to hear the law, to churches and church plants in our day. But that leap was an actual journey, and the first Christian churches grew out of these stages of gathering.

A key part of that journey was the translation of the Septuagint, a Greek translation of the Old Testament. In the Septuagint, *ekklēsia* and its variants appear as a translation of the Hebrew word *qāhāl*. This literally means an assembly, and can be used for any kind of gathering, military, political or social, as well as religious. In Greek, *ekklēsia* is similar to the Hebrew *qāhāl* in that it meant any kind of gathering of people for a variety of purposes, including non-religious ones, so the same thought process lies behind both words. Both in Hebrew and in Greek, the notion is of a gathering, which is defined by virtue of its purpose, not in the light of its inherent nature. Peter O'Brien is helpful in drawing our attention to the special nature of the occasions when *qāhāl* is used for the assembly of Israel for religious purposes:

> Of particular significance are those instances of *ekklēsia* (rendering *qāhāl*) which denote the congregation of Israel when it assembled to hear the Word of God on Mt. Sinai, or later on Mt. Zion where all Israel was required to assemble three times a year.[29]

In the history of Israel, the majority of scholars trace the beginning of synagogues to the time after the exile.[30] 'Synagogue' comes from another Greek word, *synagōgē*, which meant 'an assembly such as the Jews meeting for worship'.[31] (The Septuagint, for instance, has *synagōgē* in Exod. 12:3: 'Tell the whole congregation of Israel . . .') This seems a continuity, in the minds of the translators of the Septuagint, between God gathering the emerging nation of Israel to receive his word and the smaller worshipping groups in later history, who met for similar purposes. This continuity can be traced into the New Testament, when the church of Christ, the *ekklēsia*, stepped into the model of gathering established by the synagogues of the time. This was partly due to history, in that the first churches grew up as a sect within Judaism, and partly due to function and theology – they were gatherings for similar purposes. Derek Tidball draws out the parallels and differences:

> The early churches imitated the synagogue in their Scripture reading and exposition, prayers and common meals and in the absence of sacrifices which were common among pagan cults . . . But there were also many differences. Christians practiced baptism and not circumcision. Their worship included prophecy and tongue

---

[29] O'Brien 1993: 124.
[30] Yamauchi 1992: 782.
[31] Ibid. 781.

speaking. Women had a much greater role. And churches were not formed on the basis of race.[32]

For our purposes, the main point is that we can see a straight line from Moses and the gathering (even 'the congregation') of the people of Israel at Sinai, through the synagogue and into the earliest Christian churches. All were groups of people, defined by reference to the purpose of their meeting, and the predominant purpose was the hearing and obeying of the word of God.

This sets us up nicely for the New Testament's teaching about church, mission and church planting. The world would be fundamentally changed by the coming of Jesus, but the first Christians did not scrap all that had gone before and begin from scratch. They understood Christ and themselves in the light of the Old Testament. The shape and structure and, to some extent, function of Old Testament gatherings could be used as a wineskin into which new wine could be poured. There would be massive tensions, and much thought would go into the relationship of the two, but the sense that the people of God met, summoned by their Lord, to hear and respond to his word did not change.

So, church planters can learn many things from the Old Testament:

- God calls groups of people, gatherings of his followers, churches into being.
- He does so because his main way of working in the world is not through individuals but through groups.
- His purpose is to bring blessing (life, the healing of creation, his holy presence) to the whole world through these groups.
- He establishes these groups in relationship with himself by virtue of his own power and grace in rescuing them (through the new exodus of the death and resurrection of Christ).
- He invites them into a new way of life with him that best communicates his goodness and glory.
- He calls them to join with him in mediating his presence to the world and offering a shared experience of his love to all who will respond.

---

[32] Tidball 1993: 887.

To be summoned by God into church planting is not to engage in some newfangled, trendy and transitory thing. It is rather to step into the most ancient of paradigms and projects, into the way that God has always envisaged he would interact with his world. Church planters can be confident that they are engaging in missionary practices which align with the character and purposes of God himself. It is the way he loves to work, and we have the joy and privilege of joining him in it. This is not to say that it is easy; it will involve sacrifice and hardship, as the ways of God nearly always do. But it *is* to say that it is right and good and true. What could be more fulfilling, and a better way to spend our lives?

2

The Gospels

Counterintuitively, the Old Testament and the Gospels have at least this in common: churches are not really mentioned. There are just two occasions in which Jesus directly speaks about churches (Matt. 16:18 and 18:17). Some argue that Jesus' focus was on the kingdom of God and that he did not envisage a time beyond his death and resurrection before the consummation of all things, and that it fell to Paul and the other apostles to institute the church. In A. Loisy's famous phrase, 'Jesus foretold the kingdom, and it was the Church that came.'[1] Many scholars today rather understand Jesus as seeing himself inaugurating the kingdom of God, which will only be consummated at a later date,[2] but it remains true that we cannot read a theology of the church straight back into the teachings and actions of Jesus without care. Nonetheless, it seems palpable and undeniable that there is indeed an ecclesiology in the Gospels, and one from which church planters can learn a good deal.

Let's start with those passages where Jesus does talk about church, before locating an incipient ecclesiology more widely in his teachings and practices as interpreted in relation to Israel and to the kingdom of God.

Jesus the church planter

Matthew records Jesus twice speaking about his church, his *ekklēsia*.

The first occasion comes after Peter's confession that Jesus is 'the Messiah, the Son of the living God' (16:16):

And Jesus answered him, 'Blessed are you, Simon son of Jonah! For flesh and blood has not revealed this to you, but my Father in

---

[1] Cited in Marshall 1992: 122.
[2] See Marshall 1992: 123.

heaven. And I tell you, you are Peter [Gk *Petros*], and on this rock [Gk *petra*] I will build my church, and the gates of Hades will not prevail against it. I will give you the keys of the kingdom of heaven, and whatever you bind on earth will be bound in heaven, and whatever you loose on earth will be loosed in heaven.'
(Matt. 16:17–19)

The second is in the context of a discussion among the disciples about sin and forgiveness within the community of Jesus' followers. Jesus teaches them:

If a brother or sister sins,[3] go and point out the fault, just between the two of you. If they listen to you, you have won them over. But if they will not listen, take one or two others along, so that 'every matter may be established by the testimony of two or three witnesses' [a quote from Deut. 19:15]. If they still refuse to listen, tell it to the church; and if they refuse to listen even to the church, treat them as you would a pagan or a tax collector.

Truly I tell you, whatever you bind on earth will be bound in heaven, and whatever you loose on earth will be loosed in heaven.

Again, truly I tell you that if two of you on earth agree about anything you ask for, it will be done for you by my Father in heaven. For where two or three come together in my name, there am I with them.
(Matt. 18:15–20 TNIV)

We should not be worried by the fact that 'church' is mentioned only in Matthew. There are several uncontested and famous instances of other stories and sayings and incidents that occur in only one Gospel.[4] So, what do these mysterious sayings of Jesus have to say to us about church planting?

---

[3] The NRSV has 'If another member of the church sins against you', which of course makes the kind of leap we are cautioning against here.
[4] Schweizer 1975: 336.

Church plants belong to Jesus

In the first of the *ekklēsia* passages, Jesus says categorically: 'I will build my church' (Matt. 16:18). What is striking about this little phrase is that Jesus says not only that he will be responsible for and active in the construction of the church, but also that the church actually belongs to him. In the Old Testament, the gathering or assembly or community was the 'congregation of *God*' (e.g. Deut. 23:2, 3, 8). This is a striking claim from Jesus that he stands in the place of God in relation to this new community he is building, and all the more so for being oblique.

Jesus also says that he will give 'the keys of the kingdom of heaven' to Peter (Matt. 16:19). We will look later at what this means, but for now let's note that the authority that is to be exercised in the church is always a delegated authority: it derives from Jesus; it is his to bear and to grant. And further, when it is exercised, it is ratified by 'heaven', which is Matthew's reverent way of speaking about God.

In the second passage, Jesus promises his presence within his church: 'where two or three are gathered in my name, I am there among them' (18:20 NRSV). We have been struck, in our reflections on Exodus 19, how the hallmark of the people of God is the presence of God in the midst of them. Here, Jesus takes the same language and concept, and applies it to his presence in his church. This is a major theme of Matthew's Gospel: its first chapter describes Jesus as '"Emmanuel", which means "God is with us"' (1:23), and its last concludes with the promise of Jesus, 'And remember, I am with you always, to the end of the age' (28:20). Here it is again: Jesus is present when only two or three of his disciples are gathered together. He said this, of course, long before his resurrection and the gift of the Spirit, but he is looking forward to that time.[5] How remarkable his words must have seemed to his first hearers! And in passing, note that the Greek of 'gathered' is the verbal form of the noun 'synagogue'. This is a gathering of God's people, called together to call on the name, not of the Lord, but of Jesus.[6]

Here we have multiple assertions of a relationship between Jesus and the church, which is the exact parallel between that of God and his people

---

5 France 2007: 697–698.
6 Ibid. 698–699.

in the Old Testament and beyond. This gathering, then, is far more than one instantiated and governed by social forces and customs. It is one that comes into being and is built and inhabited by Jesus in what can only be described as his divinity. To interact, meaningfully and properly, with the *ekklēsia* is to interact with Jesus as God.

This must reinforce for church planters that sense of the specialness of church, and the privilege of working with Jesus in the establishing and nurturing of church. Our church plants are not a means to an end, perhaps a tool towards effective evangelism (although they will be that); they *are* the end, because this is where Jesus chooses to dwell. This is also a reminder never to presume! Our church plants are not ours, but his; they do not belong to us, but to Jesus.

This theological perspective also serves to galvanize our faith for what to expect in church planting. Jesus lays this out for Peter when he says that 'the gates of Hades will not prevail against [the church]' (Matt. 16:18). Although some commentators see in this the implication of 'the onslaughts the underworld powers will hurl against [the church]', and that the church 'will be at the center of the struggle to wrest the human world from the grip of Satan and reclaim it for the rule of God',[7] others see Hades as

> a metaphor for death, which here contrasts strikingly with the phrase 'the living God' in v. 16 ... The 'gates' thus represent the imprisoning power of death: death will not be able to imprison and hold the church of the living God ... The imagery is ... of death being unable to swallow up the new community which Jesus is building. It will never be destroyed.[8]

Whichever it is, the scale of the promise is staggering, and the implications enormous for the church planter. We can count on the presence of Jesus in our churches, and this is sufficient to preserve us from all manner of death and evil.

Faith is a core attribute for church planters. Often we are establishing something where currently there is nothing. Or maybe we are dealing in

---

[7] Byrne 2004: 129–130.
[8] France 2007: 624–625.

the realms of what does not yet exist, if that is the transformation or revitalization of a church. It may be that we feel our own inadequacies, whether personally, or in terms of education or training, not least if we are lay church planters. Here, in these simple words of Jesus, together with the enormity of their implications – 'I will build my church' – is a warrant for confidence, even daring, in our church-planting ventures.

This privilege of the presence of Jesus is not just for church plants, of course, but it may be something which church planters, with their call to cross boundaries, to do new things in order to reach new people, need especially to take hold of. There is something fundamentally supernatural about the constitution of the church. This is not because of our abilities or skills or backgrounds, but because the church is shot through, at every level, with the presence of Jesus. This is not to say that there will not be challenges and struggles, sorrows and reversals, but it is to say that there is a power at work in our church plants which is greater than the most powerful forces in the universe.

Church plants are about the revelation of Jesus

It is no coincidence that Jesus' teaching follows on from Peter's confession of Jesus' messiahship. Indeed, Jesus is explicit about it:

> Blessed are you, Simon son of Jonah! For flesh and blood has not revealed this to you, but my Father in heaven. And I tell you, you are Peter, and on this rock I will build my church, and the gates of Hades will not prevail against it.
> (Matt. 16:17–18)

It is the revelation of who Jesus truly is which calls out for Jesus the naming of Peter and the promise to build on him. As Brendan Byrne puts it:

> When God began to reveal to Peter the knowledge of Jesus' identity displayed by the ... confession, God began the work of founding the Church. This knowledge of Jesus and the knowledge of God that goes with it is what the Church uniquely 'knows', the primary gift it has to impart to the world.[9]

---

9 Byrne 2004: 128–129.

The revelation of Jesus is what comes out of the church, and how Jesus builds it in the world. It is a revelation that lies beyond human knowing and telling, which is why Peter's declaration of Jesus as Messiah acts almost like a starting pistol for Jesus in his launching of the church.

These verses have been the locus of much controversy in the church down the years. Without wanting to cause offence or to simplify the complexity of the issues involved, I will be following R. T. France where he argues that, strictly exegetically, there now seems to be a consensus that Jesus did indeed have Peter, and not his confession, in mind. To argue otherwise, says France, is 'the exegesis of desperation'.[10] The flow of language and sense is built around the parallels of Peter saying Jesus is Messiah, and then Jesus responding reciprocally, 'You are Peter.' The pun on 'Peter/rock' is close in Greek (*Petros/petra*), but is exact in Aramaic (*Kēphâ* for both), so making clear that the nickname for the man Peter is indicative of the rock on which Jesus will build his church. And this is exactly what happens as we read on in the Gospels and in Acts. France spells it out:

Peter comes 'first' among the Twelve. Throughout [Matthew's] gospel he is mentioned far more often than any other disciple, and he regularly takes the lead. In the early chapters of Acts it is Peter who leads the disciple group in Jerusalem, and it is he who takes the initiative in the key developments which will constitute the church as a new, international body of the people of God through faith in Jesus: note especially his role in the bringing in of the Samaritans (Acts 8:14–25) and Gentiles (Acts 10:1–11, 18; 15:7–11). By the time James takes over as president of the Jerusalem church, the foundation has been laid. In principle, all the apostles constituted the foundation, with Jesus as the cornerstone, but as a matter of historical fact it was on Peter's leadership that the earliest phase of the church's development would depend, and that personal role, fulfilling his name 'Rock', is appropriately celebrated by Jesus' words here.[11]

---

[10] France 2007: 622.
[11] Ibid. 622–623.

None of this is to rule in or out whether or not there remains a primacy for the papacy in the purposes of God in the church, and I hope my readers will hear these comments in the eirenic spirit in which they are meant. What this exegesis helps us with, as church planters, is the conviction that, in terms of this teaching of Jesus, the leadership of Peter was foundational in the way he guided the church in its proclamation and application of the revelation of who Jesus is. This is consistent with the rest of the New Testament: that the church is built on Jesus and his gospel.

This strengthens us, as church planters, in our instinct that we are all about the revelation of Jesus Christ. This is how the church is established and how it is built up. Churches can be said to exist for many reasons, but there is a case to be made that this reason, the revealing of Jesus as Messiah, King and Lord, is primary.

Church plants are communities

Jesus gives Peter three roles: '"rock foundation" of the Church; holder of the keys of the kingdom of heaven: one who binds and looses'.[12] The second and third are closely related.

I used to think that this meant Peter was the gatekeeper to heaven, admitting those who had their sins forgiven or denying entry to those who refused the forgiveness which Jesus offered them through his death on the cross. A closer look at the text shows us something different.

The phrase 'the keys of the kingdom of heaven' is an allusion to Isaiah 22:20–25. God speaks in judgment against a man called Shebna, who is a 'steward', 'master of the household' (22:15), whom God is going to replace with 'my servant Eliakim' (22:20). Eliakim's role, as he takes over as steward, comprises an authority bearing 'the whole weight of his ancestral house', which includes 'every small vessel, from the cups to all the flagons' (22:24). In the midst of this job description, God says: 'I will place on [Eliakim's] shoulder the key of the house of David; he shall open, and no one shall shut; he shall shut, and no one shall open' (22:22).

What this shows us is that the keys entrusted to Peter by Jesus in Matthew 16 are to be seen not so much as the keys of a gatekeeper, guarding admission to the kingdom of heaven, but more as a bunch of

---

12 Byrne 2004: 129.

domestic keys, given to the head steward who is in charge of running the household, what France calls 'the chief administrative officer'.[13] France also cites Ulrich Luz, in his commentary on Matthew, when he points out that whereas Isaiah talked only of a single key, Jesus here refers to the 'keys' in the plural, which is much more suited to the role of a steward, and not a gatekeeper, who would only have a single key.[14] Peter, then, does not so much have a role of determining who is to be admitted to heaven at the last judgment, but is more an authority to provide for and govern the church in the early days of its existence.

But what of the power to bind and loose, or ' "tying up" and "untying" '?[15] Again, this does not refer to people, as they respond to the gospel, either accepting or rejecting Jesus, and so being bound or freed at the judgment. Two things count against this interpretation: first, this role is broadened to include the whole community of Jesus' followers in chapter 18 (where the context is one of dealing with sin within the community, and not entry into heaven), and, second, the objects of what is to be bound and loosed are in the neuter in Matthew's Greek, and so refer to things, not to people. France explains that the phrases 'to bind' and 'to loose' (which are used in rabbinic literature) mean 'an authority to declare what is and what is not permissible';[16] it refers to deciding issues, not to adjudicating the fates of people. He helpfully reminds us that this was indeed exactly what happened in Peter's subsequent ministry, when he declared that Gentiles should be admitted into the fellowship of God's people (Acts 8:20–24), and that lying to the Holy Spirit was not permissible, as in the case of Ananias and Sapphira (Acts 5:1–11).

There is a reference in Matthew 23 to the scribes and Pharisees locking people out of heaven (23:13), which is sometimes used to interpret the keys and the binding and loosing given to Peter in chapter 16 as his teaching ministry. That passage sits equally well, however, with the sense we are suggesting here. It was the interpretation of the law given by the scribes and Pharisees which prevented both them and their hearers from entering into the kingdom of heaven. Peter has an authority to decide which issues

---

[13] France 2007: 625.
[14] Ibid., citing Luz 2001: 364.
[15] Ibid. 626.
[16] Ibid.

were the right ones and which the wrong. The binding and loosing is about the issues, not the people.

One last comment on binding and loosing. The syntax of the verbs is highly unusual, and is repeated exactly in chapter 18. Literally, what Peter declares to be bound or loosed 'will have been bound' and 'will have been loosed' in heaven. In other words, it is not that Peter decides about binding and loosing, and heaven then ratifies his decisions. Rather, it is the other way round: it is as Peter makes his decisions that he finds he is following along in something God has already decided. This is indeed the pattern in Acts with the admission of the Gentiles, when the Holy Spirit falls on them even as Peter is speaking (10:44). Peter reflects on the significance of this: 'If then God gave the same gift that he gave us when we believed in the Lord Jesus Christ, who was I that I could hinder God?' (11:17).

To sum up so far, what we have with Peter's three roles (rock foundation of the church, the keys, the binding and loosing) is not an authority to judge, but rather an authority to establish the church through proclaiming, interpreting and applying the revelation of Jesus in his fledgling community following his death and resurrection. Jesus does not have in mind the last judgment so much as the way of life of the community on earth, its boundaries and inner life.

This becomes even more apparent when we turn to Matthew chapter 18, our second passage where Jesus refers to the church, and the binding and loosing language returns. Here, what is in view is an occasion when there is sin in the community of disciples. The offender is to be engaged by an individual, then by that individual with one or two others, and then, in the last resort, in the event that the offender is not repentant, by the church as a whole. The members of the church have the power to treat the offender as they would 'a Gentile and a tax-collector' (18:18). Then binding and loosing are invoked, along with the promise of the Father who hears prayers, and the presence of Jesus.

R. T. France brings out so helpfully that this procedure is not what subsequent centuries may have come to see as excommunication. There is no hierarchy of ecclesiastical office here, nor the church operating in quasi-political ways. Rather, it is a community of disciples, each having the self-confidence to take responsibility for the spiritual and emotional health of the group as a whole. So the language (obscured by some translations) is that of family – it is brothers and sisters, looking out for one another, each on 'an equal footing' with the other.[17] When it comes to the involvement of the church as a whole (and Matthew has the local church in view here, not the more abstract idea of the church universal):

> the group share corporately in the pastoral concern which motivated the individual disciple to raise the issue, and in the event of a rebuff we may reasonably suppose that they would share that individual's attitude of disapproval and even ostracism ... but to speak of anything so formal as 'excommunication' is to import an anachronistically developed concept of ecclesiastical jurisdiction.[18]

What France is helping us to see is that the vision Jesus has for his church is of disciples having the wisdom and confidence to pastor one another, with a shared sense of mutual life.

But what of binding and loosing, which sounds much more juridical and alarming? The first thing to notice is that the verbs move from the singular to the plural. Up until now, it has been the concerned individual who has been addressed by Jesus. Now, it is the church as a whole which he has in view: 'Truly I tell you [all], whatever you [all] bind on earth will be bound in heaven, and whatever you [all] loose on earth will be loosed in heaven.' This immense responsibility and ability is given not just to Peter alone, but to the whole community. The same striking grammar ('will have been bound ... will have been loosed') gives to the members of the community as a whole the same assurance that Peter had, namely that they can expect a sense of guidance from God; similarly, as with Peter, that which is being bound or loosed is to be understood as issues and difficult questions of right and wrong, not people. And so Jesus moves naturally to assure groups within the church of answered prayer (maybe for guidance in tricky situations, or for the restoration of those in trouble) and of his presence in the community.

What these passages give to us is a vivid portrayal in Jesus' mind's eye of the lived life of the church. It is a group of people, united as his followers,

---

[17] Ibid. 691.
[18] Ibid.

who have the vision and capacity to manage their own shared life, with compassion, insight and wisdom, walking in step with heaven, even as they have to make adjustments and improvisations in the ever-changing situations of their circumstances and cultures. It is a remarkably democratic vision, with no officers or hierarchy in view,[19] and Jesus expresses astonishing confidence in the rightness of decisions that are to be made.

Stuart Murray has long been a leading light in British church planting, not least in the theological acumen and contextual insights he has brought, and he writes of this Matthew 18 passage:

> [Jesus] describes a community which is serious about discipleship; a community characterized by open and loving relationship; a community that recognizes it is composed of imperfect people and develops a style of life that remains faithful to the highest standards but realistic about failure; a community that balances individual responsibility and corporate action; a community in which there is no hint of clericalism; and, arguably, a community small enough to operate in such a way.[20]

These descriptions are exegetically challenging. For church planters, I think the main take-home is simple and powerful: our church plants are fundamentally communities of people. Jesus gives us a vision of community life, which is founded on the gospel as it is applied and interpreted in line with our circumstances and challenges, and which is not governed by authority but rather enabled democratically.

Sometimes, church planters are so focused on the mission that they lose sight of the church. Increasingly, the health of the churches we are planting is coming into view. What is a healthy church plant? One which originates in the revelation of the identity of Jesus Christ; one which has the flexibility and deep wisdom to adapt its borders and practices so that more and more people can experience God's love; and one which enables mature, adult-to-adult mutual relationships. How can we ensure that the

---

[19] Although it could be argued that Peter, in some sense, has a kind of office. Many thanks to Andy Byers for pointing this out in private correspondence.
[20] Murray 1998: 85.

churches with which we are involved in the planting have these kinds of social dynamics?

The pastoral life of church plants is important. Often, church plants will be working with people who have just come to faith or may not yet be Christians, or with people whose ethnic and social backgrounds are different from those of the people regularly seen in traditional churches. Many will find themselves in positions of leadership and responsibility far more quickly than would often be the case. There may well be difficult pastoral situations, and a stiff and unbending application of right and wrong may not be the best way forward.

Jesus' practice of 'church'

Notwithstanding the paucity of mentions of the church by Jesus, there is much that attests to his vision of what would become the church after his resurrection and ascension. The 'classical presentation' of the argument was that of R. N. Flew in his 1943 book *Jesus and His Church*, in which he described five elements in the mission of Jesus which 'encapsulated the idea of the church':

> (1) the disciples as the nucleus of the new Israel; (2) the ethical teaching given to them and the power of the Spirit; (3) the conception of Messiahship and the consequent allegiance; (4) the message as constituent of a community; (5) the mission of the new community.[21]

We will be taking a look at several of these elements below.

N. T. Wright has helpfully pointed out that when people convey a message, that message is to be heard not just in their teaching, but also in their practices and in the symbols they employ.[22] So, just because Jesus used the word 'church' on only two recorded occasions, it does not mean that the idea of church, however he defined and expressed it, was not everywhere present in the stories Jesus told, in how he lived out his life

---

[21] This is the summary in Marshall 1992: 124. Flew's book is R. N. Flew (1943), *Jesus and His Church: A Study in the Idea of the Ecclesia in the New Testament*, 2nd edn, Peterborough: Epworth.

[22] In much of his writing, but e.g. N. T. Wright 1996: 137–144.

and in the evocative, even metaphorical, practices he made central to his life. We must be aware of how communication and human interaction actually work in practice.

May we turn to how Jesus interpreted his mission and the community he came to build in the light of the history and traditions of Israel, and his understanding of the kingdom of God.

Jesus and the new Israel

Jesus was, of course, a first-century Jew and thoroughly inhabited the world of first-century Judaism. It sounds obvious to say it, but it is surprising just how many views of Jesus bypass or minimize this fact. This means that the dominant narrative within which Jesus saw himself was that of Israel in the plan of God. In many ways, he saw himself and his mission as the fulfilment of God's plans for the world through Israel. For our purposes we can state that agenda in terms of establishing God's people as the ones in whom he came to rule and reign, and through whom his compassion, peace and justice could be extended to the whole world and the whole of creation.

So, for instance, the very first words of Jesus' public ministry, according to Mark, were a summons to Israel to *be* Israel faithfully and truly: 'Now after John was arrested, Jesus came to Galilee, proclaiming the good news of God, and saying, "The time is fulfilled, and the kingdom of God has come near; repent, and believe in the good news"' (Mark 1:14–15).

James Dunn[23] draws out for us that 'repent' was an echo of the great call of the prophets to Israel to 'return' to God.[24] God's covenant people were not living out the covenant, and it was the prophetic task to call the people back to their God. Similarly, the prophets called the people once more to trust God, and not to put their faith in idols or other nations,[25] and Jesus' call to 'believe' the good news should be heard in this light.

We may conclude confidently, then, that any call of Jesus to 'repent and believe' would have been heard by his hearers as a reiteration of

---

[23] Dunn 2003: 506.
[24] E.g. Isa. 44:22; 55:7; Jer. 3:12, 14, 22; Hos. 3:5; 6:1; Mal. 3:7 – just some of the instances listed in Dunn 2003: 506.
[25] Dunn cites Isa. 7:9; 28:16; 43:10, among many examples (Dunn 2003: 502).

the prophetic call to the people of Israel to return to their God and to trust him afresh.[26]

There is, in the presentation of Jesus in the Gospels, a deliberate evocation of Israel's history and the claim that he fulfils the ancient calling of God on Israel. W. D. Davies and Dale C. Allison give an example from the early chapters of Matthew's Gospel. At the Sermon on the Mount, they link how Jesus 'went up the mountain' (5:1) with the way in which that phrase is characteristically used of Moses' repeated ascents of Mount Sinai, and trace other allusions to Israel's history in how Matthew is telling the story of Jesus:

> If the opening of the sermon on the mount be linked up with Sinai, then Mt 1–5 in all its parts reflects a developed exodus typology. The gospel opens with events recalling the birth and childhood of Moses. Then there is Jesus' baptism, which parallels Israel's passing through the waters. There follows next the temptation, in which Jesus re-experiences the desert temptations recounted in Deuteronomy. Finally, there is 4:23 – 5:2, where Jesus, like Moses, sits on the mountain of revelation. In other words, every major event in Mt 1–5 apparently has its counterpart in the events surrounding Israel's exodus from Egypt ... So when Jesus goes up the mountain to utter the sermon on the mount, he is speaking as the mosaic Messiah and delivering messianic Torah.[27]

N. T. Wright sees similar parallels, arguing that Jesus was intentionally fulfilling the true calling of Israel, becoming ever more conscious that this was something he would have to do alone and which would inevitably lead to his death on the cross, but also to his subsequent vindication by God in the resurrection. Here is a typical summary paragraph:

> Jesus, then, believed himself to be the focal point of the people of YHWH, the returned-from-exile people, the people whose sins were

---

[26] Ibid. 506.
[27] Davies and Allison 1988: 427.

now to be forgiven. He embodied what he had announced. He was the true interpreter of Torah; the true builder of the Temple; the true spokesperson for Wisdom.[28]

Peter J. Leithart develops these themes even more:

Matthew presents Jesus as Israel, as the 'son' who is called from Egypt (Matt. 2:15). His life recapitulates the life of Israel . . . He lives through the entire history of Israel. Matthew begins his Gospel with the phrase *biblos geneseos*, 'the book of genesis,' and immediately follows with a genealogy that reminds us of the *toledoth* (generations) statements of Genesis. Jesus' human father is named Joseph, and he has dreams that enable his family to escape from a murderous Pharaoh-like king, Herod. Jesus goes to Egypt and returns, is tempted in the wilderness, ascends a mountain to teach about the law, carries out a merciful conquest of the land by healing and driving out demons, forms a new Israel within Israel, is sent outside the gate to suffer exile from His Father on a Roman cross, and then returns in glory from the exile of the grave and, with authority greater than the authority of Cyrus, sends His disciples out to build the house of God in all nations.[29]

Jesus' vocation was to fulfil and complete Israel's call. Part of this was to bring Israel back to that calling, and part of it was to challenge, subvert and renew that calling. This is why, in the Sermon on the Mount, for instance, Jesus claims that he has come not to abolish but to fulfil the Law and the Prophets (Matt. 5:17), repeatedly reinterpreting Torah, saying, 'You have heard that it was said . . . But I say to you . . .' (e.g. 5:27–28, 31–32, 33–34, 38–39, 43–44).

Perhaps this is nowhere clearer than in his appointing of the Twelve. In a significant text, Jesus looks ahead to a vision of the end times. Speaking to the Twelve, he says:

---

[28] N. T. Wright 1996: 538.
[29] Leithart 2018: 1. I am grateful to my friend Darren Wolf for drawing my attention to this inventive and imaginative commentary.

You are those who have stood by me in my trials; and I confer on
you, just as my Father has conferred on me, a kingdom, so that you
may eat and drink at my table in my kingdom, and you will sit on
thrones judging the twelve tribes of Israel.
(Luke 22:28–30)

Jesus is drawing an explicit link between the twelve apostles and the
twelve tribes of Israel, and indicating that there is a sense in which
the twelve apostles fulfil the vision of the twelve tribes in a way which they
historically had been unable to do.

Howard Marshall draws the eschatological nature of this incident into
focus:

Jesus is saying in the strongest way possible that the old Israel is
coming under judgment, and that the judgment will be in the hands
of those who have been called by him as his close disciples. The
implication is that there will be what we may call a new Israel.[30]

To summarize: Jesus saw himself as fulfilling the calling of God on
Israel, but also remedying its shortcomings – since that call had not been
fulfilled. He does that supremely in himself and in his personal mission,
not shrinking from redefining that mission, or at least drawing out its true
meaning. But he also sees the fulfilment of that (new/renewed) call in the
Twelve. Jesus fulfils the calling of Israel, significantly modifies it and calls
into being a redeemed people gathered around himself to carry that
calling forward.

This means that we are justified in taking the Old Testament vision
considered in Chapter 1 and taking it forward into church planting. The
calling to be the people of God to bring his blessing to his world as we
live in covenant with him remains the basis of church planting. We must
keep in mind, though, how Jesus reframes this. Theologically speaking,
everything must now be viewed Christologically – through the lens of
Jesus, who he is and what he came to do. He reserves the right to recast
the calling of ancient Israel and to frame it around himself. While he calls

---

[30] Marshall 1992: 123. Cf. N. T. Wright 1996: 444; Dunn 2003: 510.

his disciples to be the true or the new Israel (both in continuity and in sharp discontinuity with Old Testament Israel), Jesus remains the one true (and new) Israelite, and the church takes its cue from him. And that is the case for church planting as well.

We will keep returning to this foundational theological move throughout this study, but we meet it straight away in how Jesus thought, talked and acted in relation to the kingdom of God.

Jesus and the kingdom of God

Jesus begins his public ministry in Mark with the words, 'The time is fulfilled, and the kingdom of God has come near' (1:15). This is an announcement, both of the kingdom of God as his agenda, and of himself as the agent of that agenda. In Luke's Gospel, he declares: 'I must proclaim the good news of the kingdom of God . . . for I was sent for this purpose' (4:43). In Matthew, the evangelist 'bookends' the Sermon on the Mount and a series of Jesus' healing miracles with near-identical words: 'Jesus went throughout Galilee, teaching in their synagogues and proclaiming the good news of the kingdom and curing every disease and every sickness among the people' (4:23 and 9:35); Jesus' ministry in Galilee is a proclamation and demonstration of the kingdom of God. When Jesus sends out the disciples, first the Twelve and then the Seventy(-Two), he instructs them to proclaim the good news and to heal the sick while also announcing, 'The kingdom of heaven has come near' (Matt. 10:7; Luke 10:9). Some of Jesus' most famous teaching, found in the parables, is about the kingdom of God, indeed 'the secret of the kingdom of God' (Mark 4:11, and see Mark 4 and Matt. 13). At the last supper with his disciples, Jesus says to them, 'I tell you, I will never again drink of this fruit of the vine until that day when I drink it new with you in my Father's kingdom' (Matt. 26:29). At his trial before Pilate, three times Jesus refers to 'my kingdom' (John 18:36). He is crucified under an inscription which reads, 'Jesus of Nazareth, the King of the Jews' (John 19:19). As he hangs on the cross, Jesus is asked by one of the thieves crucified with him, 'Jesus, remember me when you come into your kingdom,' to which he replies, 'Truly I tell you, today you will be with me in Paradise' (Luke 23:42–43).

The kingdom of God (or, as Matthew refers to it, 'the kingdom of heaven') is clearly central to the teaching and practices of Jesus. C. C. Caragounis calculates that there are '76 different kingdom sayings, or 103, including the parallels' in the Synoptic Gospels alone.[31] Caragounis is right to say that '[t]he kingdom of God lay at the heart of Jesus' teaching'.[32]

The kingdom of God was a concept familiar to Jews of Jesus' day from their scriptures and from certain developments that occurred in their thinking between the years when the Old Testament (as Christians call it) was completed and the years when Jesus lived and taught. Caragounis usefully summarizes them as developments of the time of David's kingship and that of the prophecy of Daniel. He is at pains to acknowledge that the distinction is oversimplified. The line of thought and expectation from the Davidic kingdom became an essentially political, even military, dream, such that God, through his anointed king, the Messiah, would free the people of Israel once more to live in peace, justice and prosperity in their own land. The picture from Daniel is an 'apocalyptic conception of an ultramundane, transcendental and everlasting kingdom'.[33] In Daniel 2, God acts sovereignly to smash the competing kingdoms of the world and to establish his kingdom in the world. In chapter 7, Daniel describes one 'like a son of man' (7:13 TNIV, ESV) who is presented to God:

> To him was given dominion
> and glory and kingship,
> that all peoples, nations, and languages
> should serve him.
> His dominion is an everlasting dominion
> that shall not pass away,
> and his kingship is one
> that shall never be destroyed.
> (Dan. 7:14)

Both the Davidic and Danielic streams of thought and expectation were alive and well, magnified under the pressure of the Roman occupation of Palestine at the time of Jesus. There were hopes both of political liberation and of the end of the world as it is known and experienced, as God's

---

[31] Caragounis 1992: 425.
[32] Ibid. 417.
[33] Ibid. 418.

universal reign of justice and peace and plenty was ushered in, usually dramatically.

With this as the background to his life and ministry, it is highly significant that Jesus chose to make the language, thought and practice of the kingdom of God central to what he was trying to do. Just as with the fulfilment of the calling of Israel, so Jesus reframed contemporary understandings and expectations of God's kingdom. N. T. Wright argues that Jesus had 'three central aspects of his own prophetic kingdom-announcement: the return from exile, the defeat of evil, and the return of YHWH to Zion'.[34] Now is not the time to examine this analysis further, save to notice just how significantly Jesus recalibrated how the kingdom of God was understood in his time. The political and military expectations of a new David are turned away from violence and dreams of an earthly geographical kingdom, and the more apocalyptic Daniel prophecies are also reframed, but without losing the intensity of Daniel's vision. Once more, we see this Christological theological move. Jesus reframes and restates a theology of the kingdom of God, built around his own person and purpose.

How might this relate to church planting? We must be careful not to overstate the case, but there are clear elements, not least in how Jesus reframed his contemporaries' understandings of the kingdom of God, which shine a light on how Jesus understood the community that would become the church after his death and resurrection. These elements have particular bearing for church planting.

The kingdom of God and community life

The first thing to say is that Jesus' vision for the kingdom of God was a social one – it involved people interacting, living together under the reign or action of God. I. H. Marshall makes the point well:

> The concept of the kingdom of God implies a community. While it has been emphasized almost *ad nauseam* that the primary concept is that of the sovereignty or kingship or actual rule of God and not a territory ruled by a king, it must be also emphasized that kingship

---

34 N. T. Wright 1996: 477.

57

cannot be exercised in the abstract but only over a people. The concept of the kingdom of God implies both the existence of a group of people who own him as king and the establishment of a realm of people within which his gracious power is manifested.[35]

This is demonstrated by the communal nature of several of the images that Jesus uses for his followers: for instance, he calls them a 'little flock' (Luke 12:32), a 'city' (Matt. 5:14), a planted field (Matt. 13:24; 15:13) and a group of wedding guests (Mark 2:19). He even describes them as his true family (Mark 3:31–35).[36] This kingdom, then, is made up of groups of people, centred on Jesus, upon whom he bestows a special status.

We can notice, as well, that much of Jesus' teaching is concerned with how people will relate to one another within his kingdom. The Lord's Prayer has the petition, 'And forgive us our sins, for we ourselves forgive everyone indebted to us' (Luke 11:4). Jesus teaches about forgiving others within the new community: 'Not seven times, but, I tell you, seventy-seven times' (Matt. 18:22). Humility, not status-seeking, is advocated (e.g. Matt. 18:3–5; Mark 10:42–45; Luke 14:10), and service and mutual love is solemnly made the keynote of the followers of Jesus (John 13:13–15, 34–35).

The kingdom of God, the crowds and the disciples

This social vision is borne out in the dynamics of the Gospels, with Jesus gathering groups around himself, most notably, of course, the twelve disciples. It is very rare that we see Jesus on his own, and the driver of the narratives of each of the Gospels is Jesus moving from place to place with the disciples. Each Gospel writer is aware, as well, of further social dynamics, which are brought into play in sometimes very sophisticated ways. Mark, for instance, shows us Jesus with the inner three of his disciples (Peter, James and John), as well as the Twelve; there is conflict with those who oppose Jesus; and then there are the crowds who follow him. The attitude of the crowds is ambivalent, though, and shifts.[37] The Sermon on the Mount, in Matthew, is introduced as being preached to the

---

[35] Marshall 1992: 123.
[36] Ibid.
[37] See e.g. Hooker 1991: 21.

disciples, in contradistinction to the crowds (5:1), but at its conclusion we read that 'the crowds were astonished at his teaching' (7:28), so they had also been listening. In John, we read that as Jesus debates with the scribes and the Pharisees in the presence of the crowds, 'many believed in him' (8:30). This is followed by Jesus' teaching on the true nature of discipleship. A similar pattern is observable in Mark: when Peter has his revelation of the identity of Jesus in the villages of Caesarea Philippi, Jesus teaches about his death, and then 'he called the crowd with his disciples' and teaches them that discipleship is patterned on his own forthcoming death on the cross (8:27–38).

So, what we see emerging is a twofold pattern: on the one hand, Jesus attracting crowds of people and teaching them, and, on the other, a focusing of that teaching onto what it truly means to follow him. The crowds come and go. In Luke, we read of Jesus entering Nain, 'and his disciples and a large crowd went with him' (7:11). In John, after the discourse on Jesus being the bread of life, 'many of his disciples turned back and no longer went about with him' (6:66). The cheering crowds of Palm Sunday may well be the same crowds who are calling for the crucifixion of Jesus on Good Friday. Jesus is constantly aware of the crowds. In Matthew we read, 'When he saw the crowds, he had compassion for them, because they were harassed and helpless, like sheep without a shepherd.' His response, intriguingly, is to encourage the disciples to 'ask the Lord of the harvest to send out labourers into his harvest' (9:36–38). This last interchange is particularly interesting, as it combines the vocabulary of the Davidic and Danielic understandings of the kingdom of God (the pre-eminent shepherd king of Israel was David, and the language of 'harvest' is common in apocalyptic literature, denoting the end of the world and God's judgment of the nations), but recasts it in terms of divine compassion, which he has just displayed in his teaching and healing.

The kingdom of God and discipleship

A strong theme of Jesus' teaching is discipleship. Mark's Gospel highlights this especially. Morna Hooker can say: 'Mark's story is a story about the meaning of discipleship (barely understood)'.[38] R. T. France writes that

---

[38] Ibid.

the passage Mark 8:27 – 10:45, in particular, is 'generally and rightly regarded as focused primarily on the nature of discipleship'.[39] Granted that this is a Gospel about the kingdom, as announced by Jesus in his first explosive public appearance when he says, 'The time is fulfilled, and the kingdom of God has come near; repent, and believe in the good news' (1:15), this prominence of the theme of discipleship is of profound significance. For Jesus, discipleship is the grammar of the kingdom of God. The one cannot be understood without reference to the other.

If we look at the central discipleship chapters in Mark, identified by France, we find several key themes.

The phrase 'the way' is used frequently and metaphorically for following Jesus on his way to Jerusalem and to his death on the cross (8:27; 9:33; 10:17, 32, 52). Discipleship and the life of the kingdom is something active. It is a literal following of Jesus along life's paths. It takes as its orientation the journey to the cross. The life of the kingdom is one of self-sacrifice, patterned on Jesus.

The whole section is framed by the healing of two blind men (8:22–26; 10:46–52). At one level, this is a lesson that we all need to have our eyes opened if we are to see and understand Jesus properly. More than that, France highlights how the disciples learn in these chapters a whole new scale of values, which are congruent with the kingdom of God but which are diametrically opposite to the values of the world. It is in these chapters that Jesus teaches, 'Many who are first will be last, and the last will be first' (10:31), and challenges the disciples to upend their understanding of power and status: 'But it is not so among you' (10:43). France argues persuasively that Jesus is training the disciples to see the world differently, which is what the life of repentance means – the theme with which Jesus began his announcement of the gospel right at the beginning. To be in the kingdom of God is to be a disciple of Jesus, and this means being trained to see the world differently. Jesus does this through a series of encounters and reflections with the disciples, culminating in the discussion of greatness as James and John ask who is to sit at the right and left of Jesus in his glory. France deftly points out that it is in this long section on discipleship that Mark recounts Jesus' three

---

39 France 1990: 49.

predictions of his passion (8:31; 9:31; 10:32–34) with their stark call: 'If any want to become my followers, let them deny themselves and take up their cross and follow me' (8:34). Hooker refers to this as 'the meaning of discipleship'.[40]

The social make-up of the kingdom of God

It is this radical recalibrating of the values of the world which is a feature of Jesus' teaching about the kingdom of God. The Beatitudes begin and end with a reference to the kingdom of God:

> Blessed are the poor in spirit, for theirs is the kingdom of heaven.
> (Matt. 5:3)

> Blessed are those who are persecuted for righteousness' sake, for theirs is the kingdom of heaven.
> (Matt. 5:10)

The bookending is a rhetorical device which shows us that everything in between is to be read through the lens of the bookends. So, meekness, mercy, righteousness, peacemaking and so on – all this is part and parcel of the life of those in the kingdom of God. How different from the political expectations of Jesus' contemporaries!

And how different was Jesus' teaching on the kingdom from the *religious* expectations of his contemporaries. For many, the coming kingdom of God was an amalgam of nationalism and religious purity, especially around the keeping of the law. Jesus challenged those who saw themselves as the custodians of the religious purity of Israel ('Woe to you, scribes and Pharisees, hypocrites! For you lock people out of the kingdom of heaven. For you do not go in yourselves, and when others are going in, you stop them' [Matt. 23:13]) and earned himself a reputation for associating with certain people whom others felt he should have kept well clear of: 'Now all the tax-collectors and sinners were coming near to listen to [Jesus]. And the Pharisees and the scribes were grumbling and saying, "This fellow welcomes sinners and eats with them"' (Luke 15:1–2).

---

[40] Hooker 1991: 110.

Jesus is questioned on this, and replies with an analogy of health and healing: 'Those who are well have no need of a physician, but those who are sick; I have come to call not the righteous but sinners to repentance' (Luke 5:31–32).

In words which they must have found as incomprehensible as they were provocative, Jesus says to the chief priests and the elders of the people, 'Truly I tell you, the tax-collectors and the prostitutes are going into the kingdom of heaven ahead of you' (Matt. 21:31). The punchline of the ensuing parable (that of the wicked tenants) is: 'Therefore I tell you, the kingdom of God will be taken away from you and given to a people that produces the fruits of the kingdom' (Matt. 21:43).

The chief priests and the Pharisees realize that he is talking about them, and look for ways to arrest him (21:45). The point is even more starkly put by Jesus after he has healed the Roman centurion's servant. The centurion was, of course, a Gentile, not a Jew, not from Israel. His faith astonishes Jesus:

> When Jesus heard him, he was amazed and said to those who followed him, 'Truly I tell you, in no one in Israel have I found such faith. I tell you, many will come from east and west and will eat with Abraham and Isaac and Jacob in the kingdom of heaven, while the heirs of the kingdom will be thrown into outer darkness, where there will be weeping and gnashing of teeth.'
> (Matt. 8:10–12)

Entry into this kingdom is not a matter of ethnicity or racial purity and descent, nor of ritual purity, but is by faith.

The kingdom of God and healing

Faith provides us with a good link into another central category of Jesus' teaching and practice of the kingdom, for he often associates healing and faith. To the woman with the flow of blood, for instance, he says, 'Daughter, your faith has made you well; go in peace' (Luke 8:48). She has touched the fringe of his clothes, power has come out of him, and immediately her haemorrhage has stopped. Healings and exorcisms are frequent in the ministry of Jesus, and he often links them to the kingdom of God.[41] In Jesus' healing work, we see his compassion, his authority over sickness, his disarming of the strong man / Satan, the approbation of God, the in-breaking of God's kingdom. This is a theme seen throughout the Gospel narratives.[42]

The kingdom of God and mission

Healings and exorcisms play a major part, as well, in the missionary mandates that Jesus gives to the Twelve and to the Seventy(-Two). The prominent place that Jesus assigns to these missionary journeys has powerful significance in our understanding of how he viewed the future of the kingdom of God. He trains his disciples, as the new or reconstituted Israel, to continue his ministry, and the Seventy(-Two) – as, at the least, a far wider grouping – to do the same. The Twelve, in Matthew's account, are given 'authority over unclean spirits, to cast them out, and to cure every disease and every sickness' (10:1). The language of authority, in the context of the kingdom of God, is interesting and revealing. Then, they are sent out on mission to the 'lost sheep of the house of Israel': 'As you go, proclaim the good news, "The kingdom of heaven has come near." Cure the sick, raise the dead, cleanse the lepers, cast out demons' (10:6–8).

As for the Seventy(-Two), they are sent in pairs by Jesus 'to every town and place where he himself intended to go' (Luke 10:1). They are commissioned: 'Whenever you enter a town and its people welcome you, eat what is set before you; cure the sick who are there, and say to them, "The kingdom of God has come near to you"' (10:8–9).

When they come back, they are rejoicing that the demons submitted to them in the name of Jesus, and the Lord says that he saw Satan fall from heaven (10:17–19).

The kingdom of God and supernatural fruitfulness

Power and fruitfulness are emphasized as well in the parables of the kingdom which Jesus tells. In Mark 4, the chapter is headed by the parable of the sower. The seed sown is the word (4:15). It has little success in the

---

[41] B. L. Blackburn (1992: 549) counts 'no less than thirty-four specific miracles (exclusive of parallels) performed by Jesus during his earthly ministry. In addition, there are fifteen texts (again, exclusive of parallels) that narrate or refer to Jesus' miraculous activity (almost always healings and exorcisms) in summary fashion'.

[42] See Matt. 12:28; Mark 1:40–42; Luke 6:19; 13:16; John 2:11 for a non-exhaustive sampling.

first three categories (on the busy paths of life, where Satan snatches it away; on the rocky ground of hearts with no root, where trouble and persecution lead to an immediate falling away; and among thorns, where the cares of the world and the lure of wealth and the desire for other things choke the word). However, where the word falls on the good soil of those who hear and accept it, the fruit is startling – 'thirty and sixty and a hundredfold' (4:20). These figures are fantastic: the average yield would have been on a ratio of 7:1, so harvests on this scale are unheard of. Brendan Byrne draws out the point:

> In this last figure ['a hundredfold'] the parable displays the kind of 'over the top' exaggerated outcome that is the feature of many of Jesus' parables. If in the end the story seems to leave the world of everyday reality, that is the point: we are not dealing with the reality of everyday life but with the power and generosity of God at work in the Kingdom.[43]

The last of the parables in Mark 4 tightens the link between the word of God and the kingdom of God. Jesus begins with the question 'With what can we compare the kingdom of God, or what parable will we use for it?' before comparing it to a mustard seed, the smallest of all seeds, which grows up and becomes 'the greatest of all shrubs, and puts forth large branches, so that the birds of the air can make nests in its shade' (4:30–32). Joel Marcus points out that Jesus would have been alluding to Ezekiel 17:23; 31:6 and Daniel 4:18, all of which refer to trees and their branches, with birds nesting in them. Ezekiel 17:23 is especially interesting:

> On the mountain height of Israel
>   I will plant it,
> in order that it may produce boughs and bear fruit,
>   and become a noble cedar.

---

[43] Byrne 2008: 81. The 7:1 figure comes from Jeremias 1972, cited by Myers 2015: 177. Myers quotes Jeremias on the super-abundance of the hundredfold yield, which reinforces Byrne's insight: '[It] symbolizes the eschatological overflowing of the divine fulness, surpassing all human measure' (Jeremias 1972: 150; Myers 2015: 177).

> Under it every kind of bird will live;
>> in the shade of its branches will nest
>> winged creatures of every kind.

Marcus points out that the cedar was the symbol of the Davidic kingdom, and that the birds coming to nest in its branches were thought to be Gentile nations. So, what we have is Jesus saying that the secret of the kingdom of God (Mark 4:11) is his word, which may appear tiny and insignificant, but which has within it the power to grow into a universal kingdom, of which King David's realm was the prototype, and into which people from all over the world would come to rest. As with the parable of the sower, we have something that appears to struggle in many ways, but which has within it the super-abundant capacity for fruitfulness of God himself.

The kingdom of God and the poor

A major incident in the ministry of Jesus comes in Luke 4. Jesus goes to the synagogue in Nazareth, and reads out words from Isaiah:

> The Spirit of the Lord is upon me,
>> because he has anointed me
>>> to bring good news to the poor.
> He has sent me to proclaim release to the captives
>> and recovery of sight to the blind,
>>> to let the oppressed go free,
> to proclaim the year of the Lord's favour.
> (Luke 4:18–19, quoting Isa. 61:1–2)

Jesus then declares: 'Today this scripture has been fulfilled in your hearing' (4:21).

Brendan Byrne emphasizes that '[i]t is hard to overstress the import-ance of this scene in Luke's gospel'.[44] In Luke, it is the launch of Jesus' public ministry. It is his manifesto, if you like, the headline under which all else is to be read and understood. Jesus announces that his ministry is to be the fulfilment of this vision of Isaiah, a bringing of good news to the

---

[44] Byrne 2015: 55.

poor. Byrne draws out that Jesus, in quoting Isaiah 61, makes some small but significant changes:

- He leaves out a reference in Isaiah 61 to binding up the broken-hearted.
- He adds in the phrase about letting the oppressed go free. This is from Isaiah 58, a passage calling the people of Israel to true (not just formal, religious) fasting, which is worth quoting:

> Is not this the fast that I choose:
>   to loose the bonds of injustice,
> to undo the thongs of the yoke,
>   to let the oppressed go free,
>   and to break every yoke?
> Is it not to share your bread with the hungry,
>   and bring the homeless poor into your house;
> when you see the naked, to cover them,
>   and not to hide yourself from your own kin?
> (Isa. 58:6–7)

- He ends the quotation with the 'year of the Lord's favour', whereas Isaiah concludes with a reference to 'the day of vengeance of our God' (61:2).

We may draw some important conclusions from this, especially given the strategic placing of this Nazareth announcement at the head of Jesus' ministry:

- Jesus, in his recasting of the role of Israel and in his redefinition of God's kingdom, has a special place for the poor. Although Jesus may well have meant more than economic poverty, he certainly did not mean less than that.[45] We have only to think of Mary's Song, the

---

[45] Joel Green is balanced in his handling of this debate. He rejects attempts to define the poor as those who are 'spiritually poor', but broadens economic poverty to other disadvantages which led to exclusion. 'Hence, although "poor" is hardly devoid of economic significance, for Luke this wider meaning of diminished status honor is paramount' (Green 1997: 211).

Magnificat, with its references to filling the hungry with good things and sending the rich away empty (Luke 1:53), and Luke's version of the Beatitudes, which begins 'Blessed are you who are poor' and includes blessings pronounced on the hungry (6:20, 21), to corroborate this. And we can trace this emphasis in Jesus' own life and ministry in the Gospels. When John the Baptist asks if Jesus is the Messiah, or if Israel should wait for another, it is noteworthy that Jesus responds by drawing his attention to his miracles and by saying that 'the poor have good news brought to them' (Luke 7:22).

• There will be a special tone of freedom and release in Jesus' ministry. The Greek word translated as 'release' is used in connection with the release from sins (e.g. in Luke 1:77; 3:3; 24:47). There is also tradition associated with this idea of freedom and release in Israel, to which Jesus was almost certainly alluding. In Deuteronomy 15 and Leviticus 25, the seventh and fiftieth years in Israel were to be years of jubilee, when debts were to be written off, slavery ended and lands restored.

• Jesus' ministry was overwhelmingly to be about acceptance with God, and not judgment. This is not to say that Jesus did not believe that God would judge the world – indeed he did – but rather that his ministry was about the offer of favour and acceptance with God for any who would take it.

The kingdom of God and the cross

To step back a bit, as we reflect on Jesus and the kingdom of God, any theology must ask how it relates to the death of Jesus on the cross, not least any theology that attempts to relate his teaching and practice of the kingdom of God to his mission and the establishing of the church.

John's Gospel writes of the crucifixion as if it were a kind of enthronement. Jesus speaks of his death as being 'lifted up', an exaltation (3:14; 8:28; 12:34), and John makes a point of emphasizing the inscription put on the cross, 'Jesus of Nazareth, the King of the Jews', which is written in Hebrew, Latin and Greek (19:19, 20). At the cross, Jesus gathers a new family (represented by Mary and the beloved disciple [19:25–27]) and bestows on them the gift of his Spirit (19:30). Some commentators see in the blood and water which flow from Jesus' pierced side 'the blood and water of Eucharist and Baptism'.[46] The Gospel's repeated reflection on honour and glory finds that the epicentre of these things for Jesus lies at the cross: 'The hour has come for the Son of Man to be glorified' (12:23). For John, then, the cross is the touchstone of the activity of God in his kingdom, and the way in which the new community of Jesus comes into being.

The Synoptic Gospels place the cross within the framework of the new covenant and the fulfilment of Old Testament prophecies and prototypes (e.g. the teaching of Jesus at the last supper [Matt. 26:26–29; Luke 22:14–23]) and present it as the ultimate pattern for discipleship (e.g. Mark 8:31–38). N. T. Wright argues that 'the central symbolic action which provides the key to Jesus' implicit story about his death is . . . the Last Supper', arguing that Jesus was accomplishing a new exodus through his death.[47]

John adds another perspective as well. At the beginning of the Gospel, Jesus cleanses the temple, driving out the traders. When he is challenged about this, he responds: 'Destroy this temple, and in three days I will raise it up.' John explains that 'he was speaking of the temple of his body' (2:19, 21). As Marianne Meye Thompson explains: 'Thus the saying in John has to do with Jesus' crucifixion ("if you destroy this temple") and resurrection ("in three days I will raise it up").'[48] She goes on to draw out the significance of this claim: 'Jesus is then both the Messiah, the guardian of the temple where the glory of God and the name of God dwell (2:13–17), and himself the locus of that indwelling glory (cf. 1:14; 2:22)'.[49]

Spiritually, the temple was where God and his people met, the place where he manifested his glory, where the sacrifices for sin were made. Socially and politically, the temple was also the centre of Jewish national pride. To speak of destroying and rebuilding the temple was thus hugely provocative. N. T. Wright likens it to burning the flag.[50] Jesus' actions in cleansing the temple were acts of judgment, direct challenges to the Jewish hierarchy, and an implicit assertion of his right to make such charges and claims. It is this assertion which John makes plain in his Gospel.

---

[46] Maloney 1998: 505. Not all commentators would read it this way.
[47] N. T. Wright 1996: 554, 557.
[48] M. M. Thompson 2015: 73.
[49] Ibid.
[50] N. T. Wright 1996: 369.

Wright encourages us to read Jesus' actions in the temple alongside those of the last supper. If the cleansing of the temple removed the greatest contemporary symbol of national and religious life from the stage, then the actions of the last supper replaced them.[51] The supper was almost certainly some kind of Passover meal, and as such commemorated the exodus as the greatest event in Israel's history. Jesus reframes it in terms of his own impending death. Just as the exodus spelled liberation for the ancient people of Israel, so Jesus' death was an announcement of freedom for the new people of Israel, and an assertion of the true nature of the kingdom of God. So, what we have is Jesus redrawing the story of Israel around himself, with his death as the climax of that narrative. The ways in which he has been reconstituting Israel and expressing the life of God's kingdom all fit within this wider understanding. Jesus is remaking the people of God, overcoming the sin and evil which has kept them in captivity, and leading them to freedom in the new Promised Land of his kingdom. As Wright puts it, reflecting on the cross:

> [Jesus] would bring Israel's history to its climax. Through his work, YHWH would defeat evil, bringing the kingdom to birth, and enable Israel to become, after all, the light of the world. Through his work, YHWH would reveal that he was not just a god, but God.[52]

The kingdom of God and church planting

So, to draw this section to a close, what theology for church planters can we draw from Jesus' teaching and practices in the Gospels? To restate, we must be careful not to draw too straight a line from the life and ministry of Jesus to the situation that pertained after his death, resurrection and ascension. Equally, we must not overstate the difference between regular churches and church plants. Nonetheless, it seems legitimate to draw out five points.

1 Church plants are built around Jesus

The new Israel and the new kingdom are delineated and created through Jesus. He reinterprets what has gone before. He establishes the new social

---

51 Ibid. 558.
52 Ibid. 609.

reality of his followers by positioning himself as the new temple and accomplishing the new exodus. The kingdom of God becomes, in an unselfconscious way, his kingdom. Whatever was to come after Jesus, it would be the fulfilment of what had gone before, dramatically recast in terms of following him. It is all about Jesus.

Jesus is the foundation of the church – all churches, including church plants. Good church theology will take pains to keep this front and centre in our thinking, praying and planning. What we want people to come away with from our churches is a sense of the greatness and wonder of Jesus Christ. All else is secondary.

Leaders of church plants will doubtless spend time thinking through their vision and values. It would be good to establish some clear link between how the church plant views itself and its core activities and Jesus himself. Often this is just assumed, but it is better for it to be made explicit, and articulated in some memorable and energizing fashion.

2 Church plants follow a way of life set before them by Jesus

Jesus made discipleship a key element of what it meant to be in the kingdom of God; church plants would be wise to do the same.

Church plants will probably be aiming to reach out to people for whom church is a foreign land and an alien culture. There will be much work to be done in helping people in the formation of Christlikeness. Many will come from backgrounds where such behaviours and practices are new and challenging. It may well be, too, that church plants will be working with people with low levels of literacy or for whom English (or whatever the dominant tongue is in your context) is not a first language. There may be destructive patterns of behaviour to deal with, and dysfunctional rela- tionships and patterns of relating. Or it may be that the assumptions of middle-class aspiration or consumerism have not been challenged in the light of Christ.

Church planters will want to think through communal practices and habits that build up discipleship and that encourage the flourishing of the kingdom of God. We are aiming to see the establishment of not just church plants, but *healthy* church plants. We will remember the 'big picture' thinking: how Jesus saw Israel's vocation as being for the world, and how self-denial and self-sacrifice took their pattern in his followers from his own life laid down on the cross.

An aspect of this is the startling way in which Jesus modelled a social life of difference. He welcomed the tax-collectors, sinners and prostitutes. He put the first last, and the last first. He placed children at the centre of the life of his community. He was scathing about a vision of purity that ended up justifying social exclusion. Church plants may well involve the challenge of including people from very different backgrounds.

Sometimes church plants take a team from one part of town and plant it in another. This may mean that members of the planting team come from socio-economic or ethnic backgrounds that are very different from those of the people they are trying to reach. Team members will need to be highly self-aware, and bring wisdom as to what is cultural and what is kingdom. Everyone will need emotional intelligence, and a high degree of intentionality about building open community between one another in the name of Jesus. It is so much easier to be part of monocultural groupings, but Jesus made a point of mixing people from all kinds of backgrounds together, without privileging one background over the others.

There should be something in the shared life of these new communities of Christian faith which is explicable only in terms of Jesus. No other cultural or sociological factors should fully account for how and why things are done in the way that they are. Hopefully, church planters will be asked why they do what they do; it may be food banks, job clubs, youth work, environmental or social justice campaigns, parties for their communities. The answer should be 'Jesus'.

3 Church plants follow Jesus in being good news to the poor

I remember addressing some Anglican clergy in Canada about church planting. Many were dubious, feeling that it was just a way of smuggling evangelical theology into the life of the wider church, with an emphasis on individual conversion and personal piety, with little or no vision for wider issues of social justice or structural and cultural change. The door for real engagement opened when I was able to tell the stories of many, many church plants which were actively committed to ministry with and among the poor. In fact, I could not think of a single church plant which was not involved in such ministries.

Church plants, like other churches, are committed to working with the poor, because this was fundamental to the ministry and vocation and practice of Jesus. Church plants, with their emphasis on reaching out to and connecting with communities which currently do not have any link with church, may well find themselves placing more of an emphasis on social justice and mercy ministries than other, more established churches.

4 Church plants depend on the power of God

A central aspect of Jesus' vision for the kingdom of God was the battle with sickness and evil. The miraculous was part and parcel of the shared life he was aiming to establish for his followers. This is true, as well, with the hundredfold fruitfulness of the word of God in his teaching. It is true, as well, in the way that suffering is borne, and in how personal preferences and priorities are made secondary to the needs of others and the mission of the kingdom. There is something in the kingdom of God that is beyond the earthly reality of day-to-day existence.

Again, this is true of all churches. Church plants, though, may find themselves with fewer alternative strategies and resources compared to more established churches, which can often rely on these. They may have less money, fewer capable and experienced people, a fuzzier sense of tradition or ecclesiastical authorization. Life can feel just that bit more exposed in a church plant. The risks and the challenges can be greater.

5 Church plants are missionary

Lastly, church plants see themselves as missionary, as they follow Jesus in his kingdom. It is striking just how much of Jesus' time with his followers is spent in training and sending them on mission. And it may be no accident that the references to the miraculous come in concentrated form around these missions.

This should apply to all churches, but there are ways in which it is specifically true of church plants. These see themselves as existing to reach those who do not, as yet, come to any church. The Gregory Centre (a Church of England centre, specializing in church planting and growth) makes the statement that church plants are to reach new people in new places in new ways. This makes them inescapably and essentially missionary.

In some ways, this clarity of purpose may give church plants a freedom that more established churches do not have. If the 'sign on the bus' is so clearly that the church plant is for the benefit of those who do not yet attend, the energy and missionary prioritization of the vision is preserved. It is striking and surprising, however, just how quickly church plants can revert to becoming self-serving, making the needs and preferences of Christians their main concern.

Jesus' vision for a missionary church

All four Gospels end with Jesus commissioning his followers to take his name and word into the world. The conclusion of his physical presence with them on earth is not the end of the Jesus-project, but is rather the signal for a whole new stage, a global extension of his kingdom and message. If we are looking for how Jesus envisaged church and mission, following on from his death and resurrection, then these four commissions are highly instructive.

We will look at each in its canonical turn, before drawing some conclusions.

Matthew

Matthew's Great Commission is the climax to his Gospel. Some see it as the key to understanding the whole Gospel,[53] others as the place in which all the narrative strands of the Gospel come together.[54] Structurally, the Gospel has been on a journey from north to south, starting in Galilee before taking the road to Jerusalem ahead of the events of the last week of Jesus' earthly life in Jerusalem; but now, we return to Galilee again, where it all started.[55] The language of Jesus 'being with' the disciples unambiguously reflects the pronouncement of the angel at his birth, namely that he will be called Emmanuel, 'which means, "God is with us"' (1:23), and there is a similar echo at the end of the Gospel, with the reference to the nations, of the Gospel's beginning, with its reference to

---

[53] E.g. Ott, in Ott, Strauss with Tennent 2010: 36, citing Köstenberger and O'Brien 2001: 87 n. 4.
[54] E.g. France 2007: 1109.
[55] See France 2007: 2–5 for this analysis.

Abraham, who was to be father of many nations.[56] The offer of earthly worship, which had been offered to Jesus by Satan, and refused, is now restored and extended (4:8–10).[57] The calling of the Twelve, which seemed to have been irreparably damaged at the cross, is now renewed. The mission, which had been previously limited to 'the lost sheep of the house of Israel' (10:6; 15:24), is now extended to 'all nations', just as baptism undergoes a shift from John, who had intended it 'as a symbol of a new beginning for a repentant Israel (3:1–12)',[58] to now being intended for the peoples of the world. We shall see the summation of the themes of kingship and discipleship. 'And, perhaps most remarkably of all, the human Jesus of the hills of Galilee is now to be understood not as the preacher and promoter of faith, but as himself its object.'[59] The mood of summation and universality is captured in the sweeping references to geography and time (to the ends of the earth, and the end of time), and by the repeated use (four times) of the word 'all':

> Now the eleven disciples went to Galilee, to the mountain to which Jesus had directed them. When they saw him, they worshipped him; but some doubted. And Jesus came and said to them, 'All authority in heaven and on earth has been given to me. Go therefore and make disciples of all nations, baptizing them in the name of the Father and of the Son and of the Holy Spirit, and teaching them to obey everything that I have commanded you. And remember, I am with you always, to the end of the age.'
> (Matt. 28:16–20)

This commission is sometimes compared to the calling of many of God's leaders and prophets in the Old Testament, men who were full of fear and a sense of inadequacy, people such as Abraham, Moses, Joshua, Gideon, Samuel, Isaiah and Jeremiah.[60] It is surely noteworthy that, in

---

[56] Ott, Strauss with Tennent 2010: 36.
[57] France 2007: 1108.
[58] Ibid.
[59] Ibid.
[60] See ibid. 1109. France cites Davies and Allison 1997: 679–680, where they argue that it is particularly the calling of Joshua which Matthew had in mind, once more showing Jesus as the new Moses.

nearly all of these cases, it is *God* who is calling and reassuring his frail messengers, whereas here it is *Jesus*, stepping into the divine role, who is commissioning his hesitant disciples.

Lucien Legrand, in an illuminating exegesis of the passage, divides the text into two: the narrative of the disciples and their mixed response to Jesus, in verses 16 and 17; and the commanding authority of Jesus, in verses 18 and 19.[61] In the first part, it is the disciples who are the subject of all the verbs, and we follow their actions and inner feelings. 'We are in the area of human initiative, then. Nor does this initiative lead far. It issues in indecision, divided between worship and doubt.'[62] The comparison serves by way of contrast with the overpowering authority of Jesus in the second part of the passage. Here, Jesus speaks, commands and promises to act, and the effect is for a tiny, troubled and isolated group of conflicted disciples to reach the whole world with their message.

The reason for this is the presence of Jesus with them, and the reason for the impact of this is the authority which has been given to him by God. Legrand writes eloquently: 'a declaration of a seizure of power and enthronement overshadows the "apostolic commission." The Christological aspect dominates the missiological.'[63] The 'enthronement' is a reference to Daniel 7:13–14, which lies behind our passage. There the prophet Daniel recounts:

I saw in the night visions,

> and behold, with the clouds of heaven
>> there came one like a son of man,
> and he came to the Ancient of Days
>> and was presented before him.
> And to him was given dominion
>> and glory and a kingdom,
> that all peoples, nations, and languages
>> should serve him;

---

[61] Legrand 1990: 80–82.
[62] Ibid. 80.
[63] Ibid. 81.

> his dominion is an everlasting dominion,
>> which shall not pass away,
>> and his kingdom one
>>> that shall not be destroyed.
> (Dan. 7:13–14 ESV)

The language of the above is alluded to seven times in Matthew, and lies behind Jesus' favourite way of referring to himself: 'the Son of Man'.[64] In Daniel's vision, one like a Son of Man comes before God and is given a universal, indestructible kingship over the nations of the world. In Matthew, on three occasions the fulfilment of this vision is said to be imminent (e.g. at the Mount of Transfiguration [16:28]), sometimes belonging to the return of Jesus and the end of the world (e.g. 19:28 and 25:31). This last reference is to the Son of Man judging between the sheep and the goats, which Brendan Byrne sees as the situation in play at the Great Commission.[65] Something has happened, then, which has led to the gift of the authority and kingdom prophesied in Daniel 7; that something can only be the resurrection. As Byrne explains:

> God's raising of Jesus from the dead has been at one and the same time his exaltation to the right hand of the Father and installation with the world authority conferred upon the 'one like a Son of Man' in Dan 7:13–14.[66]

R. T. France notes: 'what had been a vision for the future, albeit the imminent future, has become present reality.'[67]

This is the culmination of the theme of messianic kingship that has been seen throughout the Gospel. N. T. Wright lays out the argument:

> The main emphasis of [Matt. 28:16–20] is upon who Jesus is now revealed to be ... Jesus has been granted 'all authority in heaven and on earth' – virtually identical in phraseology to the kingdom-clause in the Matthean version of the Lord's Prayer. This, it seems, is

---

64 France 2007: 396–398.
65 Byrne 2004: 227.
66 Ibid.
67 France 2007: 1113.

how the prayer is to be answered; this, in other words, is how the kingdom is coming, how the will of the 'Father' is being done. The significance of the resurrection, as far as Matthew is concerned, is that Jesus now holds the role that had been marked out for the Messiah in Psalms 2, 72 and 89, which became concentrated in such imagery-laden figures as the 'son of man' in Daniel 7 . . . The world-wide commission Jesus gives the disciples depends directly upon his possessing all authority in heaven and on earth, within the kingdom which is now well and truly inaugurated. The only explanation for the messianic authority on the one hand, and this kingdom fulfilment on the other, is that Jesus has been raised from the dead.[68]

This is the authority Jesus speaks of, which lies behind this universal commission to his disciples.

What does he commission them to do? Interestingly, the emphasis is not on going to the ends of the earth. The grammatical stress is on making disciples, and the command to 'go' is subordinate to that. It could even just be an idiom for introducing an idea or some action.[69] At the most it means 'having gone', 'having left', 'having journeyed'.[70] If we take the force of the sentence to be a command to 'Go!', we are changing the emphasis of Jesus here. What he is getting at is that the mission is to make disciples, and that is done by baptizing and teaching. Legrand counsels us to picture the missionary as sitting down, like a rabbinic teacher, and not rushing off to the ends of the world.[71]

If disciple-making is the core of the Great Commission in Matthew, what could Jesus have had in mind? Byrne explains:

This means that the goal of the enterprise is that members of the nations undergo the formation the original disciples have undergone as told in the gospel: being called personally by Jesus, inducted by him into the 'family of God', learning both from his teaching and his example as healer and instrument of God's mercy, schooled in

---

68 N. T. Wright 2003: 643.
69 France 2007: 1115; Legrand 1990: 79.
70 Legrand 1990: 79.
71 Ibid. 78.

the way of service in imitation of the Son of Man who came not to be served but to serve and give his life as a ransom for many (20:28).[72]

The phrase translated 'make disciples' is also used in Matthew 13:52: 'Therefore every scribe who has been *trained* for the kingdom of heaven is like a master of a house, who brings out of his treasure what is new and what is old' (my emphasis).

R. T. France cautiously suggests that Jesus may be describing his followers as a new kind of 'scribal school'. The Jewish scribes had the task of explaining and teaching Torah to would-be followers. Jesus is showing that, in the kingdom of heaven, disciple-making is like this, except it integrates the new (the teachings and practices of Jesus) and the old (the law and history of Israel).[73]

The process is to begin with baptism, which is strikingly to be in the name (singular) of the Father and of the Son and of the Holy Spirit. We must not read back fourth-century formulations of the doctrine of the Trinity into Matthew's text, but we cannot avoid the impact of how Jesus includes himself in the same baptismal formula as the Father and the Holy Spirit. In the context of Matthew's Gospel, we are reminded of the baptism of Jesus, which has a similarly trinitarian feel: when Jesus comes up out of the water, the Spirit of God descends upon him like a dove and alights on him, and there is a voice from heaven declaring, 'This is my Son, the Beloved, with whom I am well pleased' (3:13–17). The baptism of the converts from the nations is an invitation into this same experience of the Son within the Trinity.

Note that the baptism of those from the nations comes at the beginning of the discipling process, and is not the culmination of it. France writes well:

Matthew . . . is here presenting a . . . model whereby baptism is the point of enrollment into a process of learning which is never complete; the Christian community is a school of learners at various

---

[72] Byrne 2004: 227–228.
[73] France 2007: 544–547. He also cites the rather nice theories that Matthew may himself have been a converted scribe, or that he was known as a writer/scribe; either way he may be referring to himself, and possibly to his Gospel as the archetypal disciple-making manual.

stages of development rather than divided into the baptized (who have 'arrived') and those who are 'not ready yet'.[74]

We should note, in particular in regard to a theology of church planting, that the Great Commission in Matthew necessitates the founding of churches. Disciple-making, according to Jesus, requires baptism and teaching, and neither is generally possible without a church. 'The command to baptize reminds us that conversion includes entry into the community of Christ . . . The command to teach obedience also assumes committed participation in the new community of Christ.'[75] We sometimes think of the Great Commission in individualistic terms – Christians on their own sharing their faith with individuals one to one. The call of Jesus, though, is for churches to make disciples. The context of his thought is corporate and social. We could even say that the Great Commission is a command from Jesus to plant churches.

We will note later in our study that the New Testament often links baptism and teaching. Here, too, baptism is linked with the requirement of 'teaching [the new disciples] to obey everything that I have commanded you'. In the context of Matthew's Gospel the teaching of Jesus has been especially significant. As an aside, we should note that when Jesus speaks of everything that I have 'commanded' you, that word is the one used of the commandments of God: Jesus' teaching comes with the same authority as the revelation from God on Mount Sinai. From now on, the disciples will be teaching the commandments of Jesus.

Beyond that, Matthew has seemingly gathered five blocks of Jesus' teaching, each of which is concluded with the same phrase: 'And then, when Jesus had come to the end of these sayings . . .' (see 7:28; 11:1; 13:53; 19:1; 26:1). These blocks are not the entirety of the teaching of Jesus in this Gospel (see e.g. 11:1–19; 21:28 – 22:14; ch. 23), but they do seem to have a prominence in Matthew by virtue of how he highlights them in this way. These blocks frequently have a unity and sometimes a theme to themselves, such as the Sermon on the Mount, which is carefully arranged thematically, or the training of the Twelve for mission, or the chapter of

[74] Ibid. 1, 116.
[75] Ott and Wilson 2011: 22–23.

parables. As France notes, the way Matthew has arranged things 'suggests that for him these are the main places to look for the concentrated teaching of Jesus'.[76] There is something in the careful arrangement of the teaching material which, taken together with the emphasis on training and disciple-making, makes us think that Matthew had in mind that his Gospel could be used by the new converts arising from the Great Commission in their formation as disciples of Jesus. As Byrne says, 'The Gospel of Matthew . . . is the "handbook" for that process of formation.'[77]

The Great Commission in Matthew is a call for the founding of churches that will see people from every nation under heaven formed as disciples of Jesus, in the same way that Jesus' disciples in the Gospel have been. Bear in mind Legrand's picture of the disciple-maker seated, teaching, rather than on foot, hastening from town to town to preach the gospel. The context of this spiritual formation is the new churches being founded around the globe. This is a long-term, maybe slow, careful, patient formation of new believers over time, baptizing them into these new churches, taking them through the teachings of Jesus, maybe working carefully through Matthew's Gospel with its structured arrangement of the life and words and works of Jesus. Legrand amplifies his hints:

> 'Making disciples' conjures up the image of a master initiating his disciples through an organized process in the rabbinical style, progressively communicating a teaching and lifestyle corresponding to this 'tradition' . . . In Matthew, 'mission' denotes a long-term program: sacrament, continuous formation, an ethic in accordance with the new justice . . . Proclamation was not enough. Initiation and formation were required. An ecclesial framework was required.[78]

This picture may not be quite as 'heroic' as some images of missionary work, certainly from yesteryear, but it does draw out the crucial nature of that link between mission and church which is the heart of a theology of church planting.

---

[76] France 2007: 8.
[77] Byrne 2004: 228.
[78] Legrand 1990: 78.

Jesus ends the Great Commission with a promise of his presence with the disciples wherever they travel and for however long. This assurance is not so much for individual Christians as it is for the church on mission. Once more, Jesus is taking something which in the Old Testament was a promise from God and applying it to himself: the words 'I am with you' occur frequently in Scripture, spoken by God to his people in various kinds of need (e.g. Exod. 3:12; Josh. 1:5; Judg. 6:16; Jer. 1:8). The new people of God know the divine presence, comfort and power in Jesus.

Matthew does not refer to the power of the Spirit in mission (as Luke and John will), but he rather keeps our attention on the presence of Jesus himself. This is his mission, his authority, his presence as the nations of the world are discipled.

Lucien Legrand views the Great Commission in two parts, with the first verses (16–17) being the realm of human initiative, and the latter part (vv. 18–20) being the arena of the activity and authority of Jesus; this approach means he can draw out the emphasis on the priority of Jesus in the mission of the church:

> These observations aid us in grasping the import of Christ's words: 'I am with you always, until the end of the world.' This declaration is not subordinated to the dispatch of mission, as if Jesus were promising to be present to 'help missionary work along' . . . The Messianic presence is not subordinate to mission; it dominates it. It constitutes the milieu in which mission is to be performed . . . The conclusion of the gospel of Matthew says not that Jesus abets mission, but that he performs it.[79]

Matthew's version of the Great Commission shows us how his whole Gospel may be read as a kind of training curriculum in disciple-making. The core of what Jesus intended for his church was a missionary community, actively engaged in training people of all nations in being part of that community and learning to follow Jesus. The Lord himself, clothed in resurrection power, exercises his power and right to command the allegiance of the world through the humble, collective life of his people,

---

[79] Ibid. 81.

gathered around the shared experience of being bound into the life of God by baptism and obeying the commands of this new Moses.

For church planters, Matthew puts us right at the centre of the purposes of Jesus for the world. The place of the church in mission cannot be overstated, and neither can the place of mission in the life of the church. Church planting intentionally and necessarily holds both together.

Especially striking is how Matthew puts disciple-making at the centre of missionary activity. We can tend to separate evangelism and discipling or catechesis, but Matthew sees them as being part and parcel of the same process of learning to follow Jesus. This has implications for the care and maybe length of time that church plants should invest in taking people on the journey of faith. Maybe sometimes we are just too fast, and expect too much too quickly. Courses such as Alpha helpfully emphasize disciple-making as the method of evangelism. Questions of incorporation into the life of the church are pertinent here, and this can be a huge challenge, for instance in how to help people transition from something like an Alpha course into the life of the church. Church plants which use the language of journey or process or lifelong learning would reflect the kind of approach Jesus seems to be envisaging in Matthew 28.

One of the resounding notes of the Great Commission in Matthew is of the disciples in the Gospel being themselves the ones who disciple others, as they put into practice the lessons of their own stories as narrated by Matthew. This dynamic seems built into the developing and expanding life of the church, and is frequently the experience in church plants; it is often those who have just become Christians who are the best at sharing their newfound faith with their friends who are currently outside the church. The disciple-makers for the next generation are those who themselves are recent disciples. This is often how the faith spreads, and how church plants grow.

Mark

If we can talk meaningfully of Mark's commissioning of the disciples in this context, it is linked more closely to the resurrection than Matthew. It is a commission to the women at the tomb to take the news of the risen Jesus to the disciples; they are 'the apostles to the apostles'. Let us turn to those aspects of this narrative which have a bearing specifically on church planting.[80]

> When the sabbath was over, Mary Magdalene, and Mary the mother of James, and Salome bought spices, so that they might go and anoint him. And very early on the first day of the week, when the sun had risen, they went to the tomb. They had been saying to one another, 'Who will roll away the stone for us from the entrance to the tomb?' When they looked up, they saw that the stone, which was very large, had been rolled back. As they entered the tomb, they saw a young man, dressed in a white robe, sitting on the right side; and they were alarmed. But he said to them, 'Do not be alarmed; you are looking for Jesus of Nazareth, who was crucified. He has been raised; he is not here. Look, here is the place they laid him. But go, tell his disciples and Peter that he is going on ahead of you to Galilee; there you will see him, just as he told you.' So they went out and fled from the tomb, for terror and amazement had seized them; and they said nothing to anyone, for they were afraid.
> (Mark 16:1–8)

Joel Marcus divides the passage into two: the journey of the women to the tomb (16:1–4) and the message of the young man, who must be an angel (16:5–8).[81] It is the second of these that concerns us most, and we can discern two main themes: that of fear in the women; and the message of the angel, namely that the disciples and Peter should go to Galilee to see Jesus.

It is the fear element which concerns readers of the Gospel. How can this be the last word? In what sense is fear and silence a fitting conclusion to the story of Jesus? Mark emphasizes the fear: he uses a word (which he alone employs in the New Testament[82]) in the succeeding verses 5 and 6, and the passage ends with flight, 'terror and amazement', and the concluding phrase 'for they were afraid' (16:8). Why are they so afraid?

---

[80] I am following the majority of scholars, who see Mark's Gospel ending at 16:8. The so-called 'shorter' and 'longer' endings do not appear to be canonical.
[81] Marcus 2009: 1083.
[82] Hooker 1991: 385.

One answer is that they are overcome with awe at the resurrection. They have just met an angel, and seen an empty tomb, and received a message about a living Jesus. Throughout Mark's Gospel, people have been afraid when confronted by the realities of Jesus and the kingdom of God. As Morna Hooker puts it:

> The 'trembling' and 'terror' which overcame them are familiar Markan themes: this is precisely how many other characters in the story have reacted up to this point when confronted with the power of God. Now that they are confronted with the mightiest act of all, how else could they react?[83]

What Mark is emphasizing by showing the fear of the women is the scale and magnitude of what has just happened in the resurrection. This can be seen in the message of the young man, as well, which is succinct to the point of brutality: 'You are looking for Jesus of Nazareth, who was crucified. He has been raised; he is not here. Look, there is the place they laid him. But go . . .' (16:6–7). In biblical parlance, to put something in the passive can often be a reverent way of saying that God has been the actor. That is unquestionably so here: the angel is saying that God himself has raised Jesus from death. Lucien Legrand points out that the angel says, 'He has been raised; he is not here,' whereas in Luke's account the order is the other way round: 'He is not here, but has risen' (Luke 24:5).[84] Luke is, as it were, tracking the consciousness of the women; they first register the empty tomb, and then the angel explains how it came to be empty. With Mark it is the other way round: there is the angelic announcement of the resurrection, and then the demonstration of the empty tomb as evidence that backs up the pronouncement. Mark begins with a declaration of the power and kingdom of God in its purest form – God has raised Jesus from the dead. He makes no concessions to a human perspective, which may prefer to start from our own experience and then work our way towards faith from there. This has been his approach throughout his Gospel: it begins with the uncompromising title, 'The

---

[83] Ibid. 387.
[84] Legrand 1990: 76. Legrand actually compares Mark to Matthew, but the point is the same in a comparison with Luke.

beginning of the good news of Jesus Christ, the Son of God' (1:1), and is characterized by acts of bewildering power and teaching from Jesus that frequently leave his listeners confused. For Mark, the gospel breaks into human experience and not infrequently does not seem to mesh with it. It fractures human expectations, refuses to explain itself, often offends people and sometimes leaves them excluded. Legrand writes:

> The gospel proclamation . . . is not mere human language. It is divine word . . . Before being promulgated by human beings and becoming missionary preaching, the Good News is from God and is invested with divine authority and power . . . An apocalypse founds mission.[85]

Before the message of the gospel is to be explained or fitted into a human frame of reference, it is first just to be declared in all of its otherworldliness. And there is something bewildering, something totally unexpected, even inexplicable in the gospel, and Mark has consistently drawn it out. His account of the crucifixion, for instance, shows us Jesus totally alone, deserted by friends and disciples, even (seemingly) by God, left in agony and abandonment. How can that be the climax of Jesus' mission? And yet it is. In such a light, a perplexing ending to the Gospel makes perfect sense. Rowan Williams writes:

> A Gospel of silences, of misunderstandings, of indirect and teasing communication: but this is not for the sake of making things difficult in an arbitrary or unkind way. It is to remind us that if it's the true God who is speaking and being spoken about in this book, this God is not a hugely inflated version of how we would run the universe if we had the chance . . . [Mark] shows us a Jesus who not only brings about 'regime change' in the world in which we live, but a Jesus who changes for ever what we can say about God.[86]

Tied more closely to mission, Legrand reflects, as a lifelong missionary himself, on the relationship between the gospel and evangelization:

---

[85] Ibid.
[86] Williams 2014: 50.

We are not mistaken if we detect a missionary point in Mark . . . The perspective here is less 'missionary' than 'evangelical'. As in Mark's theology generally and in Jesus' practice, the important thing is not so much evangelization as it is the gospel. Antecedent to any consideration of human cooperation is the impact of the triumphal announcement to the world: The crucified Nazarene has been raised![87]

Church plants are all about proclaiming the gospel in their new contexts. As will be emphasized later in this book, a major element of this task is the hard and patient work of contextualizing the message, doing all we can to make connections between the gospel and our hearers, putting things in terms that can most readily be grasped and applied. In many ways this encapsulates the missionary task of the church planter. Within that context, though, Mark comes as a stark reminder that the gospel is nothing unless it is the gospel of God. It is his message, and there is a sense in which the proclamation of this message is prior to any attempts to explain or apply it or to make it understood. At one level, we must beware of reducing the scope and complexity and profundity of the gospel, even in the noble service of communicating it so that it is truly heard. At another, the language of heaven will always come across as foreign to earth, and we falsify it if we translate it too idiomatically. If we come across as being able to say, 'There: that is it, neatly encapsulated and expressed for you,' or if we denude the gospel of its strangeness and even offensiveness, then Mark would remind us of the first witnesses of the empty tomb, running away from the angel, silent and overwhelmed with terror.

The second element of the second half of Mark's resurrection account is the angel's message to the women for the apostles: 'Go, tell his disciples and Peter that he [Jesus] is going ahead of you to Galilee; there you will see him, just as he told you' (16:7).

The first thing to notice is that Mark does not give us a resurrection appearance of Jesus to the disciples. Instead, we have this command to go and meet Jesus somewhere else. The angel is inviting the disciples on

---

[87] Legrand 1990: 77.

something of a journey. What that journey is will be key to understanding Mark's message.

Second, there is the inclusion of Peter in the invitation to Galilee, the only named disciple. This may be because he is the lead among the apostles and so he has a privileged place. It may also be that Peter must have had the memory of his betrayal of Jesus fresh and painful in his consciousness, perhaps even more so than the other disciples. In all likelihood, the mention of Peter carries both these connotations. This invitation is a call to a fresh start, a summons to renewed leadership and to a life and ministry lived from forgiveness. The life of the missionary is an embodying of the gospel. The message we proclaim is something we have experienced for ourselves.

Third, this is a renewed invitation; Jesus has already told them about this. He has done this in chapter 14, and the context is significant. It follows the last supper, and happens on the Mount of Olives, just ahead of Gethsemane and before the arrest of Jesus:

And Jesus said to them, 'You will all become deserters; for it is written,

> "I will strike the shepherd,
>   and the sheep will be scattered."

But after I am raised up, I will go before you to Galilee.'
(14:27–28)

This mention of Galilee is inserted into the prophecy of the resurrection as a reversal of failure and a renewal of discipleship. Not just Peter but all the disciples will desert Jesus, but the decisive act of God in raising Jesus from the dead will lead to the reconstitution of the apostolic band in Galilee. The Greek word translated 'go before you', which comes in 14:28 and 16:7, can mean 'lead' as well as 'be physically in front of'. There may be a hint here of a kind of victory procession into Galilee, with Jesus 'at the head of his assembled flock'.[88] The constitution of the church is as sure as the resurrection itself, and is a form of manifestation of it.

---

[88] Marcus 2009: 1081; Legrand 1990: 77. Marcus also, intriguingly, links 'going before' with Old Testament usages of the phrase when an angel 'goes before' individuals or the people of God (Marcus 2009: 1086).

We should not miss the significance of Galilee as the place of this reunion, because this is where it all started. It was in Galilee that Jesus first called the disciples at the start of the Gospel, and it was on the dusty roads of Galilee that so many of the lessons of discipleship were painfully learned by the followers of Jesus. By inviting them back to Galilee, Jesus is inviting them back to the life of discipleship. Mark has been unsentimental in showing us the blindness and failures of the disciples; Jesus is inviting them back to do better this time. Now that the resurrection has happened, they will be learning in a new register, seeing Jesus as the conqueror of death and the suffering servant, vindicated by God.

On this reading, Mark is not just showing how the disciples and Peter were recommissioned to a life of following Jesus; he is inviting us, as the readers of his Gospel, to include ourselves in this school of discipleship, to enrol by reading the Gospel all over again.[89] Rowan Williams says:

> At the end of his Gospel, Mark is telling us to go back and start again: read the whole story again to see how it has been preparing you for the shock of these last episodes, for the moment of stupefied terror and unimagined renewal at the empty tomb. Don't draw conclusions from Jesus' miracles or teaching; wait to see the great event taking shape as a whole, the event whose centre is the cross. And if you think that sharing this mystery is going to be simple, think again: wait for the last trauma, the miracle of miracles, the resurrection which silences even its most immediate witnesses.[90]

Some commentators pick up that Mark starts his Gospel with the introductory title 'The beginning of the good news about Jesus Christ' (1:1). This almost certainly has a double reference: to the first fifteen verses of chapter 1, and as a description of the Gospel as a whole. Joel Marcus comments: 'Mark's composition, therefore, is technically speaking not a "gospel," but the *beginning* of a gospel.'[91] This means that the end of the Gospel is in fact only the end of the beginning of the gospel; the

---

[89] This application is also made by Hooker 1991: 393. Cf. 'This is no mere rendezvous, but a call to the disciples to follow Jesus once again' (ibid. 385).
[90] Williams 2014: 50.
[91] Marcus 2000: 145; emphasis original.

resurrection launches the good news proper: 'the *beginning* of the good news is over on Easter morning; after that "the good news of Jesus" will continue through the life of the church.'[92]

This means then that, in a similar way to how Matthew has positioned his Gospel as a 'handbook' for obeying all that Jesus commanded his followers to do,[93] Mark's Gospel is presented as a training manual for what it means to be a disciple of Jesus, the crucified and risen Lord. The Gospel is written in order not just to be read, but to be reread, so that lessons of following Jesus can be applied and reapplied to the changing circumstances of life and from the different perspectives of Jesus before and after the cross and resurrection. Morna Hooker has written: 'Mark's story is a story about the meaning of discipleship (barely understood).'[94] That is why it needs to be read and pondered over and over.

We may also note, finally, that the ones who need these lessons in discipleship in the light of the cross and the resurrection are the disciples and Peter, the apostles. Mark is not just a manual in discipleship, but is, more precisely, a training curriculum for missionaries. For those of us who are church planters or in church-planting teams, Mark has written a no-nonsense account of the formation of disciples on mission. We may remember that there are no teaching sections from Jesus on mission in Mark, in the way there are in Matthew and Luke, and, in a different way, in John. Maybe that is because the whole of Mark's Gospel has this end in view. As church planters, then, we should read Mark as a practical school.

So, maybe the most significant, specific application for church planters is the emphasis in Mark's 'non-Great Commission' on training. The grand finale of the Gospel is an invitation from Jesus to the Eleven to go back to the beginning, to start over once again, learning the lessons of missional discipleship in the light of the cross and resurrection. For church planting, Mark is saying that we never really get it, we are always learning, that training is a repeated cycle of applying the discipleship lessons of Jesus into our ever-changing circumstances. Training and learning, viewing challenges in the light of Jesus, is what it means to be a church planter. There is no graduation from this school, just a continuous re-enrolment.

---

[92] Ibid. 146; emphasis original.
[93] Byrne 2004: 228.
[94] Hooker 1991: 21.

When we view missionary discipleship training in the light of the whole Gospel of Mark and its mysterious climax as the women run from the angel and the empty tomb, we may draw the following four conclusions.

1 Church-planter training is continuous and continuing

There is more and more excellent training available for church planters, but it is still mostly what we might call 'front loaded'. Mark, however, tells us that church-planter training never finishes; lessons need to be relearned – situations we thought we knew need to be revisited in the light of the cross and resurrection; our own leadership needs to be constantly challenged in the light of the perspectives of the kingdom of God and the sheer scale of the challenges mission will bring us. We never fully grasp the cross and its implications, nor are we ever fully prepared for the apocalyptic scale of the resurrection, and we need to come back to these again and again.

At one level, church plants go through distinct and discernible phases. There is the launch, the chaos of those early months and years, then the establishing of a kind of normal. And then the church plant will hopefully grow, and will change the dynamics of how it operates, which brings challenges to how it needs to be led.[95] There will almost certainly be different phases of its continuing life, dictated by changes in leadership or by events in the local contexts the church plant serves. And the leadership and core team will grow, triumph and fail, go through periods of elation and depression, grow tired, be renewed, go through life-changes, just grow older. God willing, the church plant will itself plant again, and hopefully be part of a growing network of church plants. All these are significant changes and can be challenging as well as exciting. Mark tells us that each stage and phase will need to be navigated and carefully considered in the perspective of the cross and resurrection.

All of this says to me that the church planter and his or her team would be well advised to have a coach or mentor. We are to have the attitude of a continuous, lifelong learner, says Mark: a disciple is always a disciple, and a disciple is a learner. The church-plant leadership team which

---

[95] See Keller 2010, <https://seniorpastorcentral.com/wp-content/uploads/2016/11/Tim-Keller-Size-Dynamics.pdf> (accessed 6 December 2022).

positions itself in a learning posture will do that most effectively by actively seeking out people from whom and environments in which to learn. The church-plant budget should enable the core leaders to have regular time with people who are ahead of them in the journey, or coaching for specific challenges, projects and phases of the life of the church, or time with network leaders with whom they can engage and find support, and from whom they may learn.

2 The most effective church-planter training is 'on the job'

We will be struck by just how practical Jesus' formation of missionary disciples is in Mark: there are precious few lectures, and much of the learning happens along the road.[96] This school of discipleship is a life class, a roadshow, far removed from the quiet of the library or the lecture theatre. We then, as church planters, should read Mark as a practical school. Jesus' training curriculum is to engage the disciples with whatever and whoever comes at them on the roads of Palestine, and as he sets his face for Jerusalem.

It is certainly true that the most effective church-planter training happens in planting a church. This is not to say that there is not value in other modes of training, nor is it an argument for not being as prepared as possible for the actual ministry of church planting, but it does put an emphasis on the practical, the actual lived learning of coalface ministry. This approach is still rare in the contemporary church, but there is evidence that the most effective church-planter training is of this sort.[97] If we want to be trained to plant churches, we can do no better than to join a church-planting team. And, by the same token, if we want to train church planters, we will want to involve them in church planting, working alongside more experienced practitioners.

This principle holds true for all aspects of the church-planting venture. If we want to train children's workers for our church plant, then the best way is to involve them in serving in children's church. If we want to raise up evangelists, the best way is to ask them to help lead an Alpha course.

---

[96] The phrase 'on the road' or 'on the way' (NRSV) occurs throughout Mark and stands for the path of discipleship (e.g. 10:32, 52), and is used as a technical term for the church ('the Way') in Acts 9:2.

[97] E.g. Jolley and Jones 2016; Valentine 2020.

If we want to develop preachers to reach new people outside the church, then the best way is to give them opportunities to preach and to take them with us when we are doing pioneer work beyond the walls of the church.

3 Church-planter missionary training is peripatetic

In Mark the disciples have no base; they have no settled location. The nearest to this is Galilee, but even this is provisional in the perspective of the road to Jerusalem. This is true for all the Gospels – witness Jesus' words, 'Foxes have holes, and birds of the air have nests; but the Son of Man has nowhere to lay his head' (Luke 9:58) – but feels particularly apposite to Mark. To learn to follow Jesus is to be continually on the move.

This feels very different from much of church life, at least in the West, where it is settled, largely lived around buildings. It is striking, though, how much of the biblical record describes the people of God on the move, from the wilderness wanderings to the successive exiles to Jesus' peregrinatory ministry to Paul's missionary journeys. And it is sobering to reflect on what a large proportion of Christians in today's world have no fixed abode, whether through poverty or persecution or migration. Our Western normal is probably abnormal viewed from this perspective.

This is a different model of mission and church planting from that of Matthew, though. It is a picture of mission which starts churches through kingdom encounters, and then moves on to the next village or region. It is not without strategy, but has a very different methodology.

We will find this as we look at Luke and John as well. There is no single way of doing mission, as envisaged by the Great Commissions of the four Gospels. They are strikingly different. They all have the same end in view, but the ways they adopt of getting there are by no means identical. We will think a bit about the implications of this at the conclusion of this section on the four Great Commissions.

Perhaps the fact that Mark's focus is on leadership development for mission is significant. The forum for missionary formation cannot be settled, he says. The learning for church planting is precisely in this being 'on the move', which trains and equips for mission. If this is right, the implications for church-planter training are far-reaching. Church-planter leadership teams should experience this mobile model, however it is to be applied later on. This seems to imply that the best church-planter training is in multiple contexts, and that these should be situations which combine active missionary engagement with opportunities to reflect, learn and change.

4 Church-planter training comes out of an encounter with God

Mark's 'non-Great Commission' turns out to be a revolutionary invitation to an encounter with the deep end of the miraculous, supernatural and world-changing power of God in the resurrection. In order to turn the world upside down in mission, the would-be church planter needs to have her or his world turned upside down by the bleakness of the cross and the power of the resurrection. There is something searing in the experience of the disciples and Peter; they go through a difficult journey from their first calling by Jesus to their recommissioning, implied in chapter 16, and most of it is around their own failings, culminating in the abandonment of Jesus at the cross. When it comes to thinking about mission and church planting, the qualification they bring is their own failure, but a failure more than compensated for by the scale of the cross and resurrection.

This is the secret journey of the church planter, which no-one can take for them. To arrive at a place of self-knowledge, coupled with knowledge of God in the gospel, is a difficult process. It involves bringing all we have, our very real gifts and talents, but also viewing them from the point of view of their uselessness for what the Lord has in mind. Nonetheless, this paradox is held within the framework of a depth and power in the cross and resurrection which is more than sufficient for what lies ahead.

We are on the edge of the church planter's prayer life here, how he or she engages deeply with the Lord. There needs to be the capacity for searing honesty, a real processing of life's experiences in prayer, and a confidence in the Lord, which comes from having walked through the journey of Gethsemane, the trials, the crucifixion and the empty tomb many, many times. There is a sense, says Mark, that Calvary destroys us and the resurrection terrifies us. When our emotional interiorities are remade from this encounter, then we are ready to retrace our steps, following Jesus once again through the training that is everyday life. We know that this journey will bring us, once again, to Jerusalem and that first Easter, but we also know that this is how we are progressively formed in the toughness and resilience that church planters need.

Luke

Luke's Great Commission (24:44–49) comes in the context of three encounters with the risen Jesus: the empty tomb, the road to Emmaus and the ascension of Jesus. Each has its own unique features, but all have the same basic narrative structure:

- feelings of grief and incomprehension in the disciples;
- Jesus speaking about the Scriptures and/or his own words about the cross and the resurrection;
- the dawning of faith and comprehension in the minds of Jesus' companions, followed by his leaving them.

Luke skilfully interweaves these three encounters, which build up to the Great Commission. The disciples and the readers of the Gospel all go through a kind of journey of discovery, and this journey gives the commission a force and depth. In particular, Luke is interested in two things:

1 how faith comes – it is not a foregone conclusion when confronted with the fact of the empty tomb, but needs to be explained and expounded;
2 the role of the community – the various stories from each of the encounters feed into the whole group, and fill out and confirm the perspectives of each individual encounter.[98]

We should bear these insights in mind as we reflect on the commission itself:

Then [Jesus] said to them, 'These are my words that I spoke to you while I was still with you – that everything written about me in the law of Moses, the prophets, and the psalms must be fulfilled.' Then

---

[98] Byrne 2015: 203 helpfully points this out.

he opened their minds to understand the scriptures, and he said to them, 'Thus it is written, that the Messiah is to suffer and to rise from the dead on the third day, and that repentance and forgiveness of sins is to be proclaimed in his name to all nations, beginning from Jerusalem. You are witnesses of these things. And see, I am sending upon you what my Father promised; so stay here in the city until you have been clothed with power from on high.'
(Luke 24:44–49)

Let's draw out various themes from Luke's text, thinking about how they apply to church planting.

1 Witnesses to Jesus

Witnessing is, of course, exactly what happens in Acts. The followers of Jesus repeatedly witness to his death and resurrection (e.g. 1:8; 2:32; 3:15; 5:32; 10:39, 41; 13:31).[99] What Jesus has in mind, though, is not just eyewitnesses testifying to what they have seen and heard, but also the theological context of these events. The Greek of verses 46 and 47 draws this out:

Jesus' interpretation of the Scriptures moves in three directions, designated by parallel verbs in the infinitive: (1) 'the Messiah is to suffer' and (2) 'to rise from the dead on the third day,' and (3) 'repentance for forgiveness of sins is to be proclaimed in his name to all nations, beginning from Jerusalem'.[100]

The disciples are to be witnesses of the death and resurrection of the Messiah, *and also* what the Scriptures and Jesus explain about these events. Witnessing, in Luke's commission, is about what happened with Jesus *and* what that means.

This ties in with Luke's interest in how faith comes. The resurrection chapter in Luke (24) begins with the women going to the empty tomb. They arrive, find the stone rolled away, go in and find that it is empty: 'they

---

[99] Green 1997: 858.
[100] Ibid. 856; emphasis original.

did not find the body' (24:3). This, in and of itself, did not bring them to a point of faith. Instead, Luke tells us, 'they were perplexed about this' (24:4). It takes the appearance of the two angels, and specifically their reminder of the prophecy of Jesus that he would be crucified and rise again (24:6–7), to make the difference. Luke singles out 'Then they remembered his words' (24:8) as the turning point.

A similar pattern happens in the second resurrection encounter on the road to Emmaus. Cleopas and his nameless companion rehearse all the pertinent facts about the crucifixion and resurrection (even down to the irony of saying, 'It is now the third day since these things took place' [24:21]), but they remain sad and disappointed. Jesus says how foolish they are and 'slow of heart to believe all that the prophets have declared' (24:25), before interpreting 'to them the things about himself in all the scriptures' (24:27). It is only as he breaks bread with them that 'their eyes were opened, and they recognized him' (24:31). They reflect that their hearts were burning within them 'while he was opening the scriptures to us' (24:32).

In the commission itself, this pattern finds fullest expression. After he appears to the disciples, giving proof that he is neither a revived corpse nor a ghost,[101] Jesus explains matters to them:

> 'These are my words that I spoke to you while I was still with you –
> that everything written about me in the law of Moses, the prophets,
> and the psalms must be fulfilled.' Then he opened their minds to
> understand the scriptures.
> (Luke 24:44–45)

As with the women, he reminds them of what he had said to them previously, and as with the disciples on the Emmaus road he goes through the Scriptures with them. Cleopas and his companion had the experience of burning hearts and opened eyes (24:32, 31), and the disciples have their minds opened to understand the Scriptures (24:45).

The repeated pattern underlines the point that Luke is making: faith comes by a kind of joining up of the dots between the actual events of

---

[101] Ibid. 854.

Jesus' death and the empty tomb, the reminder of his own prophecies of what would happen, the broader context of the whole scriptural testimony to Jesus, the stories of other people's experiences, and the risen Lord himself in their midst. 'Only when all this comes together in their understanding can the disciples become true witnesses of the resurrection, ready to be transformed by the Spirit into effective ministers of the word.'[102] The witnessing the disciples are called to do is a combination of all these things.

Church plants are committed to making the proclamation of Jesus central to their raison d'être, as is the calling of all churches. Maybe church plants have this in a specific way because they will often be positioned among communities which are largely unevangelized or have lost contact with any memory of the gospel there once was, if any. This perspective of Luke's is thus particularly helpful for church plants as they engage in the evangelization of their communities, networks and regions.

May we begin by noting just how much Luke reflects on what is happening. There is a definite theology of evangelism here, embedded into a practice. Luke encourages us to think carefully about what we are doing. His presentation of the factors which together add up to faith is a sophisticated one. There is a combination of what we might call an empirical approach (evidence of the empty tomb, the narration of the events) with psychological (listening carefully to the experiences of those involved, the calling to mind of previous words of Jesus) and theological (the Scriptures, the words of Jesus, the opening of hearts and minds) perspectives. Luke is aware of just what a huge shift in attitude to the world faith is: it involves rethinking who God is and how he acts in the world as much as the awesomeness of a dead Messiah raised to life. Our evangelistic strategies should reflect a similar sense of the length of journey people may have to go on, how complex human personality is and how non-linear the road to faith may be. It pays to think carefully and theologically about what is happening in evangelism.

Luke draws out, in particular, the central role of Scripture, to which the followers of Jesus are called to witness, and how multiple stories and perspectives are part of the journey towards faith.

---

[102] Byrne 2015: 203.

Jesus emphasizes the part the Scriptures play in how resurrection faith comes. Maybe the three groups in Luke 24 all had trouble in holding together the appalling sufferings of Jesus with any sense that this was God's plan to redeem the world? Maybe they could not imagine, really take on board, that he would be raised from the dead? The answer to these plausibility challenges was to be taught by Jesus that this was the story of Scripture.

'Was it not necessary that the Messiah should suffer these things and then enter into his glory?' Then beginning with Moses and all the prophets, he interpreted to them the things about himself in all the scriptures.
(24:26–27)

Then he opened their minds to understand the scriptures, and he said to them, 'Thus it is written, that the Messiah is to suffer and to rise from the dead on the third day.'
(24:45–46)

What Jesus does is to fit his story into the fuller story of the whole scriptural witness. On the one hand, he must have shown them how the Old Testament was about him, how his life and ministry are hinted at and prophesied in text and type throughout. And, on the other hand, he must have opened their eyes to read the story of Israel through the lens of what (who) was to come. What he did, in N. T. Wright's memorable phrase, was 'to tell the story differently'.[103] It is unlikely that Jesus would have proof-texted his mission; as Joel Green helpfully put it:

Which Scriptures portend messianic suffering and resurrection? One would be hard-pressed to locate specific texts that make these prognostications explicit. Even to attempt to do so would be wrong-headed, however. The point of Jesus' words is not that such-and-such a verse has now come true, but that the truth to which all of the Scriptures point has now been realized![104]

---

[103] N. T. Wright 2000: 123; emphasis original.
[104] Green 1997: 857.

Jesus, then, told the story differently, the whole story, and this enabled his hearers to shift their mental categories to give space for the miracle of the crucified and resurrected Messiah who stood in front of them.

> The disciples are witnesses not only in the sense that they have seen the wonders of Jesus' public ministry and the climactic events of the last few days. They are more fully so because they have been instructed by him to see how his story fits together and fulfils the Scriptures.[105]

Bible teaching is core to good evangelization and to healthy church planting. In all likelihood, contemporary people will have to learn to think about God, the world, themselves and Jesus completely differently if they are to come to faith in Jesus. There are multiple world views now, nearly all of which, whether implicitly or explicitly, challenge a Christian way of seeing things. The West is in a state of philosophical flux, as the modern and postmodern world views clash with each other. And now the whole world is coming to the West, with startlingly non-Western understandings of reality, morality and the nature of life. None of these competing world views exist in academic vacuums, but all find expression in culture, ritual, symbol, patterns of relating, working, worshipping. Even those from a Christian background may have very little by way of biblical knowledge, and what they may have could be atomized and piecemeal.

How wonderful then to have the privilege of telling the story differently, of laying out the big picture of the Bible and, in particular, showing how it all builds up to and revolves around Jesus. This is where themes such as blessing, covenant and kingdom, which we have traced earlier, can be so helpful. Church planters will want to give the people in their churches mental frameworks in which to help them securely locate their faith in Jesus. It is this process which gives not only a sense that Christianity is true but also an understanding of what it means.

Different church plants will have different ways of doing this. It may be that the lead planter is also an able teacher, or it may be that there are

---

[105] Byrne 2015: 210.

others on the team who could take on this role.[106] Some make midweek groups the location for this kind of study, maybe using resources from beyond the church plant. Others provide their own resources, encouraging their churches to hear this big Bible story in their own prayers and Bible study. It is the regular, consistent practice of good Bible teaching (in this sense) that contributes so markedly to the maturing of individuals and churches in faith. Church plants that are healthy, sustainable and growing will need to attend to this, to value it, and make it central to their thinking about Christian discipleship. This is not aiming to turn people into eggheads, but it is to supply them with the necessary mental furniture from Scripture to live happily, well and fruitfully in God's big story.

A particular area for thought is sermon series. This can take a lot of planning. Some church plants follow those Bible readings set by a denominational lectionary, but far more set their own plans. This is the main method by which the story of Jesus is told in the church, and a great opportunity to fit his story into the wider biblical narrative, in the way Luke is showing Jesus doing here. Various factors need to be held together in the planning:

- balancing Old and New Testaments;
- focusing on Jesus in the Gospels;
- covering major themes;
- evangelistic and discipling teaching;
- issues and subjects;
- the rhythms of the life of the church plant;
- being aware of the needs and stages of faith of the congregation(s);
- being aware of the maturity, knowledge and experience of the preachers;
- the (liturgical) time of year, and special seasons in the life of the church (e.g. prayer, giving, mission).

---

[106] It is important to make sure that the regular preachers are adequately resourced with Bible commentaries and theological books for their preaching. These are astonishingly expensive and usually beyond the salaries of church leaders and most volunteers.

2 The witnessing church

A feature of the Great Commission in Luke is that so many people are involved. There are the three separate encounters with Jesus, each with multiple people involved (the women, Cleopas and his companion, the Eleven and their companions). There is also the prevalence of meals (two of the three encounters involve meals). And the assumption of the plurality of witness: 'You are witnesses', not 'You will each individually be a witness to me'.

A narrative feature is how each of the three encounters merges into the others. So, the women tell the apostles of their experience at the tomb (24:10–11); and Cleopas and his companion report their experience on the Emmaus road to the Eleven and their companions (24:33–35). Interestingly, these conversations are not terribly fruitful – the apostles do not believe the women (24:11), and the Emmaus road disciples are met with the news that the others already know Jesus is risen (24:34), although they will struggle to accept Jesus when he appears to them. It is no coincidence, though, that Jesus appears to them all 'while they were talking about this' (24:36). As Brendan Byrne writes:

> Luke likes to build up [the] story by first describing experiences of individuals or groups separately, and then bringing them together to share their stories. In the sharing and combination, individual experience becomes community experience, creating a new sense of identity.[107]

Luke projects forward, too, into the communal experience of what will be the church in the future. The Gospel ends with worship (24:52), and surely the experience of Cleopas and his companion is programmatic of what will be the life of the church; Jesus has broken bread at the institution of the Lord's Supper (22:19) and the nascent church will do so shortly (Acts 2:42). So, when we read that he is recognized in the breaking of bread and that hearts burn as he interprets Scripture, we cannot fail to think of the two central acts of Christian worship.[108] Luke is painting a

---

[107] Byrne 2015: 203.
[108] N. T. Wright 2000: 127–128.

portrait of the Christian community, united in witnessing to the crucified and risen Jesus.

The life of church plants can be strengthened by providing space and encouragement for people to share their stories of faith. The more this can be done, the more of a culture of witnessing to the Lord as a church community can be established. It can start in small groups, maybe with the parochial church council (PCC) or other leaders taking a lead. It can grow through judicious use of testimonies in church services, on Alpha or Christianity Explored courses, and other events. Preaching can include appropriate stories about personal experience.

The aim of testimony is witness to Jesus. It is also to dovetail personal experience with the communal life of the church, and to complement the teaching of the Scriptures. When an individual speaks of his or her experience of God, then, in a sense, that individual is speaking for all of us. People's stories will add into our stories, and our faith and identity in Jesus is strengthened. And we get to see how our lives can interrelate with the story of Jesus and the big story of God's plan in the world.

3 Proclaiming to all nations

A major feature of Luke's account is the global nature of the proclamation of the gospel. This is a change from the missions of the Twelve (9:1–6) and the Seventy(-Two) (10:1–11, 17–20), which were both confined to Israel. Matthew's account of the mission of the Twelve is even clearer; Jesus tells them: 'Go nowhere among the Gentiles, and enter no town of the Samaritans, but go rather to the lost sheep of the house of Israel' (10:5–6). Now, all the nations of the world, Jew and Gentile alike, are in view.

There has also been a massive change of direction: the Old Testament, inasmuch as it envisaged mission, saw a vision for the end of time, when the nations of the world would come *to* Jerusalem (e.g. Isa. 2:3; 12:4–5; Mic. 4:2), a *centripetal* vision.[109] So, when Jesus, in Luke 24, talks about *going* to the nations, beginning *from* Jerusalem, we see here a reversal of the missionary direction, a calling which is totally new in the life of God's people. There is a switch to a *centrifugal* vision. 'It is important to

---

[109] Ott, Strauss with Tennent 2010: 22–23.

grasp the magnitude of transformation in mission that occurs with the completion of Christ's work of redemption, the coming of the Holy Spirit at Pentecost, and the birth of the church.'[110] This change of direction is signalled by the relative structures of Luke–Acts as well. In the Gospel, Luke structures his narrative around Jesus' journey *to* Jerusalem (e.g. 'When the days drew near for him to be taken up, he set his face to go to Jerusalem' [9:51]). In Acts, his second volume, Luke sees the hand of God in a journey in the other direction; Jesus said: 'You will be my witnesses in Jerusalem, in all Judea and Samaria, and to the ends of the earth' (1:8). And with the coming of the Holy Spirit at Pentecost, we see the gospel going to 'every nation under heaven' (2:5).

The nations feature explicitly in Luke's Great Commission (as they do in Matthew). Luke has already hinted at this theme in his Gospel:

- Simeon's prophecy over the infant Jesus spoke of God's salvation, 'which you have prepared in the presence of all peoples, a light for revelation to the Gentiles' (2:31–32).
- Luke quotes Isaiah's prophecy of John the Baptist's ministry to the effect that 'all flesh shall see the salvation of God' (3:6).
- He reports Jesus saying that 'people will come from east and west, from north and south, and will eat in the kingdom of God' (13:29).

It is only now, though, that these hints come fully into view with the shift to a centrifugal model of mission, moving out from Jerusalem to all nations.

When Luke picks up the story in Acts, this feature will predominate in the narrative. The promise of the Spirit is reiterated for the disciples, who will be witnesses to Jesus 'to the ends of the earth' (1:8). Luke's account of Pentecost emphasizes the global impact of this event. Those overhearing the disciples speaking in 'other languages' (2:4) remark: 'we hear, each of us, in our own native language' (2:8), and Luke then lists where each hearer comes from, going round the points of the compass, naming races and empires and cultures all foreign to Israel (2:8–11). This is the reversal of the tragedy of the Tower of Babel, where 'the LORD

---

110 Ibid. 25, and the fascinating discussion of 25–28.

confused the language of all the earth; and . . . scattered them abroad over the face of all the earth' (Gen. 11:9). The gospel is calling the nations of the earth back together again, under the lordship of Jesus, in the power of the Spirit. And Acts, of course, traces journeys around the Mediterranean, heading towards Rome. The Roman Empire is subtly compared to the kingdom of Jesus. To take just one example, Luke reports Paul quoting Isaiah 49:6 to show that the Lord has commissioned the church 'to be a light for the Gentiles, so that you may bring salvation to the ends of the earth' (Acts 13:47).[111] Richard Bauckham, in his book on the theology of mission, draws a comparison with Luke's description of the birth of Jesus, where he tells us that '[i]n those days a decree went out from Emperor Augustus that all the world should be registered' (Luke 2:1). Luke uses a very particular word for 'all the world', and it is this same word which is picked up in Acts 13:47. It is also the word in Acts 1:8 describing the progress of the gospel 'to the ends of the earth', and Luke again uses it in the report that the apostolic witness has 'been turning the world upside down' (Acts 17:6). Bauckham draws out the implications:

> So, when Luke describes Jesus' commission of his apostles 'to the end of the earth' (Acts 1:8) he evokes not only Isaianic prophecy (Isaiah 49:6) . . . but surely also Roman political ideology. What Jesus projects is a counter-narrative, an alternative to Rome's, a narrative not of coercive power but of witness.[112]

Jesus' reign is very different in kind and quality from that of the Roman emperor, but it is no less universal.

How might this speak specifically to church plants?

On the one hand, it says that global mission is as centrally on the agenda of church plants as it is on that of regular churches. Church plants, for obvious and commendable reasons, tend to be pretty focused on local or regional mission. Overseas work can feel a bridge too far for already overstretched leaders and churches. Yet Jesus is clear that this is the overall

---

[111] This quotation is behind Simeon's prophecy about Jesus, too, of course (Luke 2:29–32). We can see the church commissioned to continue the global witness of Jesus.

[112] Bauckham 2003: 106–107; also cited in Ott, Strauss with Tennent 2010: 43.

perspective within which all mission and all church life is to be viewed. If church plants lose this viewpoint, they risk vitiating the very missional energy which gave them birth in the first place. Some regular and more than token place for universal, global mission needs to be a part of the vision for church plants.

On the other hand, church plants, perhaps more often than traditional churches, may well find themselves located in highly multi-ethnic and multicultural locations. Many churches are planted for exactly this reason – a calling to love and serve those communities that have little or no connection with other churches, which may be for ethnic or religious reasons. Or it may be that the churches have been planted, for instance, in an urban environment whose population has grown dramatically in recent years but is not served by other churches, and may well include people from many nations. This kind of location makes possible all kinds of interactions between church plants and their local communities, which can be viewed as being as much in line with this commission from Jesus for all the nations as is overseas missionary work.

In all practicality, the leadership teams of church plants may not have sufficient capacity to spearhead this kind of work with the energy that they may wish, so it may be wise to appoint champions from elsewhere within the congregation who can inform and educate and inspire the church plant to be involved. Care must be taken to ensure that the nations stay clearly and gladly within the purview of the church beyond the tokenism of a missionary board at the back of a church building and an annual proportion of the budget given away. Links with people and organizations working overseas are to be encouraged, and it might be possible to forge some creative links with parts of the world from which immigrant communities in the location of the church plant originally come.

To have this theological sense that our church plants are a part of the global, universal plan that the good news of Jesus should go to all the peoples and nations of the world adds a depth and perspective to mission which is invaluable. It opens us, to a fuller extent, to what God is doing in the world, and it adds greater confidence and integrity to our own sense of being caught up in a profound work of God: our mission is a small part of his larger mission. And this takes us to our next point.

4 Witnesses in the story

A distinctive feature of Luke's account of the Great Commission is how the proclamation of the gospel is itself woven into the wider gospel story, connected to the gospel events. As we have previously seen, Joel Green drew out how the grammar of Luke 24:46–47 indicates that what was written was the suffering of the Messiah, his rising again, *and* the proclamation of repentance and forgiveness of sins in his name to all nations. He amplifies his thoughts on what is happening here:

> If one were to think of the stories of Israel, Jesus, and the early church as in one sense distinct, in these verses one would find the seam wherein they are sewn together into one cloth. Jesus first inscribes his own story, the story of the Messiah who suffers and is raised, into the scriptural story, and then inscribes the story of the early church into both his own story and that of the Scriptures.[113]

The apostolic calling is to be witnesses to *all* these things.

It feels a bit reflexive, but there is a sense in this that the church is to be clear, as part of its calling, that it has the right and responsibility to be doing what it is doing. Questions of authorization can come to the fore, especially in contested situations. The church needs to be clear that its actions in witnessing to Jesus are as a result of his commissioning and are part and parcel of the very impulse of grace which led to the crucifixion and resurrection of Jesus. In one sense, the events of the first Easter are not complete until they are proclaimed to the world by the church. This is the impulse of grace from God.

We find something of the same logic in 2 Corinthians 5. Paul is explaining, justifying and commending his apostolic ministry to his readers. He comes to the point of declaring how magnificent the new creation of God is, before continuing by locating the work of evangelization within that context:

> All this is from God, who reconciled us to himself through Christ, and has given us the ministry of reconciliation; that is, in Christ God

---

[113] Green 1997: 855–856.

was reconciling the world to himself, not counting their trespasses against them, and entrusting the message of reconciliation to us. (2 Cor. 5:18–19)

Paul is careful to distinguish between God's work (the new creation, the actual act of reconciliation accomplished in Christ) and our shared task (the ministry and the message of reconciliation). Nonetheless, the former flows into the latter. This is more than logic – that the good news of that reconciliation needs to be communicated before it can be received and actualized in the lives of men and women. There is a deeper and more organic connection – the gospel is, in its essence, a reconciling power, and so the bringing together of people around its message is a fundamental and essential aspect of the process. The ministry of reconciliation is part of the message of reconciliation. This is part of what it is to live in the new creation which God has accomplished in Christ. As Tom Wright puts it in popular tone:

The world has never seen a ministry of reconciliation. No wonder the Corinthians found Paul's work hard to fathom. It didn't fit any preconceived ideas they may have had. He was behaving like someone . . . who lived in a whole new world.[114]

Returning to Luke, we can say that the witness of the church is itself part of the grand story – Israel, Jesus and the church are all of a piece in the narrative of what God was doing in bringing forgiveness and reconciliation to the world.

This means that church plants are themselves in the very story of God that they tell. This is what God intended. So, the fact that teams have moved to other towns and cities to start new churches, and that old buildings are being given new church life and are being renewed as signs of hope and resurrection, and that churches are to be planted again among the poor in our major urban centres – these random stories of current church planting are all part of the story of God in our land, flowing right back from the history of Israel, and through the great

---

114 T. Wright 2003b: 65; dots original.

confluence of Jesus. We are part of the message, even as we live out the ministry of reconciliation.

This means that there is a quite right and proper way that we should tell the stories of our churches. What we do with individuals and their stories of lives healed and restored by the Lord, so we should do with our churches. When we hear of new churches starting or being renewed, this is a continuation of the great narrative of the Bible; and we are witnesses of these things, as we join up the dots and help people place current church planting within the context of Scripture and the life of Jesus.

It is this which Luke is drawing to our attention here: the proclamation is part of the plan. In Pauline terms, the ministry of reconciliation is itself part of the message of reconciliation. You can see it all around you. Why don't you join in, become part of what God is doing in the world? 'So we are ambassadors for Christ, since God is making his appeal through us; we entreat you on behalf of Christ, be reconciled to God' (2 Cor. 5:20).

5 The message of witness

We should not miss the fact that the risen Jesus commissions the Eleven and their companions to announce a message: 'repentance and forgiveness of sins is to be proclaimed in his name to all nations' (Luke 24:47). Luke, unlike Matthew and Mark, specifies what the apostolic message is – repentance and forgiveness, announced in the name of Jesus.

The word translated 'proclaimed' is literally 'heralded'. The task is the announcement of a message, just as there would have been declarations of victories in battle or other public communications in the ancient world. The call is for an announcement in the public square. This is, of course, just what we see Peter doing on the day of Pentecost (Acts 2:14–36), and Paul, for instance, on the Areopagus (Acts 17:22–31).

The message itself is the same as that of John the Baptist at the beginning of the Gospel (Luke 3:3). Forgiveness has featured throughout the Gospel of Luke:

- The paralysed man has his sins forgiven (5:20, 24).
- The woman who has lived a sinful life finds forgiveness (7:47–48).
- The Lord's Prayer asks that we be forgiven our sins as we ourselves forgive those indebted to us (11:4; cf. 6:37).

- The disciples are enjoined to practise the forgiveness of others (17:3–4).
- Jesus himself famously prays for the forgiveness of those who crucify him (23:34).

Similarly, repentance recurs:

- Jesus defines his mission as calling sinners to repentance (5:32).
- Chorazin and Bethsaida are chastised by the Lord for not repenting in the light of the deeds of power performed among them (10:13).
- Others are strongly admonished by Jesus that 'unless you repent, you will all perish' in like manner to the Galileans killed by Pilate (13:5).
- The parables of the lost sheep, lost coin and lost son refer to the joy in heaven over sinners who repent (15:7, 10 and, by implication, 17–19).
- The rich man, in the parable with Lazarus, argues that if someone comes back from the dead to his brothers, they will repent (16:30).

Repentance and forgiveness form a key thread in the teaching of Jesus, but we may be slightly surprised that they are not more prominent, especially given that Jesus makes this the message to be proclaimed to all the nations on his ascension. We may also be a trifle bemused at why Jesus sends out the Twelve and the Seventy(-Two) in Luke to announce not forgiveness but the kingdom of God (9:2; 10:9). Why, then, should Jesus send them in his Great Commission to announce repentance and forgiveness, and not the kingdom?

The answer lies in the fact that Jesus meant slightly different things by repentance and forgiveness of sins than we may imagine. We tend to see them as individual matters, and we may forget that Jesus was speaking into a particular historical, religious and political context.

To start with repentance, we may be surprised that this was not the kind of call to individual reformation that it is heard to be in modern Western thought; Jesus meant something else by it. Modern scholarship helps us see that the call to repentance was largely (but not exclusively) a summons to get ready for God's restoration of Israel. N. T. Wright also argues persuasively that, in the context of Jesus' day, we must hear many of the commands to repent as a turning away from nationalist

109

violence.[115] The people of God are summoned by Jesus to return to their God in the light of the conclusion of the long exile he is bringing to an end. They must not be distracted by the temptations of political violence, which can only end with swift and implacable reprisals from Rome. This is not to say that there were not individual matters to be turned away from, but the wider picture is the one that we must keep in view.

As to the forgiveness of sins, Wright interprets it similarly: '*Forgiveness of sins is another way of saying "return from exile".*'[116] He helps us enter into the world of first-century Judaism into which Jesus was speaking. Wright argues that Jesus and his contemporaries would have felt that the exile was not yet over. They might have been back in their own land, but they were ruled by a pagan power; Torah and the life of righteousness were conspicuously absent, and the temple was not yet fully restored. Wright frames this observation within the prophecies of, particularly, Jeremiah 31 and Isaiah 40 – 55, which hold out to God's people the promise of restoration and the end of exile, couched in terms of forgiveness and covenant renewal. Wright's point is that the restoration of Israel and the return from exile would happen, and that when they did, then God's people would know that indeed their sins had been forgiven. Isaiah 40 – 55 is introduced in exactly this manner:

> Comfort, O comfort my people,
>> says your God.
> Speak tenderly to Jerusalem,
>> and cry to her
> that she has served her term,
>> that her penalty is paid,
> that she has received from the LORD's hand
>> double for all her sins.
> (Isa. 40:1–2)

Again, this is not to say that individuals cannot be forgiven for their sins, but the bigger picture helps frame this. Wright puts it like this:

---

[115] N. T. Wright 1996: 246–258.
[116] Ibid. 268; emphasis original. And see the wider discussion in ibid. 268–274.

> Overarching the situation of the individual was the state of the nation as a whole; and, as long as Israel remained under the rule of the pagans, as long as Torah was not observed perfectly, as long as the Temple was not properly restored, so Israel longed for 'forgiveness of sins' as the great, unrepeatable, eschatological and national blessing promised by her [God].[117]

The original call for the people of God to be a blessing to the world was back on track, and the covenant blessings could once again be experienced. At the centre of all this is Jesus: this return from exile, this forgiveness and restoration of the people of God, was no longer to be done by the authorized leaders of Israel, particularly with reference to the temple, but instead was accomplished by him, especially through his crucifixion, now publicly and universally validated and vindicated by God in the resurrection.

So, when Jesus commissions the Eleven and their companions at the end of Luke's Gospel to announce in all the public squares of the Roman Empire that there is repentance and the forgiveness of sins in his name (24:47), it is the pronouncement that the kingdom of God is indeed present and alive and well. The significance of the little phrase 'beginning from Jerusalem' (24:47) is as much theological as it is geographical; Israel's original calling to bring the blessings of God to the world is now restored. This announcement is an invitation. Just as the Scriptures had foretold, just as Jesus himself had taught, just as the outpouring of the Holy Spirit upon all flesh will demonstrate (Acts 2:5, 17), the kingdom of God's blessing is now universal. The reason that this message is to go to 'all nations' is that it is an invitation to all people everywhere – all may come and experience the blessings of God. These blessings are no longer through the temple or through Torah or through nationalistic and moral purity, but they are in the name of Jesus. He fulfils the promises of God to Abraham, through Moses and Isaiah and Jeremiah: the kingdom has come. The king of the kingdom has been declared victorious over all that stands against the rule of God. So, repent, be forgiven, enter into this kingdom of life and healing and freedom and justice.

---

[117] Ibid. 271.

To turn to church planting, this means that we have something to say; there is indeed a message to be proclaimed. Although it is entirely true that the kingdom of God is to be demonstrated as well as declared, we cannot miss Luke's emphasis here: the church's task is to announce, to herald, to proclaim, to get up on a high mountain and raise our voice, just as Isaiah had done to announce in Jesus 'Here is your God!' (Isa. 40:9). This needs to be a public announcement because the whole public is invited; it is a universal message for all. No-one is excluded, including (perhaps especially) those who feel themselves least qualified. The sufferings of Israel's Messiah were for them, the resurrection for them to see, the proclamation precisely for their ears.

The contexts of church plants, not least in post-Christendom, postmodernist Western Europe, may be challenging.[118] It may be that the message of the gospel is misheard and mistrusted, but the answer is not to hide it, but rather to declare it more openly, more completely, so that it may be the better heard and understood. Not all will respond, of course, and there may be opposition and rejection. Church plants, though, step into the gladness of Luke's call to evangelization. There is a sense of 'at last' in this great moment, of release, of the doors being flung open. Jesus has cut through everything that kept people *out* of God's kingdom, so now is the time to press the invitation for all to come *in*.

To be any church is to share in this joyful summons, but again there are particular implications for church plants. These have a specific calling to make the good news known; this is why they exist, and why they are positioned as they are in relation to their contexts. The creativity of church plants in their evangelization is matched only by their determination. Messages can be communicated in any number of ways. Some are better than others, it is true, and some media are more conducive than others, but the overall sense is the primacy of the needs and opportunities to make Jesus known as the one who can usher us into God's kingdom through his death and resurrection. Social media, arts, video, dance – any way in which the voice of God can be heard. Come in, come in! This is the age in which God can be known and experienced by all.

---

[118] See Van de Poll and Appleton 2015.

6 The power to witness

Luke's Great Commission ends with Jesus speaking to the Eleven and their companions about the Holy Spirit: 'And see, I am sending upon you what my Father promised; so stay here in the city until you have been clothed with power from on high' (24:49). The end of the Gospel is thus a bit of a cliffhanger: we, the readers, wait to see what this power promised from the Father will be and the impact it will have on this witnessing community. If Matthew and Mark ended their Gospels with an invitation to go *back* and read them again (Matthew for the making of disciples, Mark for the training of missionaries), Luke ends by looking *forward* to the Acts of the Apostles, his second volume.

The Holy Spirit has been present in Luke. The narratives of the births and infancies of John the Baptist and Jesus see an explosion of the activity of the Spirit. John the Baptist is portrayed as one who will 'be filled with the Holy Spirit' (1:15). The angel Gabriel tells Mary that she will conceive because '[t]he Holy Spirit will come upon you, and the power of the Most High will overshadow you' (1:35). Elizabeth praises God because she has been 'filled with the Holy Spirit' (1:41), and Zechariah prophesies for the same reason (1:67). We read how 'the Holy Spirit rested on' Simeon, who had been told by the Holy Spirit that he would see the Messiah before he died (2:25, 26). In all these instances, it is the Spirit who connects people with God's plan of salvation for the world. He acts, though, in special ways with regard to Jesus, enabling his conception.

Jesus continues to be a man of the Spirit in a particular sense. John the Baptist has identified Jesus in terms of the Spirit: although he, John, baptizes with water, Jesus 'will baptize . . . with the Holy Spirit and fire' (3:16). At his own baptism, the Holy Spirit descends on Jesus 'in bodily form like a dove' (3:21), so that Jesus returns 'full of the Holy Spirit', by whom he is led into the wilderness (4:1). After the temptations, Jesus similarly returns to Galilee 'filled with the power of the Spirit' (4:14). At the Nazareth Manifesto, Jesus appropriates to himself the prophecy of Isaiah, declaring that 'the Spirit of the Lord is upon' him, anointing him to preach and enact freedom (4:18). At the return of the Seventy(-Two) from their mission, Jesus 'rejoiced in the Holy Spirit' (10:21). Jesus' ministry, though, is surprisingly described without reference to the Holy Spirit explicitly, but is rather framed in terms of the kingdom of God (e.g. 11:20).

When it comes to the disciples, Jesus concludes his teaching on prayer, which begins with the Lord's Prayer, with the triumphant declaration that 'the heavenly Father [will] give the Holy Spirit to those who ask him!' (11:13). In context, the Holy Spirit is the summation of all the needs of life, material and spiritual, for which his disciples are encouraged to ask, seek and knock. In terms of their witnessing to Jesus, the Lord promises them that 'the Holy Spirit will teach you . . . what you ought to say' (12:12). And now there is the promise of 'power from on high' to witness (24:49).

Why, though, does Luke have Jesus describe the Spirit as 'what *my Father* promised' (24:49)? This phrase is repeated by the Lord at the beginning of Acts: the disciples are to wait in Jerusalem 'for the promise of the Father' (1:4a). Jesus continues: 'This . . . is what you heard from me; for John baptized with water, but you will be baptized with the Holy Spirit not many days from now' (1:4b–5). These are strikingly similar words to those of John the Baptist concerning Jesus himself (Luke 3:16). The promise of the Father, then, is that through the Spirit the disciples will step into the ministry of Jesus himself.

Jesus also reiterates the promise of assistance he gave on the Mount of Ascension: 'You will receive power when the Holy Spirit has come upon you; and you will be witnesses in Jerusalem, in all Judea and Samaria, and to the ends of the earth' (1:8). Power and witnessing seem to go together. We see this when the Spirit is poured out at Pentecost: 'All of them were filled with the Holy Spirit and began to speak in other languages, as the Spirit gave them ability' (2:4), most notably Peter, who 'raised his voice and addressed' the massive crowd (2:14). The power is more than courage or oratorical force; it is the God-given ability to declare 'God's deeds of power' (2:11), especially as they find their focus in the death and resurrection of Jesus. The promise of the Father is to witness to the Son, and have an impact beyond that of the words themselves.

We hear the phrase of the promise of the Father again, though, in Peter's Pentecost sermon, and it is this reference which makes things even clearer: 'Being therefore exalted at the right hand of God, and having received from the Father the promise of the Holy Spirit, [Jesus] has poured out this that you both see and hear' (2:33).

Peter has just described what the observers of Pentecost in Jerusalem experienced in terms of scriptural prophecy:

This is what was spoken through the prophet Joel:

'In the last days it will be, God declares,
  that I will pour out my Spirit upon all flesh'.
(Acts 2:17)

This outpouring will see the democratization of prophecy, dreams and visions among men and women, old and young, slaves and free. It will be accompanied by portents and signs in heaven and on earth, with the sun turned to darkness and the moon to blood. These are signs of 'the coming of the Lord's great and glorious day. Then everyone who calls on the name of the Lord shall be saved' (2:20–21). The promise of the Father, the gift of the Spirit, is therefore a sign of the beginnings of the end of the world; that is what all the apocalyptic imagery means, for these are what we might call 'earth-shattering' events. And they are signs that the world has now entered what Peter quotes Joel as prophesying: 'the last days' (2:17). This is a technical term indicating that the time of the fulfilment of the kingdom of God is at hand. It is the age of the Spirit, the time when God's king has been enthroned. For Peter, the coming of the Spirit is the sign that this king is Jesus, and he is now 'exalted at the right hand of God' (2:33a). Jesus, as the exalted king, receives the promised Spirit from the Father, and pours out all that 'you both see and hear' (2:33b). And it is through the Spirit that God continues the ministry of Jesus.

The Spirit's presence is evidence that Jesus is raised and that Jesus directs his new community from the right hand of God. Luke reassures his readers, including us, that though the Messiah is dead and seemingly absent, he is present in the gift and presence of the Spirit he has sent.[119] In the Spirit, then, Peter is saying, there is the revelation of the fullness of God's promised kingdom as it has been accomplished in the life, death, resurrection and exaltation of Jesus of Nazareth. As Max Turner puts it: 'In the Gospels the term *Holy Spirit* . . . is a referring expression for the power and presence of God in action, especially as the means of God's self-revelation.'[120]

---

[119] Bock 1992: 505.
[120] Turner 1992: 341; emphasis original.

And so, we may say that Luke's Great Commission looks ahead to Pentecost, 'what my Father promised' (24:49). The Spirit is not just the help the disciples will need to witness to Jesus, to proclaim the events and meaning of his life, crucifixion and resurrection (although that is true), but is rather the demonstration that in Jesus the power and kingdom of God, long promised, is now here and is open to all. This is power as heavenly reality, invading and being manifested on earth, as the apostles witness to Jesus and continue his ministry beyond the borders of Israel to all nations.

We may thus say that Jesus envisaged the church that would come after his ascension as a 'charismatic' community. I do not mean this in a partisan way, but in the profoundly theological sense that Luke describes. The church witnesses to Jesus by virtue of the presence of the Spirit as the promise of the Father. Now that Jesus is exalted at the right hand of God, he has the authority to release the Spirit, as the last phase of the life of the world has come, following the incarnation, the cross, and the resurrection and ascension. The Spirit makes this known, through the multi-voiced testimony of the church and through the presence of God in action in its midst. This will be the story of Acts, in which Jesus continues to guide and be present in the church through the Spirit.

These are inspiring and amazing things, and happily true of all churches. Church planters are to take these perspectives to heart, and to live from their reality. They are to expect the life and ministry of Jesus to continue in their church plants, and to understand that the Acts of the Apostles is given to us not as an aspirational but as a theological blueprint of their community and missionary life. This does not mean triumphalism, as we shall see, but rather both tragedy and triumph, martyrdom as well as miracle. Both, however, express the power of the witnessing church, made possible by the promised Holy Spirit.

The important theological factor for church plants to take away from Luke's Great Commission is that this global project of establishing communities which witness to Jesus, interpreting the Scriptures about him, proclaiming that in Jesus the kingdom is here and exile is over – all this magnificent calling is dependent upon the reality of God, the fulfilling of his plan for the world, and this happens when Jesus pours out the promise of the Father. Church plants need to be 'charismatic' communities if they are to be effective witnessing communities.

John

John's version of the Great Commission comes on the evening of Easter Sunday when Jesus appears to the disciples:

> When it was evening on that day, the first day of the week, and the doors of the house where the disciples had met were locked for fear of the Jews, Jesus came and stood among them and said, 'Peace be with you.' After he said this, he showed them his hands and his side. Then the disciples rejoiced when they saw the Lord. Jesus said to them again, 'Peace be with you. As the Father has sent me, so I send you.' When he had said this, he breathed on them and said to them, 'Receive the Holy Spirit. If you forgive the sins of any, they are forgiven them; if you retain the sins of any, they are retained.'
> (John 20:19–23)

As with the other Gospel writers, the context is emphatically that of the resurrection of Jesus. John draws out just what an otherworldly experience this was for the disciples – Jesus shows them his hands and side, and, by showing the marks of his suffering, identifies himself to them as the same Jesus who had just been crucified. This same Jesus, though, is profoundly different, for he has just, in some manner which John does not describe, passed through locked doors to come and stand in their midst. However, as they reflect on the experience, John draws out the fulfilment of the promises of the upper-room discourse (in chs. 14–17): Jesus brings them peace, as he promised he would (20:19, 21; cf. 14:27; 16:33), and joy beyond grief (20:20; cf. 16:20, 22). And, more subtly, he does in resurrection life what he had done in his incarnational life – he comes and stands among them (20:19; cf. 1:26).[121]

Having established among them who he is, the risen Jesus commissions the disciples. May we look at the three elements of this commission, and think together about the implications for church planters.

---

[121] See Stibbe 1996: 199.

1 The peace of the Lord

Twice, in these few verses, Jesus speaks peace to the disciples. There is no verb in the Greek text – he merely says, 'Peace to you.' This would have been a traditional greeting at the time, but the context makes it anything but empty of meaning.

The greeting reminds us of encounters between God and heroes of the Old Testament. Gideon is one such. When the LORD appears to him, he says to him, 'Peace be to you; do not fear, you shall not die.' Gideon responds by building an altar, which he calls 'The LORD is peace' (Judg. 6:23, 24). Similarly, when an angel of the LORD appears to Daniel, he reassures him with the words, 'O man greatly loved, fear not, peace be with you; be strong and of good courage' (Dan. 10:19 ESV). Daniel is strengthened. The NRSV translates the phrase 'peace be with you' in 10:19 as 'you are safe'. In John's Gospel, we see the disciples having an encounter with the presence of God in Jesus.[122] The lack of a verb means that this is not so much a greeting or wish, as a declaration.[123]

The grounds for this are the previous promises of peace that Jesus has made to the disciples. In the farewell discourse, Jesus has prophesied that 'the Advocate, the Holy Spirit' (14:26), will be sent to them. He immediately goes on to say:

> Peace I leave with you; my peace I give to you. I do not give to you as the world gives. Do not let your hearts be troubled, and do not let them be afraid. You heard me say to you, 'I am going away, and I am coming to you' . . . And now I have told you this before it occurs, so that when it does occur, you may believe.
> (14:27–29)

The thought is very similar to that about joy which we read of two chapters later:

> Very truly I tell you, you will weep and mourn, but the world will rejoice; you will have pain, but your pain will turn into joy . . . So

---

[122] Brown 1970: 1021.
[123] Ibid.

you will have pain now; but I will see you again, and your hearts
will rejoice, and no one will take your joy from you.
(16:20, 22)

The disciples experience both the peace and the joy which the resurrected Jesus brings. They have been through the trouble, fear and pain
of seeing him killed, but now they are experiencing the peace which
he leaves with them and the joy which can never be taken from them.
The Spirit will be given to them, and the prophecy of Jesus will bring
them to faith. 'Now that he has come back to them, he grants this
peace, for in the Holy Spirit (vs. 22) they have the enduring presence
of Jesus and the gift of divine sonship that is the basis of Christian
peace.'[124]

Planting churches can be rough. How crucial does Jesus' repeated
declaration of peace become in such a context! When there might be
worry about the finances of the church plant, potential division about
the vision, concern about stakeholders in the local community, anxiety
about the reaction of local people to the first few weeks, how powerful
is a non-anxious presence among the leaders. This peace and joy from
Jesus brings perspective, resilience and an infectious confidence into all
that we do. Imagine a meeting of local clergy who are threatened by the
arrival of the new church plant; maybe tempers fray and hasty words
are spoken. Or it might be a tense meeting involving the original congregation and the church-planting team. Or maybe anger comes out in
the introductory small-group session of the first Alpha course of the
church plant. If the church-plant leadership can bring peace into these
situations, the peace of Jesus, great progress can be made.

2 The mission of Jesus

This peace is necessary for the mission itself as well. The declaration of
peace leads directly into the commission for being sent by Jesus: 'As the
Father has sent me, so I send you' (20:21). Jesus balances the sentence to
bring out the closeness of the two models of mission: '*as . . . so*'. The sending
of the disciples by Jesus is modelled on that of Jesus by the Father; the one

---

[124] Ibid. 1035.

is a pattern of the other.[125] There are different tenses to the verbs: Jesus uses an aorist (a form of a Greek past tense not available to English) for his own sending, and a present tense for the sending of the disciples. This underlines the central thought – Jesus has completed the mission for which he has been sent into the world by the Father, and now sends the disciples in like manner to undertake theirs, which is to be modelled on his.

What then has been the pattern of Jesus' being sent by the Father? This takes us right back to the beginning of the Gospel, to John's famous line: 'And the Word became flesh and lived among us' (1:14). This is the *incarnation* of the Son, which literally in Latin means a taking on of flesh. Jesus puts aside the life he had when he was 'with God' (1:1), and instead takes on a fully human life, without any loss of his deity.

The same thought can be found in the famous passage in Philippians 2, where Paul once again takes the incarnation as a pattern for Christian discipleship, this time as a model for humility:

Let the same mind be in you that was in Christ Jesus,

who, though he was in the form of God,
    did not regard equality with God
    as something to be exploited,
but emptied himself,
    taking the form of a slave,
    being born in human likeness.
And being found in human form,
    he humbled himself
    and became obedient to the point of death –
    even death on a cross.
(Phil. 2:5–8)

Jesus identifies fully with the human condition, at great personal cost. This identification is seen in his actually becoming human, but also sets

---

[125] In point of fact, different Greek words are used for the sending of the Son and the sending of the disciples, but there is no change in the meaning; the two words are used interchangeably throughout John's Gospel. See Barrett 1978: 569.

a trajectory of identification in mind and life with those among whom he came to live.

This incarnation is the manner in which Jesus was sent by the Father, and the manner in which he now sends the disciples.

We see it lived out by Paul when he defends his apostolic role to the Corinthians:

> For though I am free with respect to all, I have made myself a slave to all, so that I might win more of them. To the Jews I became as a Jew, in order to win Jews. To those under the law I became as one under the law (though I myself am not under the law) so that I might win those under the law. To those outside the law I became as one outside the law (though I am not free from God's law but am under Christ's law) so that I might win those outside the law. To the weak I became weak, so that I might win the weak. I have become all things to all people, so that I might by any means save some. I do it all for the sake of the gospel, so that I may share in its blessings. (1 Cor. 9:19–23)

Paul takes the incarnational approach to mission and applies it to a variety of contexts. For the missionary, incarnation is not something that is done once and for all, but is rather a necessary posture of entering into the worlds of the people with whom he or she comes into contact, in order to gain a hearing for the gospel.

Incarnational mission is the way in which the disciples are sent into the world by Jesus in John's Great Commission. As we apply this to church planters, it is a call to enter fully into the lives and worlds of those among whom we plant our churches.

In the evangelical world, there have been fewer more bold and articulate advocates for this approach than John Stott, who said: 'All authentic mission is incarnational mission.'[126] He describes what this meant for Jesus:

> The Son of God did not stay in the safe immunity of his heaven, remote from human sin and tragedy. He actually entered our world.

---

[126] Stott 1992: 358.

He emptied himself of his glory and humbled himself to serve. He took our nature, lived our life, endured our temptations, experienced our sorrows, felt our hurts, bore our sins and died our death. He penetrated deeply into our humanness. He never stayed aloof from the people he might have been expected to avoid. He made friends with the dropouts of society. He even touched untouchables. He could not have become more one with us than he did. It was the total identification of love.[127]

And if that is what incarnational mission meant for Jesus, then this is what it means for us who follow him too: 'It demands identification without loss of identity. It means entering other people's worlds, as he entered ours, though without compromising our Christian convictions, values or standards.'[128]

Stott goes on to spell out some of the implications of this for us, in that we are called to enter into the thought-worlds and heart-worlds of those we are called to serve.[129] Elsewhere, though, he describes a kind of journey he has been on with regard to the implications of incarnational mission for him personally. He outlines an understanding of mission that places an emphasis on 'preaching, witnessing and making disciples', and says that he himself used to advocate for this position:

Today, however, I would express myself differently ... I now see more clearly that not only the consequences of the commission but the actual commission itself must be understood to include social as well as evangelistic responsibility, unless we are to be guilty of distorting the words of Jesus.

Taking the service of Jesus as his guiding principle,[130] he traces how Jesus preached about God's kingdom but also

served in deed as well as in word, and it would be impossible in the ministry of Jesus to separate his works from his words. He fed

---

[127] Ibid. 357.
[128] Ibid. 358.
[129] Ibid. 359–360.
[130] Itself a major note of John's Gospel (e.g. 13:1–17, esp. 14–15).

hungry mouths and washed dirty feet, he healed the sick, comforted the sad and even restored the dead to life. Now he sends us, he says, as the Father had sent him.[131]

There can be few more central and more challenging aspects to church planting than this principle of incarnational mission. It is hard to overstate its importance and centrality to the whole enterprise. Church planting is all about the grounding and living out of the Christian gospel in particular neighbourhoods and in specific networks. It is the making visible of Jesus and his message and kingdom through the lived-out realities of new congregations. Often these congregations have moved into an area from another area. Occasionally, the church plant is made up of those who are very different culturally, socially, economically, maybe ethnically and religiously, from those who live in the area or in the network that the church plant is trying to reach. There is a gap – maybe there are multiple gaps – between them. A central task of the church planters is to bridge those gaps, to build bridges, to take down the barriers. This calls for an entering into the worlds of those they have come to serve. There will be strenuous efforts to understand, to connect, to build relationships. Incarnational mission demands even more. There will likely be a physical moving into the neighbourhood. There will be efforts at identification. There will be an imaginative entering into the worlds of those who live and work there, a learning of history, culture, social customs, patterns of relating. There will be an emotional connecting, feeling what others feel, stepping into others' shoes, walking alongside. Hospitality will be significant, being in one another's homes. There will be a lot of listening, hearing the local stories, unearthing the history, finding out what people's hopes and fears are. And there will be a conscious standing alongside the local communities and networks in their pains and sufferings, doing all in our power to relieve need, to enter into situations with the purpose of bringing about healing and hope. It is all part of how church plants express the love of Jesus to their communities.

There are caveats and limits to this. We must be careful to distinguish between the extent of Jesus' identification with the human race and ours

---

[131] Stott 1975: 23–24.

with our local communities. Jesus actually *became* a human being, and anything comparable is not possible for us. We should be careful not to make too ready and too exact a comparison between our efforts to incarnate the gospel and the incarnation of Jesus himself; we can too easily end up trivializing and diminishing the enormity of what Jesus did for us.[132] We need to bear in mind too the points of dissimilarity: as John Stott succinctly puts it, 'We are not saviours.'[133] Only Jesus came to die for the sins of the world. And there are questions about the limits of identification – we must be wary of losing Christian distinctiveness and of not being true to ourselves, and there are questions about how helpful it is to receiving cultures when church planters totally identify with them. And there is a growing and helpful literature around the dangers of paternalism and the damage that can be done when help is done *to* people, not *with* and *for* them.[134]

Nonetheless, we should not evade the challenge of this commission from Jesus. The shape of our church planting is to be patterned on his, both in terms of its contours and, even more centrally, its aims. Sometimes church plants are accused (usually falsely) of just being groups of middle-class people helicoptered into areas with which they make no effort to communicate and engage. Such an approach is indefensible in the light of what Jesus calls us as his disciples to do.

3 The Spirit of the Lord

The climax of this encounter is when Jesus breathes on the disciples and says to them, 'Receive the Holy Spirit,' before declaring, 'If you forgive the sins of any, they are forgiven them; if you retain the sins of any, they are retained' (20:22–23). As with Luke, John shows us the central place that the Holy Spirit will play in the mission and life of the church. Luke looks ahead to Pentecost and the coming of the Spirit, and John gives us a powerful prophetic sign from Jesus to the same effect.[135]

The act of breathing upon the disciples is an odd and striking one, and clearly intended to be a powerful action that the disciples would always

---

[132] See Ott, Strauss with Tennent 2010: 100–101.
[133] Stott 1975: 24.
[134] E.g. Corbett and Fikkert 2014; Wells 2015.
[135] See Witherington (1995: 340–341) for a concise argument for the relationship between this incident in John and Pentecost, and Brown (1970: 1038–1039) for a different understanding.

remember. Scholars show us that there are two incidents from the Old Testament to bear in mind.

The word 'breathed on' is used in the Septuagint, the Greek translation of the Old Testament, in Genesis 2:7, when God creates Adam: 'The LORD God formed man from the dust of the ground, and breathed into his nostrils the breath of life; and the man became a living being.' The point of the comparison is stunning: just as God gave the breath of life to the human race in the creation of the world, now Jesus, alive for ever from the dead, is breathing his resurrection life into the disciples at the re-creation of the world.

John's Gospel has often viewed Jesus in this light:

- Think how the Gospel begins with its famous words, 'In the beginning was the Word' (1:1). These words echo the beginning of the Bible itself: 'In the beginning when God created the heavens and the earth . . .' (Gen. 1:1). In Jesus, the world is re-created; it starts again.
- The prologue to John's Gospel sets out carefully Jesus' role in the creation of the world: 'What has come into being in him was life, and the life was the light of all people' (1:4), and emphasizes that Jesus brings this creative life-giving power with him in his incarnation: 'He was in the world, and the world came into being through him' (1:10).
- Where the Synoptic Gospels speak about the kingdom of God or the kingdom of heaven, John has Jesus speak about eternal life (e.g. 3:16; 17:3, but throughout the Gospel). For John this is more than a metaphor; it is precisely a description – Jesus makes alive, but in a dimension that is only fully comprehended after the resurrection.
- John presents Jesus' healing ministry in language that is reminiscent of the creation in the light of the resurrection. For instance, the healing of the paralysed man is referred to by Jesus by comparison with the work of the Father: 'My Father is still working, and I also am working' (5:17). Another example is the healing of the man born blind, for which Jesus spits on the ground and makes mud which he smears on the man's eyes, reminiscent of the creation of the first man from the mud of the earth (9:6, 11).

- The imagery of some of Jesus' most famous sayings in John is rooted in the experience of giving life – for instance when he describes himself as 'the bread of life' (6:35) or 'the resurrection and the life' (11:25).
- The resurrection appearances in John happen in a garden, reminiscent of that first garden of Eden (19:41; 20:15). John repeats that Easter Day is 'the first day of the week' (20:1, 19), by association drawing our minds to the beginning of the creation of the world as described in Genesis.
- John frames his purpose in writing his Gospel in terms of creation: it is written 'so that you may come to believe that Jesus is the Messiah, the Son of God, and that through believing you may have life in his name' (20:31).

Within this perspective, the breathing of Jesus on the disciples, with its clear echoes of the giving of life to the first human being at the creation, is deeply significant:

> Symbolically, then, John is proclaiming that just as in the first creation God breathed a living spirit into man, so now in the moment of the new creation Jesus breathes his own Holy Spirit into the disciples, giving them eternal life.[136]

The role of the disciples is highlighted by the second reference in Scripture to breathing, in Ezekiel's strange vision of the valley of the dry bones. We read: 'Thus says the Lord GOD to these bones: I will cause breath to enter you, and you shall live' (Ezek. 37:5). The bones came together, grew sinews and flesh, 'but there was no breath in them' (37:8).

> Then he said to me, 'Prophesy to the breath, prophesy, mortal [lit. 'son of man'], and say to the breath: Thus says the Lord GOD: Come from the four winds, O breath, and breathe upon these slain, that they may live.' I prophesied as he commanded me, and the breath

---

[136] Brown 1970: 1037. Cf. C. K. Barrett's powerful phrase: 'This was the beginning of the new creation' (1978: 570).

came into them, and they lived, and stood on their feet, a vast multitude.
(Ezek. 37:9–10)

This breath of Jesus, then, is nothing less than the resurrecting power of God, bringing the dead to life; it is the breath of the one who is, in himself, the resurrection and the life. And let's note how resurrection is viewed in terms of the restoration of life, the re-creation of creation.

Ezekiel goes on to report the significance of this vision:

Then he said to me, 'Mortal, these bones are the whole house of Israel. They say, "Our bones are dried up, and our hope is lost; we are cut off completely." Therefore prophesy, and say to them, Thus says the Lord GOD: I am going to open your graves, and bring you up from your graves, O my people; and I will bring you back to the land of Israel . . . I will put my spirit within you, and you shall live, and I will place you on your own soil; then you shall know that I, the LORD, have spoken and will act, says the LORD.'
(Ezek. 37:11–14)

With these words echoing in our ears, we see Jesus as the word and action of God, and the disciples as the restored, resurrected Israel, coming alive with hope, with fresh confidence in their calling to bring life to the world. They 'will be the nucleus of a renewed people of God, the beachhead of the new creation of the world'.[137]

'Life' is a major theme in John's Gospel, as we have seen.[138] What did John mean by it, and how might it relate to church planting? In just under half of the occurrences of the word 'life' in the Gospel, it is described as 'eternal life'.[139] This refers to the Jewish belief that the history of the world could be divided into two: 'This Age' and 'The Age to Come'. These were different, not just in terms of chronology, with the latter following on from the former, but also in terms of the quality of life. Some of the teaching of

---

[137] Byrne 2014: 336.
[138] The noun comes 36 times in John, the verb 16 times, and there are a further 3 occurrences of another grammatical form of the same word (Dodd 1968: 144).
[139] Dodd 1968: 144.

Jesus and the Gospel stands squarely in line with Jewish belief of the time, namely that the life of the Age to Come would begin after death. Some of his teaching, though, strikingly changes this, and implies that, through Jesus and belief in him, there is a kind of overlap, when the life of the Age to Come can begin in This Age. Think of Jesus speaking with Martha at the tomb of her brother Lazarus:

> Jesus said to her, 'I am the resurrection and the life. Those who believe in me, even though they die, will live [which sounds as though life after death is in mind], and everyone who lives and believes in me will never die [which is something altogether different].'
> (John 11:25–26)

As Byrne explains:

> In other words, the 'resurrection' of which Jesus has spoken is something which may take place before bodily death, and has for its result the possession of eternal life here and now . . . For John this present enjoyment of eternal life has become the controlling and all-important conception.[140]

We must not think of this eternal life, though, in purely philosophical terms, for, as we have seen, Jesus attaches to it the most material of perspectives, such as being able to walk again, to eat bread, to be in a garden.

It is into this world, this life, this Age to Come, that Jesus gives his disciples new birth when he breathes on them. The new creation begins then through Jesus giving the Spirit to his disciples. This ties in with how the Spirit has been spoken of already in John:

- In the conversation with Nicodemus, Jesus says it is necessary to be 'born from above', 'born of . . . Spirit', in order to 'see the kingdom of God' (3:3, 5).
- John the Baptist had identified Jesus as the one who 'baptizes with the Holy Spirit' (1:33).

---

[140] Ibid. 148, 149.

- Jesus describes himself as the one 'who gives the Spirit without measure' (3:34).

It is through the Spirit that Jesus enables access into the kingdom of God, into the Age to Come, and it is he who has the power to do this through the gift of the Spirit. The Spirit is given only after Jesus is glorified, which in John means the crucifixion (7:37–39).

We can go even further, though, for the gift of the Spirit is not separate from Jesus. By describing the Spirit in terms of the breath of Jesus, John is helping us see that in the Holy Spirit, Jesus is giving us nothing less than his very self. At the crucifixion, John describes Jesus' death as the giving up of his 'spirit', the same word as 'breath' in Greek (19:30). Now that Jesus is raised from death, he gives his breath, his very life, to the disciples: 'Receive the Holy Spirit' (20:22). 'Jesus is personally communicating and committing himself to the disciples in the person of the Spirit.'[141] This is how Jesus is to be personally present with the new community of the church after his ascension.

> As risen Lord [Jesus] . . . gifts his disciples with the Spirit that they may be to the world what he has been . . . The Spirit is *with* the community and *in* the community and will remain with the community for ever . . . but the community must reach beyond its borders to continue the mission of Jesus, so that the world may know and believe that he is the Sent One of the Father.[142]

The gift of the Spirit is integral to the call to mission from the risen Jesus. Just as he, in his person, brought about the beginnings of the new creation, now, through his presence in the gift of the Spirit, he enables his disciples to carry on this same work of making the world new. There is an obvious difference between the work of Jesus and that of the disciples: he *achieved* the new creation, and the disciples *implement* this new reality, just as a composer may write music and performers play it,[143] but John is at pains to draw out how Jesus, in the gift of the Spirit, is personally present in and

---

[141] Barrett 1978: 570.
[142] Maloney 1998: 532.
[143] T. Wright 2002: 149.

with the community of the disciples to carry on the work of new creation in the world after his ascension.

This explains the puzzling nature of the concluding saying of these verses: 'If you forgive the sins of any, they are forgiven them; if you retain the sins of any, they are retained' (20:23). The power to forgive sins is overwhelming enough, but also to *retain* sins? What can that mean?

More evangelical commentators see in this an allusion to the preaching of the gospel. Witherington, for instance, writes:

> Although the text may sound harsh at first, forgiving or retaining sins is simply a natural component of the calling of people to repentance and the offering of forgiveness in Christ. Those who reject the Gospel are still in their sins, as earlier texts in this Gospel stress (cf. 9:41).[144]

By contrast, Catholic commentators 'think immediately here of the penitential discipline of the church, specifically the sacrament of reconciliation'.[145] An argument for the first perspective is the consideration that only God can forgive sins (e.g. Mark 2:7) and he does so through the gospel, but against it is the absence of any mention of preaching here. And for the second interpretation is the similarity to the sayings in Matthew 16:19 and 18:18, which have the life of the church more in view, but against it is a certain anachronism in applying a later church practice retrospectively to this situation in John.

If we follow the logic of the presence of Jesus in the community of the church continuing the work of the new creation through the gift of the Holy Spirit, then these difficulties can be overcome. It is nothing less than the continued presence of Jesus in the church which is both forgiving and retaining sins, polarizing people in response to him, as has happened throughout John's Gospel. The disciples, filled with the life and breath of Jesus, will find they have the same effect. The life of creation is marred and deformed by sin, whereas the life of the new creation will bring healing, forgiveness and renewal through the presence of Jesus by his

---

[144] Witherington 1995: 342.
[145] Byrne 2014: 336.

Spirit in the community of the church. If the sending of the disciples by Jesus is patterned on the sending of Jesus by the Father, then we should look for parallels in the mission of Jesus. What we find is a judgment as a kind of disclosure of what was already present; for instance, the Pharisees are guilty because they claim to see, when in fact they are blind (9:39–41), and those in darkness choose not to come to the light because it will expose their deeds (3:19–21). This is what it is to forgive and to retain sins.

This is also true of the ministry of the Holy Spirit as Jesus describes it: he is 'the Spirit of truth', because he testifies about Jesus (15:26; 16:12–14), and he will unveil the world's wrong thinking about sin, righteousness and judgment by reference to who Jesus is and what he came to do (16:8–11). We can say, then, that in John, the Spirit of Jesus will clash with sin by virtue of the holiness of his life and the perspective of the new creation, and this will have the inevitable corollary of showing up everything that stands in opposition to the person and purpose of Jesus. 'Sanctification may lead to blessedness before God, but it also has the hard edge of exposing all that rejects the love lavished upon the world by a God who sent his only Son.'[146] As Brown writes: '[Here] the primary symbolism of the giving of the Spirit concerns the new creation, a creation that wipes out evil, for the *Holy* Spirit consecrates men [and women] and gives them the power to make others holy in turn.'[147]

This is the bigger picture of what is happening here theologically, and includes both the preaching of the gospel and the sanctifying of the life of the church. By the Spirit, Jesus is still present in and through the community that will continue after his ascension, and he will continue to bring both freedom from sin and exposure of sin. This is

> the power to isolate, repel, and negate evil and sin, a power given to Jesus in his mission by the Father and given in turn by Jesus through the Spirit to those he commissions. It is an effective, not merely a declaratory, power against sin, a power that touches new and old followers of Christ, a power that challenges those who refuse to believe.[148]

---

146 Maloney 1998: 533.
147 Brown 1970: 1043; emphasis original.
148 Ibid. 1044.

This is the mission of the church, which is a parallel of that for which the Father sent Jesus into the world, and which is made possible by the continued presence of the risen Jesus in and through the church by virtue of the gift of the Holy Spirit.

How might all this apply with reference to church plants? It ties in closely with the call to incarnational mission. Just as we are to copy Jesus in his immersing himself into and identifying himself with the world to which he was sent by the Father, so we are to do so in the power of his continued presence in the Spirit, conscious that the pattern of division caused by his mission will also likely be true in ours. The mission of Jesus is only possible by virtue of the presence of Jesus in and through his church. Churches cannot be planted without Jesus commissioning them and being present by breathing his Spirit into them.

Church plants should have the sense that they are indeed sent by Jesus. This is not their idea, nor is it an arrogant assumption of power or superiority over those communities into which they are sent. You have got to be pretty close to someone to feel their breath on you, and church plants can be confident that Jesus is very close to them when they feel his Spirit guiding and sanctifying them. Their mission is a beautiful one: the renewal of all creation, the bringing of a hope of God's future, the liberating of lives from all that mars and deforms them. This is the kind of love through which the Father sent the Son into the world, and we are privileged to stand in this succession as he in turn sends us in the power of the Spirit to continue this same work. This is Jesus remaking the world through his Spirit in and through the church, one life at a time.

Reflections on the Great Commissions

When we consider the four different versions of the Great Commission at the end of each of the Gospels, there are definite similarities. What is equally striking, particularly when we dig a bit deeper exegetically, are the differences. What conclusions may we draw from these four key moments at the climax of the Gospels?

1 The impact of the resurrection

All four Gospels show the call to mission in the light of the resurrection of Jesus. In different ways they tell us that there has been a massive turning point in the history of God's interactions with his world. We have reached the climax of the story of Israel, which is fulfilled and reinterpreted by Jesus (Matthew). With the exaltation of Jesus, we see the beginning of the last days, the age of the Spirit (Luke). The sheer awesome scale of the resurrection prompts a reappraisal of the life of discipleship and the life of mission (Mark). And the creation is made new and the human race starts again (John). The effect and impact of all this is that the kingdom of God catapults into a new phase – exile is ended, the king has come, God is shaking the most fundamental assumptions we may have about life and death, and the followers of Jesus are now sent into the whole world to demonstrate and announce this new reality. It is not that mission is a separate compartment from all this; it is actually a part of it, an extension of what it is like to experience this triumph of God in the world. It is a living out of the universal and victorious presence of Jesus in and with his community throughout the world. Lucien Legrand sums this up by saying that 'the Resurrection bestows on the Christ event *the complete extent of divine power, and, therefore, universal scope*'.[149]

We note, as well, that this new missionary life is intimately and indissolubly tied up with the life of the church. The life of Israel is transformed and continued in the life of the community of Jesus, baptizing, teaching, making disciples, telling stories, living into the narrative of Scripture, walking with Jesus on the roads of life, living lives of holiness and love in the power of Jesus. As so often in our study, we see church and mission, not as opposed to each other, but as closely interrelated. Church planting can easily locate itself at exactly this intersection.

This perspective gives a confidence for all mission, and for church planting. God has acted in Jesus Christ, and has pronounced vindication and victory through the resurrection. The life of the church and of mission lives *out of* this new reality that the life of Jesus has created. It is not for us to create something new when we plant our churches, but rather it is for us to discover the best ways of making this new life available and accessible for those we wish to serve.

Church planting is hard work and can be immensely demanding. It is frequently entrepreneurial, and it does feel as if we are making something.

---

[149] Legrand 1990: 86; emphasis original.

We are, after all, creating new communities where previously there were none. Viewed, though, from the perspective of the four Great Commissions, we need to remind ourselves that our activity is not primary, but is, theologically speaking, secondary, following on from the achievement of God. Lucien Legrand warns us against 'an unconscious semi-Pelagianism',[150] where we evangelize and engage with mission as if, somehow, everything depends upon us, rather than gratefully founding all our efforts on the colossal achievement of Christ. To quote Legrand again: 'It is not the evangelizer who carries the gospel; it is the gospel, the power of God, that carries the evangelizer.'[151] Further, all mission is actualized by nothing less than the presence of Jesus, now alive for evermore, breathing his own life into and through his church by the Holy Spirit.

The church planter works from the vantage point of the enormity of what God has done in Jesus Christ, and the sheer greatness of Jesus. The world has been fundamentally changed by Jesus. All that the Old Testament led up to is enacted in Jesus. God has acted decisively in Jesus. The enemies of the human race have been dealt a death blow in Jesus. All the deep structures of the world have been shifted as Jesus announces, inaugurates and enacts the kingdom of God. The resurrection is a demonstration of all that has happened. And it is this world-changing event which is the starting gun for global mission: 'in all four gospels, Jesus' Resurrection generates mission . . . [N]one found it possible to understand the Resurrection apart from mission.'[152]

Accordingly, church planters will sink themselves deeply and repeatedly into the theological foundations of the gospel. The more we appreciate and inhabit the life, death and resurrection of Jesus, the more confidently and effectively we will plant our churches. Our foundation is not technique, networking, the latest conference, our own personalities and skills; it is Jesus, crucified and risen. We may be able to launch a church plant through good marketing or stunning events that draw a crowd, but we will not be able to sustain and build a church from that vantage point. Our personal and spiritual lives will be oriented around the magnitude

---

[150] Ibid. 82.
[151] Ibid. 87.
[152] Ibid. 70.

of Jesus. Our imaginations and aspirations will be shaped by how the world changed on that first Good Friday and Easter Day. Our habits and prayers will revolve around the cross and the empty tomb as they encapsulate the kingdom of God and bring it to its stunning climax.

We want to be deep people. We are likely to be busy people – pragmatic, energetic activists. None of this is wrong, and goes with the territory of church planting. All the more, therefore, will we need to be proactive, intentional and determined to safeguard deep time. Make sure that there is profound time spent in the Scriptures, beyond our latest sermon series. Read some decent theology. Maybe get a small group of church planters together to introduce an element of accountability and mutual encouragement into it. Maybe book ourselves into a good theology talk or conference once a year. Give time to meditation, to slow and unhurried thought around the gospel in prayer. Make sure there is devotion to Jesus in our prayers, in our church worship, in our celebration of Holy Communion. In all of this, we are telling ourselves, 'The foundation has been laid; the world and its future have already been changed. This is not my task.' And we are fuelling ourselves for the joyous confidence of announcing God's kingdom in our work of church planting.

2 The resurrection sends us *out* to plant churches

The other main common factor in all four Great Commissions is that the church being born is sent out by Jesus, far out, to the very ends of the earth. Matthew and Luke talk about discipling 'all nations' (Matt. 28:19; Luke 24:47), Mark speaks of 'the whole creation' (16:15, in the longer ending), and John uses imagery of the re-creation of the whole human race (20:22). There may have been hints of this in the Old Testament, but only hints, and the tenor of the Gospels has been of a mission only to Israel. Now, however, at the resurrection, suddenly the perspective is global, universal, with the language of 'all', 'every', 'always', 'everything'. The resurrection enfolds all creation, all time, every tribe and tongue and nation, every person.

We have previously noted the shift from *centripetal* to *centrifugal* mission at this point of salvation history. This is a posture that is fundamental to church planting. Even though the missionary strategies of some church plants may be built around attracting people to come to

our churches, the deeper orientation is one of going. Our deepest understanding of ourselves and what we are called to do is the sense of being
sent by Jesus, sent into the world. 'Go and find them' is the dynamic out
of which we live and around which we structure our church plants.
Church planters are constantly looking for those who are not in our
churches. We are motivated by those who are not reached, do not appear
interested, those who tell us that Christianity is not for them.

Never lose that fire and that perspective! Likely as not, there will be
certain organizational dynamics which will pull your time and attention
into the internal life of the church plant, and different personalities and
spiritual gifts will resist a relentlessly outward focus. In addition, people
will get tired and run out of energy if you press too hard on the outreach
pedal all the time. Nonetheless, this direction is *the* direction of church
planting. One could argue that all churches find their origin in these
Great Commissions at the end of the four Gospels, and so all church life
should be viewed in this perspective. If you are leading the church plant,
or are part of the core team that holds the culture and ethos of the church
plant, this is a key element of your central task. Keep this question on the
agenda for every meeting: 'Where is the Lord sending us in this?' Ask
those awkward questions. Make sure this priority is reflected in the
budget, staff time, your time, the balance of the teaching, the emphasis
of the mentoring – everything that says, 'This is what our church plant
is about.' Keep your own passion alive; hang out with like-minded church
planters, apostolic and missionary types; listen to mission podcasts; read
stories that fire you up.

3 Church plants will be different from one another

What is striking about the four Great Commissions is that they are not
the same. They have the same shared dynamic – the grace and power of
God in Jesus sending the nascent church to the whole world – but each
applies this differently. So, Matthew emphasizes a church which is
structured around disciple-making, with clear roles for those who will sit
and teach the new followers of Jesus what this means in life. Mark gives
us the sheer scale and unworldliness of the resurrection, and calls us to
train church planters out on the road, applying and constantly relearning
in new contexts. Luke shows us a charismatic community, a church where

people learn together and from one another, that is constantly looking for the Holy Spirit to take the Bible story and make it new and alive in missionary contexts. And John sends the disciples into incarnational mission, identifying with those we serve, feeling their pain, but bringing resurrection hope and transformation, empowered by the presence of Jesus. There is more than one way to plant churches. Lucien Legrand writes:

> We must read all the pages of the gospels if we hope to discover the various faces of mission. These faces are as diverse as the diverse ways in which Jesus shared the hope and anguish of his fellow human beings and identified with the salvific will of God, as varied as such total freedom and such constantly astonishing creativity could inspire.[153]

I love that – church planters have freedom and creativity, rooted in the diversity of the communities that they serve and in the life and Spirit of Jesus out of which they plant their churches. This is the opposite of any 'cookie cutter' approach to planting churches.

This lesson of difference in our church plants is deeply significant. There can be a sense in which we all know what a church plant looks like: it is quite a large group, well resourced and financed by a sending church or network, dependent on young and charismatic and usually male leadership, with a worship and spirituality style built on contemporary band-led worship. Or maybe it is a smaller group, listening to the locality, building gentle links through kindness, hospitality, good works, and children's and youth work. There are, though, as many church-plant styles as there are church plants and church planters and church-plant teams. It is liberating to think that we can be different from one another, and find our own identity in planting our churches.

It is not as if we should check off each of the four Great Commissions, and make sure that we have discipleship-making, missionary training, charismatic community and incarnational mission represented. It is precisely not a formula. That said, it is hard to think of a church plant having long-term viability and sustainability if it does not include these

---

153 Ibid. 87.

elements. The different approaches and emphases of the four Gospels, however, alert us to a freedom and individuality that each church plant can and should step into.

Conclusion: the Gospels and church planting

The Gospels have given us an enormously rich insight into church planting. We have noted that we must beware of too much of a straight-line kind of thinking from Jesus to the church, or a tracing back of later historical manifestations of the church into the Gospels. Nonetheless, we have found much to encourage us in a robust theology of church planting, which can give us direction and confidence for the task.

We noted that Jesus only spoke of the church twice, both times in Matthew's Gospel (16:18 and 18:17). These passages showed us Jesus declaring that he would be the one to build his church strong enough to resist and overcome all kinds of evil. We saw how the church in these verses is built on the revelation of who Jesus is. Particularly striking, from the church-planting point of view, is the rich inner life envisaged by Jesus for the church.

We then looked at the practice of Jesus with his disciples from the perspective of what we might learn of mission and community. We saw how Jesus reoriented the story of Israel around his person and mission. We examined Jesus' teaching and practice of the kingdom of God through the lens of his social practices, the central place of discipleship, the qualification of faith rather than ethnicity, the prevalence of healings and exorcisms, his teaching in the parables, and how the kingdom of God might relate to the cross of Christ (in particular through Jesus' challenge to the temple as the central religious and nationalistic focus for Israel, and his institution of the Lord's Supper as the place of the new exodus and the coming of God's kingdom).

We concluded with the Great Commissions at the end of each of the four Gospels, noting how mission sprang from the power of the resurrection of Jesus, how each envisaged a community life in the perspective of mission, and how these missionary communities each showed an individuality and creativity.

Below are three ramifications from our examination of the Gospels and material springing from them.

1 Church plants and the kingdom of God

Scholars and commentators often remark on the prevalence of 'kingdom' language in the Gospels, and its comparative scarcity in the rest of the New Testament. Sometimes the church is compared to the kingdom, and not to its advantage. The kingdom is portrayed as dynamic, meeting human need, alive with the miraculous presence of Jesus, engaged with issues of poverty and social justice, whereas the church is portrayed as dull, institutional, and more concerned with questions of power and hierarchy than with life and growth.

Our exploration of Jesus' teaching and praxis when it came to Israel and the kingdom of God showed the extent to which these two twin concerns shaped so much of his understanding of what he was aiming to do. We unpacked how Jesus saw himself in direct continuity with the story of Israel, and how his life and ministry can be seen as an attempt to call Israel back to its true calling as the people of God. Continuity sits alongside discontinuity, for Jesus challenged conceptions of Israel as much as he fulfilled them.

Although we are right to be wary of reading 'church' back into the Gospels, we can clearly see the contours of the kind of kingdom life which Jesus was demonstrating to his followers, and these can validly be translated across into the life of church plants today. Here we can see a community of the followers of Jesus, living into the fullness of God's future as a people freed from the exile of sin, empowered to fight evil and injustice, and building a common life based on the practices they had seen modelled by Jesus. Perhaps most radical of all would be a community whose access to God was predicated not on the temple or the sacrificial system or a priestly hierarchy, but on a meeting together made possible through the life and, in particular, the death of Jesus on the cross. The central gathering of this community would be a shared meal, a remembrance of the deliverance that this death had brought them from sin, and its invitation to the life of God's kingdom, just as the Passover called the people of Israel to the remembrance of the exodus.

For church plants, this opens up a calling to build a common life deliberately patterned on that of Jesus as he expressed the kingdom of God for his disciples in the Gospels. The dynamism of life on the road with Jesus, encountering human need, battling evil and sickness, is a noble and proper aspiration. The emphasis on discipleship has its appropriate frame in the contours of the kingdom of God. The rich inner life of the community of Jesus is indeed the aim of church plants.

More specifically, the shape of the Gospels, tracing as they do Jesus' journey to Jerusalem to offer his life for the fulfilment of the kingdom of God, is a model for church plants both in terms of mission and church life. The kingdom does not stand over against church life, as if the latter is a sad declension from the former. Rather, the kingdom of God is to be seen as the pattern and the actualizing principle of the church. Church plants, with their particular self-perception as communities on mission, are exactly positioned to live into this dynamic with energy and conviction.

This means that church plants should not be embarrassed to appropriate features of the life of the kingdom of God which are sometimes lacking in church life. A radical hospitality was foundational to the practice of Jesus in the Gospels. Ministries of healing and deliverance from evil powers were central to how Jesus expressed the kingdom of God. Innovative practices of teaching, challenges to controlling religion, and resistance to codes of purity which were little more than systems of exclusion and power games – all these featured prominently in Jesus' life and ministry. Clearly, care and imagination are necessary in the work of translating these practices for today's world and particular cultures, but the principles of each of these are appropriate and even mandatory for church plants.

To sharpen the point still further, the prophetic posture of Jesus and his expression of the kingdom of God is something that church plants can adopt. Jesus challenged systems of religion and political power from the standpoint of a vision of an inclusive kingdom, where God and his healing, liberating power were the ultimate ends and values. Jesus brought the challenge of the kingdom, namely that there was only one king, and he was neither Caesar nor Caiaphas. Church plants will need exceptional humility and discernment to do this well, but they stand in the inheritance of Jesus and his interpretation of the kingdom of God. Theologically, there needs to be something disruptive in church planting if it is to express the kingdom of God as Jesus lived and taught it.

This is not a licence for bad behaviour! Sometimes church planters do have something of a reputation for being difficult and unhelpful, and sometimes, regrettably, that is justified. It is possible, though, to bring humility and grace to the table alongside the provocative questions and practices that church planting can bring. The primary challenge of the kingdom of God, as Jesus embodied and shaped it, was around those who were not yet part of it, not least when they felt excluded by the guardians and gatekeepers of Israel. If church planters can find a way of gently but insistently putting that particular question, then they will be doing well.

2 Church plants and Jesus

It has been particularly striking in our study of the Gospels how Jesus refocused and redefined and reshaped everything around himself. He is the new Moses, the new temple, the new exodus. He brings the new creation, resurrects the people of God, appoints twelve new patriarchs. He rewrites the rules of table fellowship, who may and who may not be admitted. He declares when exile is ended, and where the kingdom is to be experienced. He gives the new law and new commandments. He gives the Spirit. He takes upon himself the role of the people of Israel as the Servant prophesied in Isaiah. He is the Son of Man of Ezekiel and Daniel. He is the new David. And on we could go.

This will need further development when we look at church planting in the systematic section of this book, but here is an important and radical principle – that Christology trumps both ecclesiology and missiology. In other words, the answer to how we are to think of church and how we are to think of mission is Jesus. And how we are to define church planting theologically is likewise by reference to Jesus.

We have noted several times that the life and the mission of the Christian community are not to be fully understood without reference to each other. We cannot grasp what mission is unless we factor in the life of the church. And equally, we cannot adequately say what church is without making sure that mission is also centrally featured. This is why church planting makes so much theological sense – it combines both church and mission at the very centre of what it is. Sadly, though, it is not uncommon for there to be a theological stand-off between the proponents of church and the champions of mission, as if it were a kind of zero-sum game. Clearly that cannot be the case, because the Bible, theology and church history all alike testify to the fact that the most fruitful church and the most fruitful mission happen when the two are united. So, what can be done to help us through this seeming impasse? How can we get to that theological and practical sweet spot of ecclesiology and missiology working gladly and easily together? The answer is to transcend both, to appeal to a higher authority, and look to Christology. Just as Jesus so often in his earthly life redefined things by reference to himself and thus changed the terms of debate, so we can look to him to do the same again.

This may lead to robust debate, to disagreement and to discomfort, now as then. There will be challenges to entrenched and long-held positions, to vested interests and to cultural and community customs. The more, though, we have the theological courage to read our contemporary understandings of church and mission through the pages of the Gospels, the more we will find the freedom and creativity of Jesus to be at play. May we have the humility, faith and courage to follow him wherever he leads, not least for the sake of those outside the church who, at some level, long for the surprise and hope of the kingdom of God.

So, this is a challenge for the theologians and church leaders of our time, for thought leaders and cultural architects. Please help us all with your thinking and insights. May we all find a way through into the next phase of God's kingdom in our contexts. If we follow the example of Jesus, we may need to reinterpret the story we thought we knew so well. We may need to be open to surprising voices. We may have to move outside the places of privilege and power, and listen to the poor, the marginalized, those who have been praying and waiting all their lives for the kingdom of God. If we dare to trust Jesus, though, we will find that, through repentance and faith and the grace of the Holy Spirit, we will see the kingdom of God in a fullness we have yet to experience.

3 Community and church plants

The practice of Jesus was to gather all the wrong sorts of people together in unlikely and potentially explosive combinations. He was notorious for welcoming sinners and eating with them (Luke 15:2). The Twelve were a surprising collection, not least because of their conflicting backgrounds. Jesus taught about God's kingdom being open to those who had faith, those who asked, those who were invited or even compelled to come in. He pronounced blessings over the poor, the grieving, the hungry. He drove people away when they did not like what he had to say. He broke the taboos of purity, ethnicity, respectability, family, custom and religion. All in all, Jesus exhibited a remarkable freedom regarding those who were around him.

This, of course, is one reason why it is legitimate to take Jesus' practices in the Gospels and apply them to our church plants today. Communities of difference, based around Jesus, appear to be the essence of what it is to be church. Hence, patterns of relating, mutual grace, forgiveness, humility are directly transferable from the Gospels to today's church plants. Principles that open doors, not close them, are what the revelation of Jesus makes possible.

What is particularly challenging, though, is the commitment from Jesus to radical difference within his community. Zealots and nationalists stood alongside those who collaborated with the Romans. 'Sinful women' crashed smart dinner parties with religious high-ups. Desperate people crying out for healing, and noisy children singing his praises, all annoyed the respectable among those around Jesus. The good, the bad and the ugly all crowded round him.

Church is so much easier in homogeneous groups. Mission is so much easier in homogeneous groups. Like attracts like, and difference brings out fear and prejudice. It is, frankly, easier to build church plants with like-minded middle-class people than it is with people from different backgrounds. What do you do when young and old disagree about music style? How do 'bring and share' potluck suppers work when you have people with wildly differing levels of wealth coming to the same table? How does community work when different ethnicities and cultures assume that their way is the only way? How do you handle power, or sexuality, or spirituality, with vulnerable people, with those who have only ever known violence or prejudice or poverty?

Church planters may well start out with a very particular calling to a distinct age group or profile of those they want to reach. I do not think there is anything wrong with this. Indeed, every church in the world has a dominant culture, maybe by the sole virtue of having more people of that background or personality type than any other. And they will invite their friends, and this cultural norm is reinforced. The challenge comes when we see what a Jesus community looks like in the pages of the Gospels. It is mobile, diverse, intractable, made up of spectators, detractors, enemies, traitors, the curious, the desperate, and with so many mutual contradictions within it that it seems impossible for any kind of coherence to emerge. Church plants, to be faithful to Jesus, at some stage need to reckon with this challenge. If everyone looks and sounds and actually is alike, then there is a long way to go. The acid test is if someone new comes along and asks, 'What in the world brings these people together? They have nothing in common.' They do, of course, but only Jesus.

This argues for a different concept of community than normal. Perhaps the regular definition is around getting along or having a shared interest. In the Jesus way, though, community is about spiritual connection at a level that is deeper than family, race, politics, ethnicity, age, gender, sexual orientation, health or personal history.

This may well be the number-one challenge for church plants as they try to build community from scratch. It will have an impact on social activities, worship culture, leadership selection, evangelistic strategies, language, clothing, music, weekends away and events, pastoral support – everything. It is very difficult to get right, and will likely involve pain, anger, mistakes, much repentance, mutual tears and forgiveness. It is also massively important from the point of view of what a missionary church is all about, and of incalculable power when it comes to addressing a world that is fragmented at every level and that knows all about prejudice, racism, division, violence and atomization, but longs to be together, united and drawing the benefits of difference into a shared life. There can be few more prophetic challenges to the current practice of church planting than this. For the sake of our increasingly diverse societies, we need to respond to it.

3

Church and mission in the Acts of the Apostles

Many think of the Acts of the Apostles as a kind of manual for church planting. It is here that we read of the story of the early church and, over a thirty-year period, see churches established in Palestine, Asia Minor, Greece and other European centres, heading for Rome. As Craig Ott and Gene Wilson write: 'Everywhere in the book of Acts, where evangelism occurs, churches are created.'[1] There is much to learn and be excited about in Acts for the church planter.

Stuart Murray adds a cautionary note in observing that 'there is a New Testament basis for church planting, but it is more modest than is sometimes assumed'.[2] Murray helps us understand that while we are right to see close connections between mission and church, there are other corollaries to evangelism than church planting, and, equally, a vision for the place of the church in the plan of God does not, of necessity, mean exclusively a commitment to planting churches. He helpfully distinguishes between looking to the New Testament, and Acts in particular, for a *rationale* for church planting on the one hand, and for *guidelines* for church planting on the other.[3] He argues that the rationale for church planting is actually less explicit than is sometimes maintained, whereas there is actually far more material about the practice of church planting than is sometimes adduced. He counsels against overstating a biblical case for the rationale for church planting, not least because it opens up church-planting enthusiasts to charges of being naive in how they handle the Bible and drawing unjustifiable conclusions. Acts is one such example. Murray

---

[1] Ott and Wilson 2011: 23.
[2] Murray 1998: 71.
[3] Ibid. 63.

argues that it is not actually *about* church planting: it has wider themes and theological concerns. This is not to say that Acts is not full of church planting, but Murray is encouraging us to make sure that we do not end up distorting the biblical text by reading Acts as if church planting is its sole focus. To treat the book of Acts simply as a church-planting manual fails to recognize the author's purposes, does not do justice to the breadth of its interests and may lead to illegitimate conclusions being drawn. The result of such treatment might be that church planters, and the churches they plant, do not engage in the theological, missiological and ecclesiological reflection which Luke appears to invite, and for which the book of Acts provides resources.[4]

That said, Murray turns our attention to the plethora of New Testament material on the practice of church planting (while taking care to counsel us not to view these practices as blueprints to be slavishly imitated): 'Church planting may be peripheral theologically by comparison with a theme like the kingdom of God, but it is the primary context within which the New Testament was written, and by reference to which it should be understood.'[5] He judiciously concludes that 'many treatments of the New Testament and church planting claim both too little and too much'.[6]

Acts remains a key document for church planters, with much to inspire and instruct. Keeping Murray's warnings in mind, this chapter is in two halves, looking first at mission in Acts, and then at church.

Mission and church planting in Acts

Mission lies at the heart of the theology of Acts.

The church's universal mission is central to [Luke's] concern.[7]

For Luke, what makes the church is mission, and the reality at the heart of the church is the impulse of the Spirit for the increase of the Word.[8]

---

[4] Ibid. 74.
[5] Ibid. 79.
[6] Ibid.
[7] Senior and Stuhlmueller 1983: 276.
[8] Legrand 1990: 92.

[Acts] is governed by one dominant, overriding and all-consuming motif. This motif is the expansion of the faith through missionary witness in the power of the Spirit . . . Restlessly the Spirit drives the church to witness, and continually churches rise out of witness. The church is a missionary church.[9]

The book is itself structured around the missionary itinerary of the gospel. The headline verse contains the words of Jesus prophesying about the impact of the Holy Spirit on his followers: 'But you will receive power when the Holy Spirit has come upon you; and you will be my witnesses in Jerusalem, in all Judea and Samaria, and to the ends of the earth' (1:8). Chapters 1–7 are indeed set in Jerusalem; chapter 8 describes how persecution 'scattered [all the believers, except the apostles] throughout the countryside of Judea and Samaria' (8:1); and the rest of the book sees an acceleration of the gospel throughout Asia Minor, Greece and Europe, heading towards the centre of the Western world in Rome. More subtly, the book is divided into 'panels',[10] each of which celebrates the growth of the church and the word.[11] The first divisions pick up on the structure set out in the programme announced by Jesus in 1:8:

- 'The word of God continued to spread; the number of disciples increased greatly in Jerusalem' (6:7);
- 'Meanwhile the church throughout Judea, Galilee, and Samaria had peace and was built up' (9:31).

Later summary verses highlight the ministry of Paul and Barnabas (12:24), Paul and Timothy in Asia Minor (16:5) and Paul in Asia Minor (19:20). The last verse of the book leaves us with the sight of Paul, under house arrest in Rome, continuing to proclaim 'the kingdom of God and teaching about the Lord Jesus Christ with all boldness and without hindrance' (28:31). The narrative of the whole of Acts is the missionary advance of the word under the power of the Spirit, establishing churches across Palestine and Europe, moving from Jerusalem (the centre of Jewish

---

9 Boer 1961: 161–162, quoted in Stott 1990: 86.
10 Fee and Stuart 2002: 296.
11 See Witherington 1998: 74. The verses in question come at 6:7; 9:31; 12:24; 16:5; 19:20.

religious power) to Rome (the centre of Western political and military power). This whole book is about mission.

What might church planters learn from mission in Acts?

Mission (and church planting) is God's mission

Divine action and initiative is central. It is hard to over-emphasize the place of the Holy Spirit in Acts.

- There is the explosion that is Pentecost which kick-starts the entire book, and which serves to set the terms of reference for everything that happens thereafter.
- There is the role of the Spirit in filling the apostles (e.g. Peter in 4:11; the seven deacons in 6:3, 5; Stephen at 7:55).
- Although this is described in slightly different ways, there is the key role of the Holy Spirit in how people become Christians (such as in Samaria in 8:15, 17; with Saul in 9:17; and with the Ephesians in 19:6).
- There is the guidance of the Spirit in leading and directing the mission of the church (e.g. in leading Philip to the Ethiopian eunuch in 8:29; in leading Peter to Cornelius in 10:19–20; in setting aside Paul and Barnabas for mission from the Antioch church in 13:2; in the strange prohibitions of 16:6–7 and the vision of the man from Macedonia in 16:9; and in binding Paul to his sacrificial journey to Jerusalem in 20:22), not least in the huge moment of seeing the gospel open up for the Gentiles (e.g. 15:8, 28).

All in all, there are fifty-seven references to the Spirit in Acts. The book is frequently referred to as 'the Acts of the Holy Spirit' rather than the 'Acts of the Apostles'.[12] Thus, we begin with Pentecost.

Luke reports the events of that Pentecost in surprisingly sparing terms. All is described in four verses, and the vocabulary is circumspect and non-definite: the noise in the house is 'like the . . . wind' and the tongues are 'as of fire'. Nonetheless, the description is powerful and awe-inspiring:

---

[12] It should be noted, however, that there are long portions of Acts (e.g. chs. 21–28) which barely refer to the Spirit. To be more comprehensive of Acts as a whole, it may be better to speak of the Acts of *God* rather than the Spirit. Many thanks to Professor Steve Walton for this observation (in private correspondence).

> When the day of Pentecost had come, they were all together in one
> place. And suddenly from heaven there came a sound like the rush of
> a violent wind, and it filled the entire house where they were sitting.
> Divided tongues, as of fire, appeared among them, and a tongue
> rested on each of them. All of them were filled with the Holy Spirit
> and began to speak in other languages, as the Spirit gave them ability.
> (Acts 2:1–4)

The first thing to notice is Luke's emphasis on *unity*: 'they were all together
in one place' (2:1). In some ways, it is redundant to say that they were
together and in one place, because how could it have been otherwise?
Likewise, there is no strict need to say that they were 'all' together, because
that is what it means. Luke, however, is making a point. We do not know
where exactly they were, but the emphasis is not on location but on unity,
not where they were but who they were with.

Spiritual experiences can and do happen to individuals, but Luke is
keen to emphasize that what happened at Pentecost was the gift and
promise of the Father to the church. This is an endowment of power to
the church as a whole, not to gifted individuals within it. Where the
church is, there is the Spirit. Acts will have lots more to say about gifts of
the Spirit and experiences of the Spirit for individuals, but the foundational emphasis is on the gift of the Spirit to the church.

This has profound implications for church planters. The power lies in
the Spirit, and the Spirit lies in the church. Effective church planting is
not, theologically speaking, down to anointed individuals, leaders, gifted
speakers or flaming personalities. The most significant factor in the
planting of churches is the planting of *churches*, the gathering of a people
who see their being *together* as the most significant thing about them.
This, of course, is why the impact for those outside the kingdom of God
is most deeply felt when they encounter the church as a whole, where they
see random, very different people who have a togetherness through the
action of the Spirit among them. If we may so express it, it is what happens
between people that speaks most eloquently about the reality of God in
their midst.

Church plants will doubtless have gifted individuals, but they should
never forget that it is their common life in which the power of God is

deeply hidden. This is, of course, yet another argument for the primacy of the church as God's agent for mission. If we want mission (and we do), then it is the church which is God's chosen way of best accomplishing this. Theologically, this is because the Spirit has been poured out on the church.

There is arguably further significance in the outpouring of the Spirit happening on the day of Pentecost. This was one of the three main Jewish festivals of the year, a kind of harvest festival. There is also a suggestion that Pentecost was the time, in Jewish imagination, when God gave the law to Moses. This last is unclear, as the evidence of this practice dates to much later than Acts 2, but commentators argue persuasively that Luke had such an association in mind.[13] Neither the thought of harvest nor that of lawgiving should be pushed too far, but it is worth reflecting on how the gift of the Spirit is the supernatural equivalent of the ripening of crops (or the harvest of souls that followed), and the coming of the Spirit was a parallel (or maybe successor) to the giving of the law at Sinai.[14] With the coming of the Spirit, God is constituting an eschatological people, fulfilling all his purposes in history, gathered around Jesus, with a vision for universal mission.

The main features of Luke's account of Pentecost, though, are the phenomena of fire and wind coming upon the disciples; the fact that 'each of them' was filled with the Holy Spirit; and that they spoke in other languages. Let's consider each of these in turn, and reflect on church planting in the light of them.

The wind and fire point to the presence of God. This coming of the Spirit is nothing less than the personal presence of God with his people, echoing a biblical theme:

- When the LORD appears to Moses in the wilderness, it is in 'the bush [that] was blazing, yet . . . was not consumed' (Exod. 3:2).
- When the LORD guides the people of Israel through the wilderness, it is by means of 'a pillar of cloud by day' and 'a pillar of fire by night' (Exod. 13:21).

---

[13] See esp. Johnson 1992: 46.
[14] See a balanced and judicious discussion in Stott 1990: 62.

- At the giving of the law on Mount Sinai, the mountain 'was wrapped in smoke, because the Lord had descended upon it in fire' (Exod. 19:18).
- The Lord's appearance to Elijah is in contrast to both wind and fire: 'Now there was a great wind, so strong that it was splitting mountains and breaking rocks in pieces before the Lord, but the Lord was not in the wind . . . and after the earthquake a fire, but the Lord was not in the fire' (1 Kgs 19:11–12). And Elijah's ascent to heaven is by means of 'a chariot of fire and horses of fire', and he is taken up 'in a whirlwind' (2 Kgs 2:11).
- Isaiah portrays the judgment of God in terms of wind and fire:

> For the Lord will come in fire,
>   and his chariots like the whirlwind,
> to pay back his anger in fury
> (Isa. 66:15)

- John the Baptist prophesied that, whereas he baptized in water, Jesus would baptize powerfully 'with the Holy Spirit and fire' (Luke 3:16).

John Stott observes that each of these three elements of the Pentecostal experience was 'natural' – fire, wind and speech; but each of them was also supernatural – the fire separates and rests on each person, the sound of the wind fills the whole house, the speech is in languages not known by the speakers.[15] Luke Timothy Johnson notes that the presence of God is not to be identified with wind and flame, since in each case what happens is *compared* to wind and fire.[16] Luke is painting us a startlingly dramatic picture from the natural world, but then saying that the significance of what is happening at Pentecost goes far beyond these phenomena. As with the appearance of the Lord to Elijah, he is not in the wind and fire, although his presence is not unconnected with these stunning effects; they point beyond themselves, even by virtue of the limitations of what they can evoke – to encounter God is way beyond experiencing wind and flame. We struggle to find language and concepts to describe just what it

---

15 Ibid. 62.
16 Johnson 1992: 42.

is like to meet the living God. It is noteworthy that the imagery of fire and wind does not recur in Acts after chapter 2.

What Luke wants us to see is that mission (and so church planting) is actually the action of God before it is a human activity. Lucien Legrand puts it with his customary pungency:

> The mission of the church is first and foremost the work and *deed of God*. More specifically, in Lucan terms, it is the deed of the Spirit. Before being the Acts of the Apostles, Luke's second book is the record of the Acts of the Spirit. This is no crypto-Pelagianism. The apocalypse of the Spirit on the Day of Pentecost . . . is to demonstrate the divine origin of the deed about to be narrated. The church *en mission* will find cohesion and identity in this divine strength, which dwells within it and thrusts it forward.[17]

This has been a recurring theme of a biblical theology of mission and church planting. It is to be seen as a divine activity. And more than something that God *does*, he activates mission by virtue of his *presence*. He comes and situates himself in places and contexts and among people with the view to catalysing mission and church planting. This is both the *reason* for his presence (why he comes) and the *result* of his presence (what happens when he does). The case for the close connection between mission and church planting in Acts is yet to be seen, but what we can already say is that the personal presence of God is foundational for both the existence of the church and the existence of mission. When we speak about God, we must find ourselves inescapably talking about both church and mission. Acts will show us that the two frequently go together. To deny a proper and central place to either is the absurdity of trying to split up the presence of God into separate categories to be deployed only in particular circumstances. Church and mission are not options God can pull out of the bag when needed; both are present when he is present, because both arise from the very fact of his presence. Just as we cannot even contemplate dividing God into compartments, neither can we choose one or other of mission or church, and neither, theologically speaking, can we separate

---

[17] Legrand 1990: 105; emphasis original.

them from each other since both find their origin in the presence and being of God.

We can further observe the Spirit as God's personal presence in parallels between the beginning of Luke's Gospel and that of Acts as his second volume. Beverly Roberts Gaventa helpfully draws out how Pentecost in Acts 2 has the same role as the activity of the Spirit in Luke's Gospel as it describes the conception of Jesus. In both, the Spirit overshadows and overwhelms the key individuals, leading and guiding, and calling forth inspired speech.[18] Luke is positioning his narratives to represent the work of Jesus, called into being by the Spirit, leading to the ministry of Jesus in his first volume and the gospel and church of Jesus in his second. We should not miss the implications of the first verse of Acts, when Luke describes his 'first book' as an account of 'all that Jesus began to do and teach' (1:1 ESV), implying that Acts describes the continuance of Jesus' speech and activity through the infant church. If we compare it with Luke's account of Jesus' baptism by the Holy Spirit, we will note that it is followed immediately by the ancestry of Jesus, going all the way back to Abraham and Adam (Luke 3:21–38). In Acts, the coming of the Spirit at Pentecost is immediately followed by the list of 'every nation under heaven living in Jerusalem' (Acts 2:5).[19] Luke is pointing out to us that it is by the Spirit that Jesus' ministry continues to the end of the earth both in the incarnation of Jesus (in Luke's Gospel) and post the resurrection (in the Acts of the Apostles). So, the presence of God in the Spirit, which we see in Acts 2, is in some sense the presence and continued activity of Jesus in and through the church. This is the fulfilment of John the Baptist's prophecy: '[Jesus] will baptize you with the Holy Spirit and fire' (Luke 3:16).

What of that fire, and the 'divided tongues' (Acts 2:3)? Johnson helpfully explains: 'the tongues are separated from each other rather than divided within.'[20] The separation of the tongues of fire is a means of showing that there were *individual* tongues, one for each person present. So, what we have, to go alongside the sense of *unity* – the Spirit is given to the *whole* church – is something that establishes *individuality*. The church is both

---

[18] Gaventa 2003: 36.
[19] See Johnson 1992: 47.
[20] Ibid. 42.

one and made up of individuals, each and every one of whom has Pentecostal significance.

The dominant manifestation of the Holy Spirit was in the tongues of fire. The tongue is for speech. The Spirit was given at Pentecost to help the church communicate. The disciples *spoke* 'about God's deeds of power' (2:11), something Peter will make clearer in his sermon (2:14–36). Luke's initial point, however, is that the Spirit was given so that the church could proclaim the good news of God in Jesus Christ. This is what Jesus had led his followers to expect when he showed them from the Scriptures that 'repentance and forgiveness of sins is to be proclaimed in [the Messiah's] name to all nations' (Luke 24:47), and when he taught them that the power of the Spirit was to be given so that they could witness to him (Acts 1:8). It is also something that will be borne out in the rest of Acts; a large proportion of the book is given over to speeches. John Stott counts 'no fewer than nineteen significant Christian speeches', and estimates that '20% of Luke's text is devoted to addresses by Peter and Paul; if Stephen's speech is added, the percentage rises to about 25%'.[21] The early church was a witnessing church and a preaching church. If church plants want to tread in the steps of these first Christians, then they too will be preaching and testifying and witnessing.

Of course, there are many ways in which this can be done. It is instructive to look at the differing styles and models of the sermons and speeches in Acts, which we will go on to do. The point for now is that there can and should be flexibility in *how* the good news is communicated. That there should be proclamation and persuasion and discussion and dialogue is not something for debate.

This, too, is proving a recurring theme in the Bible's theology that can be applied to church planting, and other sections of this book have already dealt with some aspects of how it can be lived out. For now, shall we reflect on how this communication (this gift of tongues) might sit within the theological framework we have just been considering, that the Spirit is given both to the whole church and to individuals within it? A Pentecostal church plant will have simultaneously a whole-church-proclamation and an everyone-communication of the gospel.

---

21 Stott 1990: 69.

For the former, I wonder if the Spirit gives to each church its own particular way of communicating about Jesus. There are some wonderful programmes and courses available, such as Alpha and Christianity Explored, and much thought and work has gone into making these as effective as possible. I am not advocating a fiddling with these courses, or a picking and choosing of those aspects which may be the preference of individual churches. Such an approach does not really honour the hard work of those who have developed such programmes, and, paradoxically, usually leads to them being less effective. Nonetheless, when churches are able to inhabit the gospel in ways that express a mixture of the good news about Jesus and their own culture and life together, then this can come across authentically and freshly. This is an expression, in the realm of preaching, of the wider principle that is proving foundational to this book, that the more we can combine church and mission (especially in church planting), the more we will fulfil the New Testament vision of the kingdom of God.

This can be shown in how services are led, how testimonies are given, how songs and worship are positioned, in who speaks and when and for how long. It can spring to life in the approach taken in sermons and talks – whether it is experiential, rational, theological, inspirational. It will show up in the amount of technology that is used, in leaders' age, gender, length of time as a Christian, the amount of time allotted to the sermon, how long the Bible passage is and how it is related to the news and contemporary culture. It can be expressed in how the sermon is delivered – on Sundays or weekdays, live or online, from the front, discussed around tables, the extent of volume, conviction and passion demonstrated by the speaker, how many speakers there are. It will be revealed in the extent to which objections to Christianity are respectfully and coherently addressed, and how local, Western or global the vocabulary and concepts in the talk are. The ramifications are legion. These are the kinds of things that the Spirit might give to each church to help it step into its own particular gift and culture when communicating the good news about Jesus.

And, alongside that, what might the individual tongues look like? Here is a call for the encouragement of every person to take on, for himself or herself, the task and privilege of communicating the gospel.

155

Michael Green was one of the foremost evangelists of his time and a prolific scholar and author. He wrote, in his classic book *Evangelism through the Local Church*, about the impact of the Holy Spirit on individual witness:

> It is the work of the Spirit to glorify Jesus, and he builds that longing into our very being. Actually, this is a solemn barometer of our openness to the Holy Spirit. If we are full of the Spirit we will be full of the desire to share Jesus with other people. If we have no desire to share Christ with those who do not know him, there is every reason to doubt whether the Spirit is present in our lives at all, let alone filling us. For the whole purpose of the gift of the Spirit is to make us like Christ, and witness to Christ. He is given for mission. Without him the disciples would not have dared to venture out into evangelism. With him they could not hold back.[22]

Challenging words. We may wish to qualify them a bit by virtue of some being specifically gifted as evangelists by the Spirit, but we should not evade the force of Green's logic. He goes on to apply it by considering just how effective it is when everyone in a church has this understanding and vision. Reflecting on how the church in Antioch took this approach, he comments:

> This personal chatting about the subject of their greatest joy, Jesus, led many to believe in him. It still does. It is the best way of evangelism, when one person is talking about Jesus to one person who is interested in listening . . . If a church seriously wants to evangelize, my advice would not be to hire a famous preacher or invite the Archbishop; it would be to open the mouths of the people in the pews. Everyone has a story to tell, the story of God's dealings with their own soul. Everyone can invite a friend to a meeting. Everyone can say what a difference this Jesus has made to them. It is not difficult. It springs naturally to many who have recently discovered the beauty of Jesus for themselves.[23]

---

[22] Green 1993: 18.
[23] Ibid. 88–89.

This is the significance of each 'individual tongue of fire' at Pentecost: every believer has the power and potential to share God's deeds of power in Jesus with friend, neighbour, family and colleague.

The task remains challenging, not least in Western environments where faith is misunderstood or rejected as irrelevant or even malignant. Church plants will want to give confidence in evangelism to their congregations. This is partly a matter of training and partly the fostering of a culture of courage in inviting friends to hear the gospel. Environments where talking about Jesus is celebrated, where inviting others to hear about him is championed (whether or not people respond favourably), where stories of conversion are repeatedly and freshly told, tend to be places where evangelism happens fruitfully. It is the particular genius of Alpha to be a means for people who may not feel confident in explaining their faith themselves to bring people along to something attractive, sociable and effective. Many church plants will make Alpha a central feature, not just of their whole-church evangelistic strategy, but also as a means of training and energizing the witness of each and every person in the church plant.

The final main feature of Luke's description of Pentecost is not just that everyone spoke, but that everyone spoke in another tongue or language, 'as the Spirit gave them ability' (2:4).[24] He paints us a picture of the reception of this phenomenon:

Now there were devout Jews from every nation under heaven living in Jerusalem. And at this sound the crowd gathered and was bewildered, because each one heard them speaking in the native language of each. Amazed and astonished, they asked, 'Are not all these who are speaking Galileans? And how is it that we hear, each of us, in our own native language? Parthians, Medes, Elamites, and residents of Mesopotamia, Judea and Cappadocia, Pontus and Asia, Phrygia and Pamphylia, Egypt and the parts of Libya belonging to Cyrene, and visitors from Rome, both Jews and proselytes, Cretans and Arabs – in our own languages we hear them speaking about God's deeds of power.' All were amazed and perplexed, saying to

---

[24] There is debate about how the 'languages' of Acts 2 relate to the 'tongues' of Acts 10 and 1 Cor. 12 – 14. See, in particular, the relevant discussion in Fee 1987 and Thiselton 2000.

one another, 'What does this mean?' But others sneered and said,
'They are filled with new wine.'
(Acts 2:5–13)

Luke highlights the range of languages and cultures in the long list of
nations and people groups. Scholars explain this list in various ways.[25]
Common to all is the thought that Luke has in mind the table of nations in
Genesis 10 and (probably) the incident of the Tower of Babel in Genesis 11,
where the languages of the world were introduced by God to confuse the
human race and prevent a united rebellion against his rule. We note that
the crowd in Acts 2 were 'bewildered' (2:6) in hearing the languages
spoken, which may well be an echo from Babel. Now, however, they all
hear 'in [their] own languages' (repeated with minor variations at 2:6,
8, 11) about what God has done: the gift of the Spirit has made the gospel
a universal language, which is heard intelligibly within every culture,
language and people group of the world. Babel is reversed and the world
map is redrawn. It is a huge moment.

The magnitude of this shift in how global cultures relate to the gospel
needs to be reflected in the approach our church plants take to communicating the gospel. We should note that Pentecost is not astonishing by
virtue of the communication of the gospel solely, but rather because of the
intelligible communication of the gospel. The Spirit provided a means for
the disciples to declare the mighty works of God in such a way that they
could be *heard* by those who listened. They were not yet understood – the
first hearers found the announcement bewildering, astonishing, amazing
and perplexing (2:6, 7, 12), and were left wondering, 'What does this
mean?', with some mocking and sneering (2:12, 13). What they made of
it is still an open question, but that they had something solid on which to
raise that question is the miracle of Pentecost.

We will need to return to this later in our reflections on Acts and in our
theological reflections on church planting. Suffice it for now to lay down
the marker that intelligible communication and cultural awareness are
fundamental to all questions of evangelism and thus to thinking about

---

[25] E.g. Stott 1990: 63–64, 68; Johnson 1992: 43–44; Witherington 1998: 135–137; Gaventa
2003: 75.

church planting. We are not dealing with an unchanging, monolithic message which descends like Monty Python's boot from on high, squashing everything beneath it, but with something much more dynamic, communicable and even interactive. Here are huge questions, but ones which the world-changing event of the gift of the Spirit as the one who launches the church into world mission compel us to make of the first order in our theology of church planting.

The story of the people of God

One of the most striking things about Pentecost is how Peter's sermon locates it within the story of the people of God. On the one hand, he looks back, drawing out the significance of Joel's prophecy of the coming of the Spirit (2:17–21) and seeing Jesus as fulfilling the story of David (2:25–31). On the other hand, he views the events of Jesus' resurrection and the outpouring of the Spirit as the future, the start of the very last chapter of the story. Pentecost is clearly and firmly positioned within an existing plotline; in this sense, it is not a surprise, but rather something long promised and long wished for. And, at the same time, it is seen as something profoundly new, deeply disruptive, which takes the whole world into an entirely new phase of its life with God. Both these perspectives find their connection, not primarily in the Spirit, but in Jesus, as he is once and for all demonstrated to be the exalted Messiah. Beverly Roberts Gaventa comments:

> Peter's speech (2:14–40) occupies a pivotal place in Luke–Acts, because it interprets what has already happened in the death and resurrection of Jesus and because it offers essential clues for understanding what is about to unfold in Jerusalem and beyond.[26]

This can be seen within the very structure of Peter's speech.

- He starts with an explanation of what is happening as the Holy Spirit is poured out with reference to Joel's prophecy (2:14–21). He picks up on the inspired speech (2:4, 8), explaining it in terms

---

[26] Gaventa 2003: 73.

of Joel's prophecy. But then he continues with Joel, with the emphasis on bizarre and frightening 'portents in the heaven above and signs on the earth below' (2:19). The coming of the Spirit is all part and parcel of what will happen at the end of the world. This is the beginning of 'the coming of the Lord's great and glorious day' (2:20), and so the world has entered 'the last days' (2:17). That phrase is not actually part of Joel's original prophecy (which has 'Then afterward').[27] Luke is making an emphatic point: Peter is positioning the present moment of Pentecost firmly on the ancient timeline of God with the world, but locating it right near the very end.

- He then moves straight away into an account of the life, crucifixion and resurrection of Jesus (2:22–24). Jesus' life was one of power and signs from God, a witness to his significance. So, how could such a life be part of God's plan if it ended in such defeat and calumny? This too was part of what God intended, and he has now vindicated Jesus by raising him from the dead 'because it was impossible for him to be held in its power' (2:24). Peter is telling the story of Jesus from the perspective of the resurrection and the coming of the Spirit. Theologically, Peter is holding the giving of the Spirit and the resurrection of Jesus together; they are intimately connected. How come? Because for the last days to begin means the Spirit has to be poured out; and for the Spirit to be poured out, the Messiah has to come and to be glorified. Jesus has been shown to be that exalted Messiah by his anointed life and by his triumph over the power of death. So, Jesus' resurrection is a demonstration that this Pentecost event is indeed the pouring out of the Spirit predicted by Joel to be the starting gun for the last days; and the coming of the Spirit is, in turn, the sign that Jesus truly is the Messiah, and that he is now exalted by God as the Lord of the world. Jesus, in his person as the resurrected Lord, holds together both Israel's past and the world's future, and he completes the former and inaugurates the latter by pouring out the Holy Spirit.

- Peter then moves straight on to David (2:25–31). He quotes Psalm 16, with its hint of resurrection, and, 'since [David] was a prophet' (2:30),

---

27 Ibid. 76.

Peter argues that David was prophesying about Jesus. This is more than clever proof-texting. Peter is taking the high point of Israel's history with David's kingdom, and saying that it is a pointer to the even greater kingdom of the resurrected Jesus. David was Israel's greatest king. Now, there is here one greater than David.

- Peter finishes with a double declaration of the greatness of Jesus (2:32–36). God has raised him from the dead, a resurrection of which the apostles are witnesses. This means that Jesus is exalted, and it is he who is pouring out the promise of the Father. This is in line with another Davidic prophecy, this time from Psalm 110. The punchline is about Jesus: 'Therefore let the entire house of Israel know with certainty that God has made him both Lord and Messiah, this Jesus whom you crucified' (2:36).

The very structure of the sermon weaves together the events and experience of the coming of the Spirit at Pentecost, Israel's prophetic and kingly history, and the life, death and resurrection of Jesus. And it is the resurrection of Jesus which is the epicentre that holds together the meaning of everything.

May we note the language Peter uses to conclude his sermon: 'Therefore let the entire house of Israel know with certainty that God has made him both Lord and Messiah, this Jesus whom you crucified' (2:36).

- It begins with a 'therefore'. Peter is arguing something, making a case. The logic is a *theologic* – it is something that requires us to think theologically, which only makes sense with reference to God.
- It is a logic which is particularly applied to the 'house of Israel'. The essence of this theologic is the story of Israel.
- It is a logic grounded in the action of God in raising Jesus from the dead. Here we see history and theology inseparably paired. There is an event which actually happened, and this event has a meaning. God has done something and he has said something in raising Jesus from the dead.
- And the heart of that deed and word is Jesus. Peter keeps the name of Jesus to the end of the sentence in a rhetorical flourish. Jesus is the *key word* in understanding Pentecost, and he is the *last word* when it

comes to understanding the history of Israel and the action of God in the world.

From this rich blend of Christology and pneumatology we can offer some application to our focus on church planting.

First, church planters should have a sensitivity to how the activity of the Holy Spirit is inseparably tied to witnessing to Jesus Christ.

It is hugely striking that on Pentecost, Peter's sermon is focused on Jesus. When we consider just how dramatic the coming of the Spirit must have been (with sounds like a tornado inside a house, with the appearance of multiple flames on individuals' heads, with a cacophony of languages sufficiently loud to attract a crowd, the supernatural tenor of things, the volume, the numbers of people involved), it is all the more telling that Peter calmly and carefully makes the main point of his sermon about Jesus. The coming of the Spirit is testimony to the exaltation of Jesus, and a summons to recalibrate our thinking to take cognizance of his greatness and his centrality in the plan of God.

The work of the Spirit is not unique to church plants! These will, though, along with all churches, have a heightened awareness of a need of the Holy Spirit, as their raison d'être is so closely tied to mission, for which the Spirit is especially needful and so generously provided. There may well be exciting and dramatic stories of the Spirit at work, not least along the lines of Joel's prophecy – dreams and visions and prophecies, all kinds of people coming into an experience of God. There may be miracles, healings, lives radically transformed. These are giddy and heady experiences, and ones to be cherished and honoured. We should remember, though, that the Spirit will point to Jesus, that the point (if we may call it that) of so much of the Spirit's activity, not least in mission, is to make people aware that Jesus is alive. Whatever the journey the Spirit takes people (and us!) on, the destination is Jesus.

To turn the point around, if we want to see Jesus glorified in people's lives, then we will need to see this as tied inextricably to the coming of the Spirit. Acts 2 shows us that the exaltation of Jesus and the outpouring of the Spirit are two sides of the same coin. Acts is a marvellously holistic book and, with a splendid naturalness, holds together things that some-times we hold apart. The gospel and the Spirit are inseparable; the exaltation of Jesus and the phenomenon of Pentecost go together. Our theology would be wise to follow suit.

Second, Peter's sermon alerts us to a major concern of Acts as a whole – how does the story of Israel relate to the story of the church? This is a huge subject, and one marked by controversy and pain. This is not the place to enter into this too deeply, save to point out that Acts holds both stories together.

This is reflected in the narrative structure of Acts itself. The dominant human figure of the first half of the book is Peter, and the first section (chs. 1–7) is set in Jerusalem. By contrast, the main role, humanly speaking, for the second half of the book is Paul's, and the focus is the mission to the Gentiles, ending up with Paul's increasing involvement with the Roman world. The central event of the book is the Council of Jerusalem (ch. 15), which brings to a conclusion the debate of the previous chapters about the inclusion (or not) of the Gentiles into the church. Acts as a whole is deeply concerned about the spread of the gospel, and what this means for the Jewish people. We see this in the conclusion to Peter's Pentecost sermon: 'Therefore let the entire *house of Israel* know with certainty that God has made [Jesus] both Lord and Messiah' (2:36, emphasis added).

Troubling to many is the conclusion of the book, where Paul, under house arrest outside Rome, is in debate with 'the local leaders of the Jews' (28:17). The altercation ends with Paul quoting Isaiah 6 to them about the intransigence of their ancestors when it came to the message of God, and then concluding: 'Let it be known to you then that this salvation of God has been sent to the Gentiles; they will listen' (28:28). This can be interpreted as a renunciation of the Jews, as a turning away from God's ancient people in favour of the Gentiles.

In support of this approach is the location of these oracular-sounding words as the all but last words of the whole book, and the fact that Paul has already said something similar in chapter 13: 'It was necessary that the word of God should be spoken first to you [Jews]. Since you reject it and judge yourselves to be unworthy of eternal life, we are now turning to the Gentiles' (13:46).

Against that interpretation is the constant order for evangelization throughout the book. The practice of the Pauline mission was always to go first to the synagogue or equivalent, before engaging with the Gentiles. This methodology continues right to the last chapter, where Paul seeks out the Jewish leaders from Rome. They end up wanting to hear more from him, and we read that 'some were convinced by what he had said' (28:24). More widely, this is, of course, the structure of the whole of Acts, which begins in Jerusalem, before spreading far and wide as the book's story develops (Acts 1:8).

I think this latter interpretation is the more balanced of the two. Luke is looking back to the history of Israel and placing Jesus within that. His Gospel makes a big feature of how Jesus fulfils so many of the aspirations of Israel and that nation's place within the plan of God. Luke Timothy Johnson draws this out for us: 'Luke's most comprehensive way of structuring his entire two-volume work is by means of literary prophecy . . . Luke's use of "prophecy and fulfilment" goes far beyond that found in any other NT writing.'[28]

Theologically, it is unthinkable for Luke to write off all that has gone before with God's dealings with Israel. He shows us how Jesus, the Spirit and the mission of the church are to be seen as a *continuation* of all that. Equally, Luke is keen to show the theological legitimacy of the Gentile mission, how it is God himself who is leading his church to embrace the Gentiles alongside the Jews. If Luke's Gospel shows a journey *to* Jerusalem (the epicentre of salvation), then his Acts is a movement *from* Jerusalem to the ends of the earth.

This makes the Jerusalem church of outstanding importance. Here Luke must show us how God's purposes for Israel continue, while also opening the doors for the inclusion of the Gentiles who believe in Jesus. This is why there is so much detail about what happened in Jerusalem in those early days, and why Luke gives us the two sections about the inner life of the Jerusalem church (2:42–47; 4:32–37; and the summary in 5:12–16). Luke is keen to show that the gospel becomes rooted in the Jewish world, right in Jerusalem. So, Peter's Pentecost sermon is to Jews ('Men of Judea and all who live in Jerusalem', 'You that are Israelites, listen to what I have to say', 'Fellow Israelites', 'Brothers' [2:14, 22, 29, 37][29]), and

---

[28] Johnson 1992: 11–12.
[29] These appellations are how Luke reports Peter structuring his sermon; see Gaventa 2003: 73.

many thousands respond (a huge number) and are baptized in the name of Jesus Christ (2:38). Luke shows the early church continuing in 'the prayers' (2:42), which would have been the temple prayers, and meeting in the temple (3:1, 11; 5:12). The first phase of Acts concludes with a summary verse in which Luke says: 'The word of God continued to spread; the number of the disciples increased greatly in Jerusalem, and a great many of the priests became obedient to the faith' (6:7).

Luke is highlighting the fact that the church was born within Judaism. He is not just telling the story which happened to begin in Jerusalem; he is making a theological point. The Lord's agenda was that the apostolic band should be his 'witnesses in Jerusalem, in all Judea and Samaria, and to the ends of the earth' (1:8). The parallel account at the end of Luke's Gospel is even clearer, that the gospel is to be proclaimed 'to all nations, beginning from Jerusalem' (24:47). The gospel advance must begin theologically with Israel before it heads further afield, since the Gentile mission is structurally founded upon the Jewish mission. The gospel itself arises out of Israel's story and is its theological climax. As Paul said: 'It was necessary that the word of God should be spoken first to you [Jews]' (13:46). Luke Timothy Johnson sums up the implications: 'By showing that in this first community there was a "restoration of Israel," Luke can subsequently describe the Gentile mission not as a replacement of Israel but as its legitimate continuation.'[30]

Luke is also, however, opening the theological door for the Gentile mission. So, this first panel of Acts concludes with the friction between 'the Hellenists' and 'the Hebrews', and concludes with the appointment of the Seven, who will look after the food distribution in Jerusalem; significantly, all seven have Hellenistic names (6:1–6). This, in faintest outline, is what will become increasingly clear as Acts proceeds; that the gospel will go beyond not just Jerusalem, but also Judaism. When we put these perspectives together, we see that '[Luke] is . . . trying to show that Jew and Gentile united in Christ is the true Israel, not the new Israel'.[31]

It is there in some of the details too; for instance, the designations 'the Twelve' and 'the apostles'. The former harks back to the Gospels, when

---

[30] Johnson 1992: 9.
[31] Witherington 1998: 73.

Jesus renews Israel by appointing the Twelve, picking up the tradition of the twelve tribes of Israel. We have seen this already in our thinking about church planting and the Gospels. Lucien Legrand reminds us that the Twelve 'are the prototypes of a Messianic Israel in which the criterion of membership is no longer carnal lineage, but conversion and faith'.[32] The 'apostles', by contrast, looked ahead to being sent by the risen Lord to the ends of the earth. By using both titles for the twelve apostles, Luke combines the two perspectives – looking back to Israel, as it was reshaped by Jesus, and looking ahead to the global church.

How this complex relationship between the emerging church and Judaism develops is one of the core themes of Acts and, indeed, of the New Testament. As I say, this is not the place to go into it further, save to note just how significant it is. At one level, church planters may well come across Jewish populations and individuals, and they will have to be wise and sensitive in how they articulate these matters. One of the greatest pleasures for me in our church plant was to get to know one of our neighbours, who is a devout Jew. We had many discussions about 'supercessionism' and Jewish–Christian relations; I learned so much from him and his friendship. More likely, though, at another level, is the theological reflection that will be necessary about what happened in those early days, and the relationship between the old and new covenants. Whatever the complexities and sadnesses of Jewish–Christian relations,[33] for the Christian there are certain fixed points; the great theme remains the faithfulness of God and the invitation from God to all the world to believe in Jesus the Messiah, starting first with the Jews, and then the Gentiles.

A more exact application to church planting and the story of God and his people is that Acts sees itself within the wider canvas of the whole Bible. We have seen how Peter speaks from the Old Testament to explain what we would call the New: Pentecost is explicable in terms of Joel, of King David, of the last days, as all these lead up to the exaltation of Jesus the Messiah. Certainly in the first half of Acts, several of the speeches serve to put Jesus on the map of the full sweep of the Old Testament story.

---

[32] Legrand 1990: 99.

[33] See James Carroll (2001), *Constantine's Sword: The Church and the Jews – A History*, Boston and New York: Houghton Mifflin; and James D. G. Dunn (2015), *Christianity in the Making: Neither Jew Nor Greek – A Contested Identity*, Grand Rapids and Cambridge: Eerdmans.

This is most notable in Stephen's long speech in chapter 7, tracing the stories of Abraham, Joseph, Moses and David in the light of God's kingdom in Jesus, and in Paul's speech in Pisidian Antioch (13:6–41). For Luke in Acts, the Jesus story is not something which comes out of a clear blue sky, but rather something which is part of an already existing narrative. Jesus takes his place alongside the prophets and kings of the Old Testament, and Luke finds the same dynamics at work in Jesus as in his forebears. Equally, the God who raised Jesus from the dead is none other than the God of Israel, demonstrating that, in Jesus, the story is reaching its climax. The point for us is that the whole story is important in understanding the fullness of Jesus Christ. N. T. Wright puts it well:

> [For its first-century readers – and us] *the Bible was not merely a source of types, shadows, allusions, echoes, symbols, examples, role-models and other no doubt important things.* It was all those, but it was much, much more. It presented itself as a single, sprawling, complex but essentially coherent narrative, a narrative still in search of an ending.[34]

Wright's point is how Paul and his contemporaries would have looked to Scripture to understand Jesus, but we can apply it to ourselves and our situation, too.

A couple of examples. First of all, it helps to think of the Bible's story in what have been described as five acts, as if it were a play: Act 1 is the creation of God's good world; Act 2 is the entry of sin into the world, and with it the fall of humanity and the beginnings of death and alien powers enslaving the human race; Act 3 is the long history of Israel, with its triumphs and disasters, as the people of God try and fail to live faithfully with their God; Act 4 is the turning point, as Jesus is born, lives and teaches, proclaims and demonstrates the kingdom of God, is crucified, and is raised to life and exalted; Act 5 is the age of the Spirit and the church, the age of mission, looking forward to the consummation of all things, as Jesus returns and God is all in all.[35]

---

34 N. T. Wright 2013: 116; emphasis original.
35 There are variants of this structure. See e.g. Roberts 2009; Gladding 2010; Bartholomew and Goheen 2014. The five-act structure was originally set out in Tom Wright (1991), 'How Can the Bible Be Authoritative?', *Vox Evangelica* 21: 7–32.

Another example is the crucial covenant chapters at the end of Deuteronomy (30–32). Here Israel's history is laid out ahead of time, with a period of the blessings of living under the covenant (probably the reigns of David and Solomon), then the time of the curses of the covenant (the exiles of both northern and southern kingdoms) and then the longing for restoration after exile (in the prophecies of Jeremiah and Daniel, which Christians see fulfilled in the impact of Jesus and the coming of God's kingdom in him). This profound but simple pattern helps us see the wood for the trees in the Old Testament, and how all things are prepared for the coming of Jesus to bring the whole story to a climax.[36]

This is helpful for church planters because they will, God willing, be seeing people coming to faith who have no background in Christianity and for whom the Bible is a large, alien and confusing book. To give them an overview such as this is like providing a map so they can orient themselves and begin to find their way around. More than that, it helps ground the church plant theologically, as it should be, in the grand narrative of Scripture, to see how the story of Jesus relates to both Israel and the church, and how we find our place in it too.

Further, this is how we can train our preachers and leaders and the next generation of church planters. Again, God willing, we will be seeing people planting and leading churches who have grown up outside the walls of the church; these are the people who are, in all probability, going to be most effective at reaching others who are like them, with little or confused knowledge of the Christian faith. It may be that such people have little formal education, in which case the current practices of training church leaders are simply not appropriate. So, how can such capable leaders be trained? Frameworks such as those above are crucial for laying theological foundations. These not only make the avoidance of biblical 'howlers' more likely, but also provide a strength and excitement in seeing the Bible's big picture. It gives a confidence in handling Scripture, and ensures a pre-eminence for Jesus as the one to whom it all builds up, and around whom the great corner is turned.

The coming of the Spirit signals the 'last days' (2:17). When the Messiah is exalted and pours out the Spirit, as the promise of the Father, this is the

---

[36] For more detail, see N. T. Wright 2013: ch. 2.

signal that the story of the world has now entered its very last chapter. This is the beginning of the end of the story, when all the ends get tied up, when it all makes sense, when God is getting ready to put all things right. We now know the meaning of it all, what it has all been for and what it is all about – that, in Jesus, God is fulfilling the long history of Israel and bringing about the ancient calling of carrying his blessing to the ends of the earth. This is to be done by the Spirit helping the church to witness to Jesus as the one through whom all this comes to pass. There is an element not just of fulfilment but also of something new, something fresh. God's future for the world comes from ahead of us in time, but, through the Spirit, brings the fullness of Jesus and the kingdom to bear in the present. The last chapter will not be like any of the other previous chapters. This part of the story is, at one and the same time, the continuation of the Jesus story but also the consummation of that story, as we see Jesus in power working out the purposes of God all around the world through the church in the Spirit. These are heady, demanding, exciting and challenging days in which to live. These are plans in which church planters have a key and central role, because it is through the church in mission that Jesus will most profoundly and powerfully be felt to the ends of the earth.

Church planting and its opposition

All this sounds (and is) magnificent, unstoppable and self-evidently the triumph of God in the world; we know how the story ends! We all love the stories in Acts of miracles, of release from prison, of many becoming Christians, of multiple churches planted in varying cultures, of the gospel engaging the worlds of Judaism, Hellenism and Roman power. This is why Acts is such an inspiration, not least for the far-from-triumphant situations in which we may find ourselves. Theologically, Acts is set on the twin foundations of the resurrection of Jesus and the outpouring of God's own powerful and personal presence in the world; the decisive battle is won, and God's future for the world is coming into existence.

Yet Acts is also far more nuanced. To take one very obvious example: the book finishes with its hero in prison, with his future very uncertain. Paul is 'proclaiming the kingdom of God and teaching about the Lord Jesus Christ with all boldness and without hindrance' (28:31). 'Boldness' reminds us of the prayer of the apostolic band at the beginning of Acts (which we will look at in more detail in a moment) where the believers ask to 'speak [God's] word with all boldness' (4:29, 31). There is an inner freedom there, but there are plenty of outer hindrances: Paul is under house arrest, awaiting his trial before the emperor Nero. This narrative, then, is not triumphalistic; there may be victories, but they do not look the way we might expect them to.

When we look at the narrative of Acts, we find that every advance is accompanied by opposition and suffering; the road to triumph is the way of the cross.

Opposition and suffering come early on in the narrative, and continue throughout.

- There is the mockery from some of the crowd at Pentecost, saying the manifestation of the Spirit is the result of intoxication with new wine (2:13).
- Peter and John are arrested for speaking to the people about the resurrection of Jesus (4:1–3). They are released on this occasion, but warned, given orders and threatened by the Sanhedrin (4:17, 18, 21).
- The apostles are arrested by the high priest and the Sadducees, who are 'enraged and wanted to kill them', but settle instead on having them 'flogged' (5:17–18, 33, 40). The apostles 'rejoiced that they were considered worthy to suffer dishonour for the sake of the name' (5:41).
- Things change when Stephen is brought before the council, and consequently 'dragged . . . out of the city' and stoned to death (6:12; 7:58) under the direction 'of a young man named Saul' (7:58). 'That day a severe persecution began against the church in Jerusalem' (8:1).
- Saul begins preaching about Jesus. 'After some time had passed, the Jews plotted to kill him' (9:23), and the Hellenists 'were attempting to kill him' (9:29).
- Later, 'King Herod laid violent hands upon some who belonged to the church. He had James, the brother of John, killed with the sword . . . [and] proceeded to arrest Peter also' (12:1–3).
- Persecution is stirred up against Paul and Barnabas on the first missionary journey in Pisidian Antioch, and they are driven out of the region (13:50). They are threatened with stoning in Iconium

(14:5). The persecutors follow them to Lystra, where Paul is stoned, dragged out of the city and left for dead (14:19). Paul and Barnabas return there and encourage the disciples to continue in the faith, saying, 'It is through many persecutions that we must enter the kingdom of God' (14:22).

- On the second journey, Paul and Silas are arrested in Philippi on the grounds that they were, in the words of the citizens, 'disturbing our city . . . advocating customs that are not lawful for us as Romans to adopt or observe' (16:21). They are lynched by the crowd, beaten by the Roman magistrates, given 'a severe flogging' and thrown into prison, where their feet are placed in the stocks (16:22–24).

- There are riots in Thessalonica, with the apostles accused of 'turning the world upside down' (17:5–9); in Corinth, with Sosthenes beaten by the mob while the Roman proconsul turns a blind eye (18:17); and in Ephesus, where there 'was no little disturbance . . . concerning the Way' (19:23).

- Paul comes to realize that he is 'a captive to the Spirit'. He is on his way to Jerusalem, and the 'Holy Spirit testifies to me in every city that imprisonment and persecutions are waiting for me' (20:22–23). This breeds an attitude in him of not counting his life as of any value to him, 'if only I may finish my course and the ministry that I received from the Lord Jesus, to testify to the good news of God's grace' (20:24). None of the Ephesian elders will see his face again (20:25, 38). As Paul continues his journey, the prophet Agabus declares that Paul will be bound and handed over to the Gentiles (21:11). Paul announces that he is ready 'not only to be bound but even to die in Jerusalem for the name of the Lord Jesus' (21:13).

- In Jerusalem, Paul is dragged out of the temple, 'and immediately the doors were shut' (a chilling detail). They try to kill him, beating him, and are only interrupted by the swift action of the Roman tribune. 'The violence of the mob was so great that [Paul] had to be carried by the soldiers.' Paul addresses those in the crowd, but they shout, 'Away with such a fellow from the earth! For he should not be allowed to live' (21:30, 31, 35; 22:22).

- Paul testifies before the council, but 'the dissension became violent', such that the tribune feared 'that they would tear Paul to pieces', and

171

once more the soldiers have to take him out (23:10). He is moved to Caesarea once a conspiracy to kill him is uncovered (23:12–35).

• Paul is then held in captivity for over two years (24:27). After various trials, Paul appeals to Caesar and is taken by sea to Rome, where he lives under house arrest 'for two whole years' (28:30).

Here we see real violence: the abuse of religious and political power, mob uproar, corruption and bribery, judicial murder and much more. It is a consistent strain within the narrative, and no analysis of Acts can be complete without it.

The physical violence has undertones. Luke Timothy Johnson shows that Luke

> punctuates the triumph of the mission in each new territory with a symbolic conquering of evil powers. In Jerusalem, Peter strikes dead Ananias and Sapphira who had taken Satan into their hearts (5:1–11). In Samaria, Peter rejects the overtures of the magician Simon, rebukes him, and wins his recognition (8:9–24). In Cyprus, Paul overcomes the magical powers of 'the false Jewish prophet' Bar-Jesus (13:4–12) and in Philippi, the forces of divination and soothsaying (16:16–18). In Asia Minor, the 'seven sons of Scaeva' who tried to work exorcisms in the name of Jesus are routed (19:11–20). In Malta, Paul is thought to be a criminal because he is bitten by a deadly viper, but when he survives he is regarded as a god (28:1–6).[37]

The violence and opposition has a demonic parallel, or maybe undergirding.

Over against the dark side of spiritual life stands something shining and altogether more unexpected. Lucien Legrand builds up the argument (which I summarize as follows):

• Luke's narrative of Paul's ministry comes in two equal halves of eight chapters each.[38] The first half (chs. 13–20) shows Paul active in his

---

[37] Johnson 1992: 11.
[38] However, it is worth noting that, of course, our current chapter divisions are not original to the Bible's text and were not introduced until the sixteenth century.

missionary endeavours. The second half (chs. 21–28) shows Paul under the power and control of others, in captivity of various sorts. The first eight chapters, according to Legrand, cover twelve years of active ministry; the second, just three.

- Luke must regard these last three years, then, as of great significance in Paul's ministry. It is here that Paul gets to see the fulfilment of Jesus' calling for him to witness to the Gentiles, their kings and to the people of Israel, and 'how much he must suffer for the sake of my name' (9:15, 16).
- Gaventa shows us the parallels between Jesus setting his face for Jerusalem in Luke's Gospel (9:51; 13:22; 17:11) and Paul aiming for first Jerusalem (Acts 19:21; 21:13) and then Rome (25:9–12; 28:14).[39] Paul's journey to Jerusalem and Rome parallels that of his Lord, as do his trials before both religious and political bodies and leaders. As Legrand says:

> There is less passivity, then, than passion in Acts chapters 21–28. The final viewpoint of Acts on Paul's mission is an agreement with that of the Gospel of Luke. When all is said and done concerning Paul's activity, zeal, initiatives, and success, yet the essential remains unexpressed. By his suffering, Paul, like Jesus, has entered into the mystery of the pure divine power . . . Above all, [Paul] reproduced his Master's passion, and it is at the heart of this passion that he attained the goal of his course.[40]

What we are seeing is the pattern of the life and death of Jesus being recapitulated in that of Paul. His sufferings entered into those of his Lord.

So, suffering is a huge factor in the Acts of the Apostles, explicable at several different levels. It comes as the result of a challenge to religious, political, economic and social power. It is due to spiritual warfare. And, most mysteriously of all, it is part and parcel of what happens when we wholeheartedly follow Jesus in mission and church planting; the pattern of the cross becomes ever plainer and unavoidable. Suffering in Acts is

---

[39] Gaventa 2003: 52–53.
[40] Legrand 1990: 114–115.

frightening and overwhelming, violent and loud. Clamour and uproar swirl around the tiny figure of Paul, and even the power of Rome can barely control it. Yet there is a greater power, the steady journey of Paul's course, the call that the Lord Jesus had given him to fulfil (9:15–16; 20:24).

For the church planter, along with the excitement and adventure of everything, there is a sober reckoning of the costs involved. We may not know what these will be, but we can be sure that there will be something. As Henri Blocher writes: 'Church planting, we may not forget, while it means work, also means war.'[41] We would be wise to have our eyes open, to do some planning around possible contingencies, and not to be thrown when things get a bit hairy.

Church planting always involves change. It may be cultural change in the sending or receiving churches. It may be a change in the church ecology of an area. It may be social and economic change across a city or region. It will always mean spiritual change. Change is disruptive, by definition, and it can be threatening, uncomfortable and received as aggressive or invasive, even when it is not meant as such. There can be reactions from surrounding churches and church leaders, from deaneries and dioceses (in Anglican terms). Congregations can be shaken and unsettled. Patterns of belonging and behaving in an area can be disrupted, injustice and oppression exposed, greed and privilege challenged. It is small wonder that there can be reactions, sometimes anger and hostility. And Acts assures us that there will be a spiritual reaction, however it is manifested.

This is not meant to alarm us. In Acts, spiritual opposition may be real, but it is always overcome. Jesus is Lord! Whatever our vocabulary and conceptual frameworks for the suffering and opposition which church planting may provoke, we should think carefully about it, and fortify ourselves against it. God willing, we will not face the severity of physical persecution that Paul and the other early Christians endured, at least in the West. In this we are blessed, and have much to learn from our many suffering sisters and brothers around the world. And who knows if this will change in the years to come? At the very least, though, church planting is hard, tiring work, with long hours and many challenges of

---

[41] Blocher 2016: 61.

innovating and culture changing. Church planters, their teams and families, all need to think through how they will live their lives in healthy ways, protect and nurture their health and relationships, and be aware of the spiritual dynamics involved in everything they do. And they will be aware, too, of how the path to Christlikeness is necessarily the way of the cross, so how they handle suffering, hardship and opposition may well be in the Lord's good plan for them and their churches.

Let's not catastrophize every bump in the church-planting road, and start to see the demonic behind every harsh email or angry word. Equally, let's not be spiritually or emotionally naive, and never play fast and loose with our own, our families' or friends' health. Alongside that, let's not be quick to give up or throw in the towel at the first sign of trouble; may we be resilient, brave, loving and full of faith. May the Lord help us to respond wisely when we face opposition or have to endure hardship. What is required is both discernment and determination.

Church planting is rooted in prayer

The rise of persecution is met by the raising of voices to God in prayer. When Peter and John are released by the Sanhedrin, they go to the church and make a report. 'When [the believers] heard it, they raised their voices together to God' (4:24). This is the instinctive reaction of the early church – not planning or relocation or politicking, but praying. It also sets the pattern of how the first Christians are to react to unfavourable pressure. As Beverly Roberts Gaventa writes:

> [This] incident marks the beginning of the church's response to persecution. Because the petitions of the prayer are granted, the church is enabled to continue to respond to persecution with forthright proclamation accompanied by acts from God's hand.[42]

The account in Acts 4 is not just a specific answer to prayer in a specific situation, but the setting of a practice that will continue throughout the book: persecution will be met with prayer and persistence in proclaiming the gospel.

---

[42] Gaventa 1986: 80, cited in Witherington 1998: 200.

Prayer is a constant in Acts:

- We read of those in the embryonic Christian community 'devoting themselves to prayer', presumably looking for the power to be witnesses to Jesus (1:14) and asking for guidance about replacing Judas (1:24).
- The apostles see their task as being 'to devote ourselves to prayer and to serving the word' (6:4), and they commission the Seven with prayer and the laying on of hands (6:6).
- When Peter is arrested, 'the church prayed fervently to God for him' (12:5; cf. 12:12).
- The leaders of the church in Antioch 'were worshipping the Lord and fasting' (13:2). When the Holy Spirit calls Barnabas and Saul to missionary work, 'after fasting and praying they laid hands on them and sent them off' (13:3).
- When Paul and Silas are arrested in Philippi, we find them 'about midnight . . . praying and singing hymns to God' (16:25).
- After Paul has finished speaking with the Ephesian elders at Miletus, 'he knelt down with them all and prayed' (20:36).
- As Paul and his party head for Jerusalem, 'there we knelt down on the beach and prayed' (21:5).

It is noteworthy how naturally prayer comes to these early Christians, how it is so often in response to the Lord or to circumstances, how we see it on occasion combined with worship and with fasting and with the commissioning of new missionary ventures or hazardous journeys. It is only in chapter 4, though, that we hear what they pray, so may we spend a few moments looking at this justly famous passage, applying it to prayer and church planting:

After [Peter and John] were released, they went to their friends and reported what the chief priests and the elders had said to them. When they heard it, they raised their voices together to God and said, 'Sovereign Lord, who made the heaven and the earth, the sea, and everything in them, it is you who said by the Holy Spirit through our ancestor David, your servant:

"Why did the Gentiles rage,
  and the people imagine vain things?
The kings of the earth took their stand,
  and the rulers have gathered together
    against the Lord and his Messiah."

For in this city, in fact, both Herod and Pontius Pilate, with the Gentiles and the peoples of Israel, gathered together against your holy servant Jesus, whom you anointed, to do whatever your hand and your plan had predestined to take place. And now, Lord, look at their threats, and grant to your servants to speak your word with all boldness, while you stretch out your hand to heal, and signs and wonders are performed through the name of your holy servant Jesus.'
(Acts 4:23–30)

Peter and John go to 'their friends' (NRSV, ESV), 'their own people' (TNIV), and they pray together. Literally, the Greek just says 'their own'. Witherington helpfully draws our attention to other uses in the New Testament: 'This phrase would normally refer to one's own family or people (cf. Acts 24:23; John 1:11; 13:1), but here the family of faith is in view.'[43] This sense of family comes out at other times in Acts, when the church has a family feel – when Peter, released from prison, 'went to the house of Mary, the mother of John whose other name was Mark, where many had gathered and were praying' (12:12), or when Paul and his party head for Jerusalem, and 'all of them, with wives and children, escorted us outside the city. There we knelt down on the beach and prayed and said farewell to one another' (21:5–6). Prayer is the animating force of community life and its most natural expression. There can be great power in prayer between people who know one another well, love one another, and have a shared sense of mission and a willingness to face its costs.

To proceed to the prayer itself, let's consider how the disciples thought of God, how they reflected theologically on their situation, and what they asked God to do.

---

43 Witherington 1998: 201.

The praying church uses an unusual word for God; it is the Greek word from which we get our English 'despot',[44] something 'which connotes one with great power and control of circumstances'.[45] As John Stott comments: 'The Sanhedrin might utter warnings, threats and prohibitions, and try to silence the church, but their authority was subject to a higher authority still, and the edicts of [humanity] cannot overturn the decrees of God.'[46]

The next stage of prayer is to fill 'their minds with thoughts of the divine sovereignty'.[47] They declare God to be the universal Creator, and then quote Psalm 2:2 about his rule over the plans and machinations of political opposition. Stott helps us to see that 'this, then, was the early church's understanding of God, the God of creation, revelation and history, whose characteristic actions are summarized by the three verbs "you made" (24), "you spoke" (25) and "you decided" (28)'.[48]

It is highly significant that Luke's account of prayer speaks of the church raising their voices 'to God' (4:24). It sounds a truism, but it bears repetition and repays meditation that prayer is addressed *to God*. The early church's example is one of starting with God in prayer, in getting our perspective on our current situation by reflecting on God, not the other way around. This is why so much liturgy from all sections of the historic church immerses us in Scripture and the story of God before we turn to intercession, and it is why the practice of so much of Pentecostalism and many contemporary churches is to frame prayer gatherings with praise. The more we can fill our minds with the greatness and kindness of God, the more we can frame our needs and requests in terms of Scripture; the more we can cast any troubles or difficulties within the perspective of God's power and faithfulness, then the more our faith will rise and the more our prayers will be bold and appropriately confident.

This perspective continues as the believers frame their prayers with reference to Psalm 2. They quote the psalm, with its reference to the rage

---

[44] Although we should note that our English word has very different connotations from the original Greek one.
[45] Witherington 1998: 201.
[46] Stott 1990: 99.
[47] Ibid.
[48] Ibid. 100.

of the Gentiles, the vain imaginings of the peoples, and the actions of the kings and the rulers in their joint conspiracy against the Lord and his Messiah. Then, with the telling words 'in fact' (4:27), they align the psalm with the actions of the Gentiles, the peoples of Israel, and Herod and Pontius Pilate, when they all 'gathered together against [God's] holy servant Jesus' (4:25–27). They are tracing parallels between the events described in Psalm 2 and what happened in the crucifixion of Jesus. The prayer continues straight on with reference to what has just happened when Peter and John were subject to the attempted intimidation of the Sanhedrin: 'And now, Lord, look at their threats . . .' (4:29). Grammatically, the 'they' of 'their threats' should be Pilate, Herod, the people of Israel, and the Gentiles, who had conspired together to murder Jesus; but theologically, the 'they' has become the Sanhedrin. Some commentators stumble over the grammar, seeing a mistake by Luke. Beverly Roberts Gaventa helps us to see the deeper theological logic, though: 'For Luke, the persecution of the apostles *corresponds* to the persecution of Jesus. The threats against Peter and John by the Jewish leaders are the equivalent of the threats against Jesus.'[49]

Gaventa broadens this point still more in later work:

> The community's prayer in vv. 23–31 makes a strong interpretative move, in which it identifies the plight of the present community with that of Jesus and both Jesus and the community with the plight of the 'Lord' and 'his Messiah' depicted in Ps 2.[50]

What they are doing is mapping their own experience (the threats from the Sanhedrin) onto parallel experiences of Jesus, as prophesied in Psalm 2. Their use of exactly parallel language from the psalm in their description of what happened with Jesus is a demonstration of how intentional and precise they were in their meditation. It was this which helped them apply God's sovereignty into their own situation. The God who had a plan and predestined the crucifixion of Jesus, using the malice and arrogance of the Herods and Pilates of this world and the rage and empty

---

[49] Gaventa 1986: 79, quoted in Witherington 1998: 203.
[50] Gaventa 2003: 98.

thinking of religious and political leaders alike, was well able to oversee the threats of the Sanhedrin.

This ability to reflect on experience theologically has become a staple of theological training in recent years. It is a 'method of interrelating life and faith', 'a reflective linking of tradition and experience'.[51] There are many models of this, but all Christian ones involve the interaction of accurately describing an experience, bringing to bear parallels and insights from the Scriptures and Christian traditions, and moving towards fresh action.[52] Prayer, not least prayer within a Christian community, is a very good and natural way of engaging with this.

Lastly, the request of the church is striking. In the face of the power and incipient hostility of the Sanhedrin, the church was at a turning point. Luke Timothy Johnson brings out the extent of the dilemma. The word translated 'rage' ('Why did the Gentiles rage . . . ?') 'is normally used in the middle voice for the noise made by whinnying horses and by extension to human wild, wanton or arrogant behaviour'.[53] It is a vivid picture of just how alarming and intimidating the whole experience must have been for Peter and John and now for the church. These were early days; this was a small group of people with no history, no identity, no power, at least in the eyes of the Sanhedrin, which by contrast had all those things in abundance. In the face of such pressures, and the destabilizing emotional effect they must have had, the believers had extraordinary confidence and clarity in their prayers: 'Look at their threats . . . grant to your servants to speak your word with all boldness, while you stretch out your hand to heal' (4:29–30). The phrase 'stretch out your hand' calls to mind the ministry of Moses in the exodus from Egypt (Exod. 3:20; 4:4; 6:6; 7:5 etc.).[54] Here is more theological reflection: Moses and the people of Israel were likewise facing powerful opposition, and God's answer was signs and wonders. This must have been in the minds of the early church: 'stretch out your hand . . . and [perform] signs and wonders . . . [in] the name of your holy servant Jesus' (4:30). Just as Moses and the people of the exodus

---

[51] J. Thompson with Pattison and R. Thompson 2008: 3, 206.
[52] See Ward (2017: ch. 6) for a helpful description of various approaches. See also Collins' powerful critique of many approaches (Collins 2020).
[53] Johnson 1992: 84.
[54] Ibid. 85.

persevered in their freedom mission through the power of God, so would the Christians of the early church. Their courage, discernment and sense of call are astounding.

Much of the perseverance in church planting comes from this sense of calling. When the gospel burns brightly within us, when we have a vision from heaven (Acts 26:19) to plant churches and when we have a sense of walking in the footsteps of those who have gone before, then it seems natural to persevere in the face of opposition and intimidation. When this is renewed in prayer and with the support of others, we have a growing confidence that it will take more than a bit of sabre-rattling to put us off our course.

Prayer, then, has a subtle but powerful role in the planting of churches. It is a recognition of the greatness of God, and an acknowledgment that he is the sovereign, the ultimate authority. It is a calling on his power to advance his cause. And it is also an aligning of ourselves with the greater purposes of God, a way to see ourselves within the wider and longer and deeper pattern of God's own vision to plant churches around the world, to stand with Moses, Jesus and the early church in obeying God, even in the face of human power and intimidation.

The section ends with conclusive demonstrations that God has heard and is answering the believers' prayers: 'the place in which they were gathered together was shaken; and they were all filled with the Holy Spirit and spoke the word of God with boldness' (4:31), the very words of their prayer turned into action.

We will return to the practice of prayer in church plants when we consider the interior life of the early church. May we pause, though, to reflect on the cardinal place of intercession in the planting of churches.

Timothy Keller refers to the work of C. John Miller, who makes a helpful distinction between what he calls 'maintenance' as opposed to 'frontline' prayer:

Maintenance prayer meetings are short, mechanical, focused on physical needs inside the church. In contrast, the three basic traits of frontline prayer are these:

1. A request for grace to confess sins and to humble ourselves

2. A compassion and zeal for the flourishing of the church and the reaching of the lost
3. A yearning to know God, to see his face, to glimpse his glory.[55]

Keller refers specifically to Acts 4 as an instance of this extraordinary, frontline prayer.

Church planting is nothing if it is not frontline. It will need frontline prayer if it is to succeed and flourish.

The miraculous and mission in Acts

A striking feature of Acts is the number of miracles performed by the apostles and others. The life of the early church was supernatural through and through. This raises questions for the church planter – just how central should this approach be to the launching of new churches? How much should the church planter expect?

Miracles are part and parcel of the apostolic proclamation of the kingdom of God.

- In this respect, this is like the life of Jesus, 'a man attested to you by God with deeds of power, wonders, and signs that God did through him among you' (2:22).
- Early on in Acts, a disabled beggar is healed at the Beautiful Gate of the temple (3:6–8). Peter explains that the healing is in 'the name of Jesus Christ of Nazareth' (3:6), and is not a result of 'our own power or piety' but is rather the God of Israel glorifying his servant Jesus (3:13).
- After the powerful time of prayer in chapter 4, we read that 'many signs and wonders were done among the people through the apostles' (5:12). People laid out their sick in places where even Peter's shadow might fall on them as he went by, and the sick and those tormented by unclean spirits were cured (5:15, 16).
- In Samaria, Philip, not himself an apostle, performs signs of healing and deliverance, and the sorcerer Simon is 'amazed when he saw the signs and great miracles that took place' (8:13).

---

[55] Keller 2012: 73; Miller 1986, 1999: 98–101.

- In Lydda, a paralysed man called Aeneas is healed by Christ through Peter, 'and all the residents of Lydda and Sharon saw him and turned to the Lord' (9:35). In nearby Joppa, Tabitha dies and is raised to life again, and 'many believed in the Lord' (9:42).
- The demonstrable outpouring of the Holy Spirit on the Gentiles is what convinces Peter that God has accepted them through faith in Jesus (10:44; 11:15, 18).
- Peter is dramatically rescued from prison by an angel (12:6–11).
- It is the Holy Spirit who says to the leaders of the Antioch church that they are to set apart Barnabas and Saul for the work of mission (13:2).
- In Lystra, a man 'who could not use his feet and had never walked' is healed (14:8–10).
- At the Council of Jerusalem, Barnabas and Paul tell of 'all the signs and wonders that God had done through them among the Gentiles' (15:12).
- The Holy Spirit guides Paul and his companions about their missionary journey, forbidding them to speak the word in Asia, not allowing them to go into Bithynia and guiding them through Paul's vision of the man from Macedonia asking them for their help (16:6, 7, 9–10).
- In Philippi, a young female slave is exorcised (16:18).
- In Ephesus, 'God did extraordinary miracles through Paul, so that when the handkerchiefs or aprons that had touched his skin were brought to the sick, their diseases left them, and the evil spirits came out of them' (19:11–12).
- When Eutychus falls to his death from a third-storey window, Paul raises him from the dead (20:9–12).
- We read of Philip's four unmarried daughters, all of whom 'had the gift of prophecy' (21:9).
- On Malta, Paul does not die from the bite of a poisonous viper, and cures the father of Publius, the leading man on the island, and the rest of the sick (28:3–6, 8, 9).

There is an extensive vocabulary, especially of the miracles, works of power, and wonders, but maybe it is the word 'sign' which is most significant. These miracles point beyond themselves to the activity of God and the reality of his kingdom. 'A miracle was not a stained-glass window to be looked *at*, but a transparent window to be looked *through*.'[56] In addition, both Peter and Paul, when they raise Tabitha and Eutychus respectively from the dead (9:37–41; 20:9–10), follow a pattern of speech and behaviour which is exactly parallel with that of Jesus when he raised Jairus's daughter from the dead (Mark 4:35–42 and parallels). This ministry and its power is that of Jesus. 'As one studies the ministry of the apostles, it becomes apparent that they expected God to move in power whenever the gospel was preached. Their expectations were founded on their experiences with Jesus.'[57]

Sadly, signs and wonders have become something of a battleground between different approaches, although my impression is that this is less so than it used to be in the 1980s and early 1990s. John Wimber's ministry sparked extensive discussion and debate, and he and Kevin Springer wrote two influential books on the subject. On Acts, specifically, they wrote: 'Signs and wonders occurred fourteen times in the book of Acts in conjunction with preaching, resulting in church growth. Further, on twenty occasions church growth was a direct result of signs and wonders performed by the disciples.'[58]

The argument is well made that the miraculous was a regular part of New Testament evangelism and church planting. Healings and deliverances were demonstrations of the power of God, the presence of Jesus and the triumph of his kingdom over every other power, signs of the love of God, and invitations to faith in Jesus.

Not everyone is convinced of this. Eckhard Schnabel writes:

The assertion that the miracle promotes faith and should thus be an integral part of the mission and evangelism of the church is neither confirmed by Paul, by Luke's narrative of the apostles' missionary work in the book of Acts or by the history of the church. It is simply incorrect when some assert that 'there is a pattern of growth and expansion of the church that followed these recorded miracles in Scripture' ... This does not constitute a pattern. The

---

[56] Pelikan 2005: 98; emphasis original.
[57] Shenk and Stutzman 1998: 84.
[58] Wimber and Springer 1985: 117, quoted in Stott 1990: 101–102.

picture is complex . . . The ambiguity of miracles suggests that God never works only through miracles to bring people to faith in Jesus Christ. God always works through the proclamation of his Word in which the power of the Holy Spirit is present.[59]

He is tracing the link between conversion and the preaching of the gospel, as opposed to church growth resulting from miracles.

This is not the place to enter into the complexities of this debate, but we can say one or two things.

First, it is true that the miraculous is more ambiguous in Acts than is sometimes acknowledged by those arguing for the regularity and centrality of healing and other supernatural phenomena. Sometimes, miracles do not lead to faith but instead to confusion or superstition, as with the inhabitants of Lystra, who take Barnabas to be Zeus and Paul to be Hermes when a man is healed (14:12–15, 18), or with the inhabitants of Malta, when Paul is bitten by a viper but does not die (28:4, 6). Some miracles, as well, are judgments rather than healings, as with Ananias and Sapphira (5:5, 10) and the blinding of Elymas (13:10–11); these do not make their way onto too many healing-prayer training curricula!

Second, we do have the issue which every reader of Acts has to face at some stage about deciding what is *descriptive* and what is *prescriptive* in the narrative. It is not always easy to determine what is simply Luke, as author, telling us what happened, and what we are to deduce is to be normative practice for the church. All kinds of factors come into play here, from questions of interpretation to the prejudices which our own experiences bring to the text.

Nonetheless, it is hard to avoid the conclusion that the conversation sometimes has a slightly surreal air. In order to evaluate the significance of miracles in evangelism and church planting, one must first have miracles to be talking about. It is a very different conversation to be having in a lecture theatre or a library from one where a person is standing in front of you who has just been healed of a life-threatening illness. One wants to avoid superstition and overstatement and unwitting undervaluing of Jesus and the gospel by putting too great an emphasis on miracles, but

---

[59] Schnabel 2008: 454. The quotation is from Wagner 2000: 875.

the greater danger, it seems to me, is to write off the miraculous, whether in theory or practice, before we even start. John Stott writes:

If, then, we take Scripture as our guide, we will avoid opposite extremes. We will neither describe miracles as 'never happening', nor as 'everyday occurrences', neither as 'impossible' nor as 'normal'. Instead, we will be entirely open to the God who works both through nature and through miracle.[60]

Whatever our church tradition, a sense of the manifest power of God is an enormous encouragement in planting a church. To see someone from our local housing estate, known to many, healed of a long-standing medical condition is a great start. Or to see local people, far from God, being converted and added to the church is a wonderful sign of God's kingdom at work, not least, as Shenk and Stutzman remind us, because 'the greatest sign and wonder of all is the miracle of conversion and new birth'.[61]

Acts gives us a more nuanced account of the place of the miraculous than is sometimes argued. While unambiguously showing how healings and other signs and wonders played a central part in the spread of the gospel and the establishing of the early church, it also gives us a wider theological perspective within which to view miracles.

First of all, although Acts recounts many signs and wonders, it also shows us incidents in which the miraculous power of God was seemingly withheld. One such example is the murder of James:

About that time King Herod laid violent hands upon some who belonged to the church. He had James, the brother of John, killed with the sword. After he saw that it pleased the Jews, he proceeded to arrest Peter also. (This was during the festival of Unleavened Bread.) (Acts 12:1–3)

The execution of James, most likely by beheading, is recounted with shocking brevity. The Jerusalem church seemed to be enjoying a period

---

[60] Stott 1990: 104.
[61] Shenk and Stutzman 1998: 87.

of comparative peace after the persecution following the martyrdom of Stephen (8:1; 9:31), and yet Herod, the grandson of that Herod who was so involved in the events of the crucifixion of Jesus, reaches out and strikes down one of the major figures of the ministry of Jesus and the early church. The brevity of the account seems to echo the summary nature of the killing of James. Herod then proceeds to move against Peter, and has him arrested. This must all have been profoundly shocking and traumatizing to the early church.

Jesus had, of course, prophesied that James and his brother John would drink his cup and share in his sufferings (Mark 10:38–39), 'but it belongs to the mystery of God's providence why this was to mean execution for James and exile for John'.[62] Even more striking and puzzling is the contrast between James, brutally murdered for political gain, and Peter, who will be miraculously rescued from prison by the intervention of an angel (Acts 12:6–19). Why should one leader be killed and another rescued? Why should God's miraculous power be used in one instance but not in another? It reminds us of the climactic passage in Hebrews 11, the so-called roll call of the heroes of faith. The first half narrates the stories of those 'who through faith conquered kingdoms, administered justice, obtained promises, shut the mouths of lions, quenched raging fire, escaped the edge of the sword, won strength out of weakness, became mighty in war, put foreign armies to flight' (11:33–34). By contrast, Hebrews 11 continues:

> Others were tortured, refusing to accept release . . . Others suffered mocking and flogging, and even chains and imprisonment. They were stoned to death, they were sawn in two, they were killed by the sword . . . of whom the world was not worthy.
> (11:35–38)

The mystery of why some were recipients of divine power and release, and others were not, is just left to lie on the very surface of the text. Such a striking paradox should cause us to be wary of making overly bold claims for the miraculous in our church plants.

---

[62] Stott 1990: 208.

Hebrews 11, though, concludes with a reference to the promises of God: 'Yet all these [those rescued and those who were not], though they were commended for their faith, did not receive what was promised' (11:39). The focus of Scripture is not on the here and now, but remains on the fullness, the perfection, of the coming of God's kingdom. The miraculous is a stage on the journey and is not the destination in itself. The extent of powerful healings and miracles may well assist the spread of the gospel, but it does not call into question the plans and promises of God, which find their location in the world that is to come.

Acts provides further perspectives, as well, by locating the miracles within larger storylines. For instance, staying with the story of James's execution and Peter's imprisonment, the chapter is structured around Peter's miraculous release from prison but is bordered by two instances in the life of Herod. The chapter opens with his attack on the church's leaders (12:1–4), but ends with his death, a divine judgment on his failure to resist being acclaimed as a god (12:20–23). Luke concludes the chapter with another of his summary statements: 'But the word of God continued to advance and gain adherents' (12:24). He is telling us that there will be advances and defeats in the story of the life of the church, and the defeats will be real and painful, but nothing will have the power to stop the ultimate advance of the gospel. The church will mourn its Jameses, but will keep its eye on the triumphs of the kingdom. 'Such is the power of God to overthrow hostile human plans and to establish his own in their place.'[63] Miracles are to be welcomed and rejoiced in, but their presence or absence will not take the place of this wider narrative of 'the word of God [advancing] and [gaining] adherents' (12:24).

There is also a second wider theological perspective which underlies all that happens in Acts, namely that the church and her people are continuing to live out the story of Jesus. We have already noted how Luke signals this with the story of Paul and his trials. It is there with the execution of Stephen, where Stephen, while he is being stoned to death, commits his spirit to God, just as Jesus had done on the cross (Luke 23:46; Acts 7:59), and prays for the forgiveness of his killers (Luke 23:34; Acts 7:60). The shape of the story of the gospel in Acts is that of the cross, so it

---

[63] Ibid. 213.

will not be surprising if it is marked by suffering and even martyrdom. Just as the crucifixion could be seen as a moment when Jesus was abandoned by God, yet was actually nothing less than the 'definite plan and foreknowledge of God' (2:23), so the sufferings and reverses of the church can be viewed from the same double perspective.

Herod's attack and demise and Peter's rescue from prison tell the same story. We note that James's execution and Peter's arrest happen at the time of the 'festival of Unleavened Bread' or the Passover (12:3, 4), and that the followers of Jesus are the victims of the malice and abuse of power of a Herod, and this alerts us to parallels with the story of Jesus and his trial and crucifixion. Peter is taken and incarcerated, but released through the agency of angelic power, and appears after his rescue to a woman, whose tale is not believed, before he moves on to 'another place' (12:17), all of which act as parallels to the story of the death and resurrection of Jesus. The chapter is full of vocabulary shared with Luke's account of the cross and resurrection, which adds depth to the resonances between the story of Jesus and that of the nascent church. The life of the church, then, embodies both the killing of Jesus and the power of God in vindicating him and raising him to everlasting life (cf. 2 Cor. 4:10). Our church plants can expect to encounter struggle, opposition and suffering, but also the power of God in ways which astound us and confound those forces working against the gospel. An authentic New Testament pattern is to experience both of these dynamics.

> The escape of . . . Peter from prison becomes a demonstration that the resurrection of Jesus continues to empower his apostles. The story of Jesus is continued in the story of his followers, and the power at work in Jesus is now even more powerfully at work in his Church.[64]

Church and church planting in Acts

We will return to church planting and mission in Acts when we take a look at what Paul actually did, but first we must look at what Acts means when it talks about 'church'. If it is churches we are planting, then, as

---

[64] Johnson 1992: 219.

church planters, we will need to have a clear grasp of what the New Testament envisages. We will look at the two major churches of Acts, those in Jerusalem and Antioch.

The church in Jerusalem

In the Acts of the Apostles, after the ascension of Jesus and the pouring out of the Spirit at Pentecost, Peter preaches a sermon to the gathered crowd, to which about 3,000 people respond positively and are baptized and added to the number of the followers of Jesus (2:41). How were the apostles and those first 120 Christians (1:15) to think of these people? How were they to act? How were they to become church? This is a deeply significant moment in Acts. It is the hinge between the times of Jesus being physically present with his followers, and the new age, when it is the Spirit who gathers people together in response to the preaching about Jesus. In terms of a theology for church planting, this is a key and instructive moment.

There is no gap between the 3,000 being baptized and added to the number of the Jesus followers, and the account of their common life: 'So those who welcomed [Peter's] message were baptized, and that day about three thousand persons were added. They devoted themselves to the apostles' teaching and fellowship, to the breaking of bread and the prayers' (2:41–42).

Ben Witherington draws on the insights of H. J. Cadbury in noticing how Luke breaks up his narrative of the early church and structures his account.[65] There are what Cadbury calls 'summary statements', which occur throughout Acts and generally mark a movement from one phase of the action to another (and to which we will refer again in a moment). And there are also 'summary passages', which are longer and tend to refer to what is happening under the surface. These only occur in the first eight chapters of Acts, and tend to describe the interior life of the fledgling church. In Acts 2:41 we have a summary statement (informing us that those welcoming the gospel message and being baptized number about three thousand), and what follows in 2:42–47 is a summary passage, describing what was happening more deeply. It has the function, in the

---

[65] Witherington 1998: 157–159.

text, of pausing and elaborating on the narrative, helping the reader get more of a grasp on the actions of God in the particular situation. In Cadbury's words: '[The summary passages] indicate the material is *typical*, that the action was *continued*, that the effect was *general*.'[66] We can say then that these verses are significant, in Luke's mind, and are intended to give us a view of the deep currents of theology and practice in the very first days of the post-Pentecost church. This is not just a snapshot; it is, rather, a description of the general state of affairs, viewed at a particular moment.

The four things Luke uses to describe the life of the early church are the teaching of the apostles, the fellowship, the breaking of bread and the prayers. Witherington cites German theologian R. Pesch to the effect that this is, in reality, a description of only two things: the apostolic teaching and the fellowship (as expressed in breaking of bread and prayer).[67] We will follow that analysis here.

1 Church and teaching

The first mark of the church is a devotion (or being 'constant in their attention') to the teaching of the apostles. This is something we see throughout Acts:

- '[Peter and John] were teaching the people and proclaiming that in Jesus there is resurrection of the dead' (4:2).
- 'We cannot keep from speaking about what we have seen and heard' (4:20).
- 'They entered the temple at daybreak and went on with their teaching' (5:21).
- 'You have filled Jerusalem with your teaching' (5:28).
- 'And every day in the temple and at home they did not cease to teach and proclaim Jesus as the Messiah' (5:42).
- When it comes to the dispute in the emerging church between the Hellenists and the Hebrews, the people listen to the apostles with their solution to the crisis (6:1–7).

---

66 Ibid. 158, quoting Cadbury 1920–33: 401–402.
67 Ibid. 160, citing Pesch 1986: 130.

- As the debate about the inclusion of the Gentiles begins, it is Peter's apostolic teaching which holds sway (11:1–18).
- At the Council of Jerusalem, it is the letter from the apostles and elders which is decisive (15:30–35).
- We have a vignette in Troas, where Paul teaches the believers late into the night (20:7–12).
- Paul charges the elders of the church in Ephesus about their duties (20:17–35).

Apostolic teaching is a constant and central practice of the growing and expanding church throughout Acts. This is true for its evangelism, building on the apostolic witness to Jesus and his resurrection, and in the teaching of the church on how to proceed.

Cadbury's noting of the 'summary statements' of Acts is very instructive in this regard. They tend to 'indicate growth, movement, and development as repeated themes in the narrative in Acts'.[68] Witherington helpfully summarizes them:

1. 6:7 – Word of God increased, Jerusalem disciples multiplied;
2. 9:31 – Church throughout Galilee and Judea built up and multiplied in (by) Holy Spirit;
3. 12:24 – Word of God grew and multiplied, involving Paul and Barnabas;
4. 16:5 – Churches strengthened in faith and increased in numbers – Paul and Timothy going through Asia (Minor);
5. 19:20 – Paul in Asia (Minor) and Ephesus in particular – all the residents of Asia hear (v. 10); word of God prevailed mightily.[69]

Note the prominence of the word of God, in particular through the preaching of Peter and Paul. It is interesting how the summaries referring to the word are paralleled by those referencing the Holy Spirit. In Luke's mind, apostolic preaching and the work of the Spirit go hand in hand. Let's note, as well, the repeated vocabulary of multiplication (three times)

---

[68] Witherington 1998: 74.
[69] Ibid.

and increase. This reminds us of the supernatural abundance of the word we saw in the parable of the sower. It is the word of God, used by the Spirit of God, which is the engine of the growth of the church.

It is also the word of God which is the engine for the stability, strength and sustainability of the young churches. The apostles may be the primary preachers in Acts, but they are not alone. The leaders of the Antioch church, for instance, are described as 'prophets and teachers' (13:1), and following the Council of Jerusalem, when Paul and Barnabas remain in Antioch, 'there, with many others, they taught and proclaimed the word of the Lord' (15:35). Throughout Acts, the apostles are appointing leaders, among whose responsibilities is that of preaching and teaching the word:

- In Samaria, Philip is not alone in 'proclaiming the word' (8:4–5), and many accept the word of God (8:14), such that the apostles send Peter and John down to see what has been happening (8:14–24).
- The same dynamic is at play in Antioch when those scattered by persecution begin to speak the word, proclaiming the Lord Jesus to Greeks as well as Jews (11:19–20). When many turn to the Lord, Barnabas is sent to investigate, and is glad when he sees the grace of God (11:23). His response is not to leave them to it, but to go and find Saul in Tarsus, and they spend 'an entire year' teaching 'a great many people' (11:26).
- On the missionary journey through Derbe, Lystra, Iconium and Antioch, Paul and Barnabas return to strengthen the disciples and encourage them 'to continue in the faith' by teaching them about the place of persecution in the Christian life, before appointing 'elders for them in each church' (14:21–23).
- To take home the message from the Council of Jerusalem, 'Judas and Silas, who were themselves prophets, said much to encourage and strengthen the believers' (15:32).
- We see Paul sending 'his helpers, Timothy and Erastus, to Macedonia' (19:22).
- Very striking is Paul's farewell discourse to the Ephesian elders. He rehearses to them his own evangelistic and itinerant teaching ministry ('proclaiming the message to you and teaching you publicly

and from house to house' [20:20]), and encourages them to watch out for those who would 'come distorting the truth' (20:30). He commends them 'to God and to the message of his grace' (20:32).

Throughout Acts, we see an apostolic concern to preserve the truth of God's word, and to ensure that it is this message which prevails and continues, bringing encouragement and strength to the new believers.

The application to church plants is an obvious one, but no less powerful for that: the preaching of the apostolic gospel and teaching must be central to the strategy and practices of the church plant. This is not an argument for a particular theology of preaching, nor for a preferred strand of church tradition, but it is a reflection on the fact that, in Acts, new churches were planted through a bold and clear proclamation of Jesus and his resurrection, and they multiplied and increased and stayed healthy and spiritually vital through a tenacious submission to the apostles' teaching at every turn.

It could be argued that there can be fewer things more needed in my own context than a recovery of confidence in the gospel, and the conviction that when we preach about Jesus there is spiritual power to see lives changed and the multiplying of growth and congregations and churches.

When church plants get under way, there is usually an immense amount that needs doing, and it may well be that it is the senior planter who is both the main preacher and the leader of the church plant. This person and his or her core team are likely to be extremely busy, and may be overstretched, with the demands of the urgent constantly filling their in-trays. Preaching, both evangelistic and pastoral, may not feel quite so urgent, but it may well be more important in the long run. As a generalization, church plants that take their preaching seriously – biblical, accessible, clear, applied – are the ones that flourish, and those that, whether by accident or design, downplay it or give it less attention tend to struggle.

Two other facets around preaching. First of all, we could learn from the apostolic practice of training up preachers. It is striking the extent to which Paul shares the work with others. On the first missionary journeys, it is Barnabas and Silas and Timothy who share this with him, but, as time goes on, so the number of Paul's co-workers increases dramatically. The sheer number of these people is noteworthy: E. E. Ellis counts 'some one hundred individuals',[70] of whom Eckhard Schnabel identifies thirty-eight as co-workers.[71] Much of their work, in encouraging and strengthening the young churches, would have been in teaching and preaching, and in training others to take on and multiply this work. Typically, successful church plants will have a constant stream of emerging and developing leaders, and will be giving them opportunities to preach. This may not be in a main service, at least to start with, but there are plenty of other potential arenas in which they could learn their craft.

The second reflection is the apostolic emphasis on out-and-out evangelistic preaching. The majority of the speeches in Acts are addressed to those who are not Christians. In our Acts 2 passage, it is significant that verse 42 is set in the broader context of verse 47, where we read that 'day by day the Lord added to their number those who were being saved' (which picks up on the reference to Joel's prophecy – 'Then everyone who calls on the name of the Lord shall be saved' [2:21] – in Peter's sermon, and his allusion to 'everyone whom the Lord our God calls to him', just a few verses previously [2:39]). It may well be that the early house churches of Acts were made up of both believers and those who were not yet believers. It is striking how much of an emphasis is laid on those who are not Christians, giving a challenge and an invitation to belief.

Tim Keller was a church planter in New York City, where he planted Redeemer Presbyterian Church in the late 1980s. He is a very effective preacher, especially in the way he engages with the thoughts, doubts and world views of those who are not Christians. He reckons to be preaching to both Christians and non-believers at the same time in the same sermon. He thinks it is good for Christians to be hearing the gospel regularly, both to strengthen their faith and to inspire them to invite friends to church who are not Christians. And he is also assuming that not everyone present will be a Christian. Indeed, as word got round that this preacher understood and took seriously the reasons that many today do not believe, more and more people who were not Christians started to attend, and many of them did end up coming to faith. Keller aims to have a good proportion of every sermon directly addressing a concern which someone who was not a Christian would have, as it might arise from the biblical passage on

70 Ellis 1993: 183.
71 Schnabel 2008: 249.

which he would be preaching. His experience is that by preaching to both Christians and those who are not Christians every time, both groups have benefited. He writes:

> I learned these lessons ... Don't just preach to your congregation for spiritual growth, assuming that everyone in attendance is a Christian; and don't just preach the gospel evangelistically, thinking that Christians cannot grow from it. Evangelize as you edify, and edify as you evangelize.[72]

2 Church and 'fellowship'

So, the first mark of how the earliest Christians started church was a devotion to the teaching of the apostles. The second is a fellowship, expressed in 'the breaking of bread and the prayers' (2:42). In her commentary on Acts, Beverly Roberts Gaventa draws out the significance of the formation of Christian community: 'Luke displays a group of people connected to one another theologically, liturgically and socially, and those connections all derive from God's intervention.'[73]

That is a good summary of what is going on in terms of the fellowship of 2:42, and we will follow Gaventa's structure as we consider it.

'Fellowship' is in some ways a neutral word, meaning 'a participation or sharing in common of something with someone else'.[74] It is a general term which needs to be delineated further – fellowship in what? Elsewhere in the New Testament it is used to describe a spiritual communion (for instance, 'a sharing in the body of Christ' [1 Cor. 10:16]) and an economic partnership (for instance, it is Paul's word for the collection he is taking up for the Jerusalem church [2 Cor. 8:4; 9:13]), but here it is a sharing in the breaking of bread and in prayer. Verses 44–45 will show that there was a sharing of possessions too in this fellowship, and verse 46 the taking of meals together.

Before it is any of those things, however, it is a theological sharing (to take Gaventa's vocabulary). The church is the action of God and a shared reflection on that activity. It would be wrong to define it in terms of the

---

[72] Keller 2012: 79.
[73] Gaventa 2003: 41.
[74] Witherington 1998: 160.

sharing of possessions and meals before we can see it clearly in relation to God who calls it into being.

These early chapters of Acts make it clear that the fledgling church is built on two main actions of God: the resurrection of Jesus from the dead and the outpouring of the Holy Spirit. The emphasis on the resurrection is particularly striking in Peter's sermons:

- 'This Jesus God raised up, and of that all of us are witnesses' (2:32);
- 'You killed the Author of life, whom God raised from the dead' (3:15);
- 'Jesus Christ of Nazareth, whom you crucified, whom God raised from the dead' (4:10).

The emphasis is on the action of God; the crucifixion was a human act of wickedness, in this perspective, but the resurrection was a supreme act of power and vindication from God himself. Jesus is not to be thought of as the passive victim of human power, but rather the exalted (2:33) and glorified (3:13) one, who now pours out the promised Holy Spirit from the Father (2:33), bringing life instead of death (3:15), health and strength instead of sickness and lameness (3:16; 4:9–10). There is salvation (4:12), a restoration of health and vigour to a broken and ailing creation. Peter preaches that baptism in the name of Jesus means the forgiveness of sins and receiving the gift of the Holy Spirit (2:38).

It is the Holy Spirit being poured out – what 'you both see and hear' (2:33) – which is the starting gun for the witnessing life of the church, as prophesied by Jesus (1:8). It is the demonstration of the new age of the Spirit which attracts the crowd, and which Peter in his Pentecost sermon must explain in terms of the exaltation of Jesus. It is notable how he links together the resurrection and exaltation of Jesus with the gift of the Spirit. It is these two things together which constitute the theological foundation of the life of the Jesus community.

Beverly Roberts Gaventa shows just how extensively the church must be viewed in the light of the activity of God – Father, Son and Holy Spirit – in the Acts of the Apostles:

The primary assertion to make about the church in Acts [is] . . . that the church exists as evidence of God's plan and God's activity in the world. The church draws its existence from God's intervention, rather than its own initiative.[75]

When we think in terms of the narrative of the beginning of Acts, Peter's sermon draws the church into the ambit of nothing less than the power of the resurrection and the gift of the Spirit. Theologically, we are to think of the church right alongside the raising of Jesus from the dead and the outpouring of his presence in the Spirit. What binds the people of God together in this new age is the living presence of Jesus, who has conquered death and is powerfully alive and present in their midst.

This extends what we have seen throughout Scripture, that it is God who calls his people into existence and privileges them with relationship with himself, tasking them with the proclamation and demonstration of his blessing to the ends of the earth. But here things move into a different register as well. The resurrection and exaltation of Jesus changes everything, and he is made present in the midst of the renewed Israel by the Holy Spirit. God is present in new and striking ways. This is the church.

This theological fellowship is as true of church plants as it is of all churches. They exist by virtue of the will and action of God, and they are strikingly constituted and animated and activated by the presence of the risen Jesus in the Holy Spirit. This means that we must treat church plants, as we must all churches, with reverence and not a little awe, notwithstanding how unprepossessing they might sometimes appear. Can you hear this note in Paul's comments in 1 Corinthians 3? 'Do you not know that you are God's temple and that God's Spirit dwells in you? If anyone destroys God's temple, God will destroy that person. For God's temple is holy, and you are that temple' (3:16–17).

And we might also draw out how there is a mysterious connection between the action of God in both the gospel and himself and the formation of the church. When we are talking of God exalting his Son, and then the Son receiving the Spirit from the Father and pouring the Spirit out into the church and the world, are we not looking into the heart of the Trinity? And when we hear Peter preaching of the crucifixion and

---

75 Gaventa 2003: 39.

resurrection of Jesus, the outpouring of the Spirit and the formation of the church, are we not thinking of the gospel message? We must not think that God's action is somehow circumscribed around the events of the first Easter, and then the church emerged, stumbling, as human beings fumbled after some alternative society on their own. There is a theological linkage between Jesus, the Spirit and the church. The church, for all its weaknesses, frailties, oddities and sins (and we know all about those), is nonetheless a divine society. Theologically, we are bound together with this strange and awesome sense that we have been brought together by God as part of the gospel for the world.

How, then, is the church a group of people bound together liturgically (to continue with Gaventa's helpful lexicon)? Our own tradition might not make a great deal of more formal liturgies, so this language may not come naturally to us. Perhaps all the more, then, we should notice that a core element of the fellowship of the early church was a devotion to 'the breaking of bread and the prayers' (2:42).

Luke amplifies this a little in verse 46: 'Day by day . . . they spent much time together in the temple, [and] they broke bread at home'. 'The prayers' of verse 42 are the prayers recited in the temple, and the early Christians seemingly spent a lot of time there. What we have, then, is a twin focus for prayer – the more liturgical and formal and large-scale activity in the temple, and, alongside that, smaller, more informal prayers offered by the believers in one another's homes.

We will think together later in this book about the breaking of bread, so may we focus now on the aspect of fellowship in prayer. It was praying which was a key element of how the early church thought of itself, as much in terms of its identity as its activity. What was the church? The church was a group of people in which prayer happened.

It is evident that, at this stage of its history, the church saw itself as part and parcel of Judaism, and saw no contradiction between temple worship and the following of Jesus. The believers may not have taken part in the sacrifices any more, but they seemed to have gone to the temple to pray (e.g. 3:1). They favoured meeting in Solomon's Portico (5:12), and they went to witness as well as to pray (e.g. 5:42). This pattern was not to last long, of course, as the divide between the early church and Judaism widened and hardened.

The first significance of this devotion to prayer is not just that prayer happened, but *how* prayer happened. Prayer is a central aspect of the culture of church, of how things are done. The liturgical life of our church plants is going to be a key way in which people will identify themselves as part of these missionary communities.

'Liturgy' sounds formal, belonging to the more traditional parts of God's church, but of course every church and every church plant has its own liturgies. Every church tends to have repeated patterns of worship, even the most informal. Set phrases recur. The number of songs at the beginning of the service will be surprisingly similar, the children will go out to their groups at the same point each time, the same words and scriptures will be used for taking the collection or for celebrating the Lord's Supper, Bible readings will be of a similar length and number, sermons of the same length each week, and there will be similar turns of phrase to open and close services, and so on. However much we value spontaneity and creativity, these things work best (and maybe necessarily) within agreed and accepted norms of pattern. In this sense, we are all liturgical beings. It may help to identify the liturgy of our church plant and make plans to work with, not against, the grain.

How we pray together is one of the core tasks for church plants to think through, not least if they are a revitalization project, blending together two or more spiritualities. For those of us who are Anglicans, it is often noted that, in an age of confessional strife, the Church of England was founded on a practice of 'common prayer'. In the current scene, churches are often known and valued for their own particular approach to worship, be that the Book of Common Prayer, contemporary worship, contemplative prayer, or whatever. Particularly when it comes to international Christian movements, it is the style of worship and prayer which serves to define them, such as Worship Central, Hillsong, Iona or Taizé. Equally, when it comes to establishing a church-plant culture, competing approaches to prayer can be destabilizing and disruptive to the unity of the church plant. Wise and clear leadership is required, not least because assumptions about the style, culture and practice of prayer are often unexamined.

A second feature of the life of prayer of the Acts 2 church is the variety implied in the contrast between the temple prayers and the informal prayer in homes. It seems that the early church valued both formality and scale on the one hand (in the temple), and informality and intimacy on the other hand (in homes). The fellowship of our church plants might benefit from both approaches as well. As John Stott comments: 'There is no need to polarize between the structured and the unstructured, the traditional and the spontaneous. The church needs both.'[76]

It might be a bit of an exegetical stretch, but maybe there is something here, as well, about relating new movements to old. This is a tension often encountered by church plants as they tussle with their denominations and the structures of inherited church. There can be misunderstanding on both sides, and, regrettably, there can sometimes be difficulty. Stott comments wisely on this verse:

> [The early Christians] did not immediately abandon what might be called the institutional church ... Perhaps we, who get understandably impatient with the inherited structures of the church, can learn a lesson from them. For myself, I believe that the Holy Spirit's way with the institutional church, which we long to see reformed according to the gospel, is more the way of patient reform than of impatient rejection.[77]

Efforts to build cooperative and transparent relationships between church plants and their wider denominational structures can lead to mutual flourishing and enriching, and serve to advance the kingdom of God more widely. When we think in terms of 'fellowship' in this Acts 2 sense, it takes these relationships to another level, up from damage limitation to something creative and fruitful.

The third element of Gaventa's understanding of the connections in the early church, the 'fellowship' of verse 42, is social. It is the being together of the church which is such an important aspect of its life.

This comes out in the language. 'Fellowship' is the English translation of the Greek *koinōnia*, which comes from the word *koinē*, meaning 'common'. This finds concrete expression in verse 44, where we read that the Christians 'had all things in common'. In addition, there is a recurring

---

[76] Stott 1990: 85.
[77] Ibid.

phrase which does not come out in our English translations. The disciples were *epi to auto* in verses 44 and 47. The NRSV translates verse 44 as 'All who believed were *together*', and verse 47 as 'added to their *number*' (my emphasis). Witherington writes:

> The phrase *epi to auto* is an important one ... The intent of using the phrase is to say something about the unity or togetherness of the early Christians, even if its precise translation may be debated. Usually it seems to mean something like 'together,' or in v.47 'in the community,' or 'with one accord' or 'in assembly.' It refers to a gathered group in harmony with one another.[78]

Luke Timothy Johnson notes that *epi to auto* in the Greek translation of the Hebrew Old Testament is 'practically a technical term for "community"'.[79] The narrative emphasizes the believers' togetherness as well: 'Day by day ... they spent much time together' (2:46), and they are eating, praying and praising together (2:46–47).

This togetherness of life finds particular expression economically: 'All who believed were together and had all things in common; they would sell their possessions and goods and distribute the proceeds to all, as any had need' (2:44–45).

There are further details in chapter 4:

> There was not a needy person among them, for as many as owned lands or houses sold them and brought the proceeds of what was sold. They laid it at the apostles' feet, and it was distributed to each as any had need.
> (Acts 4:34–35)

All the commentators are united in explaining that this did not mean the abolition of private property, not least because the disciples still had homes in which to meet, and because of the later admonitory example of Ananias and Sapphira, whose sin against the Holy Spirit was not that they

---

[78] Witherington 1998: 161.
[79] Johnson 1992: 60.

kept back money but that they lied to God about it (5:1–11). It is doubtful if this practice survived much beyond the early days of the church. Nonetheless, it is clear that there was a radical making available of private resources to meet the needs of others within the community. The tenses of the verbs 'suggests this was not a onetime occurrence but rather a recurrent past practice, presumably undertaken whenever need arose'.[80] When the theme returns in chapter 4, it is linked to spiritual power: 'With great power the apostles gave their testimony to the resurrection of the Lord Jesus, and great grace was upon them all' (4:33), and it is followed by two stories related to economic sharing, one positive with the example of Barnabas, who will play a significant role in the rest of the book (4:36–37), and the other negative, with Ananias and Sapphira (5:1–11). Clearly, this was a major emphasis of the early church. As John Stott writes: 'we must not evade the challenge of these verses.'[81] The meeting of need, especially among the poor, was a key element of what fellowship meant when the church was in the process of being established.

There is a further aspect of this economic sharing. Contemporary literature and philosophy viewed this sharing of goods and property and being 'of one heart and soul' (4:32) as a 'foundation story',[82] the establishing of a utopian vision of what ideal society should look like. Both Johnson and Gaventa have long lists from writers such as Plato, Ovid, Aristotle, Philo, Seneca and Strabo to that effect.[83] Johnson explains the impact such statements would have had, particularly in the Hellenized world:

> [By writing in this way], Luke communicated to his readers in vivid fashion that the gift of the Spirit brought about a community which realized the highest aspirations of human longing: unity, peace, joy, and the praise of God.[84]

This is not to suggest (as Johnson himself says) that this description of the economic aspects of fellowship is a purely literary device, but it does put

---

80 Witherington 1998: 162.
81 Stott 1990: 84.
82 Johnson 1992: 62.
83 Ibid.; Gaventa 2003: 81.
84 Johnson 1992: 62.

it in the broader context of how the early church aimed to come across to the society and various cultures of its day.[85]

So, looking back on fellowship as a whole, what we have is an intertwined description of what this meant to those first Christians – a mutual, common life that was based in prayer and practical sharing, all coming out of an experience of the activity of God in their midst. It is a powerful and wonderful picture.

Lesslie Newbigin wrote: 'It is surely a fact of inexhaustible significance that what our Lord left behind Him was not a book, nor a creed, not a system of thought, nor a rule of life, but a visible community.'[86]

When it comes to a robust theology for church planting, what is central is the existence of a real, literal, physical community that embodies the message and presence of Jesus. There is an inextricable link between church and gospel, kingdom and community. The one explains the other, and together they communicate the good news of God in Jesus Christ as it is set forth in the power of the Holy Spirit. Rowan Williams speaks to this in his book on Benedictine life and ministry, here in specific regard to mission:

> The idea that apostolic witness is in itself a means of mission suggests that we misunderstand mission if we think it is a matter of persuading people to accept certain *ideas*. The *truth* of any ideas or doctrines is something that becomes apparent in the light of the sort of *life* that those ideas make possible.[87]

This is what we should expect in the light of the words of Jesus: 'By this everyone will know that you are my disciples, if you have love for one another' (John 13:35). It is more than an emotional relationality, though: it is a fellowship, a connection, which incorporates the interweaving of the presence and power of God within the patterns and practices of profound human relating. What is experienced is the risen life of Jesus, in and through a life of shared prayer and practical sharing,

---

[85] It is worth noting later examples of sharing economically – the principle doesn't go away, even if the form of it in Jerusalem changes when the gospel takes root elsewhere. See Walton 2008: 109–110 on this point.

[86] Newbigin 1953: 27.

[87] Williams 2020: 46.

within the context of apostolic teaching. At their best, churches and church plants may seem to experience the kind of life that every human polity and society aspires to, but they do so only upon the basis of the resurrection of Jesus and the life-giving, healing power of the Holy Spirit.

We must not neglect the human dimensions of our church plants, their cultures and patterns of social interaction. These are the vehicles that carry the sense of the divine for many people. The love and joy, the healthy relating, the good ways in which leaders relate to one another and to everyone in our church plants – these are striking to many people when they first come. Launching new communities gives great opportunity for building in capacity and opportunity for being together on this journey, for creating a culture that is based on prayer and profound sharing, and it really does carry extraordinary power, which is not incidental to the gospel that makes it all possible.

Many church plants are highly creative with regard to the social aspects of their life together. I can think of gyms, football and netball sessions, running clubs, nail bars, pampering sessions, as well as a lot of curry, beer and quiz nights. Many, too, give a priority to prayer, working hard to overcome the challenges of busy timetables and difficult journeys by meeting at more convenient times, using technology, setting up smaller groups for prayer. Prayer cultures fit well, too, with resources and modelling from the leadership, making for a pattern and practice that is replicated and established throughout the church.

Acts 2 (and the comparable summary passage at the end of ch. 4) is an inspiring look into the interior life of the church as it begins its Spirit-filled life. This is how the early Christians thought Jesus wanted them to be and do church – to base their life on the presence of Jesus through his resurrection and the gift of the Holy Spirit, and to devote themselves to the apostolic teaching and to a fellowship built on creative prayer and profound mutual sharing. We should beware of treating these passages as 'cookie cutter' church, as models which we just have to transfer wholesale into our own situations. The dynamism of the Spirit who constitutes and guides the life of the church in Jesus continues, and will lead to different applications of these principles in different times and contexts.

The church in Antioch

The second church to look at is that in Syrian Antioch, which we read about in Acts 11:19–30; 13:1–3 and 15:30–35. This church assumes more and more significance, not least because it is so closely tied to the inclusion of Gentiles within the church and because it acts as the missionary base for Paul and Barnabas (14:26–28). Some have seen a sense of judgment on the Jerusalem church in the increased prevalence of the Antioch church, but that seems to be overreading the case, especially when we consider the express links between the two churches, such as those provided by Agabus and his fellow prophets who come to Antioch from Jerusalem (11:27), and the collection from the Antioch church for those in need in Judea due to the famine (11:29–30; 12:25). What does seem to be the case, though, is a new emphasis on mission and church planting, and it is this which will provide us with the lens through which to view this amazing early church.

The importance of cities

Antioch itself was a significant city, probably the third city in the ancient world after Rome and Alexandria, with a population in the region of 250,000 people. It had a substantial Jewish population within a pluralistic culture, and was a centre for trade not only around the Mediterranean but also out east, being known as 'the Queen of the East', with the major city of Edessa being its access into the eastern world. The church in Antioch was to be a missionary base not only to the west, as we read in Acts, but also to the east, especially through Edessa.[88]

An interesting point is how Luke describes the history, and even, to an extent, the chronology, of the Antioch story in ethnic and geographical terms. We first read of the Antioch church like this:

Now those who were scattered because of the persecution that took place over Stephen travelled as far as Phoenicia, Cyprus, and Antioch, and they spoke the word to no one except Jews. But among them were some men of Cyprus and Cyrene who, on coming to Antioch, spoke to the Hellenists also, proclaiming the Lord Jesus. The hand

---

[88] Witherington 1998: 366.

of the Lord was with them, and a great number became believers and turned to the Lord.
(Acts 11:19–21)

The opening verse parallels the language of 8:1: 'That day a severe persecution began against the church in Jerusalem, and all except the apostles were scattered throughout the countryside of Judea and Samaria.' It seems as though the scatterings of chapters 8 and 11 are aspects of the same movement. A lot has happened theologically in the intervening chapters – the conversion of Saul, Peter's ministry in Palestine, and the momentous events surrounding Cornelius and the acceptance of the Gentiles into the church – but Luke positions his story not in terms of time but instead by reference to different people groups responding to the word of the Lord. This theology is fleshed out ethnographically. Just as Jesus laid out the agenda of Acts as a geographical movement starting in Jerusalem, moving to Judea and Samaria, and from there to the ends of the earth (1:8), so the Spirit is leading the church to embrace the Gentiles. The Cornelius narrative is paralleled by the activity of the unnamed missionaries of chapter 11, who speak to the Hellenists about Jesus. Luke is showing us a movement that is led by God, and not the strategy of any one group of people in the church.

Cities occupy a prominent place in this movement of God. We must not exaggerate this, as regions are also mentioned (such as Judea and Samaria), but urban centres feature prominently in Acts. Shenk and Stutzman put it like this:

The story of the book of Acts is the story of urban evangelism. The church moved from city to city ... A kaleidoscope of peoples comprised these cities. No wonder Jesus commissioned his disciples to begin in the city. They took his command seriously.[89]

John Stott writes:

It seems to have been Paul's deliberate policy to move purposefully from one strategic city-centre to the next. What drew him to the

---

[89] Shenk and Stutzman 1998: 141.

cities was probably that they contained the Jewish synagogues, the larger populations and the influential leaders.[90]

Tim Keller, drawing on the work of Wayne Meeks and Harvey Conn, summarizes why urban ministry was so effective in the early church:

1. Cultural cruciality. In the village, someone might win its one or two lawyers to Christ. However, if you want to win the legal profession, which will influence all lawyers, you must go to the city, where you will find the law schools and the law journal publishers – the key institutions of influence in that profession.

2. Global cruciality. In the village, someone can win over the single people group living there, since rural areas are often sociologically homogenous. But if you share the gospel in the city, you can reach dozens of different national and ethnic groups . . .

3. Personal cruciality. In the village, people live in a culture that tends to resist change and is more conservative and traditional. However, because of the diversity and mobility of cities, urbanites are more open to new ideas – such as the gospel![91]

He goes on to lay out the call of the contemporary city for church planters today. The rate of urbanization and the exponential growth of today's world cities means that this is where the vast majority of the world's population now live and will do so even more in the years ahead. Alongside that, 'cities are cauldrons of cultural reengineering and reinvention', and 'every major city is now a portal for reaching the nations of the world'. City evangelism gives special opportunities to reach the younger generation, the 'cultural elites', the accessible 'unreached' people groups and the poor.[92]

These observations raise profound questions for church planters. This is not an argument for neglecting rural or suburban environments or county towns, still less is it an assertion of the superiority of cities over other places and their peoples, but it is a thought-provoking strategic question. If Antioch was the first urban church outside Jerusalem, it

---

[90] Stott 1990: 293.
[91] Keller 2012: 148.
[92] Ibid. ch. 13.

seemed to set a pattern for the future of Paul's evangelization and church planting. Although he did indeed reach out to rural environments and he did visit less significant towns and cities, he tended to do so from bases that were urban, even metropolitan. He favoured centres such as Ephesus, Corinth, Athens and Rome, from which he could reach whole regions. We will consider Paul's church-planting strategy in more detail when we look at his missionary journeys, but we can discern its emphases in outline at this stage. In Acts 19 we read how he lectured for two years each day in the hall of Tyrannus in Ephesus, and that by this means 'all the residents of Asia . . . heard the word of the Lord' (19:10). The longer he spent in missionary journeys and church planting, the more he seems to have adopted this approach. Church planters need to think strategically and to follow the leading of the Lord. The location of church plants is a key element of how to reach neighbourhoods, cities, regions, networks, cultures and countries. It is likely that cities are to play a central role in this progress of the gospel.

It seems unlikely to be a coincidence that Antioch was, on the one hand, so culturally pluralistic, such a significant centre and so geographically and culturally strategic, and, on the other hand, became the missionary engine for Paul's work in Acts. There is much for us to learn about how church plants position themselves as missionary congregations as we look at this amazing early church, and how ethnography is a key skill and discipline for church planters.

We shall frame our examination of the Antioch church by looking at the activities of the people who comprised it.[93]

Pioneers

We note, first of all, that there were *pioneers* in the Antioch church. Whereas the majority of those scattered by the persecution following the death of Stephen 'spoke the word to no one except Jews', those from Cyprus and Cyrene 'spoke to the Hellenists also, proclaiming the Lord Jesus' (11:19–20). It is not as if those others were not evangelizing; they were speaking the word. These others, though, saw something extra and

---

[93] I am grateful to Michael Green for the framework, which he sets out in his excellent commentary on Acts (Green 2009).

did something different. The TNIV translates, 'Some of them, however . . .', and it is that 'however' which spells out the difference seen in these unnamed pioneers. Who knows why they did what they did? Was it significant that they were not mainlanders, coming from the island of Cyprus or the coast of North Africa rather than from around Jerusalem? Whatever it was, they had the vision, the theological creativity and the missionary courage to start talking to Gentiles about Jesus. They did so in new language too. Up until this point, Acts has positioned conversion in terms of recognition – seeing that in Jesus, God had anointed and vindicated his Messiah. The logic is around seeing how Jesus has poured out the Spirit, thus putting him in the same category as YHWH. This was natural terminology and an understandable conceptuality for those who were Jews or proselytes from Judaism. Now, however, these evangelists are explicitly 'proclaiming the Lord Jesus' (11:20); they are calling non-Jews to recognize the lordship of Jesus, that to speak of Jesus is to speak of God and his authority to command worship and allegiance. This is a way of announcing the good news for Gentiles, and surely came from a fresh missionary understanding, not least an actual engagement with Gentiles and their thought worlds.[94]

There is of necessity something pioneering in all church planting. It is about reaching new people in new places in new ways with the gospel of Jesus. It has within it an inescapable 'however': 'Up until now, this has been done or we have tried this. It may well have worked with this group of people. It may well be thought of as standard or accepted practice. Nonetheless [however!], we are still not reaching *this* group of people with that way of doing things. Something has got to change, and, for the sake of those who are not at the moment hearing the good news of Jesus, we will embark on a fresh course of action. It may feel somewhat daring. It may be open to being misunderstood, but we feel the grace of God with us, and we are going to do it.'

Church plants should have an edgy quality to them, something to make church folks a little nervous. The impulse should always be pioneering, daring to take risks in order to reach people for Christ. Church-planting

---

[94] This is not to argue that the gospel message changes once Acts comes more clearly into the Gentile world. And we should note that as far back as 2:36, Jesus has been declared to be Lord by the apostles.

teams should be marked with a creativity, a willingness to experiment, to break out of how things have always been done, especially when it is apparent that these methods are not or are no longer effective in connecting with communities outside the church. This is not an excuse for recklessness or for being brash or iconoclastic, but it does reflect Paul's evangelistic heartbeat: 'I have become all things to all people, so that I might by all means save some' (1 Cor. 9:22).

Church planters hold two things in tension. One is the scale and urgency of the evangelistic task. It is not an exact figure, but anecdotally 92% of the English population are not in church on any given Sunday. If we think in terms of church decline, a sobering figure is that 'the church nationally is contracting at a rate of approximately 100,000 per five years'.[95] Even more sobering are the figures for youth and children: 'Recent research tells us that whilst young people are open to faith nearly half (48%) of [Church of England] churches have fewer than 5 under 16-year olds.'[96] These figures are not quoted to depress us (and indeed there is encouraging research showing unprecedented opportunities for evangelism in our times); rather, the likelihood is that they will galvanize the pioneering church planter.

The second aspect of the tension is that the church planter will probably have something of an idea, and maybe a very specific sense of call to a particular group of people. To adopt a general evangelistic aim is probably to ensure that we fail to gain fruitful evangelistic traction. Church plants may well minister to specific groups, perhaps children and youth and young families, students and young professionals, those living on housing estates, particular ethnicities, or whatever. We think of how Paul had a vocation to the Gentiles, Peter to the Jews (e.g. Gal. 2:7).

The pioneering church plant will hold both these factors together. There will be a sense of urgency in reaching out with the gospel of Jesus, which will likely lead to the 'however' moments of reaching out to new and specific groups.

A corollary of the pioneering imperative for church plants is the affirmation of pioneers. Churches are not always the most adventurous of

---

[95] Steve Cook, 'Promoting Growth in the Church of England', June 2018 (privately written paper).
[96] General Synod of the Church of England 2018: 3.

environments, and the conservatism of church cultures can be stifling and frustrating for the more entrepreneurial and mould-breaking types. If a church plant has an ethos dominated by pastoral care or by traditionalism or bureaucracy, chances are this will scare off the pioneers. Sadly, too often the very people the church needs to lead in bold and innovative ways feel themselves not wanted or even rejected by the culture or the powers that be. Church plants, with their commitment to pioneering outreach, will need to be intentional about setting a culture that welcomes and affirms those who think and act differently, who are prepared to take risks or who privilege those who do not yet come to church over those who already do.

Pastors

Second, alongside the pioneers there are the *pastors*, pre-eminently Barnabas. We read of his role:

> News of this came to the ears of the church in Jerusalem, and they sent Barnabas to Antioch. When he came and saw the grace of God, he rejoiced, and he exhorted them all to remain faithful to the Lord with steadfast devotion; for he was a good man, full of the Holy Spirit and faith. And a great many people were brought to the Lord. Then Barnabas went to Tarsus to look for Saul, and when he had found him, he brought him to Antioch. So it was that for an entire year they associated with the church and taught a great many people, and it was in Antioch that the disciples were first called 'Christians'.
> (Acts 11:22–26)

This is a marvellous passage about the key relationship between pioneers and pastors in church plants. It can often be a cause of friction, but it is vital for the maturing of young churches and for the maintenance of a missionary trajectory for church plants. Barnabas models for us both the attitude and the actions of a pastor on the front lines of a missionary church plant.

The potentially problematic nature of church planting can be seen from the actions of the Jerusalem church. Its leaders heard about the nameless evangelists speaking to non-Jews about Jesus and about the great numbers of people turning to the Lord. They must have been concerned about both the theology and the inclusivity of the church, and their procedures for coping with a large influx of new believers. Denominations and senior staffs often have similar concerns. Sadly, not all fledgling works of God are fortunate enough to have oversight like that of Barnabas, and it is not unheard of for the 'powers that be' to be heavy-handed in the face of what can appear new and threatening. It is not wrong to have questions and to make enquiries. The answer is to do so in the spirit of Barnabas.

Barnabas is our model for how to nurture and mature church plants. His real name was Joseph, but he was known to the early church by his nickname of 'son of encouragement' (4:36). He lives up to his name with nearly every mention in Acts. Here he endorses this fresh missionary endeavour to the Gentiles, and he seeks out Saul to be their teacher. Later, he wants to give John Mark a second chance after he had abandoned the mission at an earlier stage (15:37–38). Barnabas was clearly a man with a big heart, prepared to believe the best about people, and with a willingness to stick with them when others were raising pointed questions. Maybe the reference to him here exhorting or encouraging the new believers to remain true to the Lord is an intentional play on his nickname as a 'son of encouragement' (11:23). Here in Antioch, he sees God's grace and teaches into what God is doing. Both actions are the hallmarks of missionary pastors.

He discerns the grace of God. Luke is in no doubt that what is happening is the result of the action of God: 'the hand of the Lord was with them, and a great number became believers and turned to the Lord' (11:21). The phrase 'the hand of the Lord' occurs frequently in the Old Testament and refers to the powerful action of God, to the extent that Luke Timothy Johnson sees in it a reference to miracles.[97] At any rate, Luke sees a clear linkage between God's power and large numbers of people becoming Christians. Maybe there is a hint of a two-stage response to the gospel – a believing, and then a turning to the Lord.[98] Maybe there were questions in Jerusalem about the authenticity of what was happening:

---

[97] Johnson 1992: 207.
[98] Witherington 1998: 369.

if the theology was suspect, if the gospel was not being preached accurately, then was this anything more than emotional manipulation? And suspicions about the nature of the communities being created: was this really the church, and were these large numbers, many of whom knew nothing about the law and character of God and the history of his dealings with his people, actually undermining the purity and reality of the church? Large numbers are no proof of theological truth, and this ignoring of the covenant could actually be making the progress of the gospel harder in the long term.

Such questions have an oddly contemporary ring to church planters. Is what is happening no more than a pandering to contemporary culture? Is this really God's truth that is being preached, or just a souped-up amalgam of appeals to self-help and the building of self-esteem? Are there recognizable continuities with the historic gospel? And is this actually church, particularly if its ethos seems more rooted in contemporary culture than in historic theology? Now, these are good questions, and much hinges on their answers. Sometimes, though, the answers seem presupposed in the very act of asking the questions, and there is the real possibility of missing the grace of God. That is what Barnabas saw, and it is that which made him rejoice (11:23). Discernment is needed to look beneath the surface of culture and custom to see the action of God. Church planters and denominational or other authorities alike have the responsibility to build their assessment and encouragement of missionary work on what God is doing, and not to be caught up in peripheral things, notwithstanding their historical and cultural pedigree. This takes courage, as well as wisdom. This is what Barnabas did, and Luke tells us the reason: 'he was a good man, full of the Holy Spirit and faith' (11:24). It is only here that the adjective 'good' is used of a human being in Acts,[99] and the description of him being full of the Holy Spirit and faith is the same as that used of Stephen earlier in the book (6:5).[100] More than that, Luke links Barnabas's goodness and faith with his ability to discern the grace of God in the previous verse: it takes a certain personal quality and the faith which the Holy Spirit gives to see the work of God. Faith is needed, not

---

[99] Ibid. 371.
[100] Ibid.

just for the church planter, but also for those who are trying to work out what is actually going on in new frontier situations. The result is a further wave of conversions to Christ and people being added to the church (11:24).

Barnabas is not just content to see and rejoice in what God is doing, but he proceeds to teach into the situation: he personally exhorts the new believers to 'remain faithful to the Lord with steadfast devotion' (11:23), and he goes on a considerable journey to seek out Saul, who is back in his home town of Tarsus, some seven or eight years since we last came across him,[101] bringing him to Antioch so that they could jointly teach 'a great many people' (11:26). Luke then rounds off the section by remarking that 'it was in Antioch that the disciples were first called "Christians"' (11:26). This may not have been an entirely complimentary appellation and seems to be used in the New Testament only by those who are not believers in Jesus (here, 26:28; 1 Pet. 4:16), but nonetheless is not inappropriate, as it draws out expressly the link between being a disciple and Christ. And maybe Luke is showing the connection between Barnabas's and Saul's teaching and the wider culture seeing something of Jesus in the Christian church. It is in this verse, too, that the Antioch community is called a 'church', the first time this is used of a church outside Jerusalem. Luke is making it clear that the grace of God is forming a Jesus-community here, on the missionary front line, just as truly as happened in the more religiously orthodox environment of Jerusalem.

Let us reflect for a moment on the central part of teaching in church plants, and the role of the pastors in this activity. It needed teaching, seemingly particularly about Jesus, to establish this work as a church. It will likewise need teaching in our church plants, especially in frontline situations, to see them established as viable and transformative communities. There was something about the way in which Barnabas and Saul taught that was effective in the making of disciples. This is something they will do again shortly in Derbe, where we read that they 'proclaimed the good news to that city and . . . made many disciples' (14:21). It was clearly a habit and a strategy. What can we learn from it?

It demonstrates that teaching like this lies near the heart of what it is to be a pastor in New Testament terms. Pastoral work can be thought of

---

101 Stott 1990: 204.

as kindness, support and encouragement, especially to those in some kind of crisis or trouble. It is never less than that, but the New Testament locates the kindness in the teaching. It is by teaching that Barnabas is able to encourage the new believers, something he and Saul do together in Derbe. It is worth reflecting that, in his list of the gifts of the ascended Christ to the church in Ephesians 4, Paul links pastoring and teaching together in one office (Eph. 4:11). This defines pastoral work for us, and, by the same token, teaching work; neither is separable from the other. In our church-planting work, we teach in such a way that we are actively discipling people, and we pastor in such a way that we recognize the message of Jesus as the most effective means of seeing lives transformed. We resist equally the notion of pastoral work as being wholly therapeutic, a kind of counselling role, and also that of teaching work as belonging in the classroom rather than in the rough and tumble of real life, not least missionary life.

This last point is worth underlining. The pastoring that Barnabas brings to bear in the Antioch situation is an active collaboration with the ongoing grace of God through teaching and encouragement such that the missionary growth of the church can continue. It does not act in a contrary direction, drawing people away from the mission, but sits within missionary work. Church plants will look to join with God in the momentum of lives being changed by his grace and by the powerful working of his hand. The establishing of new believers as disciples does not take them away from the front line of church growth, but disciples them exactly where they are.

One last intriguing detail is that Barnabas and Saul, at the invitation of the Antioch church, spend 'an entire year' teaching 'a great many people' (11:26). Luke tells us this as if we will be surprised that they spent so long doing this. I suspect our surprise is that they did not spend a good deal longer doing it. We must beware of overreading the text here, and we must be conscious of how different the contemporary and ancient worlds are, but it is striking to sense what a different approach Barnabas and Saul had from much of our way of doing this today. After all, many churches have a teaching pastor role (or at least as a feature of church leadership) as a permanent position and task. Luke implies that this can be done, or at least established, with a brand-new church in a year. Does this make us re-evaluate what we think we are doing in our teaching and pastoring work? It may not be like for like, of course. Maybe Barnabas and Saul were teaching in such a way that this church could go on to teach itself without them. After all, they would shortly be off to plant other churches. Nonetheless, even with this construction, there is the implication that the teaching and discipling role is something that has a specific target of self-sufficiency within twelve months. Maybe our concept of church is too static, and we should be aiming for the kind of mobility and momentum that we see in the church at Antioch?

So, what might the work of the pastor look like for church plants? How might encouragement, discernment, teaching and discipleship come together, especially on the front lines of establishing a church and engaging in missionary work?

Purely practically, let us note that this is a team exercise and a work of setting a culture. Barnabas was sent from Jerusalem, and he, in turn, went and found Saul to share in the work. They worked with large numbers and for a limited time. And the work of mission continued and accelerated. This is not something we will want to entrust to just one person, even though he or she may take the lead on it. And part of the task will be training others – this must have been what Barnabas was doing with Saul.

It will take attitudes of heart which, at first blush, we may not think sit naturally with pastors. It will take faith and the taking of risks on people. It will be in creating spaces for God to do new things with people who do not look like a natural fit, but in whom he is working and through whom he is building a real church, however unlike other churches it may appear. It will be teaching in the midst of mission and in the register of mission, not retreating into the safety of a bounded church world. This is discipling for mission in the midst of mission. This is demanding, brave work for both mind and heart; small wonder it needs women and men full of the Holy Spirit.

The time-bound nature of Barnabas's and Saul's engagement with the Antioch church leads me to think that they had a sense of precisely what needed doing, a feeling for how to go about it, and that they knew when their work was done. In our terms, they may well have had a kind of catechetical framework or programme in mind. They needed these converts to learn about Christ, in particular, and what it looked like to be his followers, such that others could begin to recognize this pattern lived out in the streets of their city – hence the description 'Christians'. This discipling had faith and knowledge elements, habits of the heart, but also a public and corporate face.

Prophets

And, third, alongside the pioneers and pastors, there were the *prophets* in Antioch. When we look at the leadership of this remarkable church in Acts 13:1–3, we will see that there were prophets among them, but in our first meeting with the church we find them interacting with prophets from Jerusalem. We read:

> At that time prophets came down from Jerusalem to Antioch. One of them named Agabus stood up and predicted by the Spirit that there would be a severe famine over all the world; and this took place during the reign of Claudius. The disciples determined that according to their ability, each would send relief to the believers living in Judea; this they did, sending it to the elders by Barnabas and Saul.
> (Acts 11:27–30)

This prophetic word alerts the church to a forthcoming need, to which it responds in action and with generosity.

There is difference of understanding in the contemporary church regarding what the gift of prophecy is for today, if it exists at all. However we understand this gift, then, there are corollaries for what we might look for in our church plants today.

The first is that a wider perspective than the current situation of the church plant is a crucial task of leadership and decision-making. It is significant that Agabus and his fellow prophets came down from Jerusalem, especially as there were prophets in the Antioch church already. This word from God came from *outside* the Antiochene church community. It came from the 'mother church'. It must have been a reminder to the Antioch Christians that they were part of something bigger, a movement, a family of churches. It led to an economic sharing, a meeting of needs. The famine did not appear to be affecting Antioch, at least to the same extent that it would affect Jerusalem. This was not an excuse to do nothing, but rather an invitation to share in the relief of need for their sisters and brothers in Jerusalem. It was also something, at the time of the prophecy, that lay in the future; it was a call to plan ahead, to set out a course of action that lay beyond the immediate circumstances and demands of the Antioch church.

The demands of life in church plants, especially in the first year, are intense and can be all-consuming. It can take something with the force of revelation to get us to lift our eyes to the needs of others beyond us and in the future. The wise church-plant leader will intentionally make space for voices that lie beyond his or her own particular church and mission front line. That may come through intentional belonging to a church-planting movement or through friendships with other church-plant leaders. It may mean deliberately seeking out voices beyond our church, listening to podcasts or sermons from other churches, or attending webinars or conferences. It may mean paying attention to those with skill and expertise at reading cultures and societal change. Whatever it means for us, it is a cultivating and nurturing of those prophetic voices that can alert us to changes and needs of which we would be otherwise unaware.

The prophetic is often the avenue down which we walk into God's future. Scholars differ over what Agabus's prophecy denoted, but there seems clear evidence to my mind that bad harvests in Egypt during Claudius's reign meant that grain prices rocketed and left the urban poor of Jerusalem, in particular, in a very grave situation.[102] Again, scholars argue about how these events link in with what we know of Paul's life and ministry outside Acts, but it seems highly likely to me that they led to what Paul describes in Galatians 2:1–10.[103] This visit was profound and epochal, setting out Paul's relationship with the Jerusalem church and the other apostles, but also setting in train some of the arguments and disputes that would lead to the Council of Jerusalem in Acts 15. Prophecy is powerful. When people hear and respond to prophecy, it can have the effect of leading them further than they ever thought they would go. It is a crucial aspect of the developing life of the church, striking not just to its programmes but also to its values and most basic ethos.

---

[102] See Witherington (1998: 372–373) for a useful summary of these arguments.
[103] See ibid. 372; Stott 1990: 206.

The second corollary is inherent in the first, in that God speaks in order to lead to action. There were results from Agabus's prophecy in the generous response of the Antioch church. There may have been certain leadership decisions – that the church would respond and that they would send their gift via Barnabas and Saul – but each person 'according to their ability' gave to the churches in Judea. The whole church had ownership of what was to be done and what every member's individual part would be in it. That sounds like good leadership – the setting of a direction, but allowing for freedom of individual response within that.

The prophetic dimension of church-plant life needs attention and discernment. The demands of pioneering and pastoring are insistent and clamour for involvement. The prophetic can invite a different dynamic, an ability to look beyond the immediate and the local and the urgent. This must have involved prayer, reflection, a turning away from the noise of what was in front of them. For church plants, it takes discipline to create space for the prophetic, to hear and formulate a response to the word of the Lord. Sometimes prophetic words come in unusual guises; we have only to think of Agabus's other prophecy in Acts when he binds himself with Paul's belt to show what would happen to him in Jerusalem (21:11). It is easy to dismiss such things as theatrical or coming from unstable people, but it may, nonetheless, be authentic prophecy. Having ways of encouraging and sifting the prophetic, all from a position of a willingness to act definitely in response, is a central plank of being a church plant moving in mission with God.

Leadership

As we read on into Acts chapter 13 about the church in Antioch, a central feature emerges: that of the nature of the leadership of this church. It is startlingly unlike the leadership structures of many of our contemporary churches, and there is much to reflect on for church plants.

In three brief verses, Luke gives us a picture into the leadership of the church:

Now in the church at Antioch there were prophets and teachers: Barnabas, Simeon who was called Niger, Lucius of Cyrene, Manaen a member of the court of Herod the ruler, and Saul. While they

were worshipping the Lord and fasting, the Holy Spirit said, 'Set apart for me Barnabas and Saul for the work to which I have called them.' Then after fasting and praying they laid their hands on them and sent them off.
(Acts 13:1–3)

The passage is structured around the interaction of the work of God and the task of the church,[104] so let us use the same approach.

Verses 1 and 3 show us the church in action. We have a list of five 'prophets and teachers' in verse 1, presumably the leadership of the Antioch church, and verse 3 shows the response of the church to the direction of the Holy Spirit. Johnson draws out a linguistic hint that there may have been several local churches in Antioch, and these five were the leaders in these churches.[105]

The list of the prophets and teachers is a fascinating one.

- Barnabas we already know. We remember that he was from Cyprus originally (Acts 4:36), and it may not be a coincidence that the Antioch church was founded by nameless evangelists from Cyprus and Cyrene (11:20).
- 'Simeon called Niger' had a Jewish name and a Roman nickname. As *niger* in Latin means 'black' it is possible that he came from North Africa. Perhaps he was one of those from Cyrene who founded the Antioch church, Cyrene being the capital of Cyrenaica in North Africa.[106]
- 'Lucius of Cyrene' was definitely from North Africa, and may well have been one of those founders of the Antioch church mentioned in Acts 11. There is another wonderful, but unlikely, possibility, namely that this may be Luke himself.[107] There is another tradition that Luke did actually come from Antioch.[108]

---

104 Gaventa 2003: 189.
105 Johnson 1992: 220.
106 Gaventa 2003: 190.
107 Ibid. He is more likely to have been the Lucius of Rom. 16:21. (Thanks to Steve Walton for this in private correspondence.)
108 Witherington 1998: 367.

- Then there is 'Manaen a member of the court of Herod the ruler'. There were particularly close links between the Herodian family and Antioch,[109] which may explain how Manaen came to be living there. The word translated 'a member of the court' can actually mean that he and Herod had been raised together as children, and carries the connotation of being intimate friends.[110] At any rate, Manaen was of high social standing.
- Then Saul is named. We know he was from Tarsus. We do not know why he is listed last and separated from Barnabas, with whom he is shortly to embark on a missionary journey. Their two names bracket the list, and from now on Saul will be taking centre stage in Luke's narrative under the name of Paul (13:9).

We note straight away that the leadership team is plural and diverse, and may well have its roots in the foundation of the church. We have men from Cyprus and North Africa, from where the evangelistic energy and vision to found the church or churches came. We have a representative from the Jerusalem church, and those who established the church through their discipling and teaching. We have Greek and Jewish and Latin names, black and white ethnicities. All in all, we have people from backgrounds as diverse as the ancient Mediterranean, who have all played a part in how the Antioch churches came into being.

We note, as well, that they were 'prophets and teachers'. We do not know who had which gift or, indeed, if some or all of them had both. What is striking, though, is that these are the gifts Luke sees as being particularly aligned with leadership in a pioneering church situation. These leaders all spoke, and spoke the word of God. As events will show, a key element in this was the ability, as a leadership cadre, to hear the word of the Lord and to respond to it. Perhaps it was this capacity, in particular, that Luke had in mind. In order to instruct, leaders have first to be inspired.[111]

Leadership is key to church planting, maybe more so than for more traditional churches. Likely, leaders will be creating something, rather

---

[109] Ibid.
[110] Ibid. 392.
[111] Ibid. 391.

than steering and developing something that already exists. They will be keen to ensure that the church plant is founded on the words and actions of God, and that the initial culture reflects the missionary movement of God which led to its creation. This concern will find expression both in the spiritual gifts of those initial leaders and in the composition of the team. I am struck by how many of the Antioch leadership team may well have played a significant role in the foundation of the church, and how their geographical origins reflect those of the genesis of the church. Although Luke draws out the significance of their prophetic and teaching gifts, their part in the evangelization of Antioch and the launching of a church or churches there shows that they may all have been more towards the pioneering end of the spectrum.

Such an approach to the selection and appointment of church-plant leaders raises some interesting questions. If these textual hints have been interpreted rightly, the best leaders for church plants are those who have played significant roles in how the church is established. There will be representation not only from the locality (we can speculate that Manaen must have been a useful source of local knowledge and networking), but also from those parts of the world which provided the evangelistic drive to get the church started (Simeon and Lucius and Barnabas), combined with perhaps more seasoned experience from a wider movement perspective (Barnabas) and spiritual giftedness (Saul). We must not push these thoughts too far, as the textual evidence is slight, but these hints are highly suggestive and seem in line with the missionary heart of the Antioch church plant.

What is clear is that the leadership was plural. There is no hint of a single leader or even one among the many. All five are named and act in concert. And although we know from chapter 11 that the church has a lovely balance of the pioneering and the pastoral, the leadership gifts are clustered around the prophetic and the didactic.

In some ways, this maps well onto the practice of many church plants being launched from sending churches that also provide the initial leadership of the plants. This ensures that the evangelistic energy and vision of the founding of the church is carried on into the establishing of the church-plant culture. What is conceivably missing is local representation in the leadership of the church plant, and maybe the contact with the wider church-planting movement (although we note how Barnabas had been sent down from Jerusalem to see what was happening in Antioch). This whole paradigm does highlight the difference between church plants and more established churches, in that leadership in the former self-consciously and intentionally situates itself within a missionary and evangelistic framework, whereas the latter may have more of a sense of wider needs within the church that should be addressed by the leadership composition.

One other reflection is the place of 'movement thinking' and dynamics in church planting. The Jerusalem church played quite a big role in the establishing of the Antioch church by sending Barnabas and in the links with Agabus and his prophetic colleagues and the arrangements for the famine collection. Maybe it was this that made it a natural thing for the Holy Spirit to send Barnabas and Saul off on a wider missionary journey, a whole new phase of missionary work. Whatever the origins of this flexibility and centrifugal energy, the leaders (and maybe the church as a whole) acted quickly in response to the Holy Spirit's direction when 'after fasting and praying they laid their hands on them and sent them off' (13:3). The words translated 'sent them off' can mean 'released them' or 'let them go', which carries the implication of 'discharging them from their teaching responsibilities in the church in Antioch, in order to make them available for a wider ministry'.[112] We can see how Antioch came to view itself as part of a wider church-planting movement.

So, when we look at the leadership of the Antioch church, we see a core group whose members share a common vision and maybe a common history for the establishing of a Gentile church in a key cosmopolitan city outside Palestine. These men knew how to walk with the Spirit of God together and how to teach the church the word of God in service to this vision. They must have had a sense of being on the verge of something new in God's purposes, and this made them all the more keen to root their leadership in prayer, worship and hearing the voice of the Lord.

The Holy Spirit and church-plant leadership

Through the way in which Luke has structured his narrative of this leadership incident at Antioch, the story of the church leadership frames the

---

[112] Stott 1990: 217.

central moment when the Holy Spirit calls for Barnabas and Saul to be set apart for mission. The human dynamics of the leadership frame the interaction with the divine. Luke tells us structurally that the heart of leading a church plant is a relationship with the Holy Spirit. There may be a list of leaders, who are good people and respond to God, but it is actually the Holy Spirit who leads the church.

Significantly, this divine interaction occurs in the context of worship and fasting. The word for worship is taken from the contemporary vocabulary for public service, and may carry implications of leadership office and activity as well as prayer and praise. This is leaders doing what leaders do, which is to worship God. The core leadership calling is to be with God. We do not know if this was the typical and regular rhythm of worship for the Antioch church leaders or if this was a time of particularly intensive seeking after God. Whatever it was, it put them in a position to interact with the Lord and to hear him when he spoke to them.

In this worship and fasting, the Holy Spirit speaks to them. We do not know how, but presumably it is through one or more of the prophets. This is the only time in Acts that the Holy Spirit speaks directly and in the first person to a church.[113] He commands that Barnabas and Saul be set apart for him, the language echoing that of the Old Testament when it speaks of separation for the purposes of God, making holy, sanctifying.[114] The Greek carries within it a sense of urgency.[115] The call is for a 'work', which is not specified. Presumably, the Antioch leaders knew of Saul's call to go to the Gentiles (Acts 9:15–16), and, even though the express activity and location is not spelt out, Barnabas and Saul have no difficulty in working out what they are to do; they at once set off on the missionary journey that will take them the next two chapters to complete. At the end of this, they return to Antioch 'where they had been commended to the grace of God for the work that they had completed' (14:26) – this was indeed the 'work' the Spirit had had in mind. To underline the point of who is in charge, the next verse spells out that Barnabas and Saul, 'being sent out by the Holy Spirit, went down' to Seleucia and on to Cyprus.

---

113 Gaventa 2003: 190.
114 Johnson 1992: 221.
115 Witherington 1998: 393; Gaventa 2003: 190–191.

This primacy of the leading of the Holy Spirit is fundamental to all missionary work, not least to church planting. We may have good ideas and smart strategies, but we ourselves cannot hope to plumb the depths of all the complexities of new and different contexts, and the Holy Spirit may have different ideas and emphases from us.

John Stott is extremely helpful in exploring how the dynamics of such an interaction may work in practice. To start with, he argues that we should not imagine that it was only the five leaders who were involved, but rather, in different ways, the whole church. Both 'the church at Antioch' and the 'prophets and teachers' are mentioned in Acts 13:1, and when Barnabas and Saul return at the end of the missionary journey, they 'called the church together' to report back (14:27). Stott traces the parallel in the similar incident when the seven deacons were chosen in chapter 6, where the whole church acts together (6:2–6). So, it seems likely that the whole Antioch church was involved here and may have been worshipping, praying and fasting, even though the five leaders, two of whom were to be commissioned for mission work, had a specific role.

This insight enables Stott to draw out a very helpful paradigm of the interaction of the Holy Spirit with the local church and its leadership. Who is it who sends Barnabas and Saul? Clearly and explicitly it is the Holy Spirit who does so (13:2, 4), but it is also the church plant through its leaders who do so when they lay hands on them and send them off (13:3). In a way, it is both the Spirit and the church plant sending the apostles.

Stott draws out the implications:

This balance will be a healthy corrective to opposite extremes. The first is the tendency to individualism, by which a Christian claims direct personal guidance by the Spirit without any reference to the church. The second is the tendency to institutionalism, by which all decision-making is done by the church without any reference to the Spirit . . . There is no evidence that Barnabas and Saul 'volunteered' for missionary service; they were 'sent' by the Spirit through the church.[116]

---

[116] Stott 1990: 218.

This helpfully locates the calling and leading of the Spirit within a kind of partnership with the church plant and its leaders, which honours both the direction of the Spirit and the involvement of the local church. As Stott draws out, we can get into trouble when we separate the Spirit from the church.

What we have in the Antioch church leadership is a fellowship caught up by the missional heart of God, with the courage and flexibility to work with him. This prayer meeting signals a seismic shift in the history of Acts. As has been mentioned, it is at Antioch that the word 'church' is first used outside Palestine. It is here that the disciples of Jesus are first called 'Christians' (11:26). From now on, mission happens in a new and more clearly defined way: an apostolic party travels to locations beyond Palestine to share the good news of Jesus with Jews and Gentiles alike, following the Holy Spirit. This will lead to the opening of the church to Gentile believers, and to the spread of the Christian gospel right around the northern Mediterranean and into Europe.

This is heady stuff for church planters. We learn that such a missionary church needs to lean equally into pioneering, pastoring and prophecy. We see that it takes a certain type of leadership, one that combines faith, humility, courage, sacrifice and obedience. The swiftness of the church's response to send away two of its most capable and gifted leaders is testimony to how much it was in tune with the missionary agenda of the Holy Spirit. Perhaps above all, we see that church planting is out-and-out missionary work. A gathering and a story like that at Antioch would only have been possible within a mental framework that saw itself as part of the bigger story of God's kingdom in Jesus reaching out to and spreading across the widest possible geographical and social and religious canvas. May our church plants, and our church-plant leadership, have a similar vision, and a similar willingness to go with all that the Holy Spirit is doing to reach the world with the love of Jesus.

Further down the line

Our last look at the Antioch church is in the aftermath of the Council of Jerusalem. It appears that Antioch was at the forefront of the question of whether Gentiles could be admitted into the fellowship of the church without effectively becoming Jews, so it is no wonder that the leaders of the council send a letter to the Christians in Antioch, Syria and Cilicia to announce their decision, to be accompanied and explained by Paul and Barnabas, Judas and Silas, and delivered to Antioch (15:22–23). After this, 'Paul and Barnabas remained in Antioch, and there, with many others, they taught and proclaimed the word of the Lord' (15:35). The work of teaching and evangelizing[117] is never done.

Our last snapshot in Antioch is both encouraging and sobering, and not untypical of the ups and downs of church-plant life:

> After some days Paul said to Barnabas, 'Come, let us return and visit the believers in every city where we proclaimed the word of the Lord and see how they are doing.' Barnabas wanted to take with them John called Mark. But Paul decided not to take with them one who had deserted them in Pamphylia and had not accompanied them in the work. The disagreement became so sharp that they parted company; Barnabas took Mark with him and sailed away to Cyprus. But Paul chose Silas and set out, the believers commending him to the grace of the Lord. He went through Syria and Cilicia, strengthening the churches.
> (Acts 15:36–41)

The encouraging aspect is Paul's invitation to Barnabas to revisit the scenes of their earlier missionary activity, to see 'how they are doing' (15:36). This is what he and Silas are eventually to do, going 'through Syria and Cilicia, strengthening the churches' (15:41). It shows us a vision of a networked church life, where there is relationship between the churches and their leaders, and where strength can be imparted. The term 'strengthened' is almost a technical term for Luke: it is what Jesus commands Peter to do for his brothers (Luke 22:32), and it describes the activity of Paul and Barnabas in Lystra, Iconium and Antioch (14:21), what Judas and Silas do through prophecy for the believers in Antioch, Syria and Cilicia (Acts 15:32) and what Paul later does with the churches in Galatia and Phrygia (18:23). On two of these occasions, 'strengthening' is linked to 'encouraging', and at the end of our current section of text, the disciples are

---

[117] The word translated 'proclaimed' by NRSV is literally 'evangelized' (Stott 1990: 252).

'strengthened in the faith and increased in numbers daily' (16:5). We can deduce that churches, especially in the early days, need strength of conviction, encouragement of heart and increase in numbers. This was central to Paul's way of working with the network of churches that he was establishing.

Networks of church plants are becoming more common nowadays. The advantages are obvious, not least when viewed within the framework of mutual strengthening. These were largely Gentile churches, so having this relationship with one another must have been an enormous encouragement to them. Paul and his apostolic companions were the link between them. When we think that the opposite of 'strength' is 'weakness', this gives us an insight into how the members of these young churches must have felt. They were finding their way in the middle of powerful political and social and religious cultures, none of which would have been understanding of or sympathetic to the Jesus-faith. To have these links through Paul and his companions with other fledgling churches in the same position must have given them inner strength and confidence.

There is learning for church plants here, especially for those which are small in number and lacking in resources. To feel themselves part of something bigger, nothing less than a movement of God, can be enormously encouraging. The same is true, on a different scale, for larger churches and their leaders. Resource churches can be misunderstood, even resented, by others, and it is a comfort and strength for their leaders on occasion to meet up with others who will understand and may have advice and encouragement for them.

The birth of such networks is a sign of the Spirit doing something new and fresh in our time, just as he was in Acts. Paul is now thinking regionally in his church planting, with churches in these regions relating to one another and to him. Originally, in our modern Western context, this must have been how dioceses started. Now, it is how church-planting movements can help and strengthen and encourage one another in the midst of what can be challenging work.

One of the challenges, sadly, occurs when relationships within church plants, not least among their leaders, come under strain and pressure. In our passage, Paul and Barnabas fall out over John Mark. They have a sharp disagreement (15:39), which is a strong word in the Greek from which we get our English 'paroxysm'. In the Greek translation of the Old Testament it has the sense of 'provoke/irritate/enrage', and has 'a strong emotional quality'.[118] This was a real conflict and quarrel, which led to Barnabas and Paul going their own separate ways. We hear nothing more of Barnabas in the rest of the Acts of the Apostles.

'Ultimately, the reasons for the separation remain unknown.'[119] They centre on John, also called Mark. He was a relative of Barnabas, probably his cousin, maybe even his nephew (Col. 4:10). He goes along with Saul and Barnabas to Cyprus 'to assist them' (Acts 13:5), but, when they come to Perga in Pamphylia, he 'left them and returned to Jerusalem' (13:13). We do not know what happened, but Luke uses a strong word about the separation, saying that John Mark 'deserted' them in Pamphylia, which implies that Mark's leaving them was a betrayal of the gospel.[120] By this time (if our claim is correct that Paul had already been to Jerusalem in the meeting described in Gal. 2), when Peter came to Antioch, 'even Barnabas was led astray by their hypocrisy' (Gal. 2:13), and, although there is no suggestion that Paul and Barnabas had fallen out prior to their disagreement over Mark, perhaps we have a suggestion that Mark was resisting the movement of the gospel among the Gentiles.

Granted the context of the Council of Jerusalem and the fact that Paul replaces Barnabas as his travelling companion with Silas, who was one of those who had come to Antioch to explain the letter about including the Gentiles in the gospel (15:27), and replaces John Mark with Timothy, who was the son of a Jewish mother and a Greek father (16:3), maybe we can guess that the falling out of Barnabas and Paul over Mark was actually about the gospel and the Gentiles. Add into this Barnabas's kind and encouraging nature, maybe wanting to give his family member a second chance, and we have a strained and delicate matter about which both men must have felt strongly. There are hints that Luke sided with Paul; he gives no reason for why John Mark deserted the mission to return to Jerusalem, and he does not say that Barnabas and Mark go on to do more church-planting work when they travel to Cyprus, which is the island of Barnabas's origins: 'in Luke's story, he has, simply, taken his relative/friend, and gone

---

[118] Johnson 1992: 282.
[119] Gaventa 2003: 231.
[120] Witherington 1998: 472.

home.'[121] By contrast, 'the believers [commend Paul] to the grace of the Lord' (15:40), and we will spend the next few chapters following their active service in missionary work and church planting.

There are few things more devastating than leadership conflicts in church plants. It is not always obvious at the time what causes them, and, as with Paul and Barnabas, the conflicts can be about a mixture of theological and personal factors. Whatever their origins, these conflicts are immensely painful for those involved, and bewildering for the rest of the church plant. Churches look to their leaders both to embody the values of the gospel and, in some sense, to hold unity and love for the church. When there is a relationship breakdown, it can be destructive of people's trust in God, as well as of their trust in one another. Potentially catastrophic though these breakdowns are, it is sometimes extremely difficult to avoid them. If it happened with Paul and Barnabas, it is likely that we will not be immune from staff and leadership conflict.[122]

Good came out of it, in that there were now not one but two missionary pairs, although we do not know for sure what happened with Barnabas and Mark. We read elsewhere in the New Testament of both Mark's and Barnabas's partnership with Paul in his work (1 Cor. 9:6 for Barnabas; 2 Tim. 4:11 for Mark). Nothing compensates for the pain of conflict with friends and close colleagues, but, equally, nothing stops the purposes of God in the movement of his grace to those who are as yet outside his kingdom.

So, this last look at Antioch for us sees a church that is becoming an engine of church planting and is at the centre of a growing network of new churches across the region. The church has a real vision for discipling, for establishing and strengthening this new movement. This feels like progress and maturation, but it happens hand in hand with the trauma of leadership conflict between its two leading lights. So often in church planting, the best and the worst happen at the same time. This whole ministry can be a violent roller-coaster. While we do all we can to ride the

---

[121] Johnson 1992: 288.

[122] Zack Eswine (2015: 223) has the interesting observation that 'more often than not, the primary leader who brought you to the church as your greatest advocate in the beginning will fight you in the end. A leader with that kind of influence will not easily give it away when you arrive'. This is, of course, exactly what happened with Paul and Barnabas, although we do not know the reasons for it.

ups and downs, we do not take our eyes off the big picture, but rather position ourselves and our church plants in the mainstream of the momentum of what God is doing.

4

Church planting in action in Acts

Acts 13 sees the launch of what are commonly referred to as Paul's 'missionary journeys'. There are three of them: the journey around Pisidian Antioch, Iconium, Lystra and Derbe in chapters 13–14; then further to Philippi and Thessalonica and into Athens and Corinth in chapters 16–18, moving into the Roman and Greek worlds; and then to Ephesus and the journey to Jerusalem in chapters 19–21. Timothy Tennent makes a good point when he writes: 'I prefer to call them "church-planting initiatives" rather than missionary journeys to clarify the misconception that Paul is rapidly traveling from town to town on an extended evangelistic campaign.' He speaks of 'Paul's ministry of church planting' in these crucial chapters that cover a thirteen-year period.[1] These journeys were extraordinarily successful:

> In little more than ten years St Paul established the Church in four provinces of the Empire, Galatia, Macedonia, Achaia and Asia. Before 47 A.D. there were no Churches in these provinces; in 57 A.D. St Paul could speak as if his work there was done, and could plan extensive tours into the far West without anxiety lest the Churches which he had founded might perish in his absence for want of his guidance and support.[2]

These chapters in Acts describing these journeys are deeply significant for contemporary church planters to reflect on. We continue to bear in mind Stuart Murray's warnings to be aware of the huge change in contexts from apostolic times to those of the modern West, especially Europe, and so

---

[1] Tennent 2010: 429.
[2] Allen 2011: 3.

we will not map what Paul did exactly and unthinkingly onto our own situations, but there will be very many principles for us to adopt, and thoughts and actions to inspire us.

One thing to note straight away is that Paul adopted different approaches in the varying situations in which he found himself, and he substantially altered his strategy over the years. We must consider this carefully, as well as the commonalities.

The first church-planting journey

The first journey (AD 45–47[3]) covered Cyprus and the southern part of the Roman province of Galatia, and is described by Luke in Acts 13:4 – 14:28. Luke concentrates his descriptions around three major incidents: the interactions on Cyprus with Sergius Paulus and the court magician Bar-Jesus, the missionary activity in Pisidian Antioch, and the events that happened in Lystra.[4]

On Cyprus

'Being sent out by the Holy Spirit' (13:4), Barnabas and Saul sail to Cyprus. We are not told why they did this, but, in all likelihood, it was because Cyprus was where Barnabas hailed from (4:36), and maybe because the gospel had already reached there (11:19, 20). They land in the east of the island, at Salamis, which was the old capital,[5] then they go 'through the whole island' (13:6), presumably on a kind of evangelistic tour, before arriving at Paphos, on the west coast, which was the new capital and the centre of Roman administration.[6] There they meet 'a Jewish false prophet, named Bar-Jesus', who would have been a kind of court magician, with the Roman 'proconsul, Sergius Paulus, an intelligent man' (13:6–7): the latter is eager 'to hear the word of God' (13:7) and so invites Barnabas and Saul to meet him. Bar-Jesus, also known as Elymas, tries to intervene, presumably to safeguard his job and influence with the proconsul, whereupon Paul calls him a 'son of the devil' (13:10), which is a play on

---

[3] Schnabel 2008: 77.
[4] Stott 1990: 218.
[5] Beitzel 2013: 302.
[6] Ibid.

his name Bar-Jesus, which means 'son of salvation',[7] and declares a temporary blindness on him. The incident is closed with the news of Sergius Paulus's conversion: 'When the proconsul saw what had happened, he believed, for he was astonished at the teaching about the Lord' (13:12). The narrative also includes a double name-change: Bar-Jesus is also named Elymas (13:6, 8) and Saul is 'also known as Paul' (13:9), the name by which he will be known in the rest of Acts and throughout the New Testament.

One of the most obvious questions for church planters as they begin is where to plant. Leaving aside, for now, questions of strategy and wider issues of geography, we can learn from Barnabas and Saul here: they started with what they knew. They weren't 'missionary novices',[8] Barnabas having evangelized in Cyprus, Jerusalem and Damascus, and Saul in Damascus, Arabia and the regions around Tarsus for many years.[9] Now they had been 'sent out by the Holy Spirit' (13:4), but with no clearer indication with regard to where they were to engage in 'the work to which [he has] called them' (13:2). In all likelihood this was Barnabas's decision, as he was the senior partner in this venture, at least at this stage,[10] and he chose to return to his native land. They covered the whole island from east to west, starting with the 'synagogues of the Jews' (13:5), perhaps making for the seat of Roman power. We should note, though, the significance of witnessing to a Gentile, and a Roman official; this was an important change from the pattern they had been following thus far, of starting with a synagogue: it was 'the great innovative development of this first missionary journey'.[11] Of course, this pattern was to become increasingly pronounced as Acts developed; maybe Cyprus was where Paul first saw what was to become a major aspect of his future work.

A church-planting strategy

This sense of how to map out a church-planting mission returns again and again in Acts, and we will regularly return to it too. Barnabas and Paul face the question as soon as they leave Paphos and Cyprus. They sail for

---

7 Stott 1990: 220.
8 Schnabel 2008: 75.
9 Ibid. 74–75.
10 Although we note that by Acts 13:13, Luke describes the little band of Paul, Barnabas and John Mark as 'Paul and his companions'.
11 Longenecker 1981: 420, quoted in Stott 1990: 220.

the northern coast of the Mediterranean, to the Roman province of Galatia, some 200 miles out from Cyprus. Luke tells us that they 'came to Perga in Pamphylia . . . but they went on from Perga and came to Antioch in Pisidia' (13:13–14). This is striking because Perga was a city with 'political and economic significance',[12] the capital of the newly constituted province of Lycia-Pamphylia, yet Paul and Barnabas do not pause there but head straight away inland to Pisidian Antioch. This was not an easy journey, involving a steep climb up mountains. It is all the more striking because, on their return journey at the conclusion of this first church-planting initiative, the apostolic band *did* stop and preach in Perga (14:25). So why not on this first occasion?

There are two theories about this. The first is that Paul contracted some disease, perhaps malaria along the coastal plain when they first landed. We know from his letter to the Galatians that 'it was because of a physical infirmity that I first announced the gospel to you' (Gal. 4:13). It seems that it was a disfiguring and repulsive disease, and may have involved Paul's eyesight (Gal. 4:14, 15). Maybe the higher elevation of inland Galatia was better for his health, and enabled him to recover there. Against that theory, a challenging climb for a sick man would have been demanding.

Another theory is that Sergius Paulus, the Roman proconsul who had become a Christian on Cyprus, had relatives in the region. There is evidence of the family of the Sergii Paulii who owned estates around Pisidian Antioch.[13] It is quite possible that the proconsul wanted his relatives to hear about Jesus, and so gave introductions to them to Paul and Barnabas. These would have been people of high social standing, wealth and local influence. Events were to intervene so that this was not possible (see 13:50), but it may well be the reason why Paul and his companions made straight for Pisidian Antioch and did not stop to preach in Perga on this initial journey. Of course, both the malaria hypothesis and the Sergius Paulus family connection theory are not mutually incompatible.

One of the things this emphasizes is that in Acts we are reading history; these things really happened. Luke writes as a theologian as well as an historian, and we must bear in mind different approaches to history in

---

[12] Schnabel 2008: 266.
[13] Ibid. 2008: 79, 264, 311.

ancient and modern times,[14] but these considerations do not take away from the fact that we are reading an account of what the Holy Spirit has done with real people in real places.

Barnabas and Saul are acting in obedience to the clear call of the Holy Spirit. Church planting was not their idea, and they did not set off on this journey on their own initiative. Accordingly, the criteria for their decision-making appear to be quite varied. There are some factors which they bear in mind – they start in the synagogues, they have an eye to the community gatekeepers – but, alongside these, they show a flexibility and spontaneity: they act at once on the Sergius Paulus family connection, and they respond to Paul's health issues.

For contemporary church planters, it could be helpful to have a similar sort of mental grid. The fixed points might be the leading of the Holy Spirit and a willingness to follow up on local connections which God makes for us. They might include a particular calling to interact with people who have existing points of contact with the gospel, to start with what we would now call the 'dechurched', those with experiences of Christianity in the past but who have drifted away over the years. Alongside these fixed points, what might the areas of flexibility include? Perhaps a willingness to follow up on one strand of pneumatological direction at once, even though it might mean postponing a longer-term strategic objective?

If the Sergius Paulus hypothesis is right, this is the first instance on the Acts church-planting journeys where we see the apostolic bands intentionally following up on personal connections from their converts. This is the principle that the apostles would have learned from Jesus' training on mission, that of the 'person of peace'. In Luke 10:5–9, Jesus instructs the missionaries to establish a relationship with any individuals who receive their offers of peace, and, through them, with those of their households and social networks. This is exactly what Paul and Barnabas are doing with Sergius Paulus: the proconsul believes in Jesus, and then introduces the missionaries to his relatives and wider family. Sergius Paulus himself is described as 'an intelligent man' (13:7), and is clearly

---

[14] See e.g. N. T. Wright 1992: ch. 4; and Meyer 2002: ch. 4, for issues of historiography, history and meaning in relation to the New Testament.

interested in spiritual matters, hence his employment of Bar-Jesus and his eagerness to hear the gospel (13:6–7). Paul and Barnabas take these connections to be a kind of marching orders from the Holy Spirit, and accept this as a more pressing invitation than starting a new work in a potentially strategic location.

This appears to be a good approach for church planters: to have a framework for their missionary strategy, but to be praying and looking for personal connections, in particular, and bringing a willingness to be flexible in response to the people in whom the Holy Spirit is clearly at work.

In Pisidian Antioch

Back to Paul and Barnabas, now in Pisidian Antioch. 'On the sabbath day they went into the synagogue' (13:14). Here is Paul's methodology in practice. In every place, he would start with the synagogue, arguing from the Scriptures that Jesus is the Christ. So, in Iconium 'Paul and Barnabas went into the Jewish synagogue and spoke' (14:1) 'as usual' (TNIV). In Philippi, Paul and Silas go looking for a place of prayer on the sabbath day, presumably because there was no synagogue there (16:13). In Thessalonica, 'Paul went in [to the synagogue], as was his custom' (17:2). At Beroea, 'when they arrived, they went to the Jewish synagogue' (17:10). In Athens 'he argued in the synagogue with the Jews' (17:17). In Corinth, 'every sabbath he would argue in the synagogue and would try to convince Jews and Greeks' (18:4). In Ephesus, 'first he . . . went into the synagogue and had a discussion with the Jews' (18:19). This is Paul's consistent practice. Right at the end of Acts, on his journey to Rome, Paul 'called together the local leaders of the Jews' (28:17).

As we have seen, this is primarily a theological commitment. Luke has shown us in the structure of Acts how God is faithful to his promises to Israel. In the words of Peter's sermon: 'When God raised up his servant [Jesus], he sent him first to you [Israelites]' (3:26). Paul shares this commitment, doubtless for the same reason. In Romans, Paul states that the gospel is 'the power of God for salvation to everyone who has faith, to the Jew first and also to the Greek' (Rom. 1:16; cf. 2:9, 10),[15] a logic that is both theological and chronological, which he will draw out in chapters 9–11.

---

[15] Stott 1990: 227.

Sadly, Antioch sees the establishing of a further pattern. Neil Cole writes:

> Paul would follow this pattern during the rest of his journeys. He would preach the Gospel in a synagogue, if one could be found. In a short time the Jews would reject this new message, and a few would join Paul as he began preaching to the Gentiles, where he would see his greatest effectiveness. The Jews who rejected him would not leave him alone, though, but would stir controversy around him until finally persecution and beatings would chase him on to the next city. Antioch of Pisidia would be the first such city.[16]

We see Paul explaining this process theologically when he and Barnabas are opposed in the synagogue on the second sabbath in Pisidian Antioch:

> Then both Paul and Barnabas spoke out boldly, saying, 'It was necessary that the word of God should be spoken first to you. Since you reject it and judge yourselves to be unworthy of eternal life, we are now turning to the Gentiles. For so the Lord has commanded us, saying,
>
> > "I have set you to be a light for the Gentiles,
> > so that you may bring salvation to the ends of the earth."'
> (Acts 13:46–47)

Paul is quoting Isaiah 49:6, the calling of the Servant of the Lord, a text which Luke has previously applied to Jesus himself (Luke 2:32). Now, Paul tells us that this text applies to the apostolic mission: 'the Lord has commanded us' (13:47), even though the 'you' of the prophecy is in the singular.[17] The ancient calling of Israel finds fulfilment in the ministry of Jesus, and continues into the early church. The rejection by the Jews is the springboard into the offer of the gospel to the Gentiles: 'Thus the word of the Lord spread throughout the region' (13:49), which Eckhard Schnabel reckons to have comprised some fifty villages.[18]

---

[16] Cole 2011: 53.
[17] See the helpful TNIV footnote to Acts 13:47.
[18] Schnabel 2008: 83.

Things had begun so well. On that first sabbath, Paul and Barnabas had been invited to speak in the synagogue. This would partly have been due to custom, but maybe also a certain excitement to have a former Pharisee with them, especially one mentored by Gamaliel, no less (22:3). Paul's sermon is well received: 'As Paul and Barnabas were going out, the people urged them to speak about these things again the next sabbath' (13:42), and Luke implies that some have become Christians (13:43). On the succeeding sabbath, 'almost the whole city gathered to hear the word of the Lord' (13:44). Schnabel brings this verse to light:

> It is not implausible to assume that Paul had the opportunity to speak to a crowd numbering in the thousands ... The crowd could have gathered in front of the synagogue, or perhaps in the plaza called Tiberia Platea in front of the temple of Augustus, or in the plaza called Augusta Platea at the northern end of the Cardo Maximus, or perhaps in the theatre located on the Decumanus Maximus.[19]

The presence of this large crowd provokes the synagogue leaders to jealousy, and they blaspheme, perhaps pronouncing a curse on Jesus,[20] and contradict Paul (13:45). The apostles turn to the Gentiles, before leaving the city, at least for now.

Reaching outsiders

These dramatic scenes raise a couple of thoughts for church planters, both centred on the approach the church plant will take to those who do not yet attend. Paul's methodology of always starting with the Jews and the synagogues raises the question of how far beyond the walls of the church the plant wishes to engage. And the vast numbers of people who came to hear Paul and Barnabas on that second sabbath in Pisidian Antioch makes us think about how we attract crowds and engage with those outside the church.

In starting with the synagogues, Paul ensured that he was conversing with people who were familiar with the Jewish God, had a moral

---

[19] Ibid. 82.
[20] Ibid. 83.

and biblical world view and were familiar with the Scriptures. Joachim Jeremias wrote:

> The overwhelming success of the mission of the apostle Paul, who in the space of ten years had established centres of Christian faith throughout almost the whole of the contemporary world, depended partly on the fact that everywhere he was able to build on ground prepared by the Jewish mission.[21]

Leaving aside the theological aspects that lay behind Paul's practice of starting with the synagogues, we have here an approach which has clear parallels with our situation in the West. Although the statistics of the decline in Christian belief in the West are alarming, there are still large numbers of people with residual elements of Christian faith. Some are in our churches, especially in mainline denominations. And large numbers are living all around us, individuals who have had some degree of contact with Christianity at some point in their lives.

This ties in with Paul starting with people who attended the synagogues. He could approach them (as we shall see when we look at his evangelistic sermons in Acts) in a different way from those who would have had no previous exposure to the God of the Old Testament. The same is true with the distinction between those in our contexts who have had experience of church and those who have not. Ralph D. Winter and Bruce A. Koch helpfully talk about units of evangelistic distance that people have to travel on the road to faith.[22] Unit 1 (or E1) involves a small and comparatively easy conceptual step – these people are familiar with language about God and Jesus, have some understanding of the world of the Bible and have a connection with traditional Christian morality. Unit 2 (E2) is more of a stretch; these people are largely unfamiliar with the church world view and have very little social contact with the church, but they are friendly towards Christians. Unit 3 (E3) is the same, but more so, having a totally unchurched background with no points of connection with church, either in personal history or in thinking. And some may

---

[21] Jeremias 1958: 16, quoted in Stott 1990: 238.
[22] Winter and Koch 2002.

have active barriers against Christianity – someone perhaps from a different religion, with questions of language and culture involved.

Different church plants will be drawn to people at different points along this scale. Many more traditional church plants will find that they land most naturally in mainly engaging with people at E1 and E2. This is not to say that the members of these churches will not share faith with those at E3, but that their evangelistic thinking and methods of communicating the gospel are largely with fringe and dechurched people. This enables them to invite people to a church service with the expectation that most of it will make sense to those invited, especially if there is careful explanation throughout. Other church plants are hoping to reach people at E3, and, for them, a church service would be too much of a reach. Here, a different approach must be taken, starting, in all likelihood, with the careful building of relationships and works of service.

So, at Pisidian Antioch, Paul was dealing with people who were at E1, whereas in Lystra and Athens, they were at E3. In all these places, though, he was able to draw a crowd, and make meaningful connections with those around him. This is a key church-planting skill, perhaps *the* key ability for church planters. After all, it does not matter how brilliant the activity or service the church plant is laying on or is engaged with is if nobody is actually coming, or if there is nobody present who is not actually a Christian. Particularly in more pioneering situations, the ability to connect with people outside the church and build relationships with them is of the essence in the church-planting task. Church plants will be looking to those who are more on the pioneering than the pastoring side of things.

Sadly, at Pisidian Antioch 'the Jews incited the devout women of high standing and the leading men of the city, and stirred up persecution against Paul and Barnabas, and drove them out of their region' (13:50). They head off to the south-east, following the Via Sebaste, 'the main Roman road connecting the Roman colonies in the region. The road was broad and well paved, built to accommodate wheeled vehicles traveling to Iconium and Lystra, both cities in the region of Lycaonia.' [23] Paul and Barnabas speak in the synagogue 'in such a way that a great number of

---

[23] Witherington 1998: 418.

both Jews and Greeks became believers' (14:1). Again, opposition is stirred up against them, 'so they remained for a long time, speaking boldly for the Lord, who testified to the word of his grace by granting signs and wonders to be done through them' (14:3). A plot of violence against them sees them move on to 'Lystra and Derbe, cities of Lycaonia, and to the surrounding country; and there they continued proclaiming the good news' (14:6–7).

At Lystra

It is the events at Lystra which provide the third main focus for Luke of the first church-planting journey. It makes for a very vivid narrative. It starts with a healing miracle, where a man 'crippled from birth' is healed – he 'sprang up and began to walk' (14:8, 10). This incident is strikingly similar to what happened in chapter 3, when God healed another man 'lame from birth' (3:2), who jumped up and began to walk (3:7). The healings are similar and Luke's vocabulary exactly the same:

> Several features of the story replay the earlier healing in Jerusalem in Acts 3. Both men are described as 'lame from birth' (3:3; 14:8). Both Peter and Paul look intently (3:4; 14:9). In both cases, the demonstration of the healing's efficacy involves leaping up (3:8; 14:10). And both connect the healing itself with faith (3:16; 14:9). In addition, both healings precipitate a response from local religious leaders, the temple authorities in Jerusalem (4:1–4), and the priest of Zeus in Lystra (14:13), although the responses differ dramatically.[24]

Witherington comments: 'One must ask why Luke has cast these two narratives in such similar language at key points.'[25]

The answer is threefold. First of all, Luke is drawing parallels between Peter and Paul:[26] the mission to the Gentiles is just as authentic and vindicated by God as that to the Jews. Second, this ministry is a continuation of that of Jesus: Luke in his Gospel has given us a story of the Lord healing a paralysed man in whom he sees faith, with the result that

---

[24] Gaventa 2003: 206–207.
[25] Witherington 1998: 423.
[26] Johnson 1992: 251; Witherington 1998: 423.

he stands up and walks (Luke 5:17–26); the apostolic mission is the same as that of Jesus. And third, Luke sees in this miracle a particularly evocative demonstration of the power of the gospel. After all, there have been other 'signs and wonders' performed just days previously in Iconium (14:3), but these are not described. There is something paradigmatic in the healing of these disabled men. In the case of the paralysed man here, Johnson comments:

> The incapacity to move, the powerlessness to walk, the weakness and the helplessness, all signify the condition of humans with respect to salvation . . . His acceptance of God's visitation in faith – and the power of that faith to 'save' him make this story . . . a literary 'sign of healing'.[27]

I wonder, as well, if these thoughts on individual conversion may not be extended to the start of the church; the first healing was a visible sign of the Jerusalem church getting onto its feet, and this second in Lystra is a similar sign for the Gentile church. It is a vivid acted parable of God opening 'a door of faith for the Gentiles' (14:27).

So, conversion to Christ is to be seen as a thoroughgoing miracle. It is not self-help or maximizing human potential. It is not even a combination of divine and human actions. Rather, it is an act of divine power to be received by faith. Likewise, the planting of churches. The church planter is totally dependent on the power of God to raise up a church, just as much as in the case of someone who has never walked in his whole life jumping and leaping up on feet and ankles made strong and well. Church planters are people of faith, looking to the word of the Lord, and they are on the lookout for others who have a similar faith that God can do something extraordinary in their midst by starting a church.

This miracle, though, causes confusion. In all likelihood, there was a local legend which told of how Zeus and Hermes had once visited the Lycaonian region in disguise and had not been welcomed into any homes, save that of an elderly couple who showed them kindness and hospitality, even though they were poor. Their reward was to be guided onto high

---

[27] Johnson 1992: 251.

ground by the gods, and so to be spared when the region was flooded as a punishment for the people's lack of hospitality to Zeus and Hermes.[28] If this is the case, it adds cogency to the question of why the priest of Zeus and the local people were so keen to welcome Barnabas and Paul, not wanting to reject Zeus and Hermes a second time (14:11–13). Lystra and its surrounding countryside is a 'cultural backwater', the people 'largely rustic and uncivilised' and 'gullible'.[29] The significant missiological factor, though, is that this is 'the first direct contact between the apostles and a purely Gentile population'.[30] The people show themselves open to the divine, to the gods coming to the earth, but misconstrue how that understanding is different from, as well as similar to, Christianity. Paul and Barnabas speak to the Lystrans, but 'even with these words, they scarcely restrained the crowds from offering sacrifice to them' (14:18).

Things are to change dramatically, for, when Jews from Antioch and Iconium arrive and turn the crowds against Paul and Barnabas, Paul is stoned and left for dead, protected (and prayed for?) by the new converts (14:19–20). The next day, the apostolic band makes for Derbe, some 60 miles further east, where 'they proclaimed the good news to that city and . . . made many disciples' (14:21), including Gaius, who will return in the story of Acts (19:29; 20:4). And perhaps it is not fanciful to think that the dramatic events in Lystra were witnessed by a young man named Timothy (see 16:1–2); towards the end of his life, Paul could write to Timothy how he had 'observed . . . my suffering the things that happened to me in Antioch, Iconium, and Lystra' (2 Tim. 3:10–11).[31] Perhaps Timothy had seen these persecutions and how 'the Lord rescued [Paul] from all of them' (3:11), and it was this which was the beginning of Timothy's own journey of faith.

At this juncture, Paul and Barnabas turn round and retrace their steps:

They returned to Lystra, then on to Iconium and Antioch. There they strengthened the souls of the disciples and encouraged them to continue in the faith, saying, 'It is through many persecutions that

---

[28] E.g. Witherington (1998: 423–424), who quotes substantially from Ovid's *Metamorphoses*, which records the story.
[29] Gaventa 2003: 206.
[30] Johnson 1992: 250.
[31] See Cole 2011: 54.

we must enter the kingdom of God.' And after they had appointed elders for them in each church, with prayer and fasting they entrusted them to the Lord in whom they had come to believe. (Acts 14:21–23)

We may wonder why they did not carry on moving east, a natural journey back to Antioch via Paul's home city of Tarsus. They may have felt that by planting a church in Derbe, they had adequately set up a road of churches from Judea and Syria, through Cilicia into Galatia;[32] thus, we see Paul and Silas beginning the second church-planting journey by going through Syria and Cilicia (15:41). More likely, though, are two weighty reasons which we must consider before returning with Paul to Syrian Antioch to mark the end of this first church-planting journey.

The significance of regions

The first reason is that Paul thought in terms of provinces. This under-lines and develops what we have already seen in the significance of cities in Paul's missionary strategy. It was not just cities, though, which lay behind Paul's thinking: it was regions, and cities as the best means of reaching them. Think how often Paul (and Luke) speaks of the provinces of Roman government or other means of provincial government and organization. In the very next verse, we read that 'they passed through Pisidia and came to Pamphylia' (14:24). References mentioning Asia, Bithynia, Macedonia and Achaia are too numerous to record.

> The object which [Paul] set before himself was the establishment of the Church in the province rather than in the city or town or village in which he preached ... [B]oth St Paul and St Luke constantly speak of the provinces rather than of the cities. In other words the unit in St Paul's view was the province rather than the city.[33]

The words are those of Roland Allen, an early twentieth-century mis-sionary, principally to China. His two books *Missionary Methods: St Paul's*

---

[32] See Allen 2011: 25.
[33] Ibid. 17–18.

or Ours? (1912) and *The Spontaneous Expansion of the Church* (1927) were ahead of their time, and continue to provoke thinking and planning for church planters. We will return to him several times in these reflections.

Allen develops his thinking on the relationship of cities and provinces in *Missionary Methods: St Paul's or Ours?*:

> St Paul's theory of evangelizing a province was not to preach in every place in it himself, but to establish centres of Christian life in two or three important places from which the knowledge might spread into the country round. This is important, not as showing that he preferred to preach in a capital rather than in a provincial town or in a village, but because he intended his congregation to become at once a centre of light.[34]

Classic examples of this are when Paul says, in Romans 15, that 'from Jerusalem and as far around as Illyricum I have fully proclaimed the good news of Christ' (Rom. 15:19), and when Luke reports that Paul's teaching activity in the lecture hall of Tyrannus meant that 'all the residents of Asia . . . heard the word of the Lord' (Acts 19:10) over a two-year period. 'When [Paul] had occupied two or three centres he had really and effectually occupied the province,' concludes Allen.[35] Not every major centre would do, however, but only those with the capacity to act as hubs of social networks which would adequately carry the gospel. Rather, it was those which were 'at the centres of Roman administration, the centres of Hellenic civilization, the centres of Jewish influence, the keys of the great trade routes'.[36]

This has profound significance for church planting. Not only does it make sense to think in terms of urban church planting to be influential in reaching cultures for Christ, but also, if we are to follow Paul's wisdom in Acts, it should be our practice to think in terms of regions, not least in how countries are divided administratively, culturally and religiously, and how they connect with one another for business and trade. Arguably, this echoes how the dioceses of the Church of England and other

---

[34] Ibid. 18–19.
[35] Ibid. 19.
[36] Ibid. 24.

denominations originated. Many of them, to start with, were based on the kingdoms of ancient kings and people groups, only being subdivided as populations increased and the manner of life developed. Dioceses, in many cases, still embody very helpful and potentially fruitful ways of thinking missiologically. Some, however, have failed to keep pace with how life and culture and populations have changed over the years. And some are far too small.

What might it be like for church-planting movements to think together about how best to reach whole regions for Christ? In Church of England terms, it is very encouraging to see increasingly joined-up thinking, evidenced by diocesan leadership teams working together with resource churches with the aim of planting churches across whole cities and their regions. The more bishops can do this, the better. In doing so, they are following in the steps of St Paul. It may be necessary to go far beyond this, though, with dioceses working together, and overcoming habits of defensiveness, where these exist. Dioceses can cooperate in thinking about major conurbations just across one another's episcopal borders, about centres of education, science, business, the arts and technology, how social geography is working nowadays, and how all this might potentially help suggest strategies for planting churches and setting up church-planting hubs.

Why plant new churches when established churches already exist?

This brings us to a central issue surrounding church planting, which goes to its legitimacy in the eyes of some: is it necessary, granted that England already has many – maybe too many – churches? As the majority of these churches are far from full for Sunday worship, would it not make more sense to concentrate on filling up these existing churches rather than start new ones? An extra factor for Anglicans is that we have a parish system whereby the whole country is subdivided into small areas, each served by an Anglican church; this means that there is a sense of redundancy in introducing extra churches, and, more than that, starting new churches carries with it a highly disruptive potential to the good work already being done by the existing churches in their parishes.

According to this argument, it is anachronistic to apply the lessons of the Acts of the Apostles to our contemporary situation. This is what lies behind Stuart Murray's reticence in how we handle Acts, for instance:

> The basic problem is the issue of context. The New Testament informs us about the mission of the earliest churches into a world without churches. Pioneer evangelism into virgin territory has, throughout history and in every area of the world, involved the planting of new churches ... But ... there are well over 40,000 churches already in England and Wales alone. Churches have existed in Britain for many centuries. The context is very different from pioneer mission elsewhere in the world, or in the New Testament.[37]

We are simply in such a profoundly different context that it is inadmissible to take New Testament models of church planting, such as those of Acts, and transpose them into our current situation.

It is worth reflecting on the long perspective of church planting. Interestingly, there is no recorded use of the term before the Middle Ages.[38] The earliest usage is the Latin term *plantatio ecclesiae*, 'the planting of the church', and refers to the initial establishing of the church in areas where previously there had been no Christian presence. From a more Catholic perspective, it carries connotations of the development and imposition of a particular style and theology of church. Interestingly, this theological angle does not start with individual churches being planted in particular locations and neighbourhoods, but is rather the expression locally of the universal reality that is the church. This means that once this is done, it is not only unnecessary to plant new churches but it is actually theologically problematic, because it tends to undermine the whole notion of the church as one, holy, catholic and apostolic. After the Reformation, Protestant churches had a different theology of church, and viewed the *plantatio ecclesiae* as the evangelization of those parts of the world which did not currently have access to the gospel, with the church being the necessary corollary to this: once people were converted,

---

[37] Murray 1998: 64–65.
[38] Paas 2016: 10.

they needed to be gathered into churches for worship and discipling. Sadly, over time, this approach degenerated into denominationalism, with different confessions planting their own brands of church in competition with other denominations.[39] This history has led to two approaches, which, broadly speaking, do not understand each other; Catholic and Orthodox theologies of the church are alienated by church planting which is not rooted in the classic understanding of the church as something that is 'given' in form, organization and practice, whereas more Protestant and Pentecostal theologies find it incomprehensible that new churches should not be planted to reach people who have no, little or inadequate exposure to the gospel. As Stefan Paas puts it:

> Many 'catholicizing' Christians are put off by the seeming lack of care with which evangelical practitioners use the word 'church', ignoring almost everything that other Christians find important in it – such as sacraments, liturgy, ecumenical dialogue, apostolic succession, ordination, confessions, sacred buildings, heterogeneous community, preaching, etcetera.[40]

There is thus a theological tension behind different approaches to church planting.

Most justifications of church planting start with the urgent needs of a rapidly changing society, driven by increasing rates of secularization and materialism. One bishop wrote:

> The Church has got to realize its missionary responsibilities. We live in a society, whether that be urban or rural, which is now basically second or even third generation pagan once again . . . We are in a critical missionary situation.[41]

The missionary situation of the UK and the diminishing impact of all sections of the church necessitated fresh missiological thinking: 'a changing

---

[39] Ibid. 16, 30, 32.
[40] Ibid. 218.
[41] Gordon Bates, Bishop of Whitby, in *Church Army News*, April 1998, quoted in Archbishops' Council of the Church of England 2004: 11–12.

culture constitutes a call from God.'[42] The influential *Mission-Shaped Church* report, produced by the Church of England in 2004, argued that it was no longer true, if it ever had been, that England could be viewed as a Christian country and its people essentially pastored by their churches, but rather that England needed to be evangelized again, taking full cognizance of the changed and changing social and cultural contexts in which the church found itself. That context was as much a part of the theological conversation as was the inherited doctrine of the church.[43]

That context has continued to demand fresh missionary thinking and acting. Consider the following features of English society:

- Churches are reaching fewer people in their parishes.
- Population increases, on the one hand, and the closure of churches, on the other, have meant that fewer and fewer churches are attempting to serve more and more people.
- Different ethnic and language groups are an increasing part of the landscapes of England, especially in its cities. These communities are not currently well served by the church.
- There are increasing cultural gaps between the church and the young, the poor and ethnic minorities. For example, our housing estates are barely reached by the Church of England, and maybe by other churches too.
- Our society organizes itself in ways other than, as well as in addition to, the geographical, so the parish system creaks more and more. Mission in and to and through networks, based in centres of education, sport, leisure and the arts, is more fruitful.

This is why church planting is so urgent and so effective. New forms of church are being born to reach new people in new ways. Traditional churches are doing fine work and ministry, but are palpably reaching only small proportions of rapidly changing local populations. New churches are springing up to reach new communities alongside those being served by more established churches.

---

42 World Council of Churches 1968: 3, quoted in Archbishops' Council of the Church of England 2004: 13.
43 E.g. Archbishops' Council of the Church of England 2004: 13, 21.

This remains a cogent argument for church planting. While it is demonstrably true that our current context in England (of hundreds of years of church presence) is totally different from that of New Testament times (with no Christian history), it is also clearly the case that England is in a missionary situation once again. It is not wise to be too sweeping and claim that everything and everyone is now secular and post-Christian, because culture is mixed and much more complex than that. We can safely say, though, that substantial (and increasing) segments of society have no meaningful contact with the existing church, and when they do hear the gospel they do so as something completely new and fresh. Church planting is one of the single most effective ways of making this possible.

What of the theological differences around the *plantatio ecclesiae*? *Mission-Shaped Church* argued for a prioritizing of mission over church, rooting this in the rich theological ground of the nature of God's involvement in the world, the call of the incarnation, the work of the Spirit in the world, and the ultimate destiny of the church and the world, as well as in the ground of traditional Anglican church thinking as being here for the people and society of England.[44] Others have argued for an understanding of God's acting in the world as being rooted in his kingdom, which is a different way of thinking than through the church.[45] And others have detected a shift in Roman Catholic theology of the church after the First World War:

> The fundamentally innovative feature of the new development was the discovery that the universal church actually finds its true existence in the local churches; that these, and not the universal church, are the pristine expression of the church.[46]

These are all encouraging signs, but much theological work remains to be done.

At the time of writing, there is an unstable but emerging praxis in favour of church planting in nearly every diocese of the Church of England. It is still true that church planting is seen as something that is substantially

---

[44] Ibid. ch. 5.
[45] E.g. Hull 2006.
[46] Bosch 1997: 380.

an evangelical activity, but, thankfully, there is increasing interest from other sectors of the church, accompanied by embryonic signs of practice. Hopefully, good practice will lead to a gathering momentum right across all spiritualities and traditions of the church.

Paul's commitment to planting churches and developing leaders

The second weighty reason to consider when we think about why Paul did not head back to Antioch via Tarsus is commitment to the establishing of leadership of the nascent churches he and Barnabas had planted. This is something to which we must return, but may we note for now the prominence Luke gives to it in Paul's decision-making. We read, at the conclusion of the first church-planting journey, that Paul and Barnabas return to Lystra and Iconium and Antioch, strengthening the disciples, warning them to expect hardship, and appointing elders for them in each church (14:21–23). This is a deeply significant section of Acts because it reveals to us how Paul was thinking (in terms of churches) and acting (appointing leaders).

We note that there are now *churches* in each place. We had heard of people urged to continue in the grace of God and Gentiles becoming believers in Pisidian Antioch (13:43, 48); of great numbers of Jews and Gentiles believing in Iconium (14:1); and of disciples surrounding the injured Paul in Lystra (14:20) – but now we read of 'each church' (14:23). Paul has not just been evangelizing, although he has certainly been doing that; he has also been establishing churches. He has been church planting.

Roland Allen draws out the significance of this: 'It is manifest that St. Paul did not go about as a missionary preacher merely to convert individuals: he went to establish Churches from which the light might radiate throughout the whole country around.'[47] And again: 'The first and most striking difference between his actions and ours is that he founded "Churches" whilst we found "Missions".'[48] And: 'Nothing can alter or disguise the fact that St. Paul did leave behind him at his first visit complete Churches.'[49]

---

[47] Allen 2011: 109.
[48] Ibid. 112.
[49] Ibid. 117.

Derek Tidball goes so far as to say: 'Paul's primary interest was not in the conversion of individuals but in the formation of Christian communities.'[50]

This means that Paul's focus was always on the planting of churches. For him, this was what mission and evangelism meant. All else flowed from this, so all needed to be directed to this primary purpose.

Even granted the difference between our contemporary context and Paul's time, here is something compelling to shape our thinking about what mission means and the legitimacy and priority of church planting. To be apostolic, in this sense, means to plant churches. Paul knew he would be moving on – his methodology was itinerant – and so he was always thinking of what he would leave behind, and that would be churches.

For those of us who are already convinced of the validity and significance of the contemporary planting of churches, there is still a major lesson here: that the existence and health of the church, and its place within the mission of God, must shape our thinking, even if outreach, mission and evangelism may fill up the foreground. We can become so focused on the mission work that we fail to place it within a wider and longer-term framework, which is the health and development of the church. We are not talking about the church existing for its own sake, but rather as being capable of carrying the good news to its region, maybe of planting further churches, and how it might be most effective in that task. We see this in how Paul will later write to the church in Thessalonica: 'For the word of the Lord has sounded forth from you not only in Macedonia and Achaia, but in every place where your faith in God has become known' (1 Thess. 1:8). Here we see him thinking in terms of a local church influencing provinces, a church that is healthy and strong in its faith, with a vision for its region.

What does this mean in practice? For Paul, it meant the appointment of leaders, those who would have oversight of these fledgling churches. We will see this practice developing in each successive journey, but here it is from the very start: in Antioch, Iconium and Lystra (and presumably in Derbe and Perga), Paul and Barnabas 'appointed elders . . . in each

---

church, [and] with prayer and fasting they entrusted them to the Lord in whom they had come to believe' (Acts 14:23).

Roland Allen is helpful in drawing out some of the implications of this:

If anyone to-day were to propose to ordain men [and women] within six months of their conversion from idolatry, he [or she] would be deemed rash to the point of madness. Yet no one denies that St. Paul did it. The sense of stupefaction and amazement, that comes over us when we think of it, is the measure of the distance which we have travelled from the Apostolic method.[51]

We can note several things about Paul's approach to leadership appointment.

1 These were local leaders. How easy it would have been to send back to Syrian Antioch for leaders! After all, these were tried and tested women and men, with knowledge of how things were done at HQ, so they offered a combination of spiritual maturity and cultural awareness. Instead, Paul goes for indigenous leaders.

Roland Allen argues that this is where the 'roots of an indigenous Church' are to be found – 'in the first converts'. He also thinks that it is precisely here 'that we come to the heart of the matter . . . of [Paul's] amazing success'.[52]

2 These leaders were newly converted. They are described by Luke as those who had just come to believe in the Lord (14:23), so they had been converted probably no longer than six months previously.

This does feel countercultural for us. We want leaders who are mature, who have the necessary knowledge and character, who won't mess things up. And usually we import: we bring leaders from the sending church or from theological college or from elsewhere in our networks. It does make me think of Alpha, though, where the practice is to ask those who have just become Christians on one course to co-lead on the next one, inviting

---

their friends and social networks to come with them. Perhaps this is one reason for the extraordinary success of Alpha around the world.

3 This was a model of plural leadership. 'Elders' are appointed 'in each church' (14:23). 'The familiar modern pattern of "one pastor one church" was simply unknown.'[53] If the leadership team of the Syrian Antioch church is anything to go by, it would actually have been quite a sizeable team (13:1). John Stott surmises that it would have comprised 'full-time and part-time ministers, paid and voluntary workers, presbyters, deacons and deaconesses'.[54] We may add that they would have had a range of spiritual gifts. Granted that these were very early days in the formation of patterns of ministry across the whole church and that Paul would only have been in each city for a matter of weeks and months, we may perhaps guess, as well, that the leadership structures would have been quite flexible and non-hierarchical.

There is much to think hard about for us as church planters. However we choose to apply these lessons from Paul, one thing is clear – that the appointment and training of leaders is a key element of how he established churches, and it will be no different for us. Following his example, this will be something which we think about right from the beginning, and see in it the engine of establishing and growing our church plants.

Personal development for the church planter

Neil Cole reflects on the first missionary journey:

> Paul and Barnabas covered 1,500 miles in one year ... The first-journey leader tends to be hurried. As when a shaken bottle of champagne is opened, the release of the pressure built up in preparation for the mission tends to explode in a flurry of activity for the new leader ... First-journey leaders go after ministry rather than letting it come to them. They expend more energy in shorter bursts, with less fruit to show for their efforts in the end ... The first journey

---

[53] Stott 1990: 236.
[54] Ibid.

is probably the least effective journey of a leader's life, but it is necessary. On the first journey, the leader gains practical know-how that later will be passed on to others. For this reason, no one can skip the first journey. It will bear fruit that lasts, one hopes, but one also hopes that it will not be the most productive period of a leader's life.[55]

It is encouraging to think that even the great church planter Paul grew in his depth and effectiveness over the years. Church planting is complex and demanding, so we can hope, too, that we will be like him in learning lessons along the way and growing in fruitfulness and in closeness to Christ.

The second church-planting journey

The second missionary journey is narrated by Luke in Acts 15:40 – 18:22, and took place between AD 49 and 53.[56] This is when the gospel first reaches what would become Europe, with all the consequences for global Christianity in the centuries to come. Luke's style changes here, too, with much more of an emphasis on individuals, and set pieces, presumably because he has already established the pattern of the missionary work from the first church-planting journey, and maybe because he was more involved personally: we now have references in the narrative to 'we' (e.g. 16:10), implying that Luke himself was one of the missionary party. The journey takes in three new provinces – Macedonia, Achaia and (briefly) Asia – with their capitals (Thessalonica, Athens and Ephesus). The main focus of Luke's description of the church-planting activity, though, is in Philippi, Athens and Corinth, and we will centre our church-planting reflections therein. In the first, we will see a church being born before our very eyes, in the second we will witness Paul engaging with a very different culture, and in the third we will reflect with Paul on the beginnings of a new strategy for the planting of churches across a region.

55 Cole 2011: 57, 59, 61.
56 Ibid. 144; cf. AD 50–52 according to Witherington 1998: 82.

In Philippi

Getting to Philippi was not totally straightforward. Paul and Silas are heading west, probably for Ephesus. Asia is squarely in their view (the Roman province, that is). Mysteriously, they are 'forbidden by the Holy Spirit to speak the word in Asia' (16:6). So, they look to go north, to Bithynia, 'but the Spirit of Jesus did not allow them' (16:6). We do not know how the Spirit closed these doors; both Silas and Paul were prophets (13:1; 15:32), so there might have been prophetic words, or there might have been a compelling inner sense, or maybe the Lord used actual events or people to prevent the progress of the church-planting band. However the guidance came, it was clear. Paul and Silas and Timothy (and by now maybe Luke) must have found this confusing. They had now covered many hundreds of miles, ending up on the coast at Troas, as far as they could go before falling into the sea, and yet were forbidden by the Lord himself from doing the very thing they had felt commissioned to do. Then Paul has his famous vision: 'there stood a man from Macedonia pleading with him and saying, "Come over to Macedonia and help us"' (16:9). This is enough to convince the apostolic party, and they immediately board a ship and cross over into Macedonia. John Stott helpfully summarizes:

> From this we may learn that usually God's guidance is not negative only but also positive (some doors close, others open); not circum-stantial only, but also rational (thinking about our situation); not personal only, but also corporate (a sharing of the data with others, so that we can mull over them together and reach a common mind).[57]

Guidance is part and parcel of church planting. There are constant decisions – about people, events, strategies, resources, priorities. It is not always clear which way is best, not least when the decision is between competing goods. On occasion, the guidance is confusing, especially when it is the Lord who closes a door into what may seem a particularly good opportunity.

Why did the Holy Spirit close down evangelism in Asia and Bithynia? We do not really know. Asia would feature in later plans, but not

---

[57] Stott 1990: 261.

yet. Maybe, Asia was not ready for the word of the Lord; more likely, as Neil Cole says, Paul was not ready for Asia.[58] Perhaps Bithynia was reserved, in the Lord's sovereignty, for Peter: his first letter is addressed to those in the Dispersion in many places, including Bithynia (1 Pet. 1:1), so maybe the Lord was reserving this ministry for him, not Paul. We cannot know for sure. We can know, however, that this was the Lord's will.

And what of Paul's vision? Who was that mysterious man from Macedonia? Again, we cannot know. Maybe he was just a representative figure. Other conjectures are that he was Alexander the Great or Luke (who was probably from Philippi)[59] or the Philippian jailer.[60] What we can be sure of is that, as Paul shared his vision with his companions, they were all of a mind that the Lord was summoning them over to 'proclaim the good news' in Macedonia (16:10).

And so, to Philippi. This was a prosperous and flourishing city, characterized by being 'a Roman colony' (16:12). Ben Witherington describes it as 'Rome in microcosm',[61] settled as it was by Roman veteran soldiers and run on Roman principles, a factor which comes to dominate the narrative (16:21, 37–39):

- The church planters begin their outreach at 'a place of prayer' (16:13) outside the city, which may indicate that there was no synagogue in Philippi; here Paul meets Lydia, and 'the Lord opened her heart to listen eagerly to what was said by Paul' (16:14). She and her household are baptized, and she invites the missionary party to come and stay with her. When they move on from Philippi, they do so after a final visit 'to Lydia's home', which is where 'the brothers and sisters' of the planted church now meet (16:40).
- The second element of the story is the deliverance of 'a slave-girl who had a spirit of divination' which was bringing 'a great deal of money' to her owners (16:16). She follows the church planters around, calling out loudly that they are 'slaves of the Most High God, who proclaim to you a way of salvation' (16:17). Paul is irritated or (better) 'deeply

---

58 Cole 2011: 69.
59 Witherington 1998: 479–480.
60 Cole 2011: 71, 72–73, 74.
61 Witherington 1998: 488.

troubled'[62] by this – concerned for the girl, and concerned at the 'ambiguous'[63] nature of this announcement, implying that this God is one among a pantheon of many – and delivers her. Her owners then bring Paul and Silas before the authorities and accuse them, with a mixture of anti-Semitism and nationalism, of being Jews and not good Romans (16:20–21). They are beaten (maybe one of the severe floggings or beatings with rods that Paul narrates in 2 Cor. 11:23, 25) and thrown into prison for the night.

- Scene 3 takes us to the 'innermost cell' of the Philippi jail, where Paul and Silas are in the stocks, singing hymns at midnight, with the other prisoners listening to them (16:24, 25). An earthquake shakes them free and flings open the prison doors. The jailer, thinking that the prisoners have all escaped, rather than suffer dishonour prepares to take his own life, but Paul calls out that 'we are all here' (16:28). The jailer falls to his knees and asks, 'What must I do to be saved?' (16:30), and believes their message. In a lovely double washing, he washes the wounds of Paul and Silas, and he and his family are baptized. The scene is completed when, the next day, Paul reveals that he and Silas are Roman citizens, and so the authorities, fearful of the consequences of having broken the law and dishonoured Roman citizenship, apologize in person and ask them to leave the city (16:37–39). They do so, pausing on the way only to encourage the church that has now been planted and meets in Lydia's house.

We see Paul and Silas putting into practice their customary pattern of starting with the synagogue (or equivalent), and being open to following up on introductions which the Holy Spirit makes for them, even if some of these were somewhat unexpected!

Do churches need to be made up of different sorts of people?

A major element of this story is the variety of people who make up the church. There would have been many other stories, but Luke draws out

---

[62] Ibid. 495.
[63] Gaventa 2003: 238.

three – Lydia, the young female slave and the jailer – and surely expects us to see the dramatic differences between them. John Stott remarks:

> It would be hard to imagine a more disparate group than the business woman, the slave girl and the gaoler. Racially, socially and psychologically they were worlds apart. Yet all three were changed by the same gospel and were welcomed into the same church.[64]

This brings into focus an issue for church planters around the composition of their church plants. On the one hand, the Scriptures give us a vision of church where difference, diversity and inclusion are the order of the day. The Philippian church is a demonstration of what Paul writes in Galatians 3:28: 'There is no longer Jew or Greek, there is no longer slave or free, there is no longer male and female; for all . . . are one in Christ Jesus.' Jesus is the only reason that these people would ever be in the same room, let alone be in the kind of depths of relationship that are experienced in the church. On the other hand, many church plants have a sense of calling to reach particular people groups or demographics, whether that be the French, Muslims, young people, the poor or young professionals. How can these two approaches be reconciled?

The Philippian church appears to encapsulate both. The vision that Paul received was to reach Macedonians (16:9), which appears to be a mission aiming at one culture. The irony is that, of the stories that Luke narrates in Philippi, two are about women (so not a Macedonian man), and of these women one (Lydia) is not Macedonian (but comes from Thyatira in Asia).[65] Maybe this is, in practice, how church planting happens.

There is fierce controversy around the work of Donald McGavran, a missiologist of the twentieth century, who developed what he called the 'homogeneous unit principle'.[66] Having seen at first hand the ineffectiveness of missionary evangelism in India, he noted that the missionaries were asking potential converts to adjust not only to the gospel but also to huge social changes. He argued that the only obstacle to faith in Christ should be the challenge of the gospel, and also noted that church growth

---

[64] Stott 1990: 268.
[65] Gaventa 2003: 236, building on an insight from John Calvin.
[66] See McGavran 1990.

was more effective when social barriers were removed. He was thrilled to see the gospel making real inroads when this approach was adopted in India, and also in other parts of the world. Others objected to this on the lines that it appeared to privilege certain people or groups over others, and that it was theologically questionable to separate joining the church from responding to the gospel. The Galatians 3:28 principle of the full diversity of the church became something around which people opposed and rejected McGavran's thinking. In classic terms, it is of the essence of the church that it is 'catholic' and 'universal', as well as 'one' and 'apostolic'. The homogeneous unit principle may have been an effective evangelistic strategy, but it was not leading to the formation of churches.

How are we to reconcile this strand of biblical thinking with the practice of Jesus and the early church in looking for 'people of peace' and following up through their social networks (Luke 10:5–7 and the households of Lydia and the jailer in Philippi, for instance)? And what of the widespread practice in contemporary churches of having youth groups, family-life ministries, groups for the over fifty-fives, all of which cater to specific demographics? And in reality, does not every church, by the existence of its very subculture, end up setting out its stall for certain sections of society more than others? For instance, an 8 am Holy Communion service attracts a different group from a 10:30 am family communion, and beautiful choir worship another group than more contemporary worship led by a band. Should we not just be honest and acknowledge that this is what is happening?

Well, yes and no. This does ring true for the kind of specific vision and calling that church plants may well have. Just as God called Peter to reach out to Jews, and Paul to the Gentiles (Gal. 2:8), so some church plants will feel called to reach young people or students or the poor, others to particular locations such as their parish or estate or city centre or group of villages. Maybe this was how the church at Philippi began: Paul felt called to reach Macedonians. But it was not how it continued, because the mission ended up reaching a far wider range of people. Where we are ending up is that church plants will, in all probability, combine specific missionary callings with the aim of being open to all and building a community that reflects, as much as possible, the local demographics of their surrounding community or city.

What about the call to reach and serve and work with the poor? If Jesus' ministry had a 'bias to the poor', how might this be made central to any church-planting strategy? Or what about issues of unconscious bias and racial prejudice, which are such a barrier to people from non-white backgrounds in many of our churches? Can we learn from Paul and his church planting to help us with these and other urgent issues?

Eckhard Schnabel analyses the texts of Acts and the Pauline letters closely, and concludes: '[The] evidence shows that Paul did not pursue a missionary strategy that focused on a particular ethnic group. He was concerned to preach the gospel to all people in any given city, irrespective of ethnic origin.'[67]

He reaches the same conclusion for the same reason with regard to any particular social groups.[68] He helpfully lays out for us what Greco-Roman society would have been like in the first century:

> In 1 Corinthians 1:26–29 Paul refers to the two main classes of Greco-Roman society. On the one hand are 'the wise', that is the educated citizens, the intellectuals. They are more or less identical with 'the powerful', that is, with those who are influential, who belong to the decision makers of the city, former or present members of the city council and their families, people whose wealth . . . [formed] the basis for their high social status. They are the people of 'noble birth', the members of the local elite who control the decisions that affect the lives of the people living in the city. On the other end of the social spectrum, comprising perhaps 95 per cent of the population of a city in the first century, are 'the foolish', that is, those who did not have the privilege of learning to read or write. They are more or less identical with 'the weak', that is, with the people who have no political or economic power and thus no influence. They are 'the despised' by the members of the local aristocracy, regarded as 'things that are not', as people who are ultimately irrelevant . . . The majority of the people living in the cities, even more so in the

---

[67] Schnabel 2008: 307.
[68] Ibid. 317.

countryside, were uneducated, powerless, without influence, of humble origins – people whom the elites would regard as foolish, weak, low, despised, indeed as 'nothing'.[69]

Paul was planting churches in a profoundly divided and hierarchical society, with a 'near abyss that existed between the local elites and the mass of the poor and disenfranchised'.[70] Paul felt a sense of obligation to every person at every level of society, because the gospel is the sole means of hope for everyone, regardless of social or ethnic background.[71]

And it is likely that both rich and poor were represented in these early churches. Reflecting on what social historians can tell us about the house churches in Rome to which Paul wrote in Romans, Scot McKnight tells us that

> the Christians of Rome were located among the poor with possible connections with high-status individuals . . . The dwelling places of the Roman Christians were at least sometimes apartments (tenements . . .) and not in a house or on villas, though there were single-family dwellings in each of those areas where Christians were found in Rome.[72]

We should note the presence of slaves in the churches of the New Testament.[73] And we also note Luke's references to the 'leading women' who responded to the gospel in Thessalonica (Acts 17:4) and 'men of high standing' in Beroea (17:12). Wayne Meeks, in his groundbreaking book on the sociology of the New Testament, concludes that 'a Pauline congregation generally reflected a fair cross-section of urban society', with those most active in these early churches being 'upwardly mobile'.[74] Paul's evangelistic vision – that the gospel was for all – is what shaped the sociological make-up of these church plants, and defines for us what church should be for us too.

---

[69] Ibid. 308–309.
[70] Ibid. 309.
[71] E.g. Rom. 1:14–16; 1 Cor. 1:26–29; 9:19–23; 12:13; Gal. 3:28; Col. 3:11.
[72] McKnight 2019: 8, 9.
[73] See e.g. McKnight 2019.
[74] Meeks 2003: 73.

Roland Allen suggests that Paul's practice of beginning with the Jews, while being theologically driven, had the effect of ensuring that those converted from this background helped set the culture of rejecting idolatry and immorality. He also notes that Paul did not, as a general rule (although with some exceptions), preach on street corners, nor did he seek out philosophers, but rather, after being rejected by the synagogues, would preach

> in the house of some man of good repute. It is curious how careful St. Luke is to tell us exactly where St. Paul lodged, or in whose house he taught . . . St. Luke evidently desires us to understand that St. Paul was careful to provide things honest in the sight of all [people], and took thought for what was honourable and of good report, as well as of what was true, and of what was pure, and of what was just.[75]

Although Paul 'did not deliberately aim at any class',[76] it is noteworthy that he may have been mindful of those who could provide solid moral and financial foundations for his church plants.

In Athens

After short and dramatic stays in Thessalonica (17:1–9) and Beroea (17:10–15), Paul is sent on by the believers to Athens. He travels alone, asking that Silas and Timothy join him as soon as they can (17:15). Athens was not what once it had been, but it was still a centre for learning.[77] Thus there is something dramatically epoch-making as Paul enters the Areopagus, 'the great Christian apostle amid the glories of ancient Greece'.[78] Athens was 'the proud capital of ancient culture, the home of philosophy, the cradle of democracy'.[79] We have moved across another cultural barrier: we are now in the heartland of Greek culture, the gospel engaging with philosophy, the good news of Jesus with life lived from the mind.

---

[75] Allen 2011: 34–35, giving the examples of Lydia in Philippi, Jason in Thessalonica, Aquila and Titius Justus in Corinth, and the school of Tyrannus in Ephesus.
[76] Ibid. 35.
[77] Witherington 1998: 513; Cole 2011: 76.
[78] Stott 1990: 276.
[79] T. Wright 2018: 195.

Paul waits in Athens for his companions, and he wanders around the city, taking in the sights (17:23). He looks more deeply than the average tourist, though, observing carefully the spiritual life of the city as it was expressed in its worship, its culture, its architecture and way of life (17:16, 23). John Stott powerfully traces the progress of Paul's observation, feeling and action, describing what Paul saw (that the city was overrun with idols), what Paul felt (a paroxysm of distress) and what Paul said (he reasoned with the Athenians in the synagogue, the marketplace every day, and then the Areopagus [17:16–17]). Learning to look and look, and to see beneath the surface of things, is a crucial skill for the church planter. How easy it would have been for Paul to be overwhelmed with the glories of the Acropolis and the Parthenon, to admire their beauty and skilful construction, and not to have thought more deeply about their impact on the culture of the people who lived there. Instead, he saw more deeply, in such a way that his heart was stirred, and he was moved to speak.

Paul ends up debating with 'some Epicurean and Stoic philosophers' (17:18). Beverly Roberts Gaventa highlights the particular points that were likely to be at issue:

> The Epicureans and Stoics were prominent among the philosophical schools of Athens. Particularly important in this context is the Epicurean emphasis on freeing humanity from the fear of the gods and the fear of death. Epicureans believed that the gods are utterly removed from human existence, and therefore the Epicureans ridiculed religious piety. The Stoics emphasized the cultivation of human virtue as the means to achieving one's goals and achieving independence from the control of the passions.[80]

Parallels with contemporary views of life, and of the relationship between God and the world, leap to mind. When you add in that the Epicureans believed that life, at its atomic level, was random and so existence was likewise random, it has an uncannily contemporary ring. 'This worldview remained the opinion of a small minority right up until the eighteenth

---

[80] Gaventa 2003: 248.

century. Since then, it has become the dominant one in modern Western culture. Many imagine it to be a modern "discovery".[81] In other words, here is the gospel engaging with a culture which is profoundly different, in all its most basic assumptions, from that of both Judaism and the agrarian, pagan, superstitious world of the countryside of southern Galatia. We have heard Paul address both these audiences before in Acts (13:16–41; 14:15–17). This speech in Athens is a companion piece to these previous speeches. The three together act as a masterclass from Paul on how to address different cultures with the gospel.

There is another element which makes Paul's speech before the Areopagus different from the previous two. Although violence ensued in both Pisidian Antioch and in Lystra, the atmosphere in which Paul initially spoke was not imminently threatening. But in all probability, it was different in Athens. We sometimes think of the Areopagus as being like a university debating society, where interesting ideas are knocked around by clever philosophers. The underlying reality in Athens was altogether more sinister. The Areopagus was actually a court, with the power to inflict severe penalties, even the death penalty, on those who were judged to be out of line.[82]

C. Kavin Rowe, in his study of the gospel's interaction with various powers and cultures in Acts, makes the careful case that Paul was in actual and potentially terrible danger. For starters, the Greek word translated 'took' in 17:19 ('so they took him and brought him') is used elsewhere in Luke and Acts with the sense of 'to lay hold of' or even 'to seize' (Luke 23:26; Acts 16:19; 17:6; 18:17; 21:30, 33).[83] Most centrally of all is the way Paul is asked about 'this new teaching' which 'sounds rather strange' (17:19, 20). The words 'new' and 'strange' are both allusions to the trial of Socrates in 399 BC at which the famous philosopher was accused of corrupting the young and introducing foreign divinities,[84] accusations of which he was found guilty and for which he was sentenced to death. Where did this happen? In the Areopagus. 'Embedded in the cultural memory of antiquity was the understanding that Socrates was brought

---

[81] T. Wright 2018: 197.
[82] See ibid. 194. Gaventa (2003: 249) disagrees, seeing nothing more than curiosity in the Athenians.
[83] Rowe 2010: 31.
[84] T. Wright 2018: 196.

to trial and received the death penalty in part for introducing "new," "strange" gods.'[85] This means that the introductory question at the Areopagus is not to be heard as a polite, intellectual enquiry, but as something chilling, along the lines of 'we have the right to know'.[86]

> We have to imagine the opening remarks said in a voice of icy calm, with just the hint of a sneer, by a presiding magistrate who knows he has the power to have the person before him beaten, banished, or possibly even killed.[87]

This means that Paul is at risk, and the stakes could not be higher. The burden of his defence, for defence it is before an unsympathetic and uncomprehending court, must be to show that his preaching about Jesus and the resurrection is not new, is not foreign to Athenian intellectual and moral culture. He succeeds triumphantly, showing courage and intelligence in equal measure.

Addressing different cultures

The three main evangelistic speeches have totally different contexts. The Pisidian Antioch address is delivered in a synagogue (13:14), addressed to 'You Israelites, and others who fear God', 'my brothers', 'you descendants of Abraham's family' (13:16, 26, 38). As such, it places the story of Jesus within the longer narrative of the exodus, Samuel and David, and then John the Baptist (13:16–26). Jesus is a descendant of David, a Saviour brought specifically to Israel (13:23, 26). The events of his trial, crucifixion and resurrection are located specifically in Jerusalem (13:27–31). His resurrection is described as fulfilment of Israel's Scriptures (13:32–36), and is compared to the life and death of David (13:36–37). The concluding argument is put to Paul's 'brothers', declaring that through Jesus there is the forgiveness of sins, freedom 'from all those sins from which you could not be freed by the law of Moses' (13:38–39), and warning them not to fulfil the denunciation of the prophets (13:40–41). The speech could not be more Jewish.

---

85 Rowe 2010: 31.
86 Ibid.
87 T. Wright 2018: 199.

We note a clear rhetorical structure, essentially a narration of Israel's history (13:17–25), scriptural proofs (13:27–37), and a final exhortation (13:38–41),[88] which Gaventa draws out for us in terms of its content: 'God's deeds for Israel' (13:16b–25), 'the death, resurrection and witness of Jesus' (13:26–37) and 'a concluding warning' (13:38–41).[89] Eckhard Schnabel helpfully indicates the main thrust: 'What Paul needed to demonstrate in his missionary sermons before Jews was the messianic identity of Jesus.'[90]

The speech in Lystra is much shorter (14:15–17) and is an attempt to correct the misunderstanding that has arisen, that Paul and Barnabas are Greek gods. The situation is rural, the people pagan, superstitious and uneducated, and for the first time Paul (in Acts) addresses a Gentile audience. Paul states that he and Barnabas are mortal (14:15), and encourages the Lycaonians to turn from idolatry ('these worthless things') to 'the living God, who made the heaven and the earth and all that is in them' (14:15). God has allowed ignorance to continue in times past in the nations, but has not left himself without witness through harvests, food and joy (14:16–17). Witherington sees a narration of what God has done for pagans in the past (14:15c–17), and argues that Paul was interrupted by the reaction of his audience and was not able to complete the speech.[91]

In Athens, Paul is once more addressing Gentiles, but this time much more sophisticated than in Lystra. Once more there is a misunderstanding – the reference to Paul being 'a proclaimer of foreign divinities' in connection with Jesus and the resurrection (17:18) is because his hearers thought that he was talking about two gods: Jesus and his female consort, Resurrection.[92] And we remember that Paul's aim is both to argue that Christianity is not 'new' and 'strange' and to declare the gospel. Tom Wright helps bring that out:

[Paul's] main point ought now to be clear: '*What I am saying to you may sound "new", but is in fact hidden within your culture. It is well*

---

88 Witherington 1998: 407.

89 Gaventa 2003: 198–202; and Schnabel 2008: 158.

90 Schnabel 2008: 162.

91 Witherington 1998: 426. Schnabel (2008: 163) would agree, seeing 14:15a–c as the narration; 14:15d–17 as the argument; and the concluding exhortation lost due to the interruption of the crowd.

92 T. Wright 2018: 198–199.

hidden; in fact, you have covered it up with foolish and unnecessary superstructures. But though the specific news about Jesus and the resurrection may be a shock to your system . . . the underlying truth that it unveils is a truth about the world and its One Creator God to which, at best, your culture dimly and distantly bears witness.'[93]

Alongside this, Paul is carefully arguing that it is in the resurrection of Jesus that we have the best way of understanding the purpose of our world.[94] Eckhard Schnabel agrees, seeing the speech as an argument that Paul was not introducing a new deity, but rather 'he is the spokesman of the unknown god whom they already worship'.[95]

Gaventa helpfully discerns a simple structure to the speech (17:16–34):

> First, Paul characterizes the Athenians as very religious people (vv. 22–23a); second, he issues a carefully worded critique of idol-worship (vv. 23b–29); third, he calls for repentance, declares that there will be a time of judgment, and connects that judgment with God's raising 'a man' from the dead (vv. 30–31).[96]

There are many rhetorical features in common with previous speeches, but, notably, there is an absence of any narration of God's dealings with the world.[97] Paul connects with the members of his audience around their religiosity, expressed in the altar to the 'unknown god' (17:23), asserting that what is unknown to them, he will proclaim. Ignorance is a recurring theme (17:23, 30), something which cannot have gone down too well in the intellectual centre that was ancient Athens. The heart of the speech presents God as the Creator of heaven and earth (17:24), and argues for the illogicality of idolatry and the notion of God living in shrines and temples (17:24–25). Again, one wonders how this would have gone down in a location overlooking the Acropolis and the Parthenon. There is an

---

93 Ibid. 202; emphasis original.
94 Ibid.
95 Schnabel 2008: 170, 182.
96 Gaventa 2003: 246.
97 Witherington (1998: 518) argues that Luke omitted it in his summary of Paul's speech on the grounds that it would just have been a repetition of what we already know of Paul's altercations in the marketplace in 17:18.

interesting allusion to how God has allotted times and locations for all peoples everywhere, which Wright sees as an allusion to the extraordinary networking and transport opportunities that the Roman Empire and its roads had given to the ancient world.[98] Paul quotes contemporary poets to back up his description of the human search for God (17:27–29), while also expressing the limits and corruptions of such a quest. Along the way, he interacts with the Epicurean and Stoic philosophers:

> Against the [Epicureans], God is said to be near and caring a good deal about human beliefs and behaviour. Against the [Stoics] God is distinguishable from his creation and true knowledge of God is not simply gained by evaluating nature. There must be proclamation of what God has revealed and is now doing. Against both of these philosophies the speech affirms resurrection, judgment, and a teleological character to human history.[99]

The conclusion is a bold application of those aspects of the gospel which the audience would find least congenial, with an urgent call for 'all people everywhere' to repent (17:30).

The speech is surprisingly Jewish: esssentially a critique of idolatry and an appeal to Jesus as the purpose of history. Although Paul nowhere quotes Scripture, the world view is unmistakably that of Isaiah and the Psalms.[100] The themes are startlingly similar to those of the short speech to the pagan Gentiles in Lystra, albeit in a much more sophisticated register. 'In both [speeches], the subjects treated included creation or natural theology, the endured ignorance of pagans, and . . . the subject of good news for Gentiles.'[101] 'The speech is a "translation" of earlier Lukan themes into the local idiom.'[102]

Eckhard Schnabel gives us a careful analysis of Paul's approach to the philosophers with whom he was engaged on the Areopagus. He shows how Paul 'employs convictions, arguments and formulations that these intellectual Athenians were familiar with and that they would have

---

[98] T. Wright 2018: 200.
[99] Witherington 1998: 534–535.
[100] T. Wright 2018: 200.
[101] Witherington 1998: 426.
[102] Gaventa 2003: 247.

acknowledged as valid',[103] but he argues that Paul must have left his hearers in no doubt that he rejected many of their ideas, describing them as ignorant, just as he had earlier called the idols worshipped by the Lycaonians 'worthless things' (14:15; cf. 17:23, 30). When we consider Paul's surroundings, the magnificent Athenian temples, and the fact that successive Roman emperors were being designated as gods and given their own temples, we see that Paul's speech was skating 'on very thin ice' and was 'positively dangerous'.[104] Schnabel's conclusion is worth quoting at length:

> Paul's response to the religious beliefs and practices of the Athenians was, ultimately, not accommodation but confrontation. While he uses terminology that could be easily understood by the intellectual Athenians, and while many of his statements and assertions are acceptable at least for some members of the council, Paul leaves no doubt that he unambiguously rejects the plurality of gods and cults and the proliferation of temples, altars and statues in the city of Athens. Paul is convinced, and he states as such, that the religious activities of the Athenians are evidence of ignorance . . . And Paul is unafraid to point to the resurrection of the dead despite the fact that he presumably knows that the resurrection is a laughable concept for the Greeks.[105]

Three very different contexts, then, for these three speeches – devoutly Jewish, superstitiously pagan, and sophisticatedly, intellectually Gentile. Paul skilfully communicates in terms, language and allusions which would have been those of his various audiences.

While we see Paul's flexibility and versatility in his approach to these different contexts (what is different each time), we can see, as well, the constants of his message and methodology (what was the same). We need to bear in mind that Luke is giving us only summaries of Paul's preaching,

---

[103] Schnabel 2008: 174.
[104] Ibid. 180.
[105] Ibid. 182. Schnabel (ibid., 181–182) tells us that many ancient tombstones had the letters *n.f.n.s.n.c.* on them, which stood for *non fui, non sum, non curo* in Latin, which means 'I was not, I am not, I care not'. How different is the Christian world view!

and so we must not overpress matters, but I think it is not outstripping the evidence to see two constants.

1 Paul had a structure to his talks. By and large, he would include:

- a narrative, either of the Old Testament story as it pointed towards Jesus (13:16–25) or of God's faithful and kind dealings with the world in nature (14:15–16);
- the main point of the talk ('to us the message of this salvation has been sent' [13:26]; 'What therefore you worship as unknown, this I proclaim to you' [17:23]);
- the argument, the proofs, sometimes about Jesus (13:26–37), sometimes the truth about God as kind and generous (14:17), sometimes the nature of the true God (17:24–29);
- a concluding exhortation – a call to faith or to repentance (13:38–41; 14:15; 17:30–31).

Paul may not have followed this outline slavishly, and he evidently felt free to adapt it and its order according to circumstances, but it seems likely that he had a mental map of what a gospel talk looked like, which both engaged his listeners and their mental worlds and got him to the point where he could talk about Jesus. When we consider that the talks at Lystra and in Athens arose from misunderstandings and in the midst of quite difficult situations, it is all the more telling that Paul appears to have had in his mind a model for communicating the gospel, one which he felt he had the freedom to adapt in the light of individual circumstances.

Is there something for us to learn here as we preach evangelistically, engaging with different and diverse cultures with a view to planting churches? The advance work of thinking through what and how we want to communicate in all situations might give us the freedom to deliver our message in contextually appropriate ways.

2 Paul's content was theological. The Pisidian Antioch talk has a clear message (that Jesus is the Messiah) and the two Gentile talks have clear similarities to each other (the true God is the Creator of heaven and earth and everything in them). It is striking how much the emphasis in both these talks is on creation, which forms the basis of the rejection of idolatry. 'The unprepared pagans first need to hear the Old Testament foundations of the New Testament.'[106]

Thinking about the origins of the world and humanity is more than a point of contact between the gospel and those, of whatever background, who do not believe, but is rather a theological foundation stone for engaging with God. To grasp that God made everything and is separate from and beyond it all, and that human beings have not made him in our image but rather the other way round, frees us from thinking of God as like us or needing us or capable of being manipulated by us. It also introduces the sense of accountability, and orients us in a world of which we are not the ultimate masters and of which we are not finally in control. It frees us to know that God is 'the living God' (14:15; cf. 17:24–25). How then are we to deal with such a God? He has shown us by raising Jesus from the dead (13:30–39; 17:31). This is where we move from ignorance (14:16; 17:23, 30) to knowing, from unbelief to the gospel, from superstition to Jesus.

Contextualization

Paul has offered us an early example of contextualization. What works well in one setting may actually be less effective (and quite likely inappropriate) in another. The size, values and strategies of church plants will and should vary considerably according to their different contexts. A critique of church planting is sometimes made that it is an imposition of an alien church culture into a very different context. Sometimes, particular models which have been widely and successfully used in similar contexts around the country are taken to be *the* way to do church planting, and these can then run into trouble, calling the whole notion of church planting into question.

Contextualization is a complex and sometimes controversial area. Christians from the Majority World have much to teach us, as their experience highlights some of the key issues. For many years, Western forms of Christianity were brought to African and Asian lands by missionaries, who planted churches that carried the gospel but did so in

---

[106] Haacker 1988: 71, cited in Schnabel 2008: 183.

a culturally Western garb; hence the anomaly of African churches which were identical to suburban English ones. Christianity was 'perceived as a foreign religion or, worse still, an effective tool of Western imperialism'.[107] This went beyond cultural forms to theological frameworks: Westerners are often blind to the historical fact that the creeds and historic formularies of, say, the Church of England arose from very particular historical situations and used culturally specific philosophical frameworks.[108] It is worth reflecting, too, that the gospel and the Scriptures come to us in culturally specific terms and stories. 'There is no context-free theology.'[109] This all raises challenging questions for church planters, but also lays out for us an important point: 'the reality . . . is that contextualization is a biblical, theological and missiological imperative.'[110] Stephen Bevans argues that contextualization is something we all do, internalizing and 'making our own' the truths of our faith, and that this is in tune with the character of the gospel itself, in which 'God is revealed not primarily in *ideas* but rather in concrete reality', not least in the incarnation.[111] This focuses the question for us: the key issue is the relationship between gospel and context, and the extent to which either or both are changed by their interaction. Tim Keller argues that 'contextualization is one of the keys to effective ministry today'.[112]

There is, of course, a primary sense in which the gospel never changes. 'Jesus Christ is the same yesterday and today and for ever' (Heb. 13:8). Alongside this, we have to recognize that 'there is no culture-less presentation of the gospel'.[113] We inescapably think and conceptualize and communicate in words, thoughts and emphases which come through our own cultures and experiences. This is true of the Bible as well: 'properly understood, the Bible is a record of contextualized revelation; a record of the way God interacted with humans in space-time history in the totality of their contexts.'[114] Contextualization is never a justification for abandoning the truth of the gospel and the Scriptures, but it raises

---

[107] Musasiwa 2007: 67.
[108] Ibid.
[109] Ibid.
[110] Ibid. 66.
[111] Bevans 2002: 5, 12.
[112] Keller 2012: 90.
[113] Ibid. 93.
[114] Musasiwa 2007: 67.

for us the realization that 'theology is both context-defined and "context-transcending"'.[115]

Tim Keller lands this for us in a carefully argued four-chapter section of his church-planting magnum opus, *Center Church*. He argues that '[e]veryone contextualizes – but few think much about how they are doing it. We should not only contextualize but also think about *how* we do it.'[116] The key is 'to do contextualization *consciously*'.[117]

An obvious point is that church planters must know what they mean when they talk about the gospel. What is the key and core message we are declaring to our neighbourhoods and contexts when we are planting our churches? What distinguishes us from other religions, other charities and philanthropic organizations? And how are we to communicate this?

Although Acts gives us more than one way of communicating the gospel, it does assume that there is only one gospel being communicated.

In his farewell speech to the Ephesian elders at Miletus, Paul can say: 'I testified to both Jews and Greeks about repentance towards God and faith towards our Lord Jesus' (20:21) and about 'the message of his grace' (20:32). This feels like a summary of his gospel ministry, regardless of audience. Interestingly, as Roland Allen points out, there is actually very little in the evangelistic speeches at Pisidian Antioch, Lystra and Athens about 'faith towards our Lord Jesus Christ'.[118] A far more likely summary of Paul's gospel preaching, certainly to Gentiles, can be found in 1 Corinthians 15 and 1 Thessalonians 1:9–10.

- In the former, Paul reminds the Corinthians 'of the good news that I proclaimed to you', that which is 'of first importance', which had been handed down to him (1 Cor. 15:1, 3): 'That Christ died for our sins in accordance with the scriptures, and that he was buried, and that he was raised on the third day in accordance with the scriptures, and that he appeared to Cephas, then to the twelve' (15:3–5). We note the centrality of the death and resurrection of Jesus, the key attestation of the Scriptures, and the witnesses to the resurrection.

---

[115] Ibid.
[116] Keller 2012: 97.
[117] Ibid. 96.
[118] Allen 2011: 93.

- In 1 Thessalonians 1, Paul talks about the reception of 'our message of the gospel' (1:5), and lays out what this response was: 'You turned to God from idols, to serve a living and true God, and to wait for his Son from heaven, whom he raised from the dead – Jesus, who rescues us from the wrath that is coming' (1:9–10). This language echoes that of Paul's altercation with the pagans of Lystra (Acts 14:15), and we note the call to abandon idolatry, the attention to the resurrection of Jesus, and the return of the Lord to put the world to rights.
- It is significant to note, as well, that the accusations against Paul from Gentiles in Acts tended to be about a challenge to the structures of authority in their lives: 'These men . . . are advocating customs that are not lawful for us as Romans to adopt or observe' (16:20–21) and 'They are all acting contrary to the decrees of the emperor, saying that there is another king named Jesus' (17:7).

When we place these summaries of Paul's preaching to Gentiles alongside that to Jews, we have an outline of his approach:

- an account of the life, teaching, miracles, death and resurrection of Jesus, as attested to by the Scriptures and witnessed by those who saw the Lord in his public ministry and after his resurrection;
- the corollaries of acknowledging Jesus as the anointed king of God in his kingdom, and leaving all other lords and reputed gods;
- the summons to work with Jesus in his kingdom, making all things new and right.

Much more could be said, but this seems to have been the core of Paul's message about Jesus, King and Messiah, fulfilling Jewish hopes, challenging Gentile power, and inviting the peoples of the world, not least the poor and dispossessed and oppressed, into the favour and anointing of God's long-promised kingdom.

This is both universal ('context-transcending', in Musasiwa's terminology) and 'context-defined'. The Scriptures fill out for us the nature of the messiahship and kingship of Jesus and his resurrection, which transcends all cultures. We also need to interpret and apply the implications for rescue and power in our own contexts. We will bring our own understanding of such things to our believing and preaching of the gospel. Our own culture will be partly affirmed and partly challenged by the gospel, and interaction with people of other cultures will help us learn from their insights those aspects of the gospel we have failed to see due to our own cultural blindness. 'Context brings to light aspects of [the gospel's] meaning which may have hitherto remained hidden.'[119] Keller uses the analogy of a bridge between the cultures of communicators and hearers, and says '[t]here should be heavy traffic back and forth across the bridge':[120] the church planter will be looking to affirm and challenge the culture of his or her hearers, but will also be open to his or her understanding of the gospel being corrected by the perspective of the receiving culture.

Biblical contextualization, then, requires a careful double task for the church planter:

- There needs to be an immersion in the gospel of Jesus Christ, such that we bring to our interaction with the living God an openness to be challenged in how our own cultures and experiences may have distorted it and blinded us to some of its aspects. This is best done in a combination of prayer and interaction with others.
- There needs to be profound interaction with the culture into which we are planting our churches, such that we understand it, empathize with it and can converse with it in ways which can be heard and felt and understood. Tim Keller talks about the need for 'CQ', or 'cultural quotient', to go alongside IQ and EQ (emotional intelligence) for the church planter. This is best done face to face, when meeting, listening to and talking with the people who we hope and pray will come to believe the gospel and join the churches we are planting.

In Corinth

Even though some of his hearers on the Areopagus say they wish to hear him again (17:32), Paul decides to leave Athens (18:1). He makes for Corinth, an action which, apart from a brief visit to Ephesus (18:19–21)

---

[119] Musasiwa 2007: 69.
[120] Keller 2012: 103.

and a journey around the Galatian churches to strengthen the disciples (18:23), signals the end of the second church-planting journey.

In connection with Paul's stay in Corinth, let's consider three points, which reflect the way the narrative is structured:[121] there are three significant pronouncements, one by Paul (18:6), one by the Lord (18:9–10) and one by Gallio, the Roman proconsul in the city (18:14–15).

Paul's pronouncement is that, here in Corinth, just as in Pisidian Antioch (13:46), he is moving on from the Jews to the Gentiles. As Luke writes: 'When [the Jews] opposed and reviled him, in protest he shook the dust from his clothes and said to them, "Your blood be on your own heads! I am innocent. From now on I will go to the Gentiles"' (18:6).

We must not exaggerate the importance of this statement. This is not a new strategy, nor a repudiation of the Jews – Paul will go straight to the synagogue when he arrives in Ephesus, after all (18:19). Nonetheless, it is a clear new aspect to his ministry. Now, he bases himself in a Gentile home, that of Titius Justus (18:7), and operates from here. It is right next door to the synagogue, so maybe Paul is continuing his witness to the Jews and God-fearers who are interested in the gospel; we read that Crispus, 'the official of the synagogue', and his household are converted, and that 'many of the Corinthians who heard Paul became believers and were baptized' (18:8).[122] John Stott underlines this for us when he remarks on how Paul moves his ministry to Titius Justus's house: '[This] is more than a geographical note. It means rather that the scene of his evangelistic labours changed from public synagogue to private house, and that so the people being evangelized changed from Jews to Gentiles.'[123]

I love the way that Paul is always thinking about his ministry, refining and developing it, listening to the Lord about how it can be done better. This seems to me to be a feature of our better church plants as well.

Stott is also helpful in drawing out a pattern that we will see in Acts 18 and 19, when Paul bases himself in Corinth and Ephesus. These are two significant centres, Corinth a place of commerce, commanding Achaia; and Ephesus a hub of religion, the focus in many ways of commercial and religious life in Asia. Paul spends significant amounts of time in both

---

121 Witherington 1998: 537.
122 And, independently, we read of Crispus's baptism in 1 Cor. 1:14.
123 Stott 1990: 298.

(around two years in Corinth [18:4, 11, 18] and over three years in Ephesus [19:8, 10]), and we will need to consider the significance of this when we reflect on the third church-planting journey. For now, we just note that Paul is doing something different, but the same thing in both places. Stott summarizes this new plan for us:

1 He starts, as always, in the synagogues (18:4–5; 19:8).
2 Then he moves to sharing the gospel with the Gentiles, basing himself in a particular place and building, Titius Justus's house in Corinth (18:6–7), and a lecture hall, owned by a man called Tyrannus, in Ephesus (19:10).
3 In both cities, large numbers of people come to faith in Christ (18:8; 19:10).
4 In both places, the Lord encourages Paul supernaturally, with a vision in Corinth (18:9–10) and with extraordinary miracles in Ephesus (19:11–12).
5 In both cities, the Roman authorities dismiss accusations made against Paul and, in effect, legitimize the Christian mission (18:12ff.; 19:35ff.).[124]

Some of these common features lie within the sovereignty of God (the response to the gospel, the miraculous occurrences, the Roman reaction), but church planters can discern an approach and an attitude in Paul that they can appropriate for themselves. Paul has not changed his strategy ('to the Jew first and also to the Greek' [Rom. 1:16]), but this seems to be a significant staging post in developing his methodology; now, he is giving time, energy and the resources of basing himself in a strategic location to reach the Gentiles. And he is looking to the Lord to vindicate this approach, both through conversions and through his protection of the mission. It may not be unconnected with the Lord's pronouncement (in 18:9–10), which we will look at in a moment.

It is worth church planters reflecting on this. To shift a location and, in particular, to stake out a base for operations is a significant moment, both in terms of strategy and also in methodology. For instance, if a mission

---

[124] Stott 1990: 294–5.

starts with meeting on the streets, as with an open youth work, things move up a gear when a hall is rented. There are pros and cons: to move into a specific location means a loss of flexibility but a gain of maturity and scale. The danger is that the building becomes the focus of the vision rather than enabling it, and that precious funds will be gobbled up by the demands of rent and maintenance. The potential advance is one of scale, and of gaining confidence from having a definite place with which to associate the mission. To have regular access to a building can be an important step towards a mission becoming a church plant. It takes wisdom to know when to make this move.

The second pronouncement of this time, transitioning to the end of the second journey, is the Lord's:

One night the Lord said to Paul in a vision, 'Do not be afraid, but speak and do not be silent; for I am with you, and no one will lay a hand on you to harm you, for there are many in this city who are my people.'
(Acts 18:9–10)

This is Jesus speaking to Paul just as YHWH had done to many in the Old Testament,[125] promising both success and protection, using the vocabulary of the people of God, which has previously been applied only to Jews but now includes Gentiles also.[126] Paul must have been strengthened, because in the very next verse we read how he stayed for eighteen months in Corinth, 'teaching the word of God among them' (18:11).

It is worth us noting that Paul, the great, lion-hearted Paul, was genuinely afraid. He writes of this experience in 1 Corinthians: 'I came to you in weakness and in fear and in much trembling' (2:3). And why else should the Lord Jesus speak to him in this vision, encouraging him not to be afraid, unless he was? He must have felt lonely ('for I am with you' [Acts 18:10]) and overwhelmed ('for there are many in this city who are my people' [18:10]). We do not know why he felt this way. Neil Cole thinks it

---

125 Such as Abraham (Gen. 21:22; 26:3; 31:3), Moses (Exod. 3:12; 4:10–12), Joshua (Josh. 1:9), Isaiah (Isa. 41:10), Jeremiah (Jer. 1:4–10); see Gaventa 2003: 258.
126 Gaventa 2003: 259.

was 'the wanton sinfulness of Corinth';[127] John Stott that it was this, combined with the pride of the Corinthians.[128] Ben Witherington wonders if it was not the accumulation of what must have been traumatic experiences of rejection and violence, which had left him 'shell-shocked'.[129] Whatever the cause, Paul was fragile and afraid, but the Lord spoke strength and hope into him.

Church planters can be and often are afraid. If Paul was, so will we be. It may surprise us, as maybe it did him. Certain things may trigger weak spots for us. Weariness may accumulate. The scale of the task, or of the wickedness with which we are called to deal, may overwhelm us. It is OK to feel like this, to be human.

By the same token, one of the key church-planter attributes is courage. Faith may often look and feel like bravery. Not to cut and run may feel as though it is the most courageous thing we have done.

Paul was strengthened by his vision from the Lord, a word that spoke to his emotions ('Do not be afraid') and to his imagined fears ('there are many in this city who are my people'); but it also gave him a strategy ('speak and do not be silent'), which led him to stay longer than usual in a place. This may have been the time when Paul took up his tentmaking again with Priscilla and Aquila (18:3), and moved to Titius Justus's house (18:7). Faith, hope and a plan are a good combination when we are under intense pressure.

The third pronouncement comes from Gallio, the Roman proconsul. The Jews from the Corinthian synagogue 'made a united attack on Paul and brought him before the tribunal' (18:12). Did Paul think back to when he had been dragged before the Areopagus (17:19)? Did he feel that his life was once more at risk? Did he wonder what the Lord had meant when he said that 'no one will lay a hand on you to harm you' (18:10)? By God's grace, Gallio refuses to hear the case, saying that this dispute about the worship of God is essentially an inter-Jewish affair, and does not fall within the jurisdiction of wider Roman civic law (18:14–16). In all likelihood, this was not wisdom and empathy, but barely concealed anti-Semitism. The aftermath is a blind Roman eye turned to an assault on the

---

[127] Cole 2011: 77.
[128] Stott 1990: 295–296.
[129] Witherington 1998: 550.

Jewish Sosthenes right outside the tribunal (18:17).[130] 'Humanly speaking, Paul escapes because of the bias or prejudice of this official . . . However, from a larger perspective, Paul escapes because God was with him and promised no harm would come to him in Corinth.'[131]

Gallio's action had potentially enormous consequences for the Christian mission and for the planting of churches in the Roman Empire. Tom Wright explains for us:

> This was a momentous event in the history of the church, and one wonders if even Paul had seen it coming. What it meant was that, unlike the authorities in the other territories he had visited, the official Roman governor of southern Greece had declared *that being a Jesus-follower was to be seen as a variation of the Jewish way of life* . . . It meant (among other things) that when non-Jewish Jesus-followers absented themselves from the civic cult – which . . . could hardly remain hidden in a proud Roman city – they would be able to claim the same exemption as their Jewish neighbours.[132]

Rome had strict parameters to its toleration of religion, and Judaism was the only permitted monotheistic religion in the empire. This put Christians in a potentially exposed and dangerous position. Gallio's ruling, though, while it might not have declared Christianity legal, did set a precedent that it could shelter under the same protected exempt status as Judaism. This had huge ramifications for Paul and his church-planting work, and for the churches he was planting in the region. They were assured, for the time being at least, that they would not be directly persecuted by the might of Rome.

One last comment on this second church-planting journey. Luke intends us to note that Paul came back to both Jerusalem and Antioch to round the journey off (18:22). It was important for Paul to maintain connection with both these bases. It will be similar for us and our church plants. Church planters can sometimes be independent-minded – pioneers and entrepreneurs often are – and the connections with sending churches

---

[130] Is this the Sosthenes we read of in 1 Cor. 1:1? It seems very likely.
[131] Witherington 1998: 554–555.
[132] T. Wright 2018: 229; emphasis original.

or dioceses or networks can feel frustrating and constraining. Sometimes, as well, there may be tensions between sending bodies and dioceses; maybe this was also true between Jerusalem (the original mother church, and the centre of Jewish Christianity) and Antioch (the leading missionary church for Paul and others, and the church with the closest links to the Gentile mission). It is a good principle, though, to honour our leaders, and diocesan officials and networks are that for church planters. Strategically, too, poor relationships and lack of communication between sending and planted churches are some of the most frequent reasons why church plants get into trouble. Let's make sure that we work hard at having strong links with our Jerusalem and Antioch churches!

The third church-planting journey

Now to the third journey, probably from AD 53 to 57,[133] narrated in Acts 19:1 – 21:26. The major centre is Ephesus (19:1–41); then comes a farewell tour of Macedonia and Greece (20:1–6), with a poignant last address to the elders of the Ephesian church (20:17–38); and finally Paul's continued journey to Jerusalem, where he is arrested in the temple (21:1–26). We will consider in turn the disaster at Ephesus, Paul's changing leadership strategy, and his plans for succession and the sustainability of the church plants.

Disaster at Ephesus – mental and emotional health for church planters

This episode is not actually narrated by Luke, but is something that was clearly of deep and profound significance for Paul. He refers to it at the beginning of 2 Corinthians:

> We do not want you to be unaware, brothers and sisters, of the affliction we experienced in Asia; for we were so utterly, unbearably crushed that we despaired of life itself. Indeed, we felt that we had received the sentence of death so that we would rely not on ourselves but on God who raises the dead.
> (2 Cor. 1:8–10)

---

[133] Cole 2011: 144.

This is profoundly dark language. Paul's affliction was beyond his capacity to bear. It was total. He thought he was going to die. Later in the letter he talks about the experience of suffering redeemed, but, as Tom Wright points out, this is the perspective of someone who has passed through such an experience; at the time, it felt very different.[134]

> We are afflicted in every way, but not crushed; perplexed, but not driven to despair; persecuted, but not forsaken; struck down but not destroyed; always carrying in the body the death of Jesus, so that the life of Jesus may also be made visible in our bodies . . . So death is at work in us, but life in you.
> (2 Cor. 4:8–10, 12)

The point is that, while he was going through these experiences, Paul felt crushed, driven to despair, forsaken, destroyed, struggling with death itself, and losing. Tom Wright talks of Paul having a breakdown.[135]

We do not know for sure what happened.

> The best guess . . . is that Paul was imprisoned in Ephesus and put on trial for his life. And that made a 'perfect storm,' because it followed hard on the heels of a nasty shock from Corinth. The church there had turned against him.[136]

Paul has already used strong language in 1 Corinthians, about fighting 'with wild animals at Ephesus' (1 Cor. 15:32), and had said that there were 'many adversaries' against the effective work that the Lord had opened up for him (16:9), but this seems to have been of a different order. The overwhelming and unrelenting nature of 'so deadly a peril' (2 Cor. 1:10) threatened to undo him completely and end both his ministry and his life.

Perhaps Acts does give us some clues. The ministry at Ephesus seems to have been marked by the supernatural to a peculiar extent. It begins with the encounter with the disciples who knew nothing of the Holy Spirit (in reality, nothing of Jesus), then comes the almost comical tale of the

---

[134] T. Wright 2018: 237.
[135] Ibid. 244.
[136] Ibid. 239.

sons of Sceva being overcome by a demonized man (Acts 19:1–16). Meanwhile, 'God did extraordinary miracles through Paul' (19:11). Any miracle sounds pretty extraordinary, but these are even more so. And all this meant awe, praise to the Lord, and new believers abandoning magic, burning their old books (19:17–19). Ephesus was clearly a centre for spiritual warfare. It is no coincidence that, when Paul writes his letter to the Ephesians, he brings it to a climax with a description of the power of the gospel to overcome evil. 'The cosmic powers of this present darkness', 'the spiritual forces of evil' (Eph. 6:12): this may be the vocabulary of someone who has experienced these things first-hand, and lived to tell the tale of both their evil and their strength.

And the riot in Ephesus must have been intensely frightening, even for someone like Paul. If Corinth led to weakness and fear and much trembling (1 Cor. 2:3), then what must it have been like for Paul to endure two hours of chanting by many thousands of people, especially when he was not allowed to do anything about it (Acts 19:23–41)? He was to face increasing violence as he neared Jerusalem (21:11, 35; 22:22–23; 23:10, 12), but this may have been the first time when such naked aggression and overwhelming strength reared its ugly head. Combined with the emotional body-blow of the Corinthian rejections and the intensity of spiritual struggle, might this have taken him to breaking point? And if, as Wright believes, he was arrested and imprisoned in Ephesus, maybe more than once, in events not reported in Acts, and Paul found himself alone in a cell of an ancient prison, frightened, perhaps ill, the victim of extreme violence and spiritual attack, would this be the time when even this great saint broke?

There will be times like this, in all probability, for every church planter. We have already reflected on the place of suffering in planting churches, the cost we may well have to pay. Let us reflect, for a moment, on how we handle things when we seem to have failed, and when our emotional and mental health might be affected.

This is far more common than one might suppose. Might we find a way in our church-planting networks to be more honest about this, to be safer places for people to talk about their struggles and failures? When we are in the midst of darkness, we do not want to have to pretend. We probably do not want to be the centre of attention either, but sensitive and sensible places to talk, to cry, to pray – these would be good. This could be where we experience a 'consolation [that is] abundant through Christ', and which we, in time and in turn, can share with others (2 Cor. 1:3–7).

Mental and emotional health is being increasingly recognized as a crucial element of all leadership, and church planting is no exception. To plant a church can be exceptionally demanding, and we can find ourselves bent out of shape every now and then. We may also find that elements of our personality and factors arising from our personal histories can be triggered when we are under pressure, not least in the kind of perfect storm that Paul experienced in Ephesus. Sometimes this damages more than ourselves: our families and friends can suffer, and it is sadly not unknown for our staffs and teams to bear the brunt of the pain of our wounds, and our congregations can find themselves on the receiving end of harsh sermons or startlingly angry conversations or emails. Paul's example should offer us a model of self-awareness, to not be afraid to get help, personal and professional – for our own sakes, as well as for our church plants and our loved ones.

Paul's evolving leadership strategy

A team has been building for some time now. We keep reading of more and more names in Paul's party. We started the second church-planting journey with Paul and Silas (Acts 15:40), swiftly joined by Timothy (16:3). Almost certainly, Luke joins the party from his native Philippi (e.g. 16:10). Then we meet Priscilla and Aquila in Corinth (18:2), who travel with Paul to Ephesus (18:18). They, in turn, mentor and disciple Apollos (18:24–28). We discover that Erastus, as well as Timothy, is one of Paul's 'helpers' and they are sent to Macedonia (19:22). By the time Paul leaves Ephesus for Macedonia, we read a magnificent list of those who went with him: 'He was accompanied by Sopater son of Pyrrhus from Beroea, by Aristarchus and Secundus from Thessalonica, by Gaius from Derbe, and by Timothy, as well as by Tychicus and Trophimus from Asia' (20:4). This list is revealing at a number of levels. First of all, that there are so many of them; we had not known that Paul was recruiting others to go with him on his church-planting journeys.[137] Then, that they all came from the churches

---

[137] E. E. Ellis (1993: 183) writes that 'in Acts and the Pauline letters some one hundred individuals, under a score of titles and activities, are associated with the apostle at one time or another during his ministry'.

he had planted; none of these come from Jerusalem or from Antioch. Finally, that he had a vision for them that went beyond where they came from; they appear to be with him on a kind of apostolic tour.

Neil Cole has written particularly helpfully about Paul's evolving strategy around leadership development and deployment.

- He notices that the churches planted on the first journey are relatively weak, not having strong leadership, which is why Paul and Barnabas have to keep going back to visit them to appoint leaders (14:23), then again to strengthen them (15:36; 16:1–6; 18:23).[138]
- On the second journey, Paul appears to be leaving people behind to look after the churches he is planting (Luke in Philippi; Timothy in Thessalonica; Silas in Beroea). This leaves Paul himself dangerously isolated, though, in Athens, and he sends for Silas and Timothy to join him there (17:15). Clearly, this strategy has limitations.[139]
- It is in Corinth that Paul makes the leap to the next stage of his strategy: 'In essence, Jesus instructed Paul not to leave so quickly. Rather than recruiting and importing a team of leaders, he is to find them in the harvest fields . . . Paul's methods would shift from an addition strategy to one of multiplication.'[140]

Alongside this new approach to leadership development and multiplication, Paul makes another major change in how he is operating between the second and third church-planting journeys. He stays for two years in Corinth, and then for three in Ephesus. This is markedly different from the ceaseless movement of the first journey.

On his first journey, Paul covered 1,500 miles in one year. On this third journey, he lived almost exclusively in Ephesus for three years (Acts 20:31), but the word of God spread in an incredible way to cover more than 4,000 miles. In fact, the success of this missionary journey is hard to fathom. Luke says that everyone in Asia, Jew and Gentile alike, heard the word of the Lord.[141]

---

[138] Cole 2011: 60.
[139] Ibid. 75.
[140] Ibid. 77, 78.
[141] Ibid. 97.

Cole notes that this success went way beyond the amazing fruitfulness in Ephesus itself, with the seven churches addressed in Revelation 2 and 3 likely planted during this time from Ephesus. So too the churches in Colossae and Hierapolis. 'These Asian churches are set apart from the ones started during Paul's previous journeys by the fact that he himself didn't start them.'[142] So, the church in Colossae was probably planted by Epaphras (Col. 1:7–8; 4:12), and the people in the church had never actually seen Paul's face (Col. 2:1). Epaphras was part of Paul's apostolic band, doubtless being trained and mentored by the apostle in how to plant churches (Col. 4:12–13). The end of the letter to the Colossians is interesting, because Paul gives instructions that it be read in Laodicea as well, and that the Laodicean letter be read in Colossae; this is now a network of churches which Paul did not plant. 'Paul learned to spread his apostolic foundation without needing to be present. He learned to work through others rather than doing it all himself.'[143] This is the generation of multiplication, learning to reproduce ourselves in and through the leaders we are raising up and investing in.

We see this in Apollos. He is clearly a gifted man, but has a way to go. In time, and after wise and caring discipling, he develops an effective and fruitful ministry in Achaia. But Paul did not do the discipling. Rather, he discipled Priscilla and Aquila, and *they* discipled Apollos (Acts 18:1–4, 24–28). Paul did not just disciple Priscilla and Aquila; he discipled them in such a way that they had the vision and ability to disciple others. This is the same pattern that we see in 2 Timothy 2:2: 'What you have heard from me through many witnesses entrust to faithful people who will be able to teach others as well.' Paul has discipled Timothy; the younger man is now to do the same with 'faithful people', but to do so in such a way that they may also be able to teach others. A virtuous cascade of grace pours out in ever-increasing circles.

Steve Addison writes of five levels of movement leadership: seed sowers, church planters, church multipliers, multiplication trainers and move-ment catalysts. He says that 'the most important and the most difficult transition of all' is in training church planters to be church multipliers,

---

142 Ibid. 103.
143 Ibid.

because 'this transition marks the boundary between addition and multiplication'.[144] Interestingly, when it comes to movement catalysts, Addison reckons that they 'should spend 60 to 90 days per year over 2 to 3 years equipping and mentoring' church planters to help them become church multipliers.[145] This sounds a colossal amount of time and a colossal proportion of a church planter's precious calendar, but, says Addison, this is how multiplication happens. This seems to be exactly what Paul did in Ephesus, and, in two years, 'all the residents of Asia . . . heard the word of the Lord' (Acts 19:10).

Succession and sustainability

One of the major speeches of Acts occurs during Paul's time with the elders of the Ephesian church at Miletus. Paul is heading for Jerusalem, hoping to be there in time for Pentecost (20:16), and he makes arrangements to meet the elders in Miletus, which is on the Aegean coast about 30 miles south of Ephesus.[146] It may be that Paul could not face going to Ephesus itself in the light of whatever terrible experiences he had had there, but it feels significant that he chooses not to meet up with the whole church, but rather with the elders. He is focusing more and more on leaders as the most effective way to multiply the work of God. His speech (20:17–35) is poignant and powerful, and is shot through with the pathos of Paul's consciousness that this is the last time he will be with them: 'And now I know that none of you, among whom I have gone about proclaiming the kingdom, will ever see my face again' (20:25). This affects them all profoundly. When they pray together after the speech, '[t]here was much weeping among them all; they embraced Paul and kissed him, grieving especially because of what he had said, that they would not see him again' (20:37–38). This is Paul's valedictory address to them, outlining the essentials of ministry in these new churches of Asia. He is ensuring that the work will continue and be healthy. It raises questions for us as church planters about sustainability and succession planning.

---

[144] Addison 2015: 101, 106.
[145] Ibid. 107.
[146] Beitzel 2013: 311.

Beverly Roberts Gaventa points out a striking feature of the speech,[147] which helps us with its structure: the phrase 'And now' comes at turning points of the speech:

- Paul begins by looking back at his ministry in Asia (20:18–21). This phase of the speech is headlined by Paul's 'You yourselves know' (20:18): he is keen to remind his listeners of their shared history.[148]
- 'And now, as a captive to the Spirit, I am on my way to Jerusalem' (20:22). Paul now lays out the uncertainty of his future, save that it will be marked by further trials and suffering (20:22–24). The reference to the journey of suffering to Jerusalem cannot but remind Luke's readers of the journey of Jesus to the cross (cf. Luke 9:51; 13:22; 17:11). This section is marked by Paul's repeated phrase 'I know' (20:23 [implied from v. 22], 25, 29); the Spirit has made these things known to him, but this aspect of his life is unknown to his hearers.
- 'And now', Paul knows that he will not be returning, and so he reveals his concerns for the future of the churches in Ephesus and Asia (20:25–31). He reminds his friends of the preciousness of the church (the church of God, bought with the blood of Christ and overseen by the Spirit [20:28]), and tasks them to be vigilant – over themselves (20:28), over the flock of the church (20:28) and over the false teachers who will threaten to savage it like wolves (20:29–31).
- 'And now I commend you to God and to the message of his grace' (20:32); Paul prays for the church and its leaders, reminding them of his own example (20:32–35).

It is a stunning and stirring speech, not least for anyone called to church leadership.

Two implications for church planters stand out.

1 Church planters' lives are a core element of their leadership

Paul begins and ends his speech with references to how he lived among the Ephesian believers. They all know how he served the Lord 'with all

---

147 Gaventa 2003: 283.
148 Stott 1990: 325.

humility and with tears, enduring the trials that came to me' (20:19). 'Humility' may well mean 'humiliations'.[149] They know how hard he worked in the gospel (20:20–21). And they know how he worked with his hands to support himself and his apostolic band, and 'in all this I have given you an example' (20:35). Of all the things Paul could have reminded them of (the spiritual victories over evil, the extraordinary miracles, the planting of many churches), he talks to them about hard work, about tears, about hardships.

There is something grounding about basing a ministry in the nuts and bolts of character. When we look to future church planters, to those who will carry on the work after us, and when we look into our own hearts, it is tempting to look for talent first and foremost, for personality. A charismatic character, someone who can shine, who will draw people by the force and splendour of his or her personality – this person, so we reason, will be the one to make sure that the work does not falter but advances by leaps and bounds. Yet here is Paul talking to the Ephesian elders about his distresses, his struggles, his attitude to money. He is looking for toughness, longevity, people whose heart is in this and for whom the church matters, those who will care for others and not exploit them.

When we disciple others and when we mentor leaders, we will of course train them in skills and model strategies and what it means to lead. We also need to look to character. At the beginning of all mentoring relationships, it is worth laying this out and making sure that it is an expectation on both sides. As mentors we will need to set the tone for this, and to be transparent with our own struggles, our own 'tears' and 'humiliations', resisting the temptation to shine in our best light with those we are mentoring. And our mentees will need to be open to challenge, to sharing more than their weekly task lists. Future church planters need to be people of depth, character, integrity, able to hold a course through upset and pressure; these are the men and women who will best build on the work that has gone before.

2 Church planters have a sure scriptural compass

When Paul talks about the need for vigilance, over ourselves, the flock and wolves, he has in mind 'the whole purpose of God', 'the truth', 'the

---

[149] Ibid.

message of his grace' (20:27, 30, 32). His concern is set against the background of his own example of diligent teaching, 'proclaiming the message to you and teaching you publicly and from house to house, as I testified to both Jews and Greeks about repentance towards God and faith towards our Lord Jesus' (20:20–21). Teaching the gospel is the bedrock of church-planting ministry, and church planters must be committed to it. If you visit the ruins of Ephesus today, you can still see the famous amphitheatre, where Paul may well have preached publicly, and the terraces of houses and shops that he would have visited. It is a lovely picture, and one to inspire church planters today.

Roland Allen poses the question for us of how Paul managed to plant churches so fast:

> The facts are these: St. Paul preached in a place for five or six months and then left behind him a Church, not indeed free from the need of guidance, but capable of growth and expansion ... The question before us is, how he could so train his converts as to be able to leave them after so short a time with any security that they would be able to stand and grow.[150]

We seem to have Paul's own answer to that question in these verses: 'And now I commend you to God and to the message of his grace, a message that is able to build you up and to give you the inheritance among all who are sanctified' (20:32). He prayed for his converts, he taught them the gospel (in all its fullest sense), and he trained leaders.

Allen summarizes a bit more fully: 'Thus St. Paul seems to have left his newly founded Churches with a simple system of Gospel teaching, two sacraments, a tradition of the main facts of the death and resurrection, and the Old Testament.'[151] He also notes, tellingly, that 'he must have concentrated his attention for a considerable part of his time on teaching teachers'.[152]

There is something fundamental here for church planters. The teaching of converts and leaders in the outlines of the gospel and the Scriptures,

---

[150] Allen 2011: 113, 114.
[151] Ibid. 121.
[152] Ibid. 120.

all within the atmosphere of faith, and a driving vision to plant other churches and reach the surrounding cities and countryside with the 'message of his grace' (20:32), is not just how churches are planted, but also how they grow and thrive and continue into the life that God has for them. This is the secret of succession and sustainability. We carry on as we have started.

Succession can be tricky. A church may be planted in a denominational area that is at odds with the passion and vision of the newly planted church. When the time comes for the lead church planter to move on (maybe to do the same thing again in another place), the diocese or the trustees or the patronage body or the denominational officials may not be in sympathy with the theology that gave rise to the church, and may try to make an appointment more in keeping with their own theological and cultural perspective. This nearly always ends in disaster. Church planters would do well to think and plan and pray ahead as much as they can. First of all, they can work hard to make sure that the members of the church, especially its leaders, its PCC and those who will liaise with the denomination over the next church leader, are quite clear about the church's theological vision and values, that they love the gospel and the Scriptures, that they cannot think of church without mission. This means that when discussions begin about succession, the church can speak clearly and with one voice. It would be a rash denominational leadership which tried to foist on a church someone out of sympathy with the people's most deeply cherished beliefs. And, second, the church planter will be building good relationships with the bishop, senior staff and denominational leaders, sharing the good things that are happening, explaining why and how the church plant does what it does. This all helps the church stakeholders understand what is happening, and why these things are important to the church. None of this need, nor should, be done with any edge; indeed, the more warmth, honour and respect the better! God willing, this enables the church plant to grow and flourish under new leadership after the initial pioneering has been done.

Church planting and cultural transformation

The final third of Acts typically gets less attention, certainly among church planters, than, say, the Jerusalem and Antioch churches or Paul's church-planting journeys. This is the narrative (21:27 – 28:31) of Paul's progress from Jerusalem and Caesarea towards Rome, in which he makes no fewer than five extensive defences before Jewish and Roman bodies, and then sails, with great adventures, to Italy. The book ends with Paul, in Rome, 'testifying to the kingdom of God and trying to convince [the Jews] about Jesus' (28:23), living under open house arrest for two years, 'proclaiming the kingdom of God and teaching about the Lord Jesus Christ [to the Gentiles] with all boldness and without hindrance' (28:31).

The significance of these later chapters is reinforced when we consider the structure of Acts. It is not just the relative length of these descriptions and speeches that is remarkable, but also how they show the outworking of the major moments of the book. Luke repeats key events – the coming of the Spirit on the Gentiles is told in chapters 10, 11 and 15, for instance. One of the other key narratives is the conversion of Paul on the Damascus road: we read of it in chapter 9, and then Paul retells the story in chapters 22 (when he is on the steps of the Jerusalem temple) and 26 (when he is before King Agrippa and Bernice and Festus), the two climactic moments of gospel defence before the Jews and the Gentiles. Luke is telling us that this is what Paul was ultimately called to do; there is a sense in which everything has led up to this. Paul's call from the risen Jesus was to be 'an instrument whom I have chosen to bring my name before Gentiles and kings and before the people of Israel', and to undergo suffering in the process (9:15–16). That threefold call has unfolded in reverse order, starting with the Jews, then the Gentiles, and now, at last, with the kings. In one sense, this is the narrative arc of the book, one of the ways in which the gospel moves from Jerusalem to the ends of the earth (1:8).

The narrative is of wider significance, though, than Paul's personal journey, although it is never separate from that. This is the story of how the gospel, and church planting in particular, makes its impact on the Greco-Roman world as the dominant culture of the day. And this is something which is urgently and significantly germane for church planting today. Any theology of church planting must think clearly about the relationship it has with the prevailing cultures, not just those of the communities into which people plant, but also the wider social and cultural scene.

C. Kavin Rowe argues that there are three fundamental 'core ecclesial practices' described in Acts: 'the confession of Jesus as Lord, the active mission "to the end of the earth", and the assembly of the "Christians".'[153] What is significant about these practices is that they link a belief with actions, a mission, and the formation of new social realities, which are called churches. Rowe argues that we should think carefully about the theology of Acts, not just as ideas, thoughts and concepts, but as real practices, as the formation of culture. He uses this approach to help us understand and interpret the relationship between the gospel, church planting and culture.

Until recently, Acts scholarship has seen the book as a kind of defence of the church before the Roman Empire, a document that Christians could use to demonstrate to the powers that be that Christianity was not a threat to them and so not worthy to be persecuted by the state.[154] This is why there are repeated verdicts of Paul's innocence before the various Roman tribunals he faces (e.g. 18:14; 23:29; 25:25), with the climactic verdict from Agrippa and Bernice: 'This man is doing nothing to deserve death or imprisonment' (26:31). This is not to say that the Roman officials are portrayed as anything less than occasionally venal – think of Gallio turning a blind eye to the beating of Sosthenes in Corinth (18:17), of Claudius Lysias rewriting history in his letter to Felix (23:27), of Felix hoping to receive a bribe from Paul and wanting to do the Jews a favour, so leaving Paul imprisoned (24:27). Luke's point is that Paul is innocent of all charges in terms of Roman justice, not that Rome is exemplary.

On the other hand, Acts shows the gospel as being profoundly subversive. There are riots practically everywhere Paul goes. There is violence in Jerusalem against the Way throughout the book. The Thessalonians are not without cause in saying: 'These people who have been turning the world upside down have come here also' (17:6), putting perhaps the most dangerous charge of all, contending that the church is 'saying that there is another king named Jesus' (17:7).

---

[153] Rowe 2010: 6.
[154] Ibid. 3.

So, which is it? Is Christianity essentially revolutionary, overturning political power and disrupting all culture? Or is it *not* a threat to these things? Or should we be looking for an uneasy and difficult-to-negotiate middle way? And how then should contemporary church planters interact with the powers that be, both political and cultural?

C. Kavin Rowe helps us see that the gospel does not force us to make a choice between competing realities (power and culture, or Christianity and the church). There can undoubtedly be a tension between the two, but Christianity does not accept the terms of such a binary choice. 'Paul engenders considerable upheaval as a part of his mission, but time and again ... the political authorities reject the accusations of his opponents ... The Christians are not out to establish Christendom, as it were. New culture, yes – coup, no.'[155]

This new culture is a result of the peaceable salvation of the new king, Jesus, and his establishing of these new social and cultural units, the churches. These do indeed challenge many of the assumptions and cultural practices of both Jerusalem and Rome, but they do so as the natural corollary of the gospel. Acts insists 'that Christianity is not a governmental takeover but an alternative and salvific way of life'.[156] And this way of life is embodied and lived out, not by means of political slogans, but in the lifestyles and practices of the churches as they are planted right across the Roman world.

Culture is an enormously powerful thing. It can be described as 'the interconnections of concepts and practices that constitute a total way of life'.[157] Very often culture is expressed in the unexamined assumptions and customs of daily personal and social life. Some of these are good and positive, some deeply harmful and antithetical to the gospel, and some are harmless. None are neutral. It has been described as being like the layers of an onion, with a core of world views, which are expressed in the next layer as values, and next embodied in institutions, finally being lived out in human behaviours and customs. This model has been criticized for not paying adequate attention to how each layer interacts dynamically with all the others,[158] but is nonetheless helpful to our thinking about how

---

155 Ibid. 91.
156 Ibid. 136.
157 Ibid. 7.
158 Keller 2012: 90.

church plants are engaging all the time with different aspects of culture and power. This may come through debates with local authorities, in arguments on the school governing body or parent–teacher association, in assessments of works of art, in behaviours in the student union. And it will be there too in the way church leadership works, in how the church handles questions of race and power, in attitudes to money, social media and social events.

Acts shows us that we should not think of questions of culture and power as a simple matter of being 'for' or 'against'; matters run much deeper than that. And what Luke gives us in Paul's various defences, as he reaches the climax of his church-planting call, is an invitation to live out a whole new culture, which is structured around the kingship of the risen Messiah Jesus and the body of diverse people he is bringing together from every part of the world and every section of society.

This makes me think of author Andy Crouch's powerful call for Christians to engage in this making of new culture. He analyses different attitudes to culture: condemning it, critiquing it, copying it and consuming it, noting that this progression has often been the path the church has travelled with regard to culture over the years.[159] He argues, though, that '[t]he only way to change culture is to create more of it'.[160] Rather than taking a position which is in reaction or opposition to something, or just a pale reflection of it, the Christian mandate (going right back to Genesis 1) is to be creative, making something new which reflects both God and his plans for the human race.

This is Paul's stance in Acts as he draws nearer and nearer to Rome, the epicentre of culture and power, whether political, commercial, military, economic, religious or social. He will be a witness to Jesus and the church, and the new way of life to which this is the door.

This is the cultural mandate for church plants as well. The church has been stronger at different aspects of these at different times in history. Church planters will aim to create cultures of the kingdom of God in their plants and then to help the members of the church to live these out in their contexts – at home, in the block of flats, in the shops, at work, in business, school and the arts, wherever they find themselves. How powerful it is

---

[159] Crouch 2008: 68–70.
[160] Ibid. 67; emphasis original.

when lives are changed by Jesus one by one, and this is accompanied by acts and programmes of compassion in the neighbourhood, and a whole way of living and relating to structures of power and culture that is somehow different and palpably better than anything else on offer. We note that it is the church, as a spiritual, social and cultural unit, which is the epicentre and engine of this new life. Once more, we see that church planting is at the centre of God's purposes for the transformation of both individuals and societies.

Something church planters have to get into pretty quickly is dealing with various stakeholders when they plant churches. There will be some stakeholders from the church world – a sending church, a denomination; some from the charity sector – funding applications, shared work with the poor or with young people or asylum seekers or people in prison; and some from the political and social world around – the town or county council, local members of parliament and councillors, the police, the local paper. Each relationship takes time and wisdom. The church planter will want to build trust and connection, to learn from these stakeholders, and to build patterns of relating which are rooted in the generosity and creativity of the kingdom of God. There may well be this uneasy combination that Paul found in Acts, of turning the world upside down and being innocent of any kind of sedition, and, hopefully, the aspiration to grow and build and make something new, something that is explicable only because of Jesus and which is lived out in the church planted in the heart of the culture and neighbourhood itself.

The Holy Spirit and church planting

Perhaps the greatest lesson of all is one we have seen again and again in our reflections on Acts. This mission, this church-planting venture, does not start with us and does not belong to us. It is God who is the great hero of Acts, even more than Peter, even more than Paul. It is the plan of the Father that is accomplished, the lordship of Jesus Christ that is the main message, and the leading of the Holy Spirit that is the chief power. Church planters will not see themselves at the centre of all that is happening, of their dreams, visions and plans. They will give priority to God in prayer, space to him in worship, glory to him in all things.

Let Roland Allen have the last word in our reflections on Acts, as he puts the power of the Spirit at the centre of our mission and church planting. 'I believe in a rushing mighty wind,' he says, 'and desire its presence at all costs to our restrictions.'[161] He contrasts the free power of the Spirit with our control:

> By spontaneous expansion [of the church] I mean something we cannot control. And if we cannot control it, we ought, as I think, to rejoice that we cannot control it. For if we cannot control it, it is because it is too great, not because it is too small for us. The great things of God are beyond our control. Therein lies a vast hope. Spontaneous expansion could fill the continents with the knowledge of Christ: our control cannot reach as far as that. We constantly bewail our limitations: open doors unentered; doors closed to us . . . fields white to the harvest which we cannot reap. Spontaneous expansion could enter open doors, force closed ones, and reap those white fields.[162]

Acts may not be an exact primer of church planting – we need to be alert to how our context today is so different from that of Paul's time – but there is still so much here for church planters. We learn about mission, and how the church is at the heart of it, and we gain a vision for church as the engine of God's kingdom in the world. We see churches being born and growing; we see how this is done; we learn about movements, about multiplication, about culture change. We discover a methodology – going to the most receptive first, following up on initiatives from the Holy Spirit, planting churches in places that have the potential to be bases of light for whole regions, investing in leaders. We see something of the cost of this work, its challenges and battles. And we see something of the triumph, of walking with Jesus, of sharing in his life. It is amazing and exciting stuff. May the Lord of the harvest release the unfettered power of the Holy Spirit as, with his help and leading, we plant churches all around the UK in the name of Jesus. Who knows what will happen then?

---

[161] Allen 1962: 12–13, quoted in Payne 2009: 402–403.
[162] Ibid.

5

How the first Christians put church into practice

If we are trying to discover how Jesus envisaged what was to become 'church' after his death, resurrection and ascension, then a good place to start is to look at how the disciples (who were to become apostles) acted on his teaching, example and inspiration. Their actions are a good indication of his intentions. From this perspective, we will consider three aspects of this quest: what we know of how the first Christians gathered together to worship; Paul's own testimony of his church-planting ministry; and his instructions to Titus and how he could church plant in Crete.

Worship in the early church

It is striking how little we actually know of the worship of the first followers of Jesus after his resurrection and ascension. There are very few descriptions of Christian worship, although there are several texts which may well be very early liturgical texts or creeds (e.g. 1 Cor. 12:3; Phil. 2:6–11; Col. 1:15–20; 1 Tim. 3:16). The dispute around the Lord's Supper in 1 Corinthians is particularly revealing, and we will start there.

The Lord's Supper

We note that in his first letter to the Corinthians Paul repeatedly uses the term 'when you come together' (1 Cor. 11:17, 18, 20, 33, 34). He also uses a similar phrase in chapter 14 about the gathering of the church (14:23, 26). These are the only times in Paul's letters that he uses these words. Gordon Fee says: 'it had probably become a semitechnical term for the "gathering together" of the people of God for worship.'[1]

---

[1] Fee 1987: 536.

Granted that most scholars date 1 Corinthians between AD 53 and 54,[2] we have an insight into what Christian worship looked like in very early Christianity.

We can learn that there was a designated gathering together. Other New Testament texts suggest that this was on 'the first day of the week' (e.g. Acts 20:7; 1 Cor. 16:2). We should not pass too quickly over this, because it indicates that Christian worship, very early on, moved from the Jewish sabbath to the Sunday, as the day of Jesus' resurrection.[3] Paul in 1 Corinthians 11 implies that this gathering was a meal, and the Lord's Supper was a part of this ('When you come together, it is not really to eat the Lord's supper. For when the time comes to eat . . .' [11:20–21]). Other New Testament texts also imply a weekly meal as the pattern of Christian worship: for instance, in Acts 20, when Paul is in Troas, Luke records: 'On the first day of the week, when we met to break bread . . .' (20:7). We will come back to how the breaking of bread may relate both to what we have come to call Holy Communion (or its variant names) and to more general fellowship meals. For now, we note that we have the probability that the Christian churches had an established pattern of meeting for worship weekly, based on the resurrection of Jesus.

Paul is dealing with an abuse of the Lord's Supper whereby the rich Christians in Corinth were eating separately from their poor brothers and sisters, and this was causing problems: 'There was over-indulgence on the part of the rich and feelings of envy on the part of the poor who were made to feel inferior.'[4] Paul sides with the poor, and castigates the rich for not 'discerning the body' (11:29). This may be a lack of recognition either of the broken body of Jesus which brings the church together (cf. 'Because there is one bread, we who are many are one body, for we all partake of the one bread' [1 Cor. 10:17]) or of the identity of the church as the body of Christ (cf. 'Now you are the body of Christ and individually members of it' [1 Cor. 12:27]). Either way, Fee is insightful when he comments: 'The primary problem was an abuse of the church itself . . . their failure truly to be God's new people when they gathered.'[5] So, here we have a clear

---

2 Fee and Stuart 2002: 324.
3 Martin 1993: 986.
4 Marshall 1993: 571.
5 Fee 1987: 532, 536.

understanding of the church of Jesus Christ, its identity as it should be reflected in its practices.

To deal with this issue, Paul calls the Corinthians back to how Jesus instituted this meal. Paul calls it 'the table of the Lord' (10:21) or 'the Lord's supper' (11:20). His emphasis is that this is the meal that has its origin in Jesus (11:23ff.); it is a meal at which the Lord is somehow present (10:16; 11:29) and which acts as a proclamation of his death (11:26). Paul draws an express link to Jesus when he describes how he heard about the Lord's Supper: 'For I received from the Lord what I also handed on to you . . .' (11:23). The vocabulary of 'receiving' and 'handing on' is the language of a tradition being passed on in the church (cf. Luke 1:2; 1 Cor. 15:3),[6] this time the words and actions of Jesus himself. This explains why Paul's rendition of the words Jesus used to institute his supper (11:23–26) are so similar to those in Luke's Gospel (22:15–20); they are both alluding to what Jesus himself actually said and did. It seems that there were two complementary but slightly different traditions, because the accounts of the last supper in Mark and Matthew are very similar to each other, but with some minor variants from the words used by Paul and Luke.[7] We should remember that Paul's account is the earliest, as 1 Corinthians was written ahead of the Gospels. We are talking about the very earliest traditions of the church. However it came down to us, we have a direct link between Jesus and the first Christians. This is explicitly something he envisaged for the gatherings of his first followers, following on from his death and resurrection and ascension. For church plants, we can say that this is fundamental to the vision Jesus had for his church.

What does it tell us? Taking the four principal accounts of the institution of the Lord's Supper together (Matt. 26:26–29; Mark 14:22–25; Luke 22:15–20; 1 Cor. 11:23–26), R. H. Stein identifies four common themes:[8]

- 'This is my body': central to this meal is the self-donation of Jesus. He came to give himself for his people and the life of the world.

---

[6] Stein 1992: 444–445. Cf. 1 Cor. 7:10; 9:14, which refer to other sayings of Jesus passed down to the church (Marshall 1993: 572).

[7] Ibid. 445.

[8] Ibid. 447–449.

- 'Do this in remembrance of me': just as the purpose of the Passover was for the people of Israel to remember how God delivered them from the slavery of Egypt, so Jesus' death was to be remembered in such a way that it brought out the new freedom he accomplished for his people.
- 'The new covenant in my blood': Jesus' giving of his life in self-sacrifice is like the 'blood of the covenant' (Exod. 24:8) which seals the relationship between God and his people. The language of Jeremiah 31:31–34 is also present: this covenant speaks of the forgiveness of sins.
- 'Fulfilled in the kingdom of God': each of the Synoptic Gospel accounts refers to the great celebration banquet at the end of time, of which the Lord's Supper is a sign of what is to come. Paul speaks of looking ahead to the return of the Lord.

These solemn and deeply moving words and actions lie at the heart of what Jesus envisaged for his church. Whatever our Christian tradition and however we may interpret these things and practise them, the main point is clear and unavoidable. All the Synoptic Gospels (and many would argue John, as well, although expressed differently) and Paul, not just in Corinth but presumably in all the churches he founded, have this act of remembrance of Jesus as a central feature of the life of the communities he envisaged following his death. It is true for all churches, of course, and for church plants no less.

What does this mean? Much might be said, but, at the least, Jesus clearly envisaged his people gathering in worship to remember him, just as the people of Israel used to meet together to remember the exodus. In particular, they are to remember his death on their behalf, their constitution as a people through the new covenant, the forgiveness and freedom of the new people of God, and their destiny within God's kingdom.

We should note that Jesus is central to these gatherings. They are done because he made provision for them. They have the account of his words at their heart, as near verbatim as is possible. They recount and celebrate his sacrifice for the sins of the world. They reflect his actions – the taking and giving thanks for, the breaking and distributing of the bread, and the sharing of the wine. The words and actions have the feeling of an act of worship to them.[9] The gatherings incorporate his practice from the days of his earthly life, when he ate and drank with so many people, and when he gathered the Twelve in the upper room. And in these gatherings (in ways which various church traditions will interpret differently), Jesus is made present as he is remembered.

This has implications for the missionary methodology of church plants. Certainly for mainline denominations, the remembrance of Jesus and the last supper is expressed in the celebration of the Eucharist, and this is tied to ordination, as only ordained priests and ministers can celebrate. All church plants will, of course, want to express and embody everything Jesus envisaged in the words of institution, but many will find it challenging to interact with how this is enacted in the wider church, with all its history and contemporary expression. There are real questions for some church plants. For starters, what if the church plant is led by a lay person? Or what if the church plant is made up predominantly of people who are on their way to faith but would not yet be comfortable calling themselves Christians and do not feel ready to take part in what seems to them an 'insider' rite? Or what about those church plants which are aimed largely at children or youth, who would not yet be confirmed and so not yet (for some denominations) able to receive communion? For some, there is a clash here, or at least a tension, between the priorities of mission and those of the church.

There are many creative solutions available, and even more conversations around ways forward.[10] What should not be lost is the significance of how Jesus provided for himself to be remembered, especially his death on the cross and coming kingdom. The first Christians made this central to how they interpreted Jesus' intentions for his church, and ways need to be found and incorporated in the life of church plants which express this with integrity.

Some have made use of 'agape meals', agape being the Greek for 'love'. The phrase is used only once in the New Testament (Jude 12), but it does seem to reflect a pattern for the early church, where what we now call

---

[9] 'The somewhat stylized nature of the accounts [of the institution of the Lord's Supper] suggests that the wording had become "fixed" as part of a liturgical statement used in church meetings' (Marshall 1993: 573).
[10] E.g. Moynagh 2012: 374–375.

Holy Communion (or variants) took place within the context of a wider fellowship meal. That was the context for the problem in Corinth in 1 Corinthians 11: there was a meal for the whole church, at which the rich were eating sumptuously and separately from their poorer sisters and brothers, with the Lord's Supper happening around that.[11] This would make sense in terms of the context of the last supper, which was a meal, and also of what the first Christians had seen and cherished in the practice of Jesus in gathering people for meals regularly. This accords, too, with what we know of contemporary practice in Corinth relating to mystery religions, and business and trade associations.[12] In the light of this, Stein argues that Acts 2:42 (which we looked at in a previous chapter) should be understood as follows: '[The first Christians] were continuing in the teaching of the apostles, and in fellowship [the love feast], the breaking of bread [the Lord's Supper] and prayers.' Likewise, Acts 2:46 could be read as: 'breaking bread [the Lord's Supper] in their homes, they partook of food with glad and generous hearts [the love feast].'[13]

Sadly, this beautiful pattern does not appear to have lasted long, maybe due to exactly the kind of issues that Paul is addressing in 1 Corinthians 11, and by the middle of the second century the Lord's Supper was completely separate from the love feast.[14] For our current purposes, we note, however, that *agape* meals are distinct from eucharistic celebrations and should not be confused with them.

What about 'breaking bread'? Does this imply a non-eucharistic Christian meal where Jesus could be remembered? The phrase is used by Luke (e.g. Acts 2:42, 46; 20:7, 11). They are the same words he uses for the institution of the Lord's Supper when Jesus breaks bread (Luke 22:19). Some of the Acts references clearly refer to acts of worship (e.g. at Troas, when the disciples gather on the first day of the week to break bread in chapter 20, and, interestingly, on the boat ahead of the shipwreck in 27:35). It seems that this was Luke's shorthand for the Lord's Supper, a practice which he describes Paul adopting in his life and ministry. Maybe it is indicative of a far more homely sharing of the bread and wine than we are used to in

---

[11] Note Paul's use of 'after supper' for when the cup is celebrated (11:25).
[12] See Marshall 1993: 570.
[13] Stein 1992: 450.
[14] Ibid. 450.

many of our churches today, but it is almost certainly another way of describing the receiving of Holy Communion.

This argues for a greater prominence for the sacrament of Holy Communion than is sometimes shown in church plants, although without losing any sense of their missionary focus.

Baptism

What of baptism, as the other sacrament that Jesus spoke of? It is prominent in the Great Commission, as Matthew reports it:

> Go therefore and make disciples of all nations, baptizing them in the name of the Father and of the Son and of the Holy Spirit, and teaching them to obey everything that I have commanded you. And remember, I am with you always, to the end of the age. (Matt. 28:19–20)

We have thought about this passage in the section on the church and the Gospels, but now may we note how baptizing and teaching are the main ways in which Jesus envisages disciples being made. The link between baptism and teaching can be found elsewhere in the New Testament, and seems to show us the outline of the practice of the early church. Paul, in his teaching on baptism in Romans 6, talks about how the Roman Christians 'have become obedient from the heart to the form of teaching to which you were entrusted' (6:17). Other letters have a similar flavour of ethical instruction, using the language of a change of clothes from an old to a new way of life, which in all likelihood comes from the practice of baptism in the early church (e.g. Eph. 4:17–32; Col. 3:1–17). Other passages refer to the teaching Paul and others gave to new converts, which may again have been part of instruction in connection with baptism (e.g. 1 Thess. 4:1–8; 2 Thess. 3:6, 11–13).[15]

More than instruction is in view, however; there is also a spiritual power. Baptism is 'in Christ' or 'into Christ', and envisages not just a symbolic washing, but also a union with Christ himself in his death and resurrection:

---

15 See Beasley-Murray 1993: 64.

> Do you not know that all of us who have been baptized into Christ Jesus were baptized into his death? Therefore we have been buried with him by baptism into death, so that, just as Christ was raised from the dead by the glory of the Father, so we too might walk in newness of life.
> (Rom. 6:3–4)

In the Gospels, baptism usually refers to the baptism of John for the forgiveness of sins, including the baptism of Jesus by John the Baptist, or, in a metaphorical way, to the baptism of fiery suffering which Jesus was to undergo on the cross.[16] At the conclusion of Matthew's Gospel, though, Jesus commands the baptism of the nations. This envisages a new kind of power, which brings about change. It unites the believer with Jesus, opens the way for conformity to the Jesus way of life and joins people to the church. This last is the basis of Paul's arguments about the way in which Christians will relate to one another, overcoming barriers of race and background:

> As many of you as were baptized into Christ have clothed yourselves with Christ. There is no longer Jew or Greek, there is no longer slave or free, there is no longer male or female; for all of you are one in Christ Jesus.
> (Gal. 3:27–28)

The practice of baptism was a universal practice among the first Christians: the New Testament assumes that all believers in Jesus will be baptized. This situation was the norm by the time of Paul's conversion on the road to Damascus and subsequent baptism. G. R. Beasley-Murray draws some conclusions: 'The conversion of Paul is commonly dated four years after the death of Jesus. Since baptism existed prior to Paul's conversion, it is reasonable to view it as coexistent with the inception of the church.'[17]

For our present argument, we can confidently see how this new form of the practice of baptism was something envisaged by Jesus before his

---

[16] See Dockery 1992: 56–58.
[17] Beasley-Murray 1993: 60.

death. He saw it as a means of forming the new people of God around himself, giving them the power both to live in the new ways of the kingdom and to be united with one another. The early church found it the universal way of being united with Christ, overcoming natural barriers of race and background to form the church, and releasing believers into 'newness of life' (Rom. 6:4).

So, in our theology of church planting, we have strong reason to say confidently that Jesus envisaged the coming into being of the church, not least through the new way of seeing and experiencing baptism.

One potential reason for this is the close connection in the New Testament between water baptism and baptism in the Holy Spirit. This can be a contested area theologically, and I have no desire to stir up debate and division. Suffice it to say that, whatever our own understandings of Spirit baptism, there are unambiguous verses in Scripture that see the Holy Spirit as the agent by which what is symbolized by water baptism comes into being. One such example is 1 Corinthians 12:13: 'For in the one Spirit we were all baptized into one body – Jews or Greeks, slaves or free – and we were all made to drink of one Spirit.'[18]

The Holy Spirit, then, was a key element in the thought and practice of the early church. We see this very clearly in the few descriptions of the worship of the early church in the New Testament.

Church services in Corinth

The fullest description of the worship of the early church in the New Testament comes in 1 Corinthians 12 and 14, where Paul gives instructions to the Corinthians on the use of spiritual gifts. His summary of the teaching comes at the end of chapter 14: 'So, my friends, be eager to prophesy, and do not forbid speaking in tongues; but all things should be done decently and in order' (1 Cor. 14:39–40). While the teaching is clearly directed to the particular Corinthian situation, it is nonetheless striking that the primary worship issues in Paul's mind are around speaking in tongues and prophecy and the orderliness of public worship.

---

[18] Another possible example would be Titus 3:5. More generally, if to be baptized is to be in Christ, and to be in Christ is only possible through the Holy Spirit (e.g. Rom. 8:9–11; 1 Cor. 12:3), then there must be some kind of profound connection between baptism and the Spirit's activity.

Paul lays the theological foundations for what is to follow at the beginning of chapter 12. While he describes a variety of gifts, he is at pains to draw out that all have their origin in the Spirit of God:

> To each is given the manifestation of the Spirit for the common good. To one is given through the Spirit the utterance of wisdom, and to another the utterance of knowledge according to the same Spirit, to another faith by the same Spirit, to another gifts of healing by the one Spirit, to another the working of miracles, to another prophecy, to another the discernment of spirits, to another various kinds of tongues, to another the interpretation of tongues. All these are activated by one and the same Spirit, who allots to each one individually just as the Spirit chooses.
> (1 Cor. 12:7–11)

There are 'varieties' of these manifestations of the Spirit (12:4, 5, 6), but there is only one Spirit, the same Spirit, working through each. Here is an important Pauline principle: in the church, '[u]niformity of experience and service is not to be expected; unity lies ultimately in the Spirit who gives, the Lord who is served, the God who is at work'.[19] The word translated by the NRSV as 'activated' is one from which we get our English word 'energy', and it implies that 'the Spirit is the source of boundless and manifold energy and power'.[20] These spiritual gifts have been variously categorized but seem to cover teaching gifts (wisdom and knowledge), power gifts (maybe faith, healing, miracles) and prophetic gifts (prophecy, spiritual discernment, tongues and interpretation of tongues). Paul's immediate concern is the healthy functioning of the church rather than services dominated by ego and self-promotion – hence his teaching on the body of Christ, which follows on in 12:12–31, and the famous chapter 13 on love after that.[21] This is an emphasis that will recur throughout these chapters (e.g. 12:7, 25; 14:1, 5, 12, 26, 31). The twin poles of his

---

[19] Barrett 1971: 284.
[20] Ibid. 286.
[21] Cf. Anthony Thiselton's (2000: 900) shrewd comment that the discussion of church practices in 1 Cor. 11:2 – 14:40 is to be read within the wider context of the whole letter's concern with the arrogance that comes with a false sense of superiority, such as was prevalent in the Corinthian churches for both economic and spiritual reasons; see 8:1 – 11:1, and 1:1 – 4:21.

argument are that every Christian has spiritual gifts, and that the Spirit is behind every such gift for the glory of Jesus and the building up of the church.

If we carry on tracing the argument of 1 Corinthians 12 – 14 as a whole, we find that there is a particular point of contention in the Corinthian churches, namely the abuse of the gift of tongues. There seems to be individual and maybe selfish use of the gift in public worship (e.g. 14:2, 5, 19). In response, 'Paul argues for *the absolute need for intelligibility* in the assembly [14:1–25] . . . In vv. 26–40, he offers some specific guidelines for *the absolute need for order* in the assembly.'[22] For our purposes, it is particularly noteworthy that Paul constantly has in mind the church as a whole. He is not against speaking in tongues per se; it is a gift of the Spirit of God, after all. It has great power for the individual (14:4), and Paul himself speaks in tongues 'more than all of you' (14:18) and 'would like all of you to speak in tongues' (14:5). Nonetheless, when it comes to public gatherings for worship, Paul is quite clear that intelligibility and order are required, not as an end in themselves but because this is how the church as a whole is most healthily strengthened and enabled to function. Here are some of the key references:

- 'One who prophesies is greater than one who speaks in tongues, unless someone interprets, so that the church may be built up' (14:5);
- 'Since you are eager for spiritual gifts, strive to excel in them for building up the church' (14:12);
- 'Let all things be done for building up' (14:26).

Paul sees the gathered church as a whole as of central importance, and argues that the consideration of this should guide all practice. In particular, he has in view the 'building up' of the church, which necessitates intelligibility and order. The noun form of the word ('building up') occurs four times in 1 Corinthians 14, and the verb three times. Perhaps Paul is harking back to the image of his apostolic ministry as the construction of the church (1 Cor. 3:10–17).[23] In chapter 8 he had said, 'Love builds up' (8:1).

---

22 Fee 1994: 148; emphasis original.
23 Barrett 1971: 316.

The thought returns with chapter 14 (and 'controls the thought of the entire chapter'[24]). Love is to be the guiding principle for the life and practice of the church,[25] practically realized through the exercise of the gifts of the Spirit to build up the church as a whole.

For a robust theology of church planting, we have a vision of the church grounded in the active involvement of the whole Trinity in the life of the church (12:4–6), especially made manifest through the energizing of the Holy Spirit (12:11), for the declaration of the lordship of Jesus (12:3). The Spirit is key to the proper and healthy functioning of the church, in particular its upbuilding and strengthening in love.

Of particular interest are Paul's comments on public worship at Corinth (1 Cor. 14:26–32): 'What should be done then, my friends? When you come together, each one has a hymn, a lesson, a revelation, a tongue, or an interpretation. Let all things be done for building up' (14:26). He goes on to say that there should be no more than two or at most three people speaking in tongues, each speaking in turn, and only where there is an interpretation. When it comes to prophecy, there should be two or three people prophesying, and others should weigh what is said. If 'a revelation is made' to someone else while another person is speaking, the speaker should give way to the other. The punchline emphasizes (once again) that the aim of everything is for the upbuilding of all: 'For you can all prophesy one by one, so that all may learn and all be encouraged' (14:31).[26]

What can we learn about the expectations of church (and church plants) from these remarkable verses?

The overall emphasis must be the central role of the Holy Spirit in Christian worship. It is the Spirit who energizes, activates and works effectively through all these diverse gifts, and who builds up the church. Paul is admittedly addressing an issue to do with spiritual gifts, but the extent to which the Spirit is in view to the exclusion of practically all else

---

[24] Fee 1994: 220.
[25] See Thiselton 2000: e.g. 1088, where he urges that 8:1, 'love builds up', and ch. 13 on love should control our understanding of the chapters on spiritual gifts.
[26] Fee (1994: 25) overcomes the apparent inconsistency between v. 29, where no more than two or three are prophesying, and v. 31, where 'all' are now potentially prophesying one by one, by explaining that there should be no more than two or three prophecies at a time before they are discerned.

is extraordinary. This is not a plea for charismatic worship,[27] but it does argue for a prioritization of the leading and activity of the Holy Spirit in every aspect of Christian worship. Without the Spirit, the life, health and growth of the church is simply impossible.

Striking in this regard is the lack of mention of any kind of leadership in the Corinthian worship services. Paul presents a vision of the life of the church which is thoroughgoing in its democratization of the gifts of God. No-one is mentioned as being 'in charge', and, when it comes to regulating and interpreting the worship, it is left to each individual (e.g. 14:30) or to the church as a whole (e.g. 14:29). It is the Spirit who leads and under whose authority and inspiration matters are carried out. This is all of a piece with the emphasis on the church as a whole – that each one present should contribute (for all have gifts, distributed by the Spirit [12:7]; for all are part of the body of Christ, constituted and animated by the Spirit [12:12–13]; each brings a hymn, lesson or revelation [14:26]; and all can prophesy, all be instructed, all be encouraged [14:31]) – and the accompanying drumbeat that all should be done intelligibly and in order for the building up of the whole church, and not just for the benefit of any particularly gifted (in their own eyes) individuals (e.g. 14:5, 12, 19, 26, 31). God, by his Spirit, is looking for maximum participation from all in church, so that everyone and the church as a whole may be strengthened, for the glory of Jesus.

Prophecy

We should note, as well, in this regard the massive emphasis on prophecy from Paul. Different Christian traditions will doubtless interpret this differently. Fee defines the gift, in relation to 1 Corinthians 14, as consisting of 'spontaneous, Spirit-inspired, intelligible messages, orally delivered in the gathered assembly, intended for the edification and encouragement of the people'.[28] He specifically rules out equating prophecy with a prepared

---

[27] Although we should note Fee's cogent argument: 'The cumulative evidence, which comes from 1 and 2 Thessalonians, Romans, Galatians, and 1 and 2 Timothy [and, of course the Corinthian correspondence, which Fee is here addressing], seems incontrovertible: that the Pauline churches were thoroughly charismatic in the full sense of that term' (Fee 1994: 270).

[28] Ibid. 170. Thiselton (2000: 962, 1091–1093) takes issue with Fee's arguing that prophecy is always spontaneous.

sermon.[29] Thiselton argues for a broad definition, including aspects of pastoral preaching: beyond the fact that prophecy involves speech, he lays the emphasis on the function of prophecy ('building up and encouragement and consolation' [14:3]) rather than its form.[30] We should perhaps note the distinction in Paul's mind between gifts of instruction (12:8) and revelation (12:10), while noting the close connection between prophecy and instruction (14:19), and his hope that orderly prophecy will lead to all being encouraged and learning something (14:31).

It is important to observe Paul's assumption that the meetings of the church would not be confined to believers but that there would be unbelievers present (14:20–25). In his view, it was one of the functions of prophecy to disclose 'the secrets of the unbeliever's heart' in such a way that he or she 'will bow down before God and worship him, declaring, "God is really among you"' (14:25).

One last observation is the assumption for Paul that the church would be of a size that there could be meaningful participation by all present. This probably means that many of our churches today are much, much larger than the Pauline churches in Corinth. Fee notes: 'Present archaeological evidence indicates that the largest house in Corinth could have accommodated only 30 to 50 guests.'[31] We will return later to this striking fact and the change of perspective that it brings.

Applications for church plants

I am reminded of a methodology adopted by the missiologist Lesslie Newbigin in his analysis of different theologies of the church. Newbigin saw three streams to understanding what constitutes the essential life of the church, which we may simplistically call the evangelical, the Catholic and the Pentecostal. He seeks to answer the question, *'What is the manner of our ingrafting into Christ?'* and draws out the three responses:

The first answer is, briefly, that we are incorporated in Christ by hearing and believing the Gospel. The second is that we are incorporated by sacramental participation in the life of the historically

---

[29] Ibid.
[30] Thiselton 2000: 956–965, 1087–1094, esp. his definition on 1094.
[31] Fee 1994: 242 n. 657.

continuous Church. The third is that we are incorporated by receiving and abiding in the Holy Spirit.[32]

I wonder if we might not see a similar pattern in our analysis of these early churches?

It must strike us just how Jesus-centred these churches and their practices were. This is expressed and experienced evangelically, sacramentally and spiritually.

The sacraments of baptism and Eucharist were central to the life of the church from the beginning, and both eloquently proclaim and enact the gospel. The Reformers had this sense strongly, calling the sacraments 'visible words'.[33] The Lord's Supper 'proclaim[s] the Lord's death until he comes' (1 Cor. 11:26). Baptism is a baptism into the death of Christ (Rom. 6:3). Both sacraments are thoroughly evangelical in the sense that they preach the gospel.

Second, the early church was sacramental, drawing Christians into a participation in Christ. 'The cup of blessing that we bless, is it not a sharing in the blood of Christ? The bread that we break, is it not a sharing in the body of Christ?' (1 Cor. 10:16). Baptism is 'the water of rebirth and renewal by the Holy Spirit' (Titus 3:5). The church met Jesus through the sacraments.

Third, the church was constituted and enlivened and strengthened through the direct work of the Holy Spirit. Worship was dominated by expressions and manifestations of the Spirit through each and every person present.

What is clear is that the early Christians did not see themselves as separated from the life of Jesus, as if they had somehow to make a fresh start now that he had ascended into heaven. Rather, they found that their life together was an expression of the continued life of Jesus in their midst. The teaching of Jesus in the Gospels as he institutes the Holy Communion finds direct corroboration in Paul and the Pauline churches. Jesus' command that the nations be baptized in the name of the Trinity is attested in the rest of the New Testament. The activity and power of the Holy Spirit, so evident in the life and ministry of Jesus, continues in the life of

---

32 Newbigin 1953: 30; emphasis original.
33 E.g. Calvin 1960: 1281, quoting Augustine.

the church. The church builds its life on Jesus, not just in the sense of continuing his legacy but also by the living out of that same life in its continuing expression. Jesus, crucified and risen, continues alive in and through the church.

Church plants are churches, and they incorporate these values and practices at their centre. Any theology of church planting must give space and voice to these continuing expressions of the life of Jesus at their heart. They live out evangelical, sacramental and Pentecostal emphases, as their organizing principles reflect and express the gospel, the sacraments and the life of the Spirit at the heart of who they are and what they are trying to do.

This, of course, is part of the joy and privilege of church planting – to see Jesus present in the midst of our meagre efforts, our ragged gatherings and all-too-ordinary practices. We may be overwhelmingly conscious of the limitations of what we are doing. We may feel that we are pale reflections of other churches, even that we are not 'real' churches. The other side of the theological coin is that, as we structure our life together and our continuing mission around Jesus, his life and death in the gospel and his continued presence with us through the Spirit, then we can confidently look for his life lived out still through the church.

Paul's own testimony to church planting

We have, of course, seen a great deal of Paul in action as a church planter in our consideration of the material in Acts. We shall now look at just two passages which seem to give us a glimpse, 'from the inside', of what he felt was happening.

Church planting is a collaborative venture with God and with others

Let's start with 1 Corinthians 3. Verse 6 is almost a slogan for church planters: 'I planted, Apollos watered, but God gave the growth.' The context, though, is far from a happy one. Paul reminds the Corinthian Christians that their church life is characterized by factionalism: some are saying they 'belong to Paul' and others that they 'belong to Apollos' (3:4). He had begun the whole letter by criticizing them for this divisiveness

(1:10–13). Then he had written to them about what might have seemed something of a digression, an exposition of Christian power and wisdom as it is demonstrated in the cross of Christ. It seems that the Corinthians thought of themselves as 'mature' (2:6), 'wise' (1:20ff.) and, especially, 'spiritual' (2:10–16). So, when Paul comes back to their factionalism at the beginning of chapter 3, he does so by stating that this divisiveness and championing of human heroes and camps is devastating evidence of immaturity, folly, and being in the flesh and all too human, the very opposite of being truly spiritual (3:1–4). All through chapter 3, he reworks their slogans: '"I belong to Paul", or "I belong to Apollos", or "I belong to Cephas", or "I belong to Christ"' (1:12). He shows them how we all (including Paul and Apollos and the rest) belong to God (3:9), and that their leaders actually belong to them in their service of Christ, not the other way round: 'For all things are yours . . . all belong to you, and you belong to Christ, and Christ belongs to God' (3:21, 22–23). Gordon Fee draws this together: 'Thus, they may not say "I belong to Paul, or Apollos, or Cephas," not only because that is to boast in mere [mortals], but because that is the precise opposite of reality in Christ.'[34]

We thus see that this whole discussion about personalities and camps within the Corinthian church is to be viewed and defused by recourse to good theology, both in undermining the criteria of superiority (wisdom, maturity, spirituality) and in making sure that Jesus and the kingdom of God are central in any thinking about church planting. As so often with Paul, we are astounded by how he traces what appear to be practical matters to fundamentally theological roots, and then proceeds to put things right from that perspective.

Sadly, of course, personalities and tribes are not uncommon in today's church. And attitudes of being more 'spiritual' or 'wise' than others similarly have a horribly contemporary ring. Paul's recalling us to the true wisdom of the cross and the glorious perspective of our shared status in Christ is a useful corrective. Sometimes church planting is advocated on the basis of its being what the Spirit is truly doing, and is resisted on the basis of its being an immature and foolish practice. Both approaches alike are ruled offside by Paul's theological perspective.

---

[34] Fee 1987: 153.

For Paul, 'wisdom' was linked to a very particular philosophy and rhetorical practice. It was the way of intelligence and superiority, but also the way to get things done, to be most effective in the world. For us today, perhaps it is being 'smart', being both clever in how things are done and pragmatically effective in achieving things – a kind of worldly wisdom. The church can still excessively revere academic brilliance, but it can also look to pragmatism, even opportunism, as a guiding principle. Paul makes us question all such approaches when they are not grounded in the true wisdom and power of the cross of Christ (1:24). Gordon Fee draws out Paul's thought that any such approaches are not only faulty theologically but will also, paradoxically, prove to be ineffective:

> It is unfortunately possible for people to attempt to build the church out of every imaginable human system predicated on merely human wisdom, be it philosophy, 'pop' psychology, managerial techniques, relational 'good feelings,' or what have you. But at the final judgment, all such building (and perhaps countless other forms, where systems have become more important than the gospel itself) will be shown for what it is: something merely human, with no character of Christ or his gospel in it. Often, of course, the test may come this side of the final one, and in such an hour of stress that which has been built of modern forms of [wisdom] usually comes tumbling down.[35]

This is not to say, of course, that academic theology or managerial insights may not have something to say to the modern church planter, but rather that these approaches should be rooted in Christ if they are to have enduring and effective value. When they become the basis of tribalism and conflict and superiority in the church, then they are potentially contributing to the destruction of the very churches which are being planted, and God takes a pretty dim view of anything that may contribute to that (3:17).

This, then, is the background to Paul's famous church-planting passage:

> What then is Apollos? What is Paul? Servants through whom you came to believe, as the Lord assigned to each. I planted, Apollos

---

[35] Ibid. 145.

watered, but God gave the growth. So neither the one who plants nor the one who waters is anything, but only God who gives the growth. The one who plants and the one who waters have a common purpose, and each will receive wages according to the labour of each. For we are God's servants, working together; you are God's field, God's building.

(1 Cor. 3:5–9)

Paul, taking the example of Apollos and himself, is arguing against the tribalism based on individuals in the ministry of church planting. He does not say, 'Who then is Apollos? Who is Paul?' but 'What then is Apollos? What is Paul?' (3:5, my emphasis). Paul is recasting the leadership discussion in terms of function, not personality.[36] He wants the Corinthians to see past the dazzling personalities, brilliance and oratorical skills of their favoured leaders to what it is, under God, that they actually do. He affirms Apollos and his ministry when he says: 'The one who plants and the one who waters have a common purpose, and each will receive wages according to the labour of each' (3:8).[37] Then, as now, it was often not the particular leaders who were the origin of conflict and partisanship within the church, but rather misguided adulation and disputes between their followers. Paul is careful to speak well of other leaders, and, in the case of Cephas (i.e. Peter), not at all, presumably so he would not be drawn into this ugly row.

Paul's main point is that there are differing tasks in the process of planting churches, but the ultimate focus in all this work is on God, who alone gives the growth (3:6, 7). It is interesting to see that Paul talks about both the planting of seeds and the watering of them, without developing the analogy. When he says that he planted and Apollos watered, both verbs are in the tense which refers to a particular completed action in the past. Presumably, he is referring to those occasions when both he and Apollos turned up and ministered in Corinth (Acts 18:1, 27). By contrast, the verb for giving the growth is in the imperfect tense, denoting a continuing work: God carries on giving growth, even after the specific times

---

[36] See Thiselton 2000: 301.
[37] And see 16:12, where he refers positively to Apollos and his (busy) timetable.

of human work in the process of church planting. So, Paul is simultaneously underplaying the ministries of Apollos and himself, and exalting the truly life-changing power of God. He does not deny that human agency is of the essence – he and Apollos did definite work – but he relativizes it over against the true source of life and growth in God. He is at pains to describe himself and Apollos as 'servants through whom you came to believe' (3:5). 'Servants' is a definitive word for 'slave' that he often uses to describe himself. The word for 'servant' is 'an *attendant*, or someone who renders *manual or other service*'.[38] Tom Wright draws this out nicely:

> The word 'servant' here, unlike the word 'slave', can mean 'the one who waits at table'; in other words, Paul and Apollos are simply the people who serve the food, while God is responsible for choosing it and cooking it. You shouldn't make a fuss about which waiter brings the food to your table. What matters is that God is in charge in the kitchen.[39]

The church-planting role involves being a person *through whom* people come to believe, not being a person *in whom* they believe.

We do note, however, that evangelistic work is clearly in view. Faith is the great object of this enterprise, whether of sowing or watering. The New Testament refers to the gospel word as 'seed', whether in Jesus' parable of the sower (e.g. Mark 4:14) or in Peter's description of the growth towards Christian holiness (1 Pet. 1:23), and it is this that is being sown. Nonetheless, it is not personal evangelism per se that Paul has in view, but the planting of gospel communities or churches. This chapter is about *churches*, not individuals.

We come away with a beautifully organic picture: church planting is an evangelistic venture, sowing the good word of the gospel in people's lives, with the view to them coming to faith and forming a church, with God acting in and through the various ministries of all involved.

Paul rounds off the point and simultaneously transitions into the next section of his letter with verse 9: 'For we are God's servants, working together; you are God's field, God's building.' He is moving from an

---

[38] Thiselton 2000: 300, quoting Hanson 1961: 67; emphasis original.
[39] T. Wright 2003a: 34.

agricultural to an architectural image. Again, we pick up the flexibility of his approach: the farming image emphasizes something organic, the construction picture something more methodical. There can be different approaches to church planting, different models, different phases in the life of the nascent churches, different gifts, different emphases; but all have a common purpose: to see churches come into existence through the preaching of the gospel. Church planters bring their differing gifts to bear at particular times and phases of the life of their church plants, relying on the continuous and continuing power of God to give life and growth to these communities of faith. What a beautiful picture!

Paul in 1 Corinthians 3 challenges those of us who plant churches with the question not so much of *whether* we have faith, as of *where* that faith is located: is it in worldly wisdom, a sense of superior spirituality and our own maturity and expertise, or is it in Christ and his cross? No church planters, of course, would say that they were putting their faith in their social media campaign for their church plant or their advertising, or that it was their organizational chart or plan for the next two years that made their plant so effective, or that their use of video or cutting-edge culture was the reason why young people were coming to faith in their services; but when we balance the amount of time and energy that goes into these things compared to, say, prayer, communicating the gospel, or working one to one with those exploring the faith outside the church, then maybe our actions are telling us some uncomfortable truths. It is not that these things are wrong in themselves. This critique should not be heard as a rejection of anything that can be learned from managerial insights or modern communications. Rather, it is affirming Paul's sense of what will deliver the power of God. We may attract more of a crowd with these things – and again, that is not to be thought of as wrong in and of itself; indeed, much of launching church plants is a consideration of the best and most appropriate ways of doing precisely this in our contexts. What is profoundly wrong, though, according to Paul, is putting our faith in these things, neglecting the gospel of Christ crucified and forgetting how things work in the kingdom of God. When we get our priorities upside down, there are terrible results, both for the church plant and for us as church planters, as Paul will go on to argue in the remainder of the chapter, to which we will now turn our attention.

Build with care

What follows is a hugely striking passage, even a frightening one for church planters. It is an unusual message – when did you last hear a talk on the need for church planters to work with reverence? – but maybe it is all the more needed for that:

> According to the grace of God given to me, like a skilled master builder I laid a foundation, and someone else is building on it. Each builder must choose with care how to build on it. For no one can lay any foundation other than the one that has been laid; that foundation is Jesus Christ. Now if anyone builds on the foundation with gold, silver, precious stones, wood, hay, straw – the work of each builder will become visible, for the Day will disclose it, because it will be revealed with fire, and the fire will test what sort of work each has done. If what has been built on the foundation survives, the builder will receive a reward. If the work is burned, the builder will suffer loss; the builder will be saved, but only as through fire.
> (1 Cor. 3:10–15)

In many ways, this is Paul developing what he has already been saying: that there is a right way and a wrong way to plant a church. To use cleverness, a spirituality that has no place for the cross, street smarts, is to use cheap materials, and these will burn easily. To make Christ our foundation, the true wisdom and power of God, is to build a temple in the Spirit that will be enduring, strong and magnificent. Now, though, Paul sharpens his focus, asking us to assess our work in the light of the day of God's judgment. *How* we plant our churches will have consequences for how durable these churches will be in the searing light of God's immediate presence, and also personally for the church planters themselves.

Paul describes his own role in the Corinthian church: 'like a skilled master builder I laid a foundation' (3:10). The initial, apostolic founding of churches is a skilful business. There is a challenge and an affirmation here for church planters; the challenge to take seriously our task, and the affirmation in God's eyes of the demands placed on us in our roles. The word translated 'skilled' is actually 'wise' in the Greek, so Paul is still working out the contrast between the Corinthians' understanding of what wisdom is and what God sees it as. This comes to the fore again when Paul goes on to explain that there is actually only one foundation for church plants, and 'that foundation is Jesus Christ' (3:11). This reminds us again of Paul's definition of 'Christ the power of God and the wisdom of God' (1:24). Wise or skilful foundation laying is thus nothing else and nothing other than 'Jesus Christ, and him crucified' (2:2). This was Paul's skill, what it meant to be a 'skilled master builder' (3:10). The word translated 'master builder' is the Greek word from which we get our English word 'architect'. Anthony Thiselton explains that the Greek word has two elements to it, the one being 'a worker in wood or stone', the other being 'chief, or leader, here perhaps as first among equals, more probably leading in experience and skill rather than in managerial status'.[40] This is a lovely image for a church planter to reflect on; church planting is like the work of a skilled craftsman, who brings wisdom and experience to bear in the work of God in starting new churches.[41]

Paul is keen to state that he had this role 'according to the grace of God given to me' (3:10). This may have the sense of 'God gave me the privilege' (REB), but seems more likely to refer to a particular spiritual gift from God for this work.[42] Either way, church planters are conscious of the sheer privilege of their work and of the equipping power of God without which they could not accomplish it.

Paul's concern, though, is not with the foundation: he knows that this church (or network of churches) in Corinth has been surely founded on Jesus and his cross. Rather, he is focusing on the fact that 'someone else is building on it' (3:10). This is not Apollos, but rather those who are influencing the church plant with their 'wisdom' and ways. The tone of the passage turns more earnest now, for 'each builder must choose with care how to build' on the foundation (3:10).

There are two ways to build; one is with 'gold, silver, precious stones', and the other is with 'wood, hay, straw' (3:12). Although the first three are superior in value to the second three, the main point of the contrast is that the last three are combustible, whereas the first trio would not be burned

---

40 Thiselton 2000: 308; emphasis original.
41 See Selvaratnam 2022.
42 Fee 1987: 137.

up in a fire. Paul is viewing the work of those building on the foundation in the light of 'the Day', the day of judgment, which is characterized by fire. This day will reveal things in its brightness (daylight, as opposed to darkness) and will also be the ultimate test of the value and durability of the ministries that went into building the church plant; the work characterized as gold, silver and precious stones will endure, and that described as wood, hay and straw will be burned up (3:13, 15). Of the two ways to build up a church plant, then, one is ultimately worthless, and the other of supreme, enduring, eternal worth, and the day of God's judgment will show clearly which it is.

The urgent question then becomes: 'What does Paul mean when he talks about building with gold, silver and precious stones, and what does he mean when he describes the worthless work as building with wood, hay and straw?' He does not specify in any detail, but the outline is clear.

> With Paul's own concern in view, and in light of the argument as a whole, one may rightly argue, therefore, that for Paul the 'gold, silver, and costly stones' represent what is compatible with the foundation, the gospel of Jesus Christ and him crucified; what will perish is [wisdom] in all its human forms. It belongs only to this age, and this age is passing away, along with all that belongs to it.[43]

This is reinforced by the way in which Paul returns to a denunciation of worldly wisdom to round off the section. He uses the same phrase in the Greek ('let no one'[44]) to criticize the Corinthians in the two (related) areas of their church life that are causing him such concern:

- 'Let no one delude themselves' when it comes to worldly wisdom, because 'the wisdom of this world is foolishness with God' (3:18, 19);
- 'So let no one boast about human leaders' (3:21).

Factionalism, in Paul's analysis, is an expression of the worldly wisdom. The Corinthians are putting their trust in a power and a wisdom that are

---

[43] Ibid. 140.
[44] Ibid. 150.

different from that of the cross of Christ. This is the stuff of wood, hay and straw. It is very much 'of this world', not the kingdom of God. By contrast, Christ crucified is the true wisdom and power of God. When the Corinthians move away from this, divisions and factions arise, built on all-too-worldly criteria. Then there is a real risk, not just that the church is being built with shoddy and combustible materials, but that the whole building may be torn down (3:17).

Further to this, gold, silver and precious stones were the building materials of Solomon's temple.[45] Paul makes this connection explicit at the conclusion of the building materials section of our passage: 'Do you not know that you are God's temple and that God's Spirit dwells in you? If anyone destroys God's temple, God will destroy that person. For God's temple is holy, and you are that temple' (1 Cor. 3:16–17). The pronouns are in the plural; Paul is talking about 'you all', everyone at the church in Corinth. His concern – God's concern – is the building up of this group of people, founded and taught in the gospel, not weakened by worldliness, pragmatism, a competitive tendency to impress and destroy one another. The Spirit of God no longer inhabits the Jerusalem temple, but chooses instead to make his home within the church of Jesus Christ.

Tom Wright draws out the implications beautifully:

If you come upon a foundation already laid, but without any plans for the superstructure, you will have to choose what sort of building to build. Paul's basic answer is that this must be a building for *worship*: a Temple, in other words (verses 16–17). That's the question every church worker should ask: is what I'm doing encouraging and enabling people to worship the true and living God, in holiness and truth? If not, am I perhaps being untrue to the foundation that has been laid?[46]

This is the new temple, the place where people meet God, built on the sure foundation of the cross of Christ, and animated and sanctified for worship by the Holy Spirit living in each believer. What a wonderful vision!

---

45 Ibid. 140.
46 T. Wright 2003a: 34–35; emphasis original.

We have the outline, then, of the business of a church plant:

1 Establish it through the gospel alone, the only foundation that has been and can be laid. Be apostolic about this, depending on God's enabling grace.
2 Build something that will last, in keeping with Jesus. Don't look to worldly wisdom, pragmatism or personality to get the results that truly count.
3 Aim for worship, the praise and honour of God.
4 Be acutely aware of the Holy Spirit, not least as he lives in others, especially as we gather for worship.
5 Make unity a priority. Relate to one another, especially leaders, within the perspective of the greatness of Jesus Christ. Leaders belong to the people, not the other way round. We are servants, waiters, through whom people come to believe.
6 View everything through the lens of the judgment and evaluation of the holiness of God.
7 'Each builder must choose with care how to build on' the foundation of Jesus Christ (3:10).

We cannot avoid the seriousness with which Paul writes. There will come a day when our work will be tested. It will be shown for what it is, and if it is not kingdom-work, it will be burned up in front of our eyes. And we too will be singed, even if not burned (3:15). This is not the same as saying that we will not be saved, nor that there is a kind of purgatory; this is a testing of church leadership, of the work that has been done, not the condemnation of those who reject Christ. Nonetheless, this is a solemn and alarming note.

Church planting can be a short-term game; at least it carries pressures that drive us to evaluate it in the immediate. 'Will this work? How many people will come this Sunday? Can we report back to our funders an increase in attendance, baptism and giving for this quarter?' It is not that these are bad questions or wrong metrics. It may well be, though, that we are in danger of missing the ultimate evaluation: is this a thoroughly Jesus community, a gathering in which God lives, and is worshipped and honoured? Paradoxically, this short-term approach to church planting can lead us away from the full glory of what a church is and can and should be. Gordon Fee writes:

> One of the desperate needs of the church is to recapture this vision of what it is by grace, and therefore also what God intends it to be . . . Seldom does one sense that it is, or can be, experienced as a community that is so powerfully indwelt by the Holy Spirit that it functions as a genuine alternative to the pagan world in which it is found. It is perhaps not too strong to suggest that the recapturing of this vision of its being . . . is its single greatest need.[47]

Church planters should aim for nothing less, and should build with care and skill towards that aim. What a vision and what a privileged calling!

And what a responsibility. The church is greatly precious to God, and so he will be watching particularly closely those who are tasked with its upbuilding, its holiness (3:16–17). There will be real (although not ultimate) loss for those who build as if the church was a variant of the world, and worldly wisdom and techniques can be used to make it fly. Equally, there will be rewards for those who lay the foundation of Jesus Christ, the true wisdom and power of God, and build with care, in such a way that it will not be out of keeping in the presence of God. 'Each will receive wages according to the labour of each' (3:8).

Church planting is the most effective missionary strategy there is

Towards the end of Romans, Paul is treading on delicate ground, bringing up the matter of the collection for the poor Christians in Jerusalem (Rom. 15:26), suggesting that the Roman churches might support his continuing work in some way (15:24) and gently justifying how it is that he is writing so fully to churches he has not founded (15:15; cf. 1:8–15). Central to his answers relating to all these matters is that he has been given an apostolic mission to the Gentiles by the Lord, and, as we shall see, this mission is essentially fleshed out as a church-planting ministry. Here is the passage:

---

[47] Fee 1987: 149–150.

I myself feel confident about you, my brothers and sisters, that you yourselves are full of goodness, filled with knowledge, and able to instruct one another. Nevertheless, on some points I have written to you rather boldly by way of reminder, because of the grace given me by God to be a minister of Christ Jesus to the Gentiles in the priestly service of the gospel of God, so that the offering of the Gentiles may be acceptable, sanctified by the Holy Spirit. In Christ Jesus, then, I have reason to boast of my work for God. For I will not venture to speak of anything except what Christ has accomplished through me to win obedience from the Gentiles, by word and deed, by the power of signs and wonders, by the power of the Spirit of God, so that from Jerusalem and as far around as Illyricum I have fully proclaimed the good news of Christ. Thus I make it my ambition to proclaim the good news, not where Christ has already been named, so that I do not build on someone else's foundation, but as it is written,

'Those who have never been told of him shall see,
and those who have never heard of him shall understand.'
(Rom. 15:14–21)

John Stott summarizes the content of this passage under three helpful headings: a priestly ministry (15:16–17), a powerful ministry (15:18–19a) and a pioneer ministry (15:19b–22).[48] As we look at this text through the lens of church planting, we will take these themes in reverse order.

Paul's startling claim is that, in his missionary career, he has fully proclaimed the gospel in an arc all around the eastern Mediterranean (15:19). This is an enormous area, summarizing his missionary work (what we have been calling his three church-planting journeys). Some are puzzled that he puts down Jerusalem as the starting point, when it seems from Acts that Antioch in Syria was his sending church (Acts 13:2, 4). Paul did, however, begin his evangelistic ministry in Jerusalem (Acts 9:28). Perhaps, as well, there is the theological perspective on his work which we have had frequent cause to note, namely that the gospel is 'to the Jew first and also

---

[48] Stott 1994: 378–383.

to the Greek' (e.g. Rom. 1:16; 2:9). Equally, some are thrown by the reference to Illyricum. This was the area on the western coast of Macedonia, 'the Balkan coast opposite Italy on the Adriatic sea'.[49] The source of puzzlement is that we have no record of Paul ever having gone there. It may be, though, that Illyricum was known as the end of the eastern Mediterranean, and perhaps Paul had indeed conducted an evangelistic and church-planting tour in that region which is simply not recorded in the New Testament.[50] It seems likely, therefore, that Paul is speaking in terms comparable to the missionary agenda laid down at the beginning of the Acts of the Apostles: both theologically and geographically, the gospel has been preached 'in Jerusalem . . . and to the ends of the earth' (Acts 1:8). Paul adds a term meaning 'circle' or 'ring', so perhaps he is laying out the rough sense of his regular missionary journeys, which could be traced from Jerusalem, through Galatia, into Asia, across into Macedonia and Achaia (and Illyricum), and then back again. However we construe this verse, the main impact is clear and astonishing:

> Before Paul began, neither Asia Minor nor Greece had heard of Jesus of Nazareth; by the time he was writing this letter, there were little communities all over that part of Caesar's empire . . . in which Jesus was being celebrated as the risen Messiah, the world's true Lord. That is in itself an astonishing achievement, and Paul must have known it.[51]

The vastness of this area makes Paul's claim that he had fully preached the gospel here the more remarkable:

> Taken at face value, the claim is extraordinary: Paul's preaching, as far as we can judge, was confined to the great cities and even in them probably reached only a small proportion of the population, leaving the vast rural hinterland virtually untouched.[52]

---

[49] N. T. Wright 2002: 754.
[50] Ibid.; and Schnabel (2008: 112–113), who has the intriguing suggestion that Paul may have visited Illyricum in order to experience a region in which Latin was spoken and thus prepare himself for his proposed visit to Spain.
[51] N. T. Wright 2002: 754.
[52] Byrne 1996: 436–437.

So, as one commentator writes: 'Could Paul really claim to have preached everywhere in such a vast area? Plainly he could not; the idea is so absurd that it cannot be what he is saying.'[53]

Paul underscores the same point when he goes on to say that there is 'no further place for me in these regions' (Rom. 15:23). The same commentator expostulates: 'Why ever not? Surely there must have been large numbers of towns and villages left which had not been evangelized.'[54]

So, what is Paul saying? Surely he is stating that he has planted churches sufficient within these regions that the gospel would inevitably permeate or fill the whole region (and perhaps was already doing so). Granted what we have seen throughout the New Testament of how the gospel is rooted in places through the establishing of churches, this is Paul laying out the fulfilment of his evangelistic strategy for reaching regions – to plant churches, which would themselves go on to plant other churches, and this would continue until there were no places, networks or people groups without the witness of a gospel church reaching out to them.

Douglas Moo states that this is 'the only reasonable' explanation of what Paul can mean, and goes on to quote John Knox:

[Paul] could say that he had completed the preaching of the gospel from Jerusalem to Illyricum only because this statement would have meant for him that the message had been proclaimed and the church planted in each of the nations north and west across Asia Minor and the Greek peninsula – 'proclaimed' widely enough and 'planted' firmly enough to assure that the name of Christ would soon be heard throughout its borders.[55]

Viewed in this light, Romans 15 is a parallel to Luke's statement in Acts, that by his daily ministry in the hall of Tyrannus in Ephesus, over a two-year period, Paul ensured that 'all the residents of Asia . . . heard the word of the Lord' (Acts 19:10). It was not that Paul himself travelled to all the places of Asia (or from Jerusalem round to Illyricum), but rather that he trained leaders who could plant churches, which would in turn

---

[53] Ziesler 1989: 343.
[54] Ibid. 344.
[55] Moo 1996: 896, quoting Knox 1964: 3.

plant further churches and so on, thus ensuring that whole regions were evangelized.

So, when Paul claims that he has 'fully proclaimed the good news of Christ' all around the eastern Mediterranean (Rom. 15:19), he is actually saying that he has preached the gospel in such a way that churches were planted that would carry on this apostolic work throughout the region. He is saying that his work was a church-planting work.

Missiologists Craig Ott and Gene Wilson raise an interesting implication for church planters:

[Paul] demonstrated an obvious concern for the *entire process* of planting – in the sense of laying a foundation of new kingdom communities led by local leaders *and* guiding those leaders and communities so that they might have a broad and powerful impact for years to come.[56]

If we are to follow Paul in our church planting, then:

- we will be concerned to hold church and gospel together – evangelism will be integral to church life, and the establishing of churches will be a key aspect of evangelism;
- we will view the development of local leaders who can succeed us and pick up the baton of mission and church planting as an essential aspect of our ministry – Ott and Wilson go on to say that 'leadership development constitutes the sine qua non of church growth and church-planting movements';[57]
- we will have a heightened strategic sense of how church planting is the way to reach regions, to build a sense of momentum into our church planting, so that we do not just plant churches, but rather we plant churches which plant other churches which go on to plant further churches and so on.

It is encouraging that there is more and more of a practice growing up that when churches are planted, they start with a person on the initial

---

[56] Ott and Wilson 2011: 55.
[57] Ibid. 59.

planting team who has the brief to be the planter for that church plant's first church plant. In this way, potential church planters gain the experience of being in on the very beginning of a church plant. When they themselves come to plant, perhaps in three to five years' time, they do so with the first-hand experience of having lived through it previously. And of course, when they come to plant they replicate this pattern, taking someone with them on their church-planting team who will lead off the first of the next generation of church plants, planting out of this church plant. This can be done in intervening years, as well, maybe on a smaller scale. Perhaps the initial church can have an ambition to start some form of new Christian community each year – perhaps a youth congregation, or a missional community in a local care home, or gathering around a new football team. The methodology of multiplication is that each of these new ventures is launched with a kind of trainee planter as part of the core team. These people will have the beginnings of a vision for this but may feel that they do not yet have the skills or maturity to lead such a venture themselves. By taking a role in the launch of something, they grow in these areas and in confidence, such that they will shortly be ready (or as ready as any of us ever feel) to launch off with their own team to start another venture in a year or so. And of course, when they do so, they include their own apprentice planter on their core team with a view to having that person start something similar in due course. In that way, church plants multiply, and we move towards being able to say with Paul that a whole area or network has been evangelized.

The power of God

But how did Paul do what he did? It really was an extraordinary achievement to evangelize such a vast area from nothing, often in the teeth of heated opposition, and to do so in about a decade. He is in no doubt about how he did it – he planted churches solely through the power of God. There is the outline of a trinitarian theology in his words.

- He speaks of his 'work for God' (15:17), and 'the grace given me by God' (15:15) for this work, which he fulfils through 'the power of the Spirit of God' (15:19).

- What is done, he says, is 'what Christ has accomplished through me' (15:18).
- The sanctifying of the Gentile converts is through the 'Holy Spirit' (15:16), and the church planting happens through 'the power of the Spirit of God' (15:19).

Father, Son and Holy Spirit, then, are all involved in this remarkable ministry of apostolic church planting.

Paul spells out in more detail what has happened: Christ has accomplished the obedience of the Gentiles 'by word and deed, by the power of signs and wonders, by the power of the Spirit of God' (15:18–19). This is how he did his church planting. He draws our attention not to techniques and strategies, but to the underlying power.

We note the combination of both word and deed; it is not just by preaching, but by a combination of the message and the living out of that message in love and service of others. When Paul follows this up with a reference to 'signs and wonders' on the one hand and 'the power of the Spirit of God' on the other, as Moo says, '[i]t is tempting to connect the first of these phrases with "by deed" and the second with "by word"':

> Paul would then be identifying the 'deed' part of his ministry with 'signs and wonders' and the 'word' part of his ministry as accomplished by 'the power of the Spirit'. However, Paul would obviously attribute all that he accomplishes in ministry – whether 'by word' or 'by deed' – to the power of the Spirit.[58]

The point is well made, but it is hard to escape the sense that Paul (at least primarily, if not exclusively) had in mind that the evangelistic deeds were the 'signs and wonders' that Christ did through him. Moo is helpful, though, in drawing out Paul's main point, namely that the totality of his church-planting work should be seen as a result of nothing less than the power of the Spirit. By repeating the word 'power' in successive clauses – 'by the *power* of signs and wonders, by the *power* of the Spirit of God' (15:19, my emphasis) – it is hard to miss Paul's theme here: Christ's work in and through him was one of awesome power.

---

[58] Moo 1996: 892–893.

What an encouragement for church planters, and what a challenge! If ever there was a church planter who could have begun to develop a sense of self-sufficiency and self-reliance in his ministry, surely it must have been Paul. The success of church planting the whole of the eastern Mediterranean could easily have gone to his head. And he would have learned a great deal about what worked and what did not. He was abundantly gifted, had a determined personality, was super-smart. Yet, he is at pains to attribute his achievement, in as many ways as he can, to God, to Christ accomplishing things through him, to the power of the Holy Spirit.

Although the power comes through God's grace that is specifically tied to Paul's apostolic calling (15:15–16), there is no reason to limit it solely to Paul and the apostles. The grace is to do with pioneering and church planting, not apostolic ministry in this strict sense. So, here is the encouragement, that the full resources of the Holy Trinity are available for church planting. This is how God has chosen to show his grace and kindness to those outside the church: by reaching them in and through newly planted communities of faith, and for that to happen, God makes available his grace and power, his miracles, and an anointing on the preaching of the gospel. The power for planting churches is not ours. The 'success' is not down to our experience, cleverness, smarts, personalities, abilities, personal charisma, youth or age, amazing teams, or whatever. The deeper factor is nothing less than the power of the Spirit of God.

The challenge, of course, is the flip side of this: how can we avail ourselves of this power? How can we so position ourselves to live and minister in this power? How can we make sure that we do not disqualify ourselves in some way from this power? There is a call here for us as church planters to be passionate and deliberate in giving ourselves first and foremost to the Lord in prayer, to make sure that we are not in any way implying that it is us and not Christ who is accomplishing the planting of these churches.

Church planting is as much worship as it is mission

The last section from this key passage shows us a further aspect of Paul's vision for his apostolic church-planting mission. In a startling and surprising way, he uses language taken from the worship of the temple to describe what we would normally think of in evangelistic terms.

- Paul calls himself 'a minister of Christ Jesus to the Gentiles' (15:16). 'The Greek word [translated "minister"] does not in itself have a sacral sense but designates one who performs a task under a supervisor.[59] Yet in the biblical literature both the noun and its cognate verb . . . are used "exclusively of religious and ritual services".'[60]
- 'The verb that follows . . . [translated "in the priestly service"] is always used . . . with respect to priestly offering of sacrifice.'[61]
- The final phrase of Paul's self-description of his ministry in 15:16 makes even more explicit the priestly framework he is using: the Gentiles are described as an 'offering' which will be made 'acceptable' to God through the sanctifying work of the Holy Spirit.

Paul thus sees his church-planting work as analogous to how the Old Testament priests made sacrificial offerings to God in the temple, except he is not offering an animal or a part of a crop, but presenting the Gentile converts of his churches to God. Thus, the church planter, in these terms, is as much a worship leader as an evangelist. The fruit of our church-planting work becomes an offering of praise to honour the God of the gospel.

This is all the more striking in our modern context when evangelism and worship can seem to be separate from or even at odds with each other. John Stott spells this out for us:

All evangelists are priests, because they offer their converts to God. Indeed, it is this truth more than any other which effectively unites the church's two major roles of worship and witness. It is when we worship God, glorying in his holy name, that we are driven out to proclaim his name to the world. And when through our witness people are brought to Christ, we then offer them to God. Further, they themselves join in this worship, until they too go out to witness. Thus worship leads to witness, and witness to worship. It is a per-petual cycle.[62]

---

59 Or a public servant (Stott 1994: 379).
60 Stott 1994: 379, quoting Bauer 1979: *leitourgos / leitourgeō*.
61 Byrne 1996: 437–438.
62 Stott 1994: 379–380.

Partly it is the same logic as the biblical proverb which says: 'The glory of a king is a multitude of people' (Prov. 14:28); in mission terms, the church planter wants Jesus our king to be honoured by as many people as possible. But it is not mere quantity; it is also quality that Paul has in mind. In 2 Corinthians, he can describe his evangelistic ministry as a kind of matchmaking process: 'I feel a divine jealousy for you, for I promised you . . . as a chaste virgin to Christ' (2 Cor. 11:2). He has a calling to offer to God a people who are holy and wholly devoted to Christ. Hence the language in our passage of the sanctifying work of the Spirit. The thought here is not so much the growing holiness of life of believers over time and through ever-deepening experience of Christ, but rather the offering to God through Christ in the Spirit of lives gladly surrendered to him in conversion: 'you were washed, you were sanctified, you were justified in the name of our Lord Jesus Christ and in the Spirit of our God' (1 Cor. 6:11).

There are several implications for church planters from this magnificent line of thought, which we examine in the next two subsections.

1 Church planting is focused on what God thinks and wants

We, of course, have reversed Paul's line of thought in our consideration of this passage. Paul *begins* with his description of his apostolic work as a priestly ministry, before going on to state how it is God who has been acting through him, and then concluding with showing how his ministry has essentially been one of a multiplying church-planting movement. For Paul, his view of his ministry must start with its being an offering of worship to God. For us, the train of thought has been in reverse, but we must not miss the foundational point: church planting is Paul's key methodology, it is carried out through the power of God working through us, and it is rooted in worship – in the desire that God be honoured and worshipped by many people through it.

Listen again to Paul's language.

- He describes himself as 'a minister of Christ Jesus to the Gentiles' (Rom. 15:16). He serves Christ, not the Gentiles. He is solely a minister of Christ. This service finds expression in being an apostle to the Gentiles, but it is fundamentally an obedience to Christ, a service to him only.

- He goes on to talk about 'the priestly service of the gospel of God' (15:16). He describes his ministry once again in relation to God. The Gentiles are not even in view yet in this phrase. Paul thinks of himself like the priests of the Old Testament, serving God in the temple at Jerusalem, coming to offer sacrifices in worship to God. Notice how he recalibrates that picture totally by reference to the gospel: now this service of worship takes the shape of evangelization, not of ritualistic sacrifice. The motivation and orientation of his ministry stays the same, though – it is worship to God.
- When we get back to the Gentiles, he positions them as an 'offering' (15:16). Once again ministry is framed in terms of relating to God; it is not described as human activity or even in missionary terms (something *to* the Gentiles), but as an offering of worship to God (the offering *of* the Gentiles *to* God).
- The key thing about this offering, says Paul, is that it be 'acceptable' to God, 'sanctified by the Holy Spirit' (15:16). Paul's focus is on the pleasure of God; his concern is whether the church-planting work results in something pleasing and acceptable to God.

When we apply this to church-planting work, we have an orientation towards worship and an eye to the last day. The line of thought is parallel to what we have just seen in 1 Corinthians 3. Is this work worthy of God? Is it holy work? Will we be able to offer our church plants back to God (and they have always been his, of course) with a sense of them bringing honour and glory and pleasure to him?

Sometimes church planters are so focused on the mission, outreach and evangelism of the church plant that the worship can almost feel secondary. Paul encourages us not to set the two (mission and worship) over against each other, but to see them flowing beautifully into each other. So the fruit of evangelism is lives and voices lifted to God in church worship. And equally, church worship finds expression in the everyday, throughout the week, in lives of holiness, service and witness to the glory of God.

2 Church planting has a vision for a holy quality of church life
Paul emphasizes the holiness of the offering of the Gentiles, which is why it is dependent on the sanctifying work of the Holy Spirit (15:16). This

reflects back to the Old Testament insistence on the offering of sacrifices that were without blemish to God. Here is just one example, and there could have been many:

> O priests, [you] despise my name. You say, 'How have we despised your name?' By offering polluted food on my altar. And you say, 'How have we polluted it?' By thinking that the LORD's table may be despised. When you offer blind animals in sacrifice, is that not wrong? And when you offer those that are lame or sick, is that not wrong? . . . I have no pleasure in you, says the LORD of hosts, and I will not accept an offering from your hands.
> (Mal. 1:6–8, 10)

This is the vocabulary that Paul applies to the power of the gospel in establishing churches that are themselves pure offerings to God:

> Christ loved the church and gave himself up for her . . . by cleansing her with the washing of water by the word, so as to present the church to himself in splendour, without a spot or wrinkle or anything of the kind – yes, so that she may be holy and without blemish.
> (Eph. 5:25–27)

And elsewhere: 'And you who were once estranged and hostile in mind, doing evil deeds, he has now reconciled in his fleshly body through death, so as to present you holy and blameless and irreproachable before him' (Col. 1:21–22).

Repeatedly, Paul applies the language of sacrifices in the Old Testament to the work of church planting and development; just as the former had to be without 'blemish', so do the latter. To offer blemished sacrifices is a mark of disrespect to God, something which offends him. It is a sign of hearts that do not really love and worship him. Paul aspires to have the same high standards when it comes to the quality of his church-planting work.

It is noteworthy again how this ties in with Paul's thoughts in 1 Corinthians 3, when he challenges church planters to use only the highest-quality materials in building their churches. Here, Paul is actually defining his whole church-planting ministry around this notion of the holiness of the church plants he is offering to God in worship. Consider the logic of this sentence: '[God has given me grace] to be a minister of Christ Jesus to the Gentiles in the priestly service of the gospel of God, *so that* the offering of the Gentiles may be acceptable' (15:16, my emphasis). God's grace called Paul to this apostolic ministry of church planting; this ministry is to offer new churches of Gentile believers to God; and the whole point is that these offerings/churches be acceptable to God. In terms of the offerings-language Paul uses, this means that they must be holy, without blemish. How can this be? They need to be 'sanctified by the Holy Spirit' (15:16).

Paul, of course, would have had an uncomfortable awareness of how his church plants fell short of this sublime vision. Think of the substance of his letter to the Galatians, where the church seemed to have lost hold on the gospel itself; or the moral issues in the church in Corinth; or his exhortations to the Colossians to keep going in the gospel (e.g. 1:23; 2:6); or his grief over those who deserted his apostolic missionary cadre, such as Demas (2 Tim. 4:9); or his telling comment about 'daily pressure because of my anxiety for all the churches' (2 Cor. 11:28).

This must be why Paul looks to the power of the Holy Spirit to sanctify this offering of the Gentile church plants (Rom. 15:16). It takes the holy power of God himself to make us and our churches holy. For sure, we do all we can, and we have as our aim that the church plants be acceptable to God and without blemish, but we do so in the conviction that only the Holy Spirit can make us holy in this way.

This brings out an element in church planting that we also see in 1 Corinthians 3. Paul, by and large, planted churches and then moved on. He was a starter of church plants, which he would then leave in the hands of leaders he had raised up and appointed. Nonetheless, Paul has a vision of church planting as a *process*. There is a definite beginning; there was a time when the church was not, then it comes into being through the preaching of the gospel. Paul had an eye, though, to the rest of the story. So, in 1 Corinthians 3, he talks about a foundation being laid, and then the need to build on it. In 1 Corinthians he talks about the 'building' or 'building up' of the church, almost as a technical term. In Romans 15, he can talk about foundations being laid (15:20) and an offering made to God in holiness.

It seems that the heart of what this meant for Paul could be summed up in the word 'obedience'. He can describe the work Christ accomplished through him as winning 'obedience from the Gentiles' (15:18). This is a big word in Romans, bookending the letter as it does. In the opening section of the book, Paul describes his ministry as 'grace and apostleship to bring about the obedience of faith among all the Gentiles for the sake of [Christ's] name' (1:5). And in the closing section of the book, he praises God for the revelation of the gospel, which is now made known 'to all the Gentiles, according to the command of the eternal God, to bring about the obedience of faith' (16:26). And, in the heart of the letter, he can talk about how through Christ's obedience 'many will be made righteous' (5:19). As he describes union with Christ, he talks of Christians becoming 'obedient slaves' to righteousness, and says to the Roman believers: 'you . . . have become obedient from the heart to the form of teaching to which you were entrusted' (6:16, 17). This is how church plants become holy, sanctified by the Holy Spirit: by being obedient in faith to the revelation of Christ's gospel. In terms of Paul's own mission, this is particularly true of Gentiles coming to faith.

Brendan Byrne writes interestingly about the light that this perspective sheds on Paul's relationship with the Roman Christians:

> The image [of priestly ministry] suggests not so much the role in which Paul usually depicts himself – that concerned with original preaching and conversion – but rather that of subsequent 'sanctification' of those who were originally unclean.[63]

Although we must not overpress the distinction, can we not see something of a longer process than is usually thought of? The gospel comes not just with justifying but also with sanctifying power – it is in Christ that we find 'righteousness and sanctification and redemption' (1 Cor. 1:30), and the Corinthians 'were washed . . . were sanctified . . . were justified in the name of the Lord Jesus Christ and in the Spirit of our God' (1 Cor. 6:11) – so we must not separate conversion and sanctification completely, at least theologically. Nonetheless, in chronological terms, Byrne is right

---

[63] Byrne 1996: 436.

to see Paul thinking of himself as both the initial evangelizer (the layer of the initial foundation through the gospel) and the one who has a concern for continuing life and development (sanctification through the Holy Spirit).

With our church-planting hats on, we can thus see a longer process than is sometimes spoken of. The church planter not only establishes the church plant but also develops it, looking to foster its spiritual health. There is a growing to maturity in discipleship, a discovery and use of the gifts of God for the continuing life and growth of the church plant. Paul's image, though, is striking in the emphasis he puts on holiness, on being an acceptable offering to God through the sanctifying work of the Spirit, of lives that are marked by a heart-obedience to the good news of Christ.

Bear in mind that the priestly vocabulary would take his initial readers back to the world of the Jerusalem temple. Here is another overlap with Paul's thought in 1 Corinthians 3. His concern is that these church plants be places of worship, holy offerings to God in Christ through the Holy Spirit. They are communities characterized by obedient self-offering to Christ, to the honour and glory of God in this world and the next. Church planters have a vision not just for people coming to faith, but also for those people growing more and more holy throughout their lives and forming more and more churches that are holy and for whom worship is their joy and raison d'être. Church planters have an eye to churches not just *forming*, but *conforming* to the life of Jesus. And their vision reaches its culmination in heaven, where these churches stand together to praise their God and Saviour through all eternity.

Church planting anticipates heaven

We have found our thoughts turning to heaven, guided by the contours of Paul's thought in Romans 15, and the occasions when we have picked up parallels to his thinking expressed in 1 Corinthians 3. There are further hints in Romans 15 which are worth drawing out, not least in connection with church planting.

Paul uses an interesting word when it comes to his church planting around the eastern Mediterranean: 'from Jerusalem and as far around as Illyricum I have fully proclaimed the good news' (15:19). More literally, what he says is that he has 'fulfilled' the preaching of the gospel in these regions.[64] It is not just a sense of filling, but of completing. Some think this might mean that he has finished his work in the regions, which is true, but it is not what this particular phrase is getting at; grammatically, the fulfilment has to do with the preaching of the gospel, not the geographical areas. Others think Paul may be referring to the manner in which he preached the gospel (usually interpreted as the presence of signs and wonders as well as words in the proclamation), but this does not explain the sense of something being 'fulfilled'. Douglas Moo summarizes another view which adequately takes on board the significance of Paul's choice of this unusual word: 'Paul often uses this verb in an eschatological sense . . . Paul is hinting again at his special role as an eschatological preacher, destined to bring Gentiles into the kingdom and hence usher in the end.'[65]

We can pick up a sense that Paul saw in the response of the Gentiles to the gospel how God was fulfilling his promise that both Jews and Gentiles would flock into his kingdom. He has already written about this in Romans chapter 11. Now, he sees his own church-planting work in this light, and the significance of the Gentiles' collection for the relief of their Jewish-Christian sisters and brothers in Jerusalem similarly.[66]

Paul quotes from Isaiah to round off this section of the letter: 'Those who have never been told of him shall see, and those who have never heard of him shall understand' (Rom. 15:21, quoting Isa. 52:15). Paul is seeing in this prophecy a prediction of his own pioneer work, founding churches only where there were not previously churches in existence; but there is also the sense that Isaiah's prophecy speaks of the Servant of the LORD, through his suffering and death, bringing the nations into the covenant of God.[67] Paul had a clear vocation to bring the gospel to the Gentiles;[68] he viewed this as playing a significant part in how God would fulfil his plan that the whole world, Gentiles as well as Jews, would come to worship God at the end of time. For Paul, then, his church-planting work had a

---

[64] See Moo 1996: 895.

[65] Ibid. 896, although we should note Moo's own reluctance to overstress this aspect.

[66] See Ziesler 1989: 341, 342.

[67] See e.g. the first part of the verse Paul quotes, which speaks of 'many nations' being startled by the Servant, and kings shutting their mouths because of him.

[68] E.g. Acts 9:15; Rom. 1:5; 15:16; Gal. 2:8, 9.

further dimension in seeing God's good purposes for his kingdom coming to completion.

Church planting in our contexts can carry similar resonances. We may not have the same epoch-making convictions as Paul in relation to his work – after all, these were the very early days of Gentiles coming into God's kingdom – but we live under the same trajectory of the fulfilment of God's plans for the world. Jesus pronounced that 'the good news must first be proclaimed to all nations' before the end (Mark 13:10), and Paul had a similar sense of the significance of the gospel going out 'to all the earth . . . to the ends of the world' (Rom. 10:18). When we church plant, particularly to reach those who have no meaningful access to existing churches, and we have a heart for those outside our current churches or present way of doing things, we are joining Paul in a church-planting ministry that is drawing in the nations and the Gentiles to participate in the worship of the people of God in the heavenly Jerusalem. We are fulfilling the gospel promise that this kind of evangelism is hastening the fullness of God's kingdom.

This kind of perspective is strange to the ears of most Western Christians, but it seems to have been a powerful motivator and encouragement for Paul in his church-planting ministry among predominantly Gentile populations. When, in our day, such an alarmingly large proportion of contemporary Western society is alienated from the church and can accurately be described as 'far off' (Eph. 2:13, 17), we can be sure that faithful and effective church planting among these populations is not only close to the missionary heart of God but also bang on track for his plans for the world. The gospel is a 'fulfilment' of the purposes of God, and Paul tells us in Romans 15 that church planting is among the most effective ways of joining with God in what he, in love, purposes for human history.

Perhaps the key aspect of this for Paul was not just the inclusion of the Gentiles in God's kingdom, but that Jewish and Gentile Christians *together* would join in worshipping the God and Father of our Lord Jesus Christ. In Ephesians he writes: 'So [Jesus] came and proclaimed peace to you who were far off and peace to those who were near; for through him both of us have access in one Spirit to the Father' (Eph. 2:17–18).

In Romans 15 Paul writes of how 'together you may with one voice glorify the God and Father of our Lord Jesus Christ' (15:6). He writes that

Christ came to serve the circumcised *and* that 'the Gentiles might glorify God for his mercy' (15:8–9). He quotes Deuteronomy 32:43, 'Rejoice, O Gentiles, with his people' (15:10). The glorious vision is for Jew and Gentile *together* to join in the praise of God. This is what John sees in Revelation:

> After this I looked, and there was a great multitude that no one could count, from every nation, from all tribes and peoples and languages, standing before the throne and before the Lamb, robed in white, with palm branches in their hands. They cried out in a loud voice, saying,
>
> 'Salvation belongs to our God who is seated on the throne,
>   and to the Lamb!'
> (Rev. 7:9–10)

We note the double emphasis on worship as the goal of all mission (including church planting) and on united worship among differing groups. It is worth bearing in mind that the Greek word in the New Testament that is translated into English as 'Gentiles' literally means 'the nations'. Paul's vision is for a global gathering, all praising the God of Israel. This serves to underline for us once more the beauty and significance of multi-ethnic church planting, of new Christian communities which embody God's future where every tribe, nation and language group is united in Christ to worship him. Church plants where this is the case anticipate the worship of heaven.

As John Piper has cogently written:

> Missions is not the ultimate goal of the church. Worship is. Missions exists because worship doesn't. Worship is ultimate, not missions, because God is ultimate, not [humanity]. When this age is over, and the countless millions of the redeemed fall on their faces before the throne of God, missions will be no more. It is a temporary necessity. But worship abides forever. Worship is, therefore, the fuel and the goal of missions.[69]

---

[69] Piper 2003: 17, quoted in T. Wright 2007: 244.

344

Church planting an entire island

Our last snapshot from the New Testament is Paul's letter to Titus. We have seen Paul reflecting on the practice of church planting generally in 1 Corinthians 3, and on his own life's work of planting new churches in Romans 15. Titus gives us a window on him as he briefs one of his loyal colleagues about church planting. It is like a senior pastor, minister or priest sitting down with his or her 'planting curate' or associate to talk through what they are going to do to establish a whole network of churches across a region. It is a remarkably helpful little letter for church planters.

The occasion for the letter is set out in chapter 1, verse 5: 'I left you behind in Crete for this reason, that you should put in order what remained to be done, and should appoint elders in every town as I directed you.' This implies that Paul and Titus had been on mission together in Crete, and had seen churches established right across the island, but Paul had been called away before leaders could be appointed in the churches. George W. Knight III sets the scene for us:

> That Paul left Titus behind implies that he was with Titus on Crete. The occasion for this that best fits into Paul's life would be during a journey after Paul's release from his first Roman imprisonment.[70] From what follows, one can surmise that the two were successful in evangelizing various cities on the island but did not have time to return and strengthen the believers by setting the churches in order and seeing that elders were elected (for Paul's pattern see Acts 14:21–23).[71]

Alternatively, Paul is putting into practice the methodology he learned in the second and third church-planting journeys: he is encouraging local churches to appoint their own leaders (albeit under the helpful eye of an experienced overseer) and taking care himself not to become the one around whom everything else revolves.

Paul uses a mixed metaphor to describe Titus's task: literally, he is to 'straighten out what was left unfinished'. As John Stott comments: 'one

---

[70] John Stott agrees; see Stott 1996: 171–172.
[71] Knight 1992: 287–288.

straightens out what is crooked, whereas what is unfinished needs rather to be completed.'[72] Nonetheless, the picture is comprehensible: things were out of line and needed to be put right, and the churches on Crete were like fishing nets with tears in them; their way of life needed to be sewn up. The answer was to appoint elders in each of the churches in each of the towns. Leadership is key to church life, and to church planting. Titus's job was to attend to this.

We know very little about Titus. Sir William Ramsay called him 'the most enigmatic figure in early Christian history'.[73] Apart from the letter that bears his name, he comes up in connection with the dispute in Galatians 2, and in connection with two 'diplomatic mission(s)'[74] elsewhere in the New Testament: the delivery of 'the severe letter' to the Corinthians (see 2 Cor. 7:8, 12) and the collection in Corinth for the relief of the Jewish Christians in Jerusalem (see 2 Cor. 8:16). It seems Titus was a 'safe pair of hands', someone Paul could rely on. At any rate, he was one of Paul's converts who had stayed with him, and whom Paul trusted completely; he was 'my loyal child in the faith we share' (Titus 1:4).

This letter is a privileged 'listening in' to how Paul instructed a trusted lieutenant in the training of leaders for a network of church plants. It seems likely that these were fresh plants, new churches, but there may well be things to learn too for revitalizations. Key elements are leadership, preaching and teaching, and good works. We shall look at them in turn.

Leaders in church plants

Paul directs Titus to appoint 'elders' (1:5) for each church, who are the same as 'overseers' (1:7).[75] These leaders are set over against false leaders who are already troubling these new churches. Verses 5–10 describe the kind of elders that Paul wants Titus to appoint; and verses 10–16 describe the others who were doing so much damage. The two sections are linked by the Greek word which means 'because'. In other words, good leadership is needed *because* there is bad leadership. The solution to a leadership

---

[72] Stott 1996: 173.
[73] Ramsay 1900: 284, quoted in Stott 1996: 170.
[74] Stott 1996: 171.
[75] NRSV translates as 'bishop', with a footnote about overseers.

that Paul lambasts as 'detestable, disobedient, unfit for any good work' (1:16) is good, healthy leadership.

The good leader is described in many ways, all of them searching. The key word, repeated when Paul talks about the elders (in 1:6) and overseers (1:7), is 'blameless'. This, needless to say, does not mean perfect, for who then could ever qualify? But it does mean that they have a good reputation in the church and wider community. They should be 'above reproach'.[76] To summarize the areas of life that Paul draws attention to, he talks about a blameless home life (1:6–7), blameless self-mastery (1:7–8) and 'a firm grasp of the word that is trustworthy' (1:9). They are to be people who do not show character traits that would call their message and the reputation of the church into question, but are instead positive adverts for the faith, with an ability to understand, commend and defend the Christian message.

How might we apply this to church planting?

First of all, how striking it is to see the prominence that Paul gives to leadership in these nascent churches! Indeed, he has no other strategy. In our church plants, once again, we see the cardinal importance of paying close attention to the development and deployment of leaders. When we plant churches, a fair proportion of our time will go to seeking out and investing in leaders and supporting them in their work. The lead planter would be well advised to carve out space in his or her already busy diary to give attention to leadership development in others. The staff meeting is never just a functional meeting; it is an opportunity to train others, to spot potential, to give opportunity for real leadership to those who work with us. There will probably be continuing leadership investment too, both for those who are already leading and for those who are emerging and can act as a kind of pipeline for future leaders.

Training is about more than skills too. Paul's qualifications for leadership are largely moral and ethical in nature. He is concerned about temper, about a love of money and alcohol, and about hypocrisy. The description of the poor leaders is bracketed by the adjectives 'rebellious' (1:10) and 'disobedient' (1:16),[77] which goes to an attitude that kicks against authority, especially in this case that of the trustworthy word (1:9).

---

[76] Knight 1992: 289.
[77] See Stott 1996: 183.

This helps us when it comes to spotting leaders. Paul begins with family life. John Stott quotes Donald Guthrie's insight that 'the home is regarded as the training ground for Christian leaders',[78] before concluding himself with the suggestion that 'before being accepted for a wider ministry, [candidates for leadership] should have proved themselves in a narrower one, for example Sunday School or youth club'.[79] This is not to denigrate such vital ministries, nor to view them merely as stepping stones onto the 'real deal' of 'wider' leadership, but it is taking Paul's admonition seriously, particularly for those who happen to be single or who do not have children, that they be seen among the challenges, joys and opportunities of working with children and young people. I always think that a person who can give a talk to a bored and vaguely hostile youth group can preach to anyone. Paul's point is wider and deeper, though; he would be looking at how we react temperamentally to the cauldron that children's and youth work can be. If we do not cope well, then we should probably seek out ways of growing in character before taking on other ministry in the church plant. Church-planting teams could do worse than train up promising leaders in youth work.

They will also need to grasp some nettles, and ensure that character development is a recognized core element of leadership development. Most of us fight shy of this, but Paul puts it front and central. Tom Wright gives a humorous but telling example:

People are watching all the time . . . [Take] the seminary rugby team – a formidable proposition. Will there be bad language in the scrum? Will there be cheating when the referee's back is turned? If there is, people will look at each other and smile knowingly. Maybe these priests-in-training aren't so holy after all.[80]

His – and Paul's – point, of course, is that 'if you can't rely on church leaders to model Christian character, how can you expect anyone else in the church to bring their lives into the pattern of Christ?'[81]

---

[78] Guthrie 1990: 195, quoted in Stott 1996: 175.
[79] Stott 1996: 176.
[80] T. Wright 2003c: 151.
[81] Ibid. 144.

We can widen the view. At the time, Christianity was an all but totally new phenomenon on Crete. There would have been close scrutiny of this new religion, not least because it could come across as subversive – undermining an ancient way of life and posing a threat to the Roman authorities of the time. Leaders of these church plants all over the island would have been the primary example of the Christian way, enabling outsiders to evaluate the message of this Messiah whose death and resurrection had altered history. The same was true of those in the church plants too. This is why Paul is doubly concerned about the bad leaders, not just because of their false teaching which is 'upsetting whole families' (1:11)[82] but also because they 'deny [God] by their actions' (1:16). It is why Paul is concerned about family dynamics 'so that the word of God may not be discredited' (2:5) and so that critics may have 'nothing evil to say of us' (2:8). And why he homes in on the behaviour of slaves 'so that in everything they may be an ornament to the doctrine of God our Saviour' (2:10). We will come back to this thought when we think of 'good works' in the letter, but for now let's note how the life of the church, and especially the life of leaders, has a powerful evangelistic function in Paul's thinking.

Sometimes Paul's approach here is ridiculed as rather dull and bourgeois. Where has the revolutionary language of Jesus gone to, the fire that was turning the world upside down? Why this focus on family life, on good behaviour, on not getting drunk or losing your temper? This criticism is not true to the way in which church planting actually works, however. Just as Paul and Titus's churches on Crete were scrutinized by a suspicious and maybe hostile audience, so will our church plants be. New churches, congregations or fresh expressions of church can appear strange and not quite the real thing to outsiders. Anything to do with church is increasingly suspect in our Western culture, and gatherings which do not appear to conform to more traditional church gatherings can be thought of as cultish. It is genuinely surprising just how much church plants are closely observed and discussed by the local communities into which they are planted. If the house of the senior planter is regularly heard to ring with bad-tempered shouting and terrible arguments, or if his or her kids are dealing drugs, or if the worship band gets wasted in the pub after

---

[82] These 'families' may actually have been house churches.

rehearsal, or the curate gets into a heated exchange at the school gates, these things will all be noted and conclusions drawn. It may seem harsh and not fair, but it is what it is. This is why Paul urges Titus, at some length, to appoint only leaders who will not blow up the reputation of the church.

One other feature of Paul's leadership strategy in church plants is that they 'may be able both to preach with sound doctrine and to refute those who contradict it' (1:9). Church-plant leaders are teachers of God's word.

We will go on to consider what Paul has to say to Titus about this under the next point, but for now let's note that the Christian message is the meat and drink of church-plant leaders. Paul puts the matter in pretty absolute terms throughout the letter.

- He talks repeatedly of 'the faith' (e.g. 1:1, 4, 13; 3:15).
- He writes of 'the truth', or the message being 'trustworthy' or 'sure' (1:1, 9, 14; 3:8).
- He speaks of Christian teaching or doctrine as if there is already a recognized and accepted sense of what this is (1:3, 9; 2:1, 10).

Paul states that Titus is only to appoint to leadership those who have 'a firm grasp of the word that is trustworthy in accordance with the teaching' (1:9). They are to have two complementary functions: 'to preach with sound doctrine and to refute those who contradict it' (1:9).

There is a strong emphasis on not just positive teaching but also what we might call negative or corrective preaching. The whole discussion is framed in terms of confronting and overcoming bad leadership, characterized by being deceptive (1:10), 'teaching . . . what is not right to teach' (1:11), promoting 'myths' (1:14), being 'those who reject the truth' (1:15). This approach is not universally popular today. In truth, sometimes, where such preaching and teaching exists, it is conducted with arrogance and aggression and a lack of sympathy. Many more, however, keep their heads below the parapet, and the result is a generation of new churches and Christians who are all at sea on some of the major ethical issues of our time. Finding a way that both commends the Christian faith and also defines it over against other philosophies, even within the church, is a challenging but necessary task.

John Stott draws a powerful conclusion from his reflections on what he calls 'the true elders' and 'the false teachers':[83]

> This is why the key institution in the church is the seminary or theological college. In every country the church is a reflection of its seminaries. All the church's future pastors and teachers pass through a seminary. It is there that they are either made or marred, either equipped and inspired or ruined.[84]

We thank God that the standards of theological education and the vision for the equipping of priests and pastors with a bit of fire about them to re-evangelize our nation are dramatically improving in these days. We need to pray for our training institutions and do all we can to support and encourage them. That may well mean the occasional challenge, not least when they seem skewed towards a purely academic training and when they lose touch with the real life of the ministry or do not adequately equip people for evangelistic and church-planting work. We stand at an interesting point at the time of writing. The current way of training and deploying ministers is financially unsustainable and quite possibly theologically unjustifiable. The next few years will see many new approaches to training and deployment. Many of these developments will come from the energy of church plants and fresh expressions of church. There is a key task to see that theological education and formation are adequate to the challenges of the hour.

Church plants and their message

The next major emphasis is on what Titus is to preach. He has a message for the members of the church plants in relation to their home lives (2:1–15), and one for them as they look out to play their part in wider society (3:1–8). He introduces these sections with the telling words 'But as for you', which sets Titus apart from the bad leaders Paul has just been excoriating. This is a distinctively Christian leadership pattern, and one from which all church planters might benefit.

---

[83] Stott 1996: 173, 179.
[84] Ibid. 184.

Paul uses another telling phrase at the beginning of chapter 2: Titus is to 'teach what is consistent with sound doctrine' (2:1). Other translations bring out some of the flavour of these words: 'teach what is appropriate to sound doctrine' (TNIV), 'teach what accords with sound doctrine' (ESV), 'you must instruct people how to conduct themselves in accordance with healthy teaching' (NTE). The emphasis is on the sound doctrine, literally that which is healthy, hygienic, health-giving and healing, but especially on its application. This becomes even clearer when we look to the rest of the chapter and see that Paul gives Titus instructions on what to say to six distinct categories of people 'according to age, sex and occupation'.[85] This is all application – detailed, practical, unequivocal. Titus is included in the recipients, encouraged to be a good example, particularly to the younger men (2:6). As with the qualifications for leadership in the church plants, the repeated refrain is on self-control (2:2, 3, 5, 6, 12).

The instructions with regards to Christians in wider society are briefer: 'Remind them to be subject to rulers and authorities, to be obedient, to be ready for every good work, to speak evil of no one, to avoid quarrelling, to be gentle, and to show every courtesy to everyone' (3:1–2). In other words, the members of these church plants are to be model good citizens, centres of reconciliation, gracious to all. Some of these words are the exact opposite of the terms Paul will go on to use when he describes how these new Christians once were.

> A deliberate antithesis seems to be developed between the kind of people Christians should be (1, 2) and the kind of people we once were (3). It is a contrast between submissiveness and foolishness, between obedience and disobedience, between a readiness to do good and an enslavement to evil, between kindness and peaceableness on the one hand and malice and envy on the other, between being humble and gentle and being hateful and hating.[86]

In other words, these new believers are to show that their lives have been transformed by the way in which they conduct themselves towards the

---

[85] Ibid. 186.
[86] Ibid. 202.

state and in society. Again, we notice the concrete ethical nature of the teaching Titus is to give.

Both of these ethical sections are followed by majestic doctrinal passages, and each is linked by the Greek word translated 'for' or 'because' (2:11; 3:3). These passages are linked: the ethics grows out of the doctrine; the ground and reason for the behaviour is the teaching about God our Saviour (2:13; 3:4). 'Thus doctrine inspires duty, and duty adorns doctrine. Doctrine and duty are married; they must not be divorced.'[87]

The first of these doctrinal passages is helpfully described by John Stott as involving two 'epiphanies' or appearances.[88] The first is the epiphany of grace and the second an epiphany of glory:

- 'For the grace of God has appeared, bringing salvation to all' (2:11). Here, the word translated 'has appeared' is the Greek word of which 'epiphany' is the English equivalent.
- 'We wait for the blessed hope and the manifestation of the glory of our great God and Saviour, Jesus Christ' (2:13), where the word translated 'manifestation' is the 'epiphany' word in Greek once again.

God's grace has appeared in Jesus Christ, who saved us, redeeming and purifying us, training us to say no to any rejection of God and his ways, and to live lives of goodness and good works. This life can be characterized by three words: 'self-controlled, upright, and godly' (2:12).

God's grace, then, in which Titus is to instruct these new church plants, is the power of the two manifestations of Christ, and they lead to the transformation of our lives. It is Jesus, who has come and who has died and who will come again, who enables the kind of lives lived well towards ourselves, others and God in the arena of family and home and church life.

The second doctrinal section (3:4–7) is a very long sentence in the original Greek, but the meaning depends on 'he saved us' in verse 5. Paul shows what we once were (3:3), but dwells on the 'goodness and loving-kindness of God our Saviour' (3:4), the action of the Holy Spirit in baptism and regeneration through Jesus Christ. Just as the first doctrinal section

---

[87] Ibid. 213.
[88] Ibid. 192–197.

told us that 'the grace of God' saved us (2:11), so the second section tells us that we have been 'justified by his grace' (3:7), saved for eternal life by the Father, the Son and the Holy Spirit. Just as the grace of God changing us is the ground for our living changed lives, so his salvation is why we can hope for social change as other lives are changed the way ours have been by God. 'The only reason we dare instruct others in social ethics is that we know what we were once like ourselves, that God nevertheless saved us, and that he can therefore transform other people too.'[89]

Both passages teach us what God has done for us in Christ by the Spirit, how our lives have been definitively changed by the action of God, and how this in turn can lead to an impact on others.

So, how might these chapters teach us as church planters?

First of all, we need to know our doctrine! When Paul speaks of 'the faith', 'the truth', 'sound doctrine', this appears to be what he means. In 2:1 he tells Titus to 'teach what is consistent with sound doctrine', and proceeds to give ethical instruction rooted and grounded in the doctrinal sections on the two comings of Christ and the salvation that he brought. Church planters will love the gospel, will be clear and confident in it, will be shaped by it at the deepest level of who they are, and will consistently communicate it to others.

Second, church planters will teach their churches applied ethics in a very concrete way. They will be aware of the social realities of their congregations, and give people a vision for home and personal life and how they can contribute in wider society. Paul could not be more down to earth, less easy to misunderstand, more direct in a teaching that is applied to life and meant to make a robust and actual difference to how life is lived.

It is the third point, though, which is perhaps the most telling: that doctrine and application go together in the teaching of the church and in preaching. To caricature, I would say that it is possible to divide church preaching into two approaches; one is expository and the other topical. The emphasis in expository preaching, quite rightly, is the biblical message. Often, though, it is rare that this touches the ground, and applications tend to be predictable and just a bit thin. Topical preaching

---

[89] Ibid. 200.

is stronger on application, using various 'How to' titles – how to handle your finances, build a strong relationship, deal with anxiety, and so on. Frequently, however, the exegetical foundation is poor or lacking, just a case of taking a particular verse and spinning the topic out of that. Neither approach is particularly doctrinal in the way that Paul is thinking of in Titus.

So, how could church plants adopt and model Paul's approach to preaching and teaching here? How could they be strong on teaching actual doctrine, teaching about God, the Trinity, salvation, the incarnation, the return of Christ, the power of the cross, while clearly linking it to life change and to the arenas of people's actual lives? How could we ensure that Paul's magnificent 'because's come into play, linking doctrine with the power to change life and to live fully and gratefully for God?

That brings us to our next point, that Paul's whole theme is around transformation. While chapter 3 is explicit about this ('For we ourselves were once . . .' [3:3]), the whole letter radiates the change that Jesus brings. Both doctrinal sections major on the impact of grace in a human life. Both envisage a movement from 'impiety and worldly passions . . . from all iniquity' (2:12, 14) to 'lives that are self-controlled, upright, and godly' (2:12). It is noteworthy how often God and Jesus are described as Saviour (1:3, 4; 2:10, 13; 3:4, 6); Paul's great theme is that 'he saved us' (3:5).

Church plants are generally brilliant at building a culture where conversion and transformation are the norm. They tell stories of change – in the lives of individuals and communities and situations. Faith is high that God does save, he intervenes, he changes things. It is the norm; it is expected. This is Paul's drumbeat in this short letter too. He wants leaders whose lives have been changed by Jesus, and he is looking for people who can say the same. This is how Crete too will be transformed through these multiple church plants.

One last application from this emphasis on teaching and preaching from Titus: Paul wants the Cretan Christians to think theologically and to view the world from the perspective of living halfway between the two epiphanies of Jesus, his coming in grace and his coming in glory. This is how Christians and their church plants position themselves in the world. They know that with the coming of Jesus in grace (his incarnation, crucifixion and resurrection) everything has fundamentally changed, but that all the earth is not yet fully healed, not everything has been put right; that will only come at the epiphany of glory.

> This deliberate orientation of ourselves, this looking back and looking forward, this determination to live in the light of Christ's two comings, to live today in the light of yesterday and tomorrow – this should be an essential part of our daily discipline.[90]

Tom Wright detects a similar positioning right at the start of the letter, with its talk of 'the hope of eternal life . . . promised [by God] before the ages began' (1:2). This reflects the Jewish belief that history could be divided into two ages: 'the present evil age' (Gal. 1:4) and the age of the kingdom of God or the age to come. In Jesus, Paul and the early Christians believed, God had inaugurated the age of the kingdom but right in the midst of the present age.

> Thus, even in the introduction to a short letter, Paul locates his work and his writing within the larger framework of God's overall plan – like someone sketching a map of the entire country in order to pinpoint a single small village.[91]

This is why Christianity – and church planting – is built on an irreducible sense of wild hope that God is putting all things right, summing up and uniting everything in Jesus Christ. This is what Paul means by 'the hope of eternal life' (Titus 1:2; 2:13; 3:7) – not just personal immortality, wonderful as that is, but the promise of the salvation and renewal of all things in Christ.

Wouldn't it be marvellous if church plants made a name for themselves as places of profound theological truth and wisdom, the kind that leads to changed lives, to a clear view of Jesus and his trustworthy word? Paul took this very seriously; twice he charges Titus to preach in this way:

- 'Declare these things; exhort and reprove with all authority. Let no one look down on you' (2:15);

---

90 Ibid. 196.
91 T. Wright 2003: 140.

- 'I desire that you insist on these things, so that those who have come to believe in God may be careful to devote themselves to good works' (3:8).

This is the way to see churches changed by Jesus our Saviour and communities profoundly impacted by his grace. May our church plants teach and preach more and more like this.

Church plants and their impact

A third major emphasis for the church plants of Crete is their engagement with their local communities and the impact that Paul wants them to have. Gordon Fee and Douglas Stuart call this the theme of 'doing good', which they say 'permeates' the letter.[92] In his commentary on Titus, Gordon Fee goes even further, describing it as 'the dominant theme' and 'the recurring theme of the entire letter'.[93] This is immensely striking for church planters: when Paul sat down with his 'planting curate' and laid out the plan for church planting a region, his major emphasis was on the good works with which these churches would be engaged. This is the core of his church-planting regional strategy.

It is worth tracing the theme, if only fully to register the scale of Paul's emphasis:

- Negatively, the poor leaders are 'unfit for any good work' (1:16). By implication, good leadership is aligned to the practice and fostering of good works in the churches. By contrast, Titus is to show himself 'a model of good works' (2:7).
- When it comes to the doctrinal passages of the letter, Paul goes so far as to say that Christ's death on the cross had the aim of 'purify[ing] for himself a people of his own who are zealous for good deeds' (2:14). Literally, God's redeemed people are to be 'enthusiastic' for good works.[94]
- And in the ethical sections, Paul asks Titus to remind the Cretans that, in relation to those in authority, they are to be 'ready for every

---

[92] Fee and Stuart 2002: 384.
[93] Fee 1988: 12, 215, quoted in Stott 1996: 207.
[94] Stott 1996: 195.

good work' (3:1), and, more generally, 'those who have come to believe in God [should] be careful to devote themselves to good works' (3:8); specifically they should 'learn to devote themselves to good works in order to meet urgent needs' (3:14).

The phrase 'good works' echoes throughout the letter, chiming in with the other major emphases we have noted: good leadership is a model for good deeds, and the teaching has as its aim a people eager to do good things. The whole life of these church plants is oriented around good works. This is why Christ redeemed them; this is the hallmark of their stance towards secular authorities and of their attitude to those all around them outside the church. There is nothing grudging about this. It is not a duty, but it is a devotion, a zeal, an enthusiasm.

What then are these 'good works'? Fee defines them as 'exemplary Christian behaviour, and that *for the sake of outsiders*'.[95] Paul refers to the meeting of 'urgent needs' (3:14), which may have a financial resonance, but the phrase generally seems to refer to behaviours and attitudes. Often these are set over against the ways of the poor leaders, or the way the Cretan Christians used to live before they were changed by Christ. It is things like hospitality, loving goodness (1:8), as opposed to being arrogant, quick-tempered, addicted to wine or financially greedy (1:7). It is the attitudes and actions in which Titus is to instruct the various groups within the churches, things like loving spouses and children (2:4), being sexually pure and being kind (2:5), being loyal and true, not answering back or pilfering (2:10). And it is the rejection of a lifestyle that is querulous and argumentative, enslaved by passions, characterized by resentment, malice and hate (3:2–3). It is to live the redeemed lifestyle of being 'self-controlled, upright, and godly' with reference to ourselves, others and God (2:12), to be good citizens living 'consistent lives of peace, courtesy and gentleness'.[96]

Fee emphasizes that this exemplary behaviour is specifically for the benefit of outsiders.[97] This comes out in the instructions to the various categories of people in the church plants; they are to live this way 'so that

---

[95] Fee 1988: 200, quoted in Stott 1996: 207; emphasis original.
[96] Stott 1996: 209, summing up Titus 3:1–2.
[97] Fee 1988: 200, quoted in Stott 1996: 207.

the word of God may not be discredited' (2:5), 'so that in everything they may be an ornament to the doctrine of God our Saviour' (2:10). It is also the dominant feature of their relation to the authorities and to wider society in chapter 3 (3:1, 8, 14). Paul is keen that these church plants on Crete should be positioned as forces for good on the island.

There is another emphasis too, namely that the believers' lifestyle of goodness, nobility and beauty should display their gratitude to Christ and represent an outworking of his grace to them through the cross, baptism and the work of the Holy Spirit in their lives (2:14; 3:5–8). Tom Wright explains the theological logic:

> [Jesus] is welcoming us into a way of life for which he has set us free. His own death on our behalf has unlocked the door of ethical possibilities, and we are now invited to go through into his new world, the world of genuine purity, the world where we can begin to contribute positively to people and society around us.[98]

We take on the trajectory of the life of Jesus, we have our original vocation as human beings (to live well for the sake of God, others and our world) restored to us, and we have the power of the cross and the Spirit within us to make this possible. The life of good works is the life for which we were originally created and for which we have been redeemed.

All this seems less than dramatic, rather ordinary, even dull. Yet it is the primary emphasis of Paul's instructions to Titus: make sure these church plants have good leaders, who will preach and teach the people to live lives characterized by good works. The aim is the good works – the characters, attitudes and behaviours that are genuinely pure, kind and good, that stand out against the social norms of selfishness, self-indulgence and sensuality, hatred and divisiveness. Paul wants the island of Crete to take note of these new Christian communities and, whatever else the inhabitants may say about them, the first and last word should be: 'They are good people.'

This is telling for church plants. How can we make sure that, when people from the communities we serve come to any gatherings in our

---

[98] T. Wright 2003: 158.

plants, they notice there is something different about the people we are and the way we relate to one another? They should pick up a kindness and gentleness, a purity, an absence of querulousness and argumentativeness. They should feel safe, that this is somewhere they would like to make a home.

Intermezzo: Moving from biblical to systematic theology

We are now changing tack in terms of our methodology in this book. Part I has proceeded on an exegetical basis: we have looked squarely at some key scriptures to see what they have to say about church planting. Certain themes have emerged, and these have given us a strong framework for thinking about the practice of starting new Christian communities, and arguing not just for their legitimacy from a biblical point of view but also for a more positive mandate for the church to be engaging intentionally and energetically in this practice. Part II reverses the telescope, as it were, and looks at church planting within the context of wider theological themes. We are in the land of systematic theology.

For some readers this may be a challenging shift, requiring us to think in what feels like a different register. Systematic theology (or dogmatic theology) enables us to pull together some of the themes we have seen emerging from our biblical exegesis and to articulate them. This stage of our thinking prepares us to cast a vision for church planting and to engage in the practice of actually planting churches. It also sets up a virtuous circle, and returns us to Scripture to test our understanding of what we are about in the light of what the Bible says to us.

A key thought is that we all actually have systematic theologies in our minds. Some may be examined, some subconscious. Some may reflect biblical principles and priorities closely, and others less so. An important aspect of the systematic-theological enterprise is to bring these assumptions and systems to the surface, so that we can examine them in the clear light of Scripture.

John Calvin wrote his *Institutes of the Christian Religion*[1] to occupy a particular place alongside his biblical commentaries. He was clear that the

---

[1] Calvin 1960.

Institutes were not to replace the core work of biblical exegesis, nor to supplement it, as if the Scriptures were insufficient, but rather to provide a framework of thought within which the Bible could be studied more fruitfully and effectively. In Calvin's mind, systematic theology had a clear role to play in developing our understanding and practice of the Christian life.

Some fear that systematic theology artificially closes down the richness of Scripture, and imposes a flattening of the variety of teachings and perspectives we find in the Bible. That can certainly be a danger. Certain systems of Christian thought have justly been critiqued as effectively negating some aspects of biblical teaching by prioritizing others and so effectively ignoring them. That is why good dogmatics are intimately and inextricably tied to exegesis, precisely to safeguard us from such dangers.

Responsible systematic theology, however, provides us with a broader framework within which to consider our concerns. Christian faith is certainly not monochrome or reducible to simplistic formulae, but it is coherent and holds together. It is imperative too, as a core theological task, to see how different aspects of Christian truth relate together. For instance, if our understanding and practice of church planting contradicts or falsifies our doctrine of God, then something is amiss, and we will need to return to our exegesis to see what has gone wrong.

Systematic theology also gives us some other key benefits.

- It enables us to articulate what we mean when we talk about the Bible and church planting. We will not want to go beyond Scripture, nor to say less than the Bible does, but it is helpful for our own faith to be able to discern, distil and disseminate some, at least, of the major strands of biblical teaching about church planting. This will give us confidence in our own understanding, and also coherence when we attempt to articulate it for others. For the church-planting practitioner, vision-casting is a key skill and a prerequisite to good practice. A clear and healthy systematic theology of church planting enables us to communicate with greater effectiveness.
- By the same token, much of the debate (initially at least) around church planting takes place at the level of systematic theologies. The level of discourse can be considerably enhanced when we have a thought-through, clear and coherent systematic theology of our

own, through which we may engage with those who disagree with us or our practices of church planting. To argue from pragmatics alone is not sufficient when it comes to a fruitful discussion about practices which may be threatening and disruptive to others in the church.

- To do this well also serves to enhance the credibility of church planting. To demonstrate congruence and continuity with some of the great theological themes and thinkers of our own and previous Christian ages can give confidence to others who may be asking for deeper thought about these things. To show that our thinking is biblical and sits clearly within highly regarded streams of Christian thought, and that our principles are not primarily derived from purely secular, management or marketing frameworks, is to move us all into a place where agreement and confidence may flourish right across the various strands of the Christian church.

- Lastly, systematic theology can help protect us from error. Part of the reason why Augustine of Hippo preached and wrote so prolifically was to safeguard the church from heresies. There are similar challenges in our day. The enthusiasm of many in the church-planting movements around the world is greatly to be admired and celebrated. Nonetheless, there are causes for concern, namely that unexamined assumptions upon which some churches are being planted may prove in time to lead to distortions, disfigurements and dysfunctions in the life and health of these churches, their leaders, people and practices. Robust systematic theological thinking is a useful corrective to these assumptions, even if it may prove challenging initially.

The second part of the book thus looks at church planting from the point of view of systematic theology. It has two main approaches: the first is to tease out the nature of the relationship between the church and mission when it comes to church planting. Much of the disagreement around church planting comes from different starting points and differing arguments about this. Unless we are diligent, we can end up in a stand-off of mutual incomprehension. A deep engagement with the question of how church and mission relate in the purposes of God to glorify himself and bless his world can, by contrast, lead to fruitful and exciting thinking and practice.

The second approach is to locate the practice of church planting in God himself, specifically in relation to the doctrine of the Trinity. If there is little by way of connection, then we have raised a profound challenge to church planting. If these new church plants have little to say about God (or even end up saying things which are at variance with what we know of the God of Jesus Christ), then we must question the legitimacy of any such enterprises. And by the same token, if we can show profound connections between church planting and the Trinity, then we are acknowledging and arguing for something healthy and theologically compelling about it, and, even more, asserting that church planting must be of theological and practical importance in our age.

Readers may find that some of the language and approaches in this part of the book come less naturally to them than those of the first part. Systematic theology may indeed be challenging, but, in its own way, it is as fruitful and essential as exegesis in giving us a framework within which to pray, plan and practise our church planting.

Part II

IS THERE A THEOLOGY OF CHURCH PLANTING?

Can we talk meaningfully about a theology of church planting?
We have traced church planting throughout the Scriptures.

- The Old Testament gives us a foundation by demonstrating how God works in the world through communities of his people who bring his blessing to the world. The people of God have a covenantal vocation to live, proclaim and demonstrate his kingdom. Communities of God's people are inextricably linked to the declaration of God's rule and ways in the world.
- While Jesus himself spoke of 'church' only twice in the Gospels, it is clear that his priority towards mission in the world was linked in his mind to the communities that would be gathered in his name. He anticipated a quality of communal life which was based on his own mission and values, and which would transcend the model of synagogue gathering around the ancient world. In his person he fulfilled Israel's story, and provided for his followers to continue that vocation. Particularly in the events surrounding the cross, we see Jesus establishing a culture that would lie at the heart of the post-resurrection church. In the imagery of his teaching, the praxis of the emerging Christian community and the global missionary agenda he laid down, Jesus established the means and method and ultimate goal of the kingdom of God through the church.

- In Acts, we see this vision become a reality. We see the church born as a missionary body, and we see mission having the church as its means and goal. We see church planting as the way in which God fulfils his plans for the world, and the Holy Spirit leading and directing that mission by means of a combination of evangelism and church life.
- In the rest of the New Testament, we see church planting as the core of Paul's strategy to reach his world, and we glimpse something of his motivation as well as methodology for all he is doing.

The Bible is remarkably consistent in how it links mission and community. Although our Western individualism can blind us to much of the shared life of God's people, it is nonetheless striking how God's desire for a people of his own is inseparable from his will to love and heal his world. It is not just that the church is the *aim* of mission, but it is also that the church is the *means* of mission. God's way of loving and reaching the world is precisely in and through the people he has gathered to love and trust and worship him. And so it becomes a virtuous circle: the message of Jesus is declared to the world, calling out a people who will live this message; then they themselves become the way in which the message of the gospel rings out to their communities and regions; those who come to believe also establish new communities of faith, which continue to reach out further yet; and so on, to the ends of the earth. The church is where Jesus is most clearly seen and known, and so it is that the church is how 'the word of the Lord has sounded forth' (1 Thess. 1:8) to whole regions. Biblically, we cannot talk about mission without talking about church, and we cannot fully talk about church without making mission central. And church planting is at the epicentre of both mission and the church. Church planting is what God is doing in the world, establishing outposts of his kingdom which will exponentially increase in number and influence, loving and serving whole regions of the earth in word and deed.

We need to dig a bit deeper into these great themes. In the next chapter, we consider the interplay between church and mission, of which church planting is the epicentre. And the succeeding chapter will reflect on Trinitarian theology, seeing church planting as it is – an expression of nothing less than the heart of God himself.

6

Church planting, and the doctrines of church and mission

There is agreement between many theologians and missiologists about the need for clarity around the relationship between the doctrines of church and mission when it comes to church planting. Steven Croft writes about the 'hard questions' that are asked about church planting and fresh expressions of church, and reflects that 'the key areas that need serious theological resourcing . . . are in the two areas of reflection on mission on the one hand and on the life of the church, and particularly the interface between the two'.[1]

Craig Ott and Gene Wilson put the matter more dogmatically:

Church planting is where missiology and ecclesiology intersect. Unfortunately many missiologists and mission practitioners have a weak ecclesiology, as if mission could exist without the church or as if the church were a practical but imperfect and bothersome necessity. On the other hand, many standard systematic theologies and ecclesiologies devote few pages, if any, to the topic of mission. A missionless church is no church, and a churchless mission is not biblical mission. In the words of Lesslie Newbigin, 'An unchurchly mission is as much a monstrosity as an unmissionary Church.'[2]

Some are quick to point out how church planting has a crucial role in reconnecting church and mission. Stuart Murray writes:

The practice of church planting may serve to strengthen cross-fertilization between ecclesiology and missiology. Church planting

---

1 Croft 2009b: 14.
2 Ott and Wilson 2011: 26, quoting Newbigin 1953: 169.

reminds missiologists that the church plays a pivotal role in mission. It is possible for mission strategists, enthusiastic evangelists and academic mission theologians to concentrate on other dimensions of mission – such as the conversion of individuals, the transformation of society or relationships with other faith communities – but to ignore or marginalize the church in relation to these dimensions. Church planting reminds ecclesiologists that mission is the primary task of the church. It is possible for local church leaders, denominational representatives and ecclesiastical commissions to concentrate on other aspects of church life – doctrinal, sacramental, relational and institutional – but to fail to relate these to the calling of the church to be a missionary community.[3]

From the perspective of more mainland Europe, Stefan Paas concludes his whole book with an optimistic sense of the theological role of church planting:

> The strongest theological defense of church planting in Europe can be found in the relationship between mission and church. As an intersection of ecclesiology and missiology, church planting provides the Western church with a rich potential for missionary experience and reformation.[4]

To sever the connection between church and mission is theologically perilous. It has led to the loss of missionary confidence and identity within many churches, and to the proliferation of many para-church evangelistic organizations. It is not that these last are a bad thing, but the weakening of the church and its sense of mission is palpable. We can also see that the rise of the church-planting movement has led to an exciting reconnection between church and mission, in both theory and practice, and this is a cause for profound theological and missionary optimism. Jürgen Moltmann has written: 'Today one of the strongest impulses towards the renewal of the theological concept of the church comes from the theology

---

[3] Murray 1998: 48–49.
[4] Paas 2016: 265.

of mission',[5] and maybe church planting can do the same for ecclesiology in our day.

Mission

Let's start with mission. If church planting is part of the mission of God to his world, it is important we know what that is. The answer may not be as obvious theologically as we suppose.

The two major books of missiology of the last twenty-five years are arguably David Bosch's *Transforming Mission*,[6] written from a Protestant stable, and *Constants in Mission* by Catholic missiologists Stephen Bevans and Roger Schroeder.[7] Both are written from the widest perspectives, ecumenically, historically and theologically. Both take as their methodological starting point the fact that the church has had differing views on what constitutes mission down the ages. Bosch points out that 'until the sixteenth century the term was used exclusively with reference to the doctrine of the Trinity, that is, of the sending of the Son by the Father and of the Holy Spirit by the Father and the Son'.[8] He states that 'at no time in the last two millennia was there only one single "theology of mission"'.[9] While acknowledging that 'the Christian faith ... is intrinsically missionary', he argues that 'ultimately, mission remains undefinable; it should never be incarcerated in the narrow confines of our own predilections'.[10] He begins his magisterial book with a look at the different but complementary theologies of mission found in Matthew, Luke and Paul, before proceeding to an historical analysis through the framework of six epochs or paradigms within which mission has been viewed in the history of the church. The six paradigms are:

1 the apocalyptic paradigm of primitive Christianity;
2 the Hellenistic paradigm of the patristic period;
3 the medieval Roman Catholic paradigm;

---

5 Moltmann 1977: 369.
6 Bosch 1997.
7 Bevans and Schroeder 2004.
8 Bosch 1997: 1.
9 Ibid. 8.
10 Ibid. 8, 9.

4 the Protestant (Reformation) paradigm;
5 the modern Enlightenment paradigm;
6 the emerging ecumenical paradigm.[11]

His argument is that mission means something different in each of these eras, not least because the world is 'fundamentally different' in each of these time periods.[12] He counsels against leaping directly from the world of the New Testament to our own times:

> The magnitude of today's challenge can really only be appreciated if viewed against the backdrop of almost twenty centuries of church history. In addition, we need the perspectives of the past in order to appreciate the scope of the present challenge and to be able really to understand the world today and the Christian response to its predicament.[13]

Bosch's book traces the history of mission, in its assumptions and practices, through these twenty centuries, before an engagement with what he sees as the emerging ecumenical contemporary understanding of mission.

Bevans and Schroeder adopt a similar approach. They cite the justly famous essay by Andrew Walls, 'The Gospel as Prisoner and Liberator of Culture'.[14] 'Let us imagine a long-living, scholarly space visitor – a Professor of Comparative Inter-Planetary Religions perhaps – who is able to get periodic space-grants which enable him to visit Earth for field study every few centuries.'[15] The space visitor sees Christians in Jerusalem in around the year AD 37, the Council of Nicea in 325, some Irish monks in the fifth and sixth centuries, a missionary conference in London in the 1840s and a church service in Lagos, Nigeria, in 1980. Walls imagines the consternation of the space professor as he notices that these Christians have different concerns and that there is a 'wild profusion of the varying statements of

---

[11] Ibid. 181–182. Bosch is following the work of Catholic theologian Hans Küng in Küng 1984; 1987: 157.
[12] Bosch 1997: 189.
[13] Ibid.
[14] Walls 1996.
[15] Ibid. 3.

these differing groups'.[16] Walls detects two fundamental continuities, however, down the ages: an 'historical connection' and a 'continuity of thought', this last about Jesus, a 'certain consciousness about history', about the Scriptures, and the sacraments.[17] Bevans and Schroeder discuss the essay and, interestingly, reframe Walls's first continuity, which he calls 'historical', as 'the continuity of Christianity's *missionary* vision'.[18] They develop Walls's approach for their book on mission, identifying certain 'constants' in Christianity's relationship to the world down the ages. They also position this discussion with reference to three 'types of theology': these are orthodox/conservative ('mission as saving souls and extending the church'), liberal ('mission as discovery of the truth') and radical/liberation theology ('mission as commitment to liberation and transformation').[19] With the grid of their own 'constants' in mission and these three theological approaches, they analyse how differing ages viewed and expressed mission. Like Bosch, they conclude with an exploration of contemporary understandings of mission in the light of the theology and history of previous ages.

Both books are acutely alive to the lessons of history and to the crucial shaping influence of context. This opens them to wider definitions of mission than are perhaps common in the local church. Both, however, conclude in not dissimilar places, emphasizing the kingdom of God as it is discovered and expressed in the gospel of Jesus Christ. Bevans and Schroeder conclude by saying that 'to preach, serve and witness to the reign of God is to preach, serve and witness to the gospel *about* and *of* Jesus, and it is to participate as well in the very life of the triune God'.[20] They encourage Christians to view their missionary stance as a kind of 'prophetic dialogue' with the world.[21] Bosch, while still opining that 'it remains extraordinarily difficult to determine what mission is' and 'that there is a constant need for mission itself to be transformed', concludes that

mission is, quite simply, the participation of Christians in the liberating mission of Jesus, wagering on a future that verifiable experience

---

16 Ibid. 5, 6.
17 Ibid. 6–7.
18 Bevans and Shroeder 2004: 33; emphasis original.
19 Ibid. 35–72.
20 Ibid. 396.
21 Ibid. ch. 12, and 398.

seems to belie. It is the good news of God's love, incarnated in the witness of a community, for the sake of the world.[22]

These and similar theological works have influenced contemporary understandings of mission. Andrew Kirk, for instance, posits seven aspects of Christian mission: evangelism, cultural engagement, justice for the poor, encounter with world religions, overcoming violence and bringing peace, care for the environment and partnering with other churches in mission.[23] Even more influential have become 'the five marks of mission' adopted by the Anglican Communion:

The mission of the Church is the mission of Christ

1. To proclaim the Good News of the Kingdom.
2. To teach, baptise and nurture new believers.
3. To respond to human need by loving service.
4. To transform unjust structures of society, to challenge violence of every kind and pursue peace and reconciliation.
5. To strive to safeguard the integrity of creation, and sustain and renew the life of the earth.[24]

Interestingly, the first of these five marks of mission is privileged above the rest:

The first Mark of Mission, identified with personal evangelism at the Anglican Consultative Council in 1984 ... is a summary of what all mission is about, because it is based on Jesus' own summary of his mission. This should be the key statement about everything we do in mission.[25]

For the church planter, then, committed to mission, there is much encouragement here. There is a clear theological mandate that the core

---

[22] Bosch 1997: 511, 519.
[23] Kirk 1999.
[24] Anglican Consultative Council 2022.
[25] Ibid.

calling of the church is to mission. There is a breadth of definition that opens the way for missionary creativity. There is even a sense of invitation from the Holy Spirit to lean into what God is doing in the world in our time.

There are also questions which require careful thought. This is the case for the lead church planter, but also for the team, and for the shared theological culture of the church plant. What do we mean when we talk about mission?

- How do evangelism and social action relate to each other?
- What is the place of the church in mission?
- Is the kingdom of God the centre of mission or the cross of Christ? How do the two relate to each other?
- What do we mean when we talk about the gospel?
- What is the relationship of mission to the physical, economic, social and political worlds? Where does the spiritual begin and end?
- Is there a danger that 'If everything is mission, nothing is mission'?[26]

As Craig Ott and Stephen Strauss put it: 'The need is for nothing less than a biblically grounded theological perspective on God's work in the world and the participation of the church in that work today.'[27] Too many church plants unthinkingly adopt what they see to be mission projects and partnerships, without reflecting clearly enough on how what they are doing does or does not align with the mission of Jesus and the kingdom of God. This is particularly true when they enter into partnerships with secular organizations, such as the local council or major charities. This is not to say that this practice is wrong per se, but merely that a robust theological investigation ahead of time may well rescue the church plant from subsequent difficulties. A sadly not untypical pattern is for a church to set up a charity in one generation, and then, when economic difficulties or a paucity of volunteers or an increase in the complexity of the task and the legislation surrounding it kicks in, the second generation enters into a partnership with a more skilled and better resourced but secular

---

[26] Neill 1959: 81, quoted in Ott, Strauss with Tennent 2010: 200.
[27] Ibid. xiii.

organization. Things start well with a sense of equality in partnership, but, by the time of the third generation, the values and even presence of the church have vanished.

We have discussed some of these issues previously in this book, but it is the relationship of mission to the church which will occupy us in this chapter. Let's turn now to what we mean when we talk about 'the church'.

The church

According to the historic creeds, the church is 'one, holy, catholic and apostolic'. Since then, in Protestantism at least, Article XIX of the Church of England is representative, building on the typical Reformation definition of the church: 'The visible Church of Christ is a congregation of faithful [people], in the which the pure Word of God is preached, and the Sacraments be duly administered according to Christ's ordinance.'[28]

Similar developments have followed down history. The Anglican Quadrilateral of 1886 is an interesting one. Episcopal churches in the United States were exploring what it meant to be Anglican when not in England, and with a view to future ecumenical developments. They adopted a four-point declaration of Anglican identity: a belief in the holy Scriptures; in the creeds; in the practice of the sacraments of baptism and Holy Communion; and in leadership by the historic episcopate.[29]

The divisions and disunity of the church, with different emphases and historic disagreements, led to all kinds of good work on the theology of the church in the second half of the twentieth century, much of it under the aegis of the World Council of Churches (WCC). Arguably, the three most influential books on the church in ecumenical circles since the Second World War are Lesslie Newbigin's *The Household of God*,[30] Paul Minear's *Images of the Church in the New Testament*[31] and Avery Cardinal Dulles's *Models of the Church*.[32] All of these works speak to the highly contested understandings of the church from the points of view of Protestant and Roman Catholic positions (and Pentecostal too in Newbigin's

---

28 The Book of Common Prayer.
29 This Quadrilateral was subsequently adopted by the 1888 Lambeth Conference.
30 Newbigin 1953.
31 Minear 1960.
32 Dulles 1974.

work) and achieve ways of seeing the church which can be fruitfully adopted by each section of the church.

Each author is careful to step back and to adopt as wide a perspective as possible on the church. Minear finds no fewer than ninety-six images of the church in the New Testament, before isolating what he considers to be the four lead images: the people of God, the new creation, the fellowship in faith and (the most central) the body of Christ. Newbigin asks what constitutes the church, and answers under a rubric which he generalizes as the Protestant (the church is constituted by the word of God), the Catholic (by the sacraments), and the Pentecostal (by the Holy Spirit). Dulles lays out five models: the institutional (which alone of the models he argues is not ultimate), that of mystical communion, the sacramental, the kerygmatic and the church as servant. This breadth of view, demonstrated by all three authors, is not always a characteristic of contemporary debates about the place of ecclesiology in church planting.

A serious critique of the 'fresh expressions of church' movement has been made by Andrew Davison and Alison Milbank.[33] Among many trenchant comments, they argue that fresh expressions of church are so different from what has previously been seen and experienced as church, at least in the mainline denominations, that they cannot be thought of as the same animal. In a philosophically sophisticated argument, they suggest that 'the meaning is in the form':[34] 'the message and purpose of the Church are to be found *in* the way she lives and worship (*sic*).'[35]

> In the Church as in the poem, the message is in the form. In neither case can we simply extract the meaning and rearticulate it in a new form without loss . . . The traditional patterns and disciplines of the life of the Church embody the Faith and they do so on many different levels.[36]

This line of thought is shared by Angela Tilby in her essay, 'What Questions Does Catholic Ecclesiology Pose for Contemporary Mission and

---

[33] Davison and Milbank 2010.
[34] Ibid. 5.
[35] Ibid.
[36] Ibid. 9.

Fresh Expressions?'[37] She argues that, from a Catholic point of view, 'in a very real sense the Church *is* its history . . . So Catholics will want to say that history, Church and mission go together. Where there is no history there can be no Church and no mission.'[38] Tilby (and Davison and Milbank) deplore how church history and tradition have been ignored or taken piecemeal without what they see as due regard for the whole garment, as it were, of what God has given the church to be within Western history and tradition. Tilby goes on to raise concerns about how liturgy is often abandoned in fresh expressions of church and in church plants. Faith and prayer go together, she argues, and so 'what keeps our new movements potentially orthodox is our liturgy'.[39] This has widespread ecumenical impact as well. Orthodox and Catholic ecclesiologies are closely linked with their liturgical, especially eucharistic, traditions and practices. John Zizioulas writes: 'Ecclesiology in the Orthodox tradition has always been determined by the liturgy, the eucharist.'[40] This makes for profound ecumenical difficulties in dealing with expressions of church which have little or no formal liturgy, an irregular eucharistic practice, and a form of ministry which does not conform to the traditional system of bishops, priests and deacons from some of the mainline denominations. Steven Croft points out that, for Anglicans at least, there is already a considerable variety of liturgical practice, and that recent years have seen a shift from shared liturgical texts to shared liturgical shapes to shared liturgical values.[41]

Davison and Milbank go on to bring specific criticisms of a view of salvation and church embodied in fresh expressions of church, and, by extension, in church plants. They argue that such approaches individualize salvation and take it out of the biblical realm of seeing salvation as essentially corporate, a joining of the church: 'Union with God "in Christ" is not an individualistic matter, but corporate and ecclesial.'[42]

So, church planters need to think carefully about what they mean when they say they are planting churches. There are the biblical questions, to

---

[37] Tilby 2008: 78–89.
[38] Ibid. 79.
[39] Ibid. 84.
[40] Zizioulas 1985: 131.
[41] Croft 2006: 180.
[42] Davison and Milbank 2010: 43.

which we have kept returning in this book, but there is also the theological expression of those concerns, and how matters of unity, liturgy and salvation find their place.

Some of these objections to what church planting and fresh expressions of church do to ecclesiology can actually be turned on their heads. Good points made, but misapplied. So, it is true that meaning and form go together, as Davison and Milbank argue so well. What is not logically true, however, is that the meaning and form in question are serving the correct purposes, at least as they are currently employed. The meaning and form of so many churches are those of an enclosed club, of cultural, educational and class privilege. What is required is a recalibration of both form and meaning such that the shared life of the church better serves those who do not yet attend or those who do not yet believe. This is precisely the ecclesiological challenge being made by church plants and fresh expressions of church. The separation of mission from church has evacuated the form of its meaning, established as it was in very different cultural times. One has only to read the thinness of Davison and Milbank's missionary suggestions in the parish model to see just how in need of radical overhaul it is.

Similarly, the argument that salvation is understood corporately and ecclesially, not individualistically, in the New Testament is an argument *for* church planting, not against it. By losing the connection between church and mission, we are left with a theological and practical vacuum at the centre of much church life in the West. It is by placing mission once more as the very heartbeat of church life that both church and mission find their proper place.

Some of the arguments around these matters are stronger than others, and we hear cultural values as much as theological argument, on occasion. Nonetheless, the discussions and concerns around ecclesiology are often conduits for wider matters which need to be handled with care, thought and mutual respect.

Church and mission

It is at the intersection of church and mission, ecclesiology and missiology, that church planting has its greatest contribution to make. It has the potential to restore and to reinvigorate both disciplines, and to liberate churches for mission and to generate practices of mission that are more church-shaped.

There is an undeniable tension between the two emphases, and some of the rhetoric on both sides has a certain 'zero sum' flavour.

Some argue that, in the relationship between church and mission, it is mission that must take the lead. So, the *Mission-Shaped Church* report quotes Tim Dearborn (in bold): **'It is not the Church of God that has a mission in the world, but the God of mission who has a Church in the world.'**[43] The writers go on to say:

> Those who start with questions about the relationship to the existing church have already made the most common and most dangerous mistake. Start with the Church and the mission will probably get lost. Start with mission and it is likely that the Church will be found.[44]

Alan Hirsch quotes the above passage from *Mission-Shaped Church*, and prefaces it by saying:

> By my reading of the scriptures, ecclesiology is the most fluid of the doctrines. The church is a dynamic cultural expression of the people of God in any given place. Worship style, social dynamics, liturgical expressions must result from the process of contextualizing the gospel in any given culture. *Church must follow mission.*[45]

Stuart Murray quotes Anglican church planter Bob Hopkins as saying: 'We must stop starting with church.'[46]

By contrast, others argue that church should take priority in this relationship. Once again, Davison and Milbank write with clarity and vigour:

> We cannot separate the Church from who Christ is and what he does. As Ephesians puts it, Christ's reconciling work has made him

---

[43] Dearborn 1988, quoted in Archbishops' Council of the Church of England 2004: 85.
[44] Archbishops' Council of the Church of England 2004: 116.
[45] Hirsch 2006: 143; emphasis original.
[46] Murray 2010: 18.

'the head over all things for the church, which is his body, the fullness of him who fills all in all' (Eph. 1.22–23). This makes it all the more strange that writing about Fresh Expressions *of Church* has so little place for the Church in what it says about salvation. As often as not, when the Church features among the *dramatis personae* of salvation's story, it is as a hindering force or as a merely human construction.[47]

For Davison and Milbank, the church cannot be seen as a human construct or the product of cultural expression of a common life: 'This will not do. The Church is not simply part of the order of this age, destined to pass away . . . For Ephesians, the consummation of all things involves *more* Church, and not less Church.'[48] They discern that much of the thinking behind fresh expressions of church and church planting views the church as a *means* to something else, as of purely instrumental value. By contrast, they argue, mission becomes a 'be all and end all', in a bizarre kind of way existing for its own sake: 'Mission is the goal, and the Church is only for the sake of mission . . . It will not do to orientate mission towards anything outside itself. Secretly, mission becomes about nothing but itself . . . Mission is a self-justifying good.'[49] In a more measured way, they say:

> Fresh Expressions theorists call us to separate the Church and her mission – to downplay the first and concentrate on the second. This is a false distinction, not least because the Church is central to what she proclaims in her mission. We cannot write the Church out of the gospel.[50]

I suspect we can all see both sides of the argument. Church planters will, in all likelihood, have a strong conviction of the missionary imperative of our times, coupled with a sense of how the contemporary church in the West is failing to reach people in our contexts. They will also have

---

47 Davison and Milbank 2010: 48.
48 Ibid.
49 Ibid. 52–53.
50 Ibid. 60.

a love for the church, and an inescapable theological commitment to the place of the church in God's acting in the world. To speak honestly, though, many church planters may also carry with them bad experiences of church; they will have specific instances of missionary failure or complacency, and maybe, sadly, personal examples of having been misunderstood or even mistreated on account of their missionary zeal. On the other side of the conversation, there will be many in inherited church who have been criticized, sometimes rudely, by church planters, or who feel themselves written off as 'part of the problem', not 'part of the solution'. When we add in the complexities of new approaches to church and mission operating within the large-scale institutional mechanisms of the mainline denominations, there can be a recipe for conflict, mutual misunderstanding and mistrust. In addition, different personalities can be drawn to different approaches. So, we have the all-too-human aspects, the impact of organizational systems and cultures, plus differing theological emphases all combining to make for the kind of 'zero sum' stances and conversations we have previously noted.

Part of the sadness of this divided approach is that it forces us all into false positions. There cannot be a thoughtful Christian anywhere who does not see that the church has a missionary aspect to it, and, by the same token, there cannot be a missionary who has no place for the church. I love how Paul, in Colossians 1, can say within a matter of a few verses how he 'became a servant of this gospel' (1:23) and that he also 'became [the church's] servant' (1:25). He felt an obligation to both mission and church; they were not set over against each other in either his mind or his ministry. So, how can we, particularly if we are church planters, fruitfully develop and treasure a similar commitment to both? We can say two things.

1 The church is inescapably missionary

First of all, we can lean into a more dynamic, and less static, view of the church than is sometimes taken. Debates about the nature of the church can be driven by history or a more abstract view of doctrine, rather than by an effort to see the church living and active in our own contexts. Whatever one's view of the church, the static approach does not do justice to what is actually happening day in, day out, in churches up and down the land. Bevans and Schroeder write: 'Mission happens wherever the church is; it is how the church exists.'[51] Catholic theologians have, in recent years, been at the forefront of emphasizing that the church is 'missionary by its very nature', and that mission is the church's 'deepest identity'.[52] The ancient creeds speak of the church as being 'one, holy, catholic and apostolic', where apostolic means *both* adhering to the apostles' teaching *and* being sent out by God into the world on mission. John Flett defines apostolicity as 'faithfulness to origins expressed in the continuity of mission'.[53] He sees a tension between these two aspects of the definition, and quotes Rowan Williams to this effect: '[this tension results from] the tendency to think of "mission" and "spirituality" as pointing in different directions – the communicating of the faith and the cultivation of the faith.'[54] Flett sees a priority being given to 'the cultivation of the faith' over 'the communication of the faith', which has established a 'range of controls' over mission:[55]

> The general necessity of mission might be granted, but when considered in relation to unity, to historical continuity or to the processes variously termed 'inculturation' or 'contextualization', it is evaluated against its potential negative effect over the cultivation of, and maturity in, the faith. Mission, by this binary, is not only properly distinguished from Christian spirituality – it is to be approached with an enduring theological caution.[56]

But what if the two, cultivation and communication of faith, could be seen as equally significant and operative in the life of the church?

Our examination of many biblical themes and texts through the lens of church planting has shown that this is precisely the way in which Scripture views the interrelationship of church and mission. We have consistently seen the gospel leading to the establishing of churches, and

---

51 Bevans and Schroeder 2004: 9.
52 Pope John XXIII, *Ad Gentes*, 2; Pope Paul VI, *Evangelii Nuntiandi*, 14, quoted in Bevans and Schroeder 2004: 7.
53 Flett 2016: 16.
54 Williams 1995: 221, quoted in Flett 2016: 16.
55 Flett 2016: 16.
56 Ibid. 16–17.

churches being the central aspect of the virtuous circle of the gospel continuing to reach out to their regions and contexts. Theologians and practitioners alike have found this to be fundamentally true of their convictions about and experience of the church.

In our time, Lesslie Newbigin has written most eloquently about the evangelistic power of the church: 'It is surely a fact of inexhaustible significance that what our Lord left behind Him was not a book, nor a creed, nor a system of thought, nor a rule of life, but a visible community.'[57] Reflecting on his experience, as a long-term overseas missionary returning to life in the British Midlands, he wrote:

> I have come to feel that the primary reality of which we have to take account in seeking for a Christian impact on public life is the Christian congregation. How is it possible that the gospel should be credible, that people should come to believe that the power which has the last word in human affairs is represented by a man hanging on a cross? I am suggesting that the only answer, the only hermeneutic of the gospel, is a congregation of men and women who believe it and live by it.[58]

C. Norman Kraus puts it pithily: 'The life of the church *is* its witness. The witness of the church *is* its life. The question of authentic witness is the question of authentic community.'[59]

There is something ineluctably missionary in the very nature of the church; it is part of its DNA. This is true for each and every church that has ever been or ever will be. And so, every church will be missionary and will witness to its community. This is the fundamental premise of any church-planting theology: through the church the gospel rings out to the world, and God's kingdom is made manifest. The question that inescapably follows, though, carries a sting in the tail: what is the nature and quality of that witness? Every church will be a witness; but will it be a good or a bad witness?

---

[57] Newbigin 1953: 27.
[58] Newbigin 1989: 227.
[59] Kraus 1978: 156, quoted in Bevans and Schroeder 2004: 355.

Church plants are established with this question in the foreground, an explicit challenge from day one. This acknowledges that apostolicity, in both senses, is a crucial element of the identity of any church, and, by virtue of its praxis, the church plant is drawing this effectively to the surface of church and missionary life. It is not that other churches do not have this inherent dynamic, still less that they are incapable of effective mission; but church planting does, de facto, catapult this missionary aspect of what it is to be a church into an active and intentional mode.

Bevans and Schroeder have an interesting extra element to add. They say: 'The church only becomes the church as it responds to God's call to mission, and to be in mission means to change continually as the gospel encounters new and diverse contexts.'[60] They are arguing for the missionary element of the church's identity to be necessarily leading in order for the church to be in essence what it is. They are also suggesting that this is a continuous and a continual process. Later in their book, they write of 'the radical missionary nature' of the church, 'for it is only in mission that the church continues to be what it is'.[61] They are saying that, just as the church most fully becomes itself only in mission, so can it lose its essence by ceasing to be a missionary church. Andrew Kirk puts it even more strongly:

> Mission is so much at the heart of the Church's life that, rather than think of it as one aspect of its existence, it is better to think of it as defining its essence. The Church is by nature missionary to the extent that, if it ceases to be missionary, it has not just failed in one of its tasks, it has ceased being Church.[62]

By this token, church plants are more profoundly and essentially ecclesial than other less missionary churches. A church which has as its very raison d'être the missionary engagement of its community and context is, in this perspective, as authentic an expression of church as one can find anywhere. And, by the same token, the more church planting that existing churches

---

[60] Bevans and Schroeder 2004: 72.
[61] Ibid. 319.
[62] Kirk 1999: 30.

can do, the more in touch they will be with their ecclesial as well as missionary essence.

So, the first thing to say about the interface of church and mission in church planting is the challenge to live up to the essential missionary nature of the church. Church planting has done the wider church the service of highlighting this, and giving us a concrete practice that ensures we recapture the full potentialities of this missionary stance. Theologically, church planting is not saying anything new about the nature of the church, but has the quality of a prophetic call to the wider church to inhabit in practice what it already is in its essence.

2 Mission is inescapably ecclesial

If the challenge of the previous point is more towards those who have reservations about church planting, and why it is that the starting of new churches is legitimate in the service of the mission of God, then this point may be more challenging to those who have no issues with leading with mission but who struggle to see why the church should be a necessary part of the equation. The cardinal importance of the missional link to the church is, by and large, harder for Protestants and evangelicals to see than it is for their Orthodox and Catholic brothers and sisters. For the latter, the church is more of a given, and a natural locus for the primary work of God's grace in the world. For the former, the major defining moments of their history tend to be around missionary movements or revivals, where 'the formation of the Church on the mission-field was a corollary of their labours, but not their primary target'.[63] Also, by methodology and culture, they are more individualistic, emphasizing personal commitment and experience, and not the corporate and ecclesial. Church planting, however, properly understood, brings the church much more centrally into view when we think of mission. It is the *means* and *goal* of mission, and it is also a central part of the message of the gospel.

May we briefly retrace some biblical themes. First of all, the story of Israel is all about the calling out of a people, the people of God, to live in his presence and to represent him to the world. Their mission was always tied up with their shared life and identity. Jesus himself took and

---

[63] Berg 1956: 159, quoted in Bevans and Shroeder 2004: 232.

developed the centrality of a shared life as something to be experienced and communicated to the world, when he invited 'sinners', the poor, the despised and other marginalized people to occupy an honoured place within his people. He also took the language of kingdom and made it central to his redemptive mission. 'The revolutionary nature of the early Christian mission manifested itself, *inter alia*, in the new relationships that came into being in the community.'[64] It was, indeed, a 'sociological impossibility'.[65] This is reflected in the emphasis in the teaching of Jesus on mutual forgiveness, mercy and other relational emphases for life within his kingdom. By the time we come to Paul, we find the church represented, among other metaphors and descriptions, as nothing less than the body of Christ (e.g. 1 Cor. 12). To be in the church is, in some sense, to be in Christ. When we look at Ephesians, we read that the aim of the cross was to make 'one new humanity' out of Jews and Gentiles (Eph. 2:15), so that all the nations could come to share in the promises and privileges of Israel (2:19–20). This is nothing less than 'the mystery of Christ' (3:4), 'that is, the Gentiles have become fellow-heirs, members of the same body, and sharers in the promise in Christ Jesus through the gospel' (3:6). And how is this mystery to be declared to the world? 'Through the church the wisdom of God in its rich variety might now be made known to the rulers and authorities in the heavenly places' (3:10). The word translated 'rich variety' by the NRSV literally means 'many-coloured'. John Stott traces out the implications: 'The church as a multi-racial, multi-cultural community is like a beautiful tapestry. Its members come from a wide range of colourful backgrounds. No other community resembles it. Its diversity and harmony are unique. It is God's new society.'[66]

Stott goes on to castigate those who see the church as incidental or even optional to God's work in the world: 'How can we take lightly what God takes so seriously? How dare we push to the circumference what God has placed at the centre?'[67] And he draws out how the church is a part of the gospel message:

---

[64] Bosch 1997: 48.
[65] Hoekendijk 1967, quoted in Bosch 1997: 48.
[66] Stott 1979: 123.
[67] Ibid. 129.

It is evident from Ephesians 3 that the full gospel concerns both Christ and the 'mystery' of Christ. The good news of the unsearchable riches of Christ which Paul preached is that he died and rose again not only to save sinners like me (though he did), but also to create a single new humanity; not only to redeem us from sin but also to adopt us into God's family; not only to reconcile us to God but also to reconcile us to one another. Thus the church is an integral part of the gospel. The gospel is good news of a new society as well as of a new life.[68]

This has massive implications for church planting. It is not only that we preach the gospel and see people added to the church, true though that is. Rather, it is also that the being added is a part of the invitation and demonstration of the gospel's power. According to theologian John Knox, the difference in the world before and after Jesus is that 'now there is a group of people who believe in him and what God did and is doing through him. They make a difference. The world is different if there is a genuine Church in it.'[69] And part of the genuineness of this church is its diversity, its 'sociological impossibility'.[70] If we do not find a way for people to experience this 'many-coloured' quality of the life of the local church, then there is a sense in which we have not adequately preached the gospel. Without the church, we do not properly do mission.

Still more fundamentally, there is the theological claim that God – Father, Son and Holy Spirit – has chosen to dwell in the church, and to act through the church in the world. As St Irenaeus wrote: 'Where the church is, there is the Spirit of God; and where the Spirit of God is, there is the church, and every kind of grace.'[71] We have only to trace the use of temple language in the New Testament to see how fundamental was this sense for the first Christians. Just two examples from Paul: he tells the Corinthian Christians that they are God's holy temple (1 Cor. 3:17), and he describes the church in Ephesus in similar terms: 'In [Christ] the whole

---

[68] Ibid. 128–129.
[69] Quoted in Bevans and Schroeder 2004: 358. Their footnote says: 'The quotation is from Joseph Komonchak, "Christians Must Make a Difference," *The Tablet* (September 28, 2002), 4. Komonchak makes the reference to Knox in the article.'
[70] Hoekendijk 1967, quoted in Bosch 1997: 48.
[71] Irenaeus, *Against Heresies*, 3.3.1, quoted in Bevans and Schroeder 1977: 65.

structure is joined together and grows into a holy temple in the Lord; in whom you also are built together spiritually into a dwelling-place for God' (Eph. 2:21–22).

The New Testament shows us Jesus as the new temple, the meeting place of God with humankind, and whenever we read of the Holy Spirit in the church, this is how the Old Testament paradigm of the presence and glory of God with his people has been actualized in New Testament theology and experience. The presence of Jesus, by his Spirit, is primarily (but not exclusively) presented in the New Testament to be in the church. 'The Christian mission is always Christological and pneumatological, but the New Testament knows of no Christology or pneumatology which is not ecclesial.'[72] Bosch writes:

> The era of the Spirit is . . . the era of the church. And the church in the power of the Spirit is itself part of the message it proclaims. It is a fellowship . . . which actualizes God's love . . . We cannot ignore this community, indeed are forbidden to do so.[73]

When we come to talk about mission, then, about finding God or about God's action in the world, we must talk about the church. It is in the church that we most clearly find and see and encounter God.

Paul Minear's classic 1960 study, *Images of the Church in the New Testament*,[74] analyses over ninety different ways in which the New Testament describes the church. In a thorough and nuanced discussion, he comes to the conclusion that the church as the body of Christ is the most significant of the images: '[The] panorama [of the images for the church in the New Testament] is dependent upon another panorama, the portraits of the Messiah. The story of Jesus as Messiah defines the church as his people.'[75] And, in a fascinating move, he goes on to say that '[t]he images as a whole fuse together the ministry of Christ, variously conceived, with the ministry of his people as a whole'.[76]

---

72 Bosch 1997: 385.
73 Ibid. 517.
74 Minear 1960.
75 Ibid. 262.
76 Ibid.

This has huge implications for our view of mission and church planting. Minear quotes Alan Richardson to that effect:

> The church is thus [as Christ's body] the means of Christ's work in the world; it is his hands and feet, his mouth and voice. As in his incarnate life, Christ had to have a body to proclaim his gospel and do his work, so in his resurrection life in this age he still needs a body to be the instrument of his gospel and of his work in the world.[77]

Therefore, theological logic demands that we never separate mission from church, that the one is unintelligible without the other.

This also means that, as we move from theory to practice, theology to action, church planting should never be without a significant ecclesial dimension. The shared life of the people of God is an essential aspect of not just the aim of church planting but also the means by which we get to it. The clue is in the name: it is *churches* we are planting.

Church and mission in tension

Imagine that a group of Christians from a commuter community are planting a church into a far poorer part of their parish, which has no church connections and a population that is as much unchurched as dechurched. The church planters have worked out that people in this community will not come to anything which they put on in 'the church'; the barriers – social, ethnic, economic and cultural, let alone spiritual – are all too great. They therefore cannot 'set up' church in any way that is normal to them, but instead are focusing on the building of relationships and the establishing of various social action projects, being very careful of any unhelpful power dynamics which may be at play. Bit by bit, over some considerable period of time, individuals and families come to faith. It would be alienating, though, to start holding church services, with singing and the sacraments. What then are they to do, and how is this to be thought of as 'church'? Are they really 'church' planting at all?

This is a very real dilemma for many church planters, and even more so for pioneers and those starting fresh expressions of church. Sometimes

---

[77] Richardson 1958: 256, quoted in Minear 1960: 239.

there are painful discussions about the legitimacy of what they are doing. Say some planters are looking to start a youth congregation, or a messy church,[78] or a lay prayer-community on a housing estate; or maybe two families are setting up a youth project in their local school. There is no doubting the Christian vision that has given birth to such projects. There is no question that Christians are involved, and that the ethos and culture are Christian. Those involved talk about Jesus, they pray to him, there is Bible study and evangelism, and people are coming to faith. They may even talk about 'our church'. If there is a sponsoring or sending or planting church, its leaders may talk about 'our church plant'. But there are other conversations which cast doubt on the legitimacy of what has been happening. 'It is not a church,' is the argument. 'We love what you are doing, and admire you for doing it, but we cannot define your project as a church. It is not led by ordained people. There are no sacraments. There is no liturgy. The leadership is amateur and untrained. There are no links to other churches or any meaningful allegiance to our denomination. Where is the oversight? You don't even have a name, or at least one that the local community recognizes as a church.' And so the conversation goes on. Sometimes the church plant is described as a 'staging post' on the way to becoming a 'proper' church, but this can just make matters worse, and the plant is left feeling defective and deficient. Or the new community is justified by the analogy of being the shallow end of a swimming pool; it has all the elements of genuine church already present, albeit in embryo, but they are not yet visible or operative.[79] Pain and discouragement result, and strained relationships.

There can also be a real sense that the work of the Spirit is being held back. People are coming to Christ, people who would never darken the doors of a more traditional church; new kingdom relationships are being formed. The work is growing, and new Christian communities are springing up. The 'interference' of those who are giving or withholding

---

[78] According to its website, 'Messy Church is a way of being church for families and others. It is Christ-centred, for all ages, based on creativity, hospitality and celebration': <www.messychurch.org.uk> (accessed 17 December 2022).

[79] This raises the question of which elements of church are still 'shallow', of course. Usually, the sacraments or the liturgical life of the church are in mind. If mission or every-member ministry are brought to the fore, however, then it raises the question of the shallowness of the more established church.

'accreditation' of these new 'churches' is felt as a brake or, at the least, an irritation by the new communities. Can't they see that God is doing a new thing? Why can't they be like Barnabas in Acts 11, and see the grace of God, be glad, and come and help (Acts 11:23), rather than criticize from the sidelines? The energy is all flowing the wrong way: God is clearly pulling 'out' into the community with the message of Jesus, and the established church is pulling back. And why are they so hung up on some doctrinal points rather than following the Spirit? Doesn't it stand to reason that, if the Spirit is in it, he will be bringing people round Jesus, and isn't that what the church *truly* is? And if sacraments and ordination and liturgy really are essential, why can't we find new ways of expressing these things, rather than being bound by old models, which are palpably not working in this context?

This brings us to a crunch point regarding what we mean when we talk about church planting being the intersection of both church and mission. What we mean by mission and by church are of more than academic interest. We are coming to the point where we refuse to privilege one over the other. Ecclesiology and missiology are *equally* essential to any theology and approach to church planting. So, how do we navigate those tricky waters, when the two appear to be in tension or even conflict?

Future directions

What is to be rejected is our 'unchurching' of one another. To hear traditional churches written off as irrelevant failures to be censured and abandoned, or church plants as theologically inauthentic or inappropriate, is both distressing and counterproductive. There is talk within my own Church of England of the 'mixed economy' or 'mixed ecology', where traditional and innovative churches are alike to be thought of as expressions of what God is doing in our contexts at this time. We can go further, and say that toleration must give way to collaboration. We need each other. There is much to learn from each other. It is not that the past belongs to the traditional church, and the future to the emerging church. The future belongs to a glorious tapestry of both.

One thing to say is that we are in a period of huge cultural transition. This is affecting the churches as much as every other sector of society. Change and experimentation are taking place in the midst of a landscape which is as much made up of what is ancient and historical as it is of what is new and innovative. A large part of today's challenge, not least for denominational, network and regional leaders, is how to marry the two perspectives together in such a way that a fruitful and united missional future comes into being for the church. We are to be like Jesus' scribes, trained in the kingdom, and bringing out from our treasure 'what is new and what is old' (Matt. 13:52). We note David Bosch's striking warning that 'it remains extraordinarily difficult to determine what mission is', and that 'there is a constant need for mission itself to be transformed'.[80] This means that the church, because we must always think in terms of mission whenever we think of the church, is likewise in a place of change and challenge and exploration. 'In its mission, the church affirms its own preliminariness and contingency . . . Aware of its provisional character, it lives and ministers as that force within humanity through which the renewal and community of all people is served.'[81]

Oliver O'Donovan helpfully distinguishes between the church's 'outer' and 'inner' life, where the latter is its essential identity derived from the gospel and the presence of Jesus, and the latter its outward expressions, which have more of a historical and cultural contingency. 'The Church's openness to reformation is first and foremost a matter of appraising and evaluating the service rendered by traditional forms, keeping the subservience of the outer to the inner in view.'[82]

Daniel Hardy sees the church as already having the necessary resources within itself for this work of continuing and continuous reformation:

In a world of ever increasing social complexity the church cannot simply adhere to fixed traditional forms. It must reach more and more deeply into its own realities and dynamics within the purposes of God for the world, and invite the Holy Spirit to stir its heart, soul, mind and strength. If it does so, it will learn to participate more fully in the energy of the Spirit of Christ by which God, through his church, is drawing all human society to its fulfilment in the kingdom of God.[83]

---

[80] Bosch 1997: 511.
[81] Ibid. 518.
[82] O'Donovan 2007: 186, discussed in Moynagh with Harrold 2012: 181.
[83] Hardy 2001: 4, quoted in Archbishops' Council of the Church of England 2004: 86.

We need to do two very different things at the same time: to take what we know to be theologically true and key for both church and mission, and to follow the lead of the Spirit in the challenges of our contexts as he takes the church deeper into the fresh arenas of mission in our time. We hold with equal tightness the theological conviction that the church's fundamental character is apostolic and missionary, and the theological conviction that the mission of Jesus to and in and for his world is essentially ecclesial. And, by his grace, we pray, talk, experiment and lean into the missionary future that the Lord is opening up for us. Church planting, it seems to me, has a particularly prophetic role in these explorations. It is imperative for the church to provide space and grace for this emerging movement to try things out, things which may well be alarming, even threatening, to the ways that Christendom did them. And equally, it is incumbent on church planters to hold tightly to the precious unity of the wider church, and to stay in good relationship with the more traditional church as it does so.

Another thing to say is that, by God's good grace, we in the West are being given the gift of the experience and perspective of our sisters and brothers in the Majority World.

Philip Jenkins, in his influential *The Next Christendom*,[84] predicts that the future of world Christianity will, if current trends are to continue, be linked to its life and expression in the Global South: 'Very soon, the two main centers of Christianity will be Africa and Latin America.'[85] The predominant expression of Christianity in these continents is Pentecostal or Catholic, and, in both, the miraculous and the experimental take precedence over a more cerebral approach to faith. In addition, the vast majority of Christians are from the world's poorest people.[86] Jenkins draws out some interesting consequences: 'For the foreseeable future, the characteristic religious forms of Southern world Christianity – enthusiastic and spontaneous, fundamentalist and supernatural-oriented – look very different from those of older centers in Europe and North America.'[87]

---

[84] Jenkins 2011.
[85] Ibid. 15.
[86] Ibid. 98.
[87] Ibid. 100.

Western Christianity appears to be feeling the impact of this, not simply because of the weight of numbers in global terms shifting to the South, but by virtue of European demographic changes too:

> People of African and Asian stock now play a crucial part in European societies, especially in major cities. About half of London's people are now nonwhite, and by 2050, around 20 percent of the population of Great Britain will be from ethnic minorities, with origins in Africa, Asia, or the Caribbean.[88]

It is churches rooted in these ethnic communities that are growing fast in the West: 'these congregations perhaps represent the future face of Christianity in Western Europe.'[89]

The significance of these trends is more than demographic; it may also presage a theological shift, not least in regards to ecclesiology and missiology. Jenkins remarks:

> This global perspective should make us think carefully before asserting 'what Christians believe' or 'how the church is changing.' All too often, statements about what 'modern Christians accept' or what 'Catholics today believe,' refer only to what that ever-shrinking remnant of *Western* Christians and Catholics believe. Such assertions are outrageous today, and as time goes by they will become ever further removed from reality.[90]

The Western church is likely to be made up numerically of a majority of people from non-white backgrounds, with different theological traditions and emphases from those of their white sisters and brothers. Worship and mission may well take on a much more non-white character. What emerges in such a process is that the questions, language and even cultural origins of world Christianity are not the same as those of Western Christianity; and this has enormous implications for our theologies of church and mission.

---

[88] Ibid. 120.
[89] Ibid. 123.
[90] Ibid. 3; emphasis original.

Zimbabwean theologian Roy Musasiwa writes:

> The traditional theologies that have originated from the West and are uncritically consumed by the rest of the world are in fact a product of Western culture and philosophy. These theologies are neither exhaustive nor absolute, nor should they be regarded as standard theologies suited to every context.[91]

This perspective enables us to view our theological definitions in a more flexible way, without losing the central truths to which they point. Michael Moynagh comments:

> Just as Jewish believers had to modify their assumptions about what it meant to be a Christian and how this was to be expressed in the life of the church, so too the Western church – as it responds to new cultures at home and overseas – must be open to question its inherited life and assumptions.[92]

By avoiding absolutizing theological positions on church and mission, we see a freedom that permits fruitful dialogue. This in turn may open up fresh ways of church planting that could be on the leading edge of the church's missionary encounter with the West in the future.

Where we have got to is that theologies of church and mission are both equally vital for a theology of church planting, and neither should be privileged over the other. It is the essentially missionary nature of the church and the essentially ecclesial nature of mission that lends power and authenticity to the theology and practice of church planting. By seeing ecclesiology as fundamental to missiology, we bring mission firmly and clearly into the centre of church life, rather than exiling it to the periphery or to the realm of enthusiasts for whom that is 'their thing'. And, in defining mission by reference to an essentially 'church' category, mission is rescued from being separate from the virtue and vigour of the heart of the church's life, history and future. We have recognized, though, the

---

[91] Musasiwa 2007: 67.
[92] Moynagh with Harrold 2012: 117.

tensions that exist in holding church and mission together in such a determined fashion, in terms of both theology and practice. Often it is the practice of church planting which brings to the surface the theological assumptions and questions that lie beneath. We have advocated a practice of listening and learning from both sides regarding the questions which arise, seeing the need for mutual dialogue and learning as critical for the future of church planting and Western mission. We have argued for an approach which holds together cherished biblical truth with a certain humility and provisionality as we explore models of church planting, and have found the experience of the Majority World churches to be instructive by way of examples of this approach. We now need to see if there are theological moves which will enable us to transcend the conflicts between theologies of church and mission which seem to have landed us in practical cul-de-sacs.

Transcending the conflicts

Let us start with where we will end up in the next chapter of this book, with the Trinity. It is when we locate church and mission, and their intersection in church planting, in the context of a broader theology that we release a way of thinking that sees them working freely and fruitfully together. Specifically, the broader theological rationale is nothing less than the nature and being and purposes of God, with their focus on the life, ministry and triumph of Jesus.

Michael Moynagh has done us all a great service by proposing the use of the language of self-donation. He sees a danger of focusing on the church as the origin of mission in that the world begins to be viewed as a kind of gift to the church, which is cannibalized to sustain the church's own existence. This is at variance with the Bible's view of God's covenant people serving the world, and with the mission and practice of Jesus himself. Moynagh cuts through debates over the priority of church or mission by appealing to the nature of God as we see it in the gospel. Jesus demonstrates for us 'the essence of mission – going out to others in self-giving generosity'.[93] He sees the life of Jesus as an expression and a

---

[93] Moynagh 2017: 144.

demonstration of God's own nature of self-giving love. And, within this framework, church plants are themselves gifts from this self-giving God in love to the world. 'As part of God's outflowing of generosity, new ecclesial communities are divine gifts. They are gifts through the church to the world.'[94] This perspective enables church plants to see themselves as part of the same trajectory of self-donation: 'The Spirit turns the church into a gift by enabling it to give itself to others . . . New ecclesial communities follow the logic of divine generosity, which is the core of the gospel.'[95] The perceived tension between church and mission is resolved; the church is itself the mission, understood as a gift from the self-giving God to the world.

Moynagh's framework also bestows on the church the freedom of sacrificing its own culture for the sake of the context it serves. 'The church corresponds to the divine self-donation when it, too, gives itself in mission – when it generates new entities that reflect the self-giving character it has received from God.'[96] The self-donation of the church can be seen in church planting, as churches give away people, resources and love to start new worshipping communities in their own neighbourhoods, regions and contexts. It can also be seen in the forms these church plants take: the culture will be geared to that of the people they serve, rather than their own. The self-donation of God runs through the very centre of both the church plant and its mission; the one cannot be understood without reference to the other, as this 'community-in-mission' is used as the frame of reference.[97] Theologically, it is when we think of the intersection of church and mission through the frame of the character and purposes of God in Jesus that the two cease to compete and a unified theology of church planting as both ecclesiology and missiology makes sense.

We find the same theological move in what are arguably the three most influential books on church and mission from the second half of the twentieth century, to which reference has already been made: Lesslie Newbigin's *The Household of God* (1953), Paul Minear's *Images of the*

---

94 Ibid. 148.
95 Ibid. 148, 158.
96 Moynagh with Harrold 2012: 128.
97 Ibid. 140–150, citing Bevans and Schroeder 2004: 294. Bosch (1997: 512) has the similar phrase 'Church-in-Mission'.

Church in the New Testament (1960) and Avery Cardinal Dulles's *Models of the Church* (1974).[98] Even more significant is how each author locates the essence of the discussion in something beyond the church, but never without losing a sense of the local and concrete. For Newbigin, it is the eschatological and missionary nature of the church 'and only in that perspective can the deadlock of our present ecumenical debate be resolved'.[99] For Minear, the nature of theological language – a kind of imaginative poetics, necessitated by the theological realities to which the language points – is a reflection of how the life and existence of the church is nourished by God himself.[100] He refines this insight, seeing how the 'panorama [of the images] is dependent upon another panorama, the portraits of the messiah. The story of Jesus as Messiah defines the church as his people.'[101] As for Dulles, he argues for a methodology which is congruent with the supernatural nature of the church. He reaches for definitions which allow for the life of Christ by his Spirit in the church, and resists rigid classifications for something which is alive by virtue of the action of Jesus. He calls this 'mystery' and argues that it 'rules out the possibility of proceeding from unclear and univocal concepts'.[102]

These insights and methodologies have potential for the development and exploration of any ecclesiology of church planting. There is something provisional in the way all three theologians proceed, which generates a flexibility when it comes to reflecting on the nature of the church. This flexibility is not born of pragmatism but is rather rooted theologically in the life and action of the triune God in the church, not least its missionary life. It enables genuine dialogue with different theological positions.

We note the kind of questions these theologians are asking: they are seeking to understand the church by virtue of its interaction with God and his purposes. Their starting point is emphatically theological rather than practical. Yet it is this approach which ends up yielding a flexibility and breadth of vision which makes all kinds of practical outcomes possible. This divine perspective makes our human definitions of church

---

[98] See above in the section headed 'The church'.
[99] Newbigin 1953: 25.
[100] Minear 1960: 12.
[101] Ibid. 262.
[102] Dulles 1974: 10.

and mission provisional, but roots any discussions of the interaction of ecclesiology and missiology in the most concrete theological foundation of all – God himself and his purposes in the world.

Rowan Williams has adopted a similar approach to understanding church and mission. He has described church in the New Testament as

> what happens when the news and presence of Jesus, raised from the dead, impact upon the human scene, drawing people together in a relationship that changes everyone involved, a relationship which means that each person involved with Jesus is now involved with all others who have answered his invitation, in ways that are painful and demanding but are also lifegiving and transforming beyond imagination.[103]

He makes the same point in his foreword to the *Mission-Shaped Church* report, arguing that this approach makes possible in both theology and practice a freedom to experiment and to learn:

> If 'church' is what happens when people encounter the Risen Jesus and commit themselves to sustaining and deepening that encounter in their encounter with each other, there is plenty of theological room for diversity of rhythm and style, so long as we have ways of identifying the same living Christ at the heart of every expression of Christian life in common.[104]

From a different theological perspective, Alan Hirsch argues for the same approach. Hirsch observes that frequently ecclesiology has been given a theological primacy, which enables it to define missiology. Instead he argues for

> the following 'formula' for engaging in mission in a post-Christian culture: *Christology determines missiology, and missiology determines ecclesiology.* This is just a smart-aleck's way of saying that in order to

---

103 Williams 2008–9: 13, cited in Moynagh with Harrold 2012: 107.
104 Archbishops' Council of the Church of England 2004: v.

align ourselves correctly as a missional movement, we first need to return to the Founder of Christianity and, having done that, re-calibrate our approach from that point on . . . Jesus is our constant reference point – we always begin and always end with him.[105]

Hirsch argues for a missional priority over ecclesiology, whereas I am saying that we must not set one over against the other, but it is striking to see Hirsch agreeing with Williams that the way to understand church and mission is to submit them both to the priority of Jesus.

Such an approach is in line with the way in which Jesus himself recalibrated Israel's story around himself. As we have seen, he reframed the law around his teaching, reconstituted the twelve tribes of Israel around himself, fulfilled the sacrificial system, and declared himself the new temple, the new Passover and the one in whom Israel could encounter its covenant God. It is all of a piece for church planters to see church and mission through this same Christological lens. Indeed, not to do so is to fall out of step with Jesus.

Ways of thinking to take us forward

What might this mean in practice? Michael Frost and Alan Hirsch have written a provocative book, *ReJesus: A Wild Messiah for a Missional Church*,[106] in which they imaginatively try to answer just that question. They explain the purpose of their book as being 'the recovery of the absolute centrality of the person of Jesus in defining who we are as well as what we do',[107] but they also concede that this is surprisingly hard to do, given our own prejudices and limited perspectives.

> Surely the challenge for the church today is to be taken captive by the agenda of Jesus, rather than seeking to mold him to fit our agendas, no matter how noble they might be. We acknowledge that we can never truly claim to know him completely. We all bring our biases to the task. But we believe it is inherent in the faith to keep trying and to never give up on this holy quest. The challenge before

---

[105] Hirsch 2006: 142.
[106] Frost and Hirsch 2009.
[107] Ibid. 8.

us is to let Jesus be Jesus and to allow ourselves to be caught up in his extraordinary mission for the world.[108]

We might do worse than bring four perspectives to bear.

1 To read the Gospels to help us view church and mission Christologically. As we discovered, there is a strong case that the Gospels were written for precisely this purpose, particularly Matthew and Mark. Matthew can be seen as a carefully structured curriculum for new disciples in those churches planted in the light of the resurrection of Jesus, whereas Mark can be read as leadership training for churches-in-mission. The more we focus on the Gospels to help define the essence and purpose of our missionary churches, the more closely we will draw to Jesus and his kingdom as expressed in our church plants.

2 To think of the whole Christ. Frequently, it is the incarnation which is taken as Jesus' model for ministry, and, as we have seen, quite rightly so. New Testament mission, though, is of course undertaken from the perspective of the incarnate Lord who is now risen and ascended, and who has sent his Spirit to empower mission in the light of the resurrection. We remember our discussions of each of the 'great commissions' at the end of the four Gospels, and how mission is viewed in terms of Jesus-communities living out life from the perspective of the victory and triumph of Jesus over death.

Michael Moynagh, for instance, writes that he

> understands the incarnation in terms of the whole of Jesus' earthly and ascended life. Jesus became and remains a human being ... Contextual churches echo the whole sweep of Jesus' life when they mirror not only his identification with culture, but also his mission in community within ordinary life, his community's Good Friday fragmentation and Easter resurrection, his letting go and sending out, and his completion of all 'places' when he returns.[109]

---

[108] Ibid. 10.
[109] Moynagh with Harrold 2012: 182.

This is helpful, and draws us back into the way in which Minear was able to frame his four master images of the church in the New Testament around the underlying picture of the crucified and risen Messiah, and how Newbigin urges us to see the church in terms of both mission and eschatology. We must not underestimate the greatness of Jesus, and how he carries within himself Israel's story and the world's future. Rowan Williams significantly speaks of shared encounters with the *risen* Jesus, when he speaks of the church coming into existence.

3 To think of Jesus from the perspective of the whole church. Each tradition of the church brings its own invaluable insights, but each also brings its own limitations. This tendency is compounded when culture is also brought into the reflections. We have constantly noted the impact of context in this book: views, visions and values in an inner-city church plant will be different from those in a rural one; Christians working with postmodern students will emphasize different aspects of the gospel from those evangelizing a retirement community; Christians dealing with white working-class culture will bring different approaches from those engaging with immigrant communities, and so on. This current chapter has also reflected on the startlingly different approaches of Majority World perspectives from the unexamined views of most post-Christendom Western contexts. The more we can listen to and learn from one another, the more likely it is that we will build up a more comprehensive view of Jesus, and the kind of missional church planting he envisages for his followers.

4 To make the cross of Jesus the centre-point of our thinking. We can see that this was Paul's approach. He declares to the Corinthian Christians that he decided to 'know nothing among you except Jesus Christ, and him crucified' (1 Cor. 2:2), and that what is 'of first importance' is 'that Christ died for our sins . . . and that he was buried, and that he was raised on the third day' (1 Cor. 15:3–4). In 2 Corinthians he describes his apostolic ministry as 'always carrying in the body the death of Jesus, so that the life of Jesus may also be made visible in our bodies' (2 Cor. 4:10). What we have here is both the message and the methodology of the cross: we preach the crucified Messiah, and we do so in line with his sufferings and weakness. Theologian Ernst Käsemann argued that this was the only authentic way in which the language of the church as a sign of God's kingdom could be used.[110]

We are moving towards a theological approach to church planting which views both church and mission together in terms of the incarnate and eschatological life of Jesus. Moynagh's concept of self-donation fits well within this framework. We are finding the constitution and the activity and the agency of the church by thinking in this way, and we are discovering that 'not only our purpose is defined by the person and work of Jesus, but our methodology as well'.[111] Church planting will bear the stamp of *what* Jesus was about, and *how* he went about it.

The great freedom of this approach is that each tradition of the church is able to express its own emphases in how the presence of the living Jesus is experienced today. Of course, these are not mutually exclusive approaches. The central conviction is that Jesus is alive, risen from the dead, and present among his people in word and sacrament by his Spirit, and he is fulfilling the purposes of God for his creation. Rowan Williams is especially helpful in pointing out that such encounters with the living Lord Jesus, even though they may be individual, will necessarily draw us into relationship with others who are having their own encounters with the Lord. It is in this sharing of experience of Christ that the church comes into being. What is in view is the completeness of who Jesus is, both for the church and for the world. His ultimacy, even in the face of our provisionality, is what grounds church-planting theology. He is the king of the kingdom of God, and by his Spirit he is healing and redeeming and judging the world. He has chosen to fulfil the biblical pattern by displaying his glory and accomplishing the fullness of his work on the cross and the empty grave through the church. In himself he continues to embody both the cultivation and the communication of faith. It is as the church is constantly and intentionally on the lookout for the presence and activity of Jesus that it is simultaneously and appropriately ecclesial and missionary. The more we make Jesus central to our church

---

[110] Käsemann 1974: 130, discussed in Bosch 1997: 375.
[111] Hirsch 2006: 143.

planting, the more we will have the capacity to resolve tensions around ecclesiology and missiology.

In the next chapter, let us delve more deeply into how the very person and heart of God, notably expressed in the person and mission of Jesus, are fundamental to the theology and practice of church planting.

7

The Trinity and church planting

In this book, we have seen that God's characteristic way of working in the world has been through communities, whether that be the nation promised to Abraham, the covenant people revealed to Moses, the kingdom led by David and Solomon, the renewed people prophesied by Isaiah and Jeremiah, the restored and recalibrated people of God gathered around Jesus, or the new Jesus-communities planted by Paul. Always, mission and community go together. In the New Testament, we have seen the leading of God in the planting of the church, and the activity of God in sustaining and developing these churches. And, in the previous chapter of this book, we found that the best way of viewing church planting (as it holds church and mission together) is to see it through the lens of who Jesus is and what he does. We may wonder at how God's action in the world is so consistently carried out through communities on mission, and how this activity is so intimately linked with his own personal action, even seemingly his own character, as expressed in Jesus.

This chapter draws these themes together. In a nutshell, church planting is central to God's action in the world because it reflects and arises from his being as Trinity. Church planting most fully parallels and incorporates who God is, and so how he acts in the world. Bevans and Schroeder summarize some of the ground we are to cover, as they reflect on the papal encyclical *Ad Gentes* (AG):

> In AG, God the Father is pictured as a life-giving fountain of love who freely creates the world and calls humanity in particular to share in the fullness of divine life. God does this by generously pouring out the divine goodness in history (the mission of the Son) and never ceasing to do so as history continues (the mission of the Spirit). Since humanity is created in God's image and is called to

share in God's fullness, the end of God's action is not that men and women are taken up individually; rather, like God in God's innermost mystery, they too are formed into a community, a people, an 'icon' of the Trinity. God is the community of Father, Son and Spirit, constantly involved in the world; salvation, human wholeness, is life lived in a community that reflects the community and self-giving that is God.[1]

In other words, mission and community are not coincidentally or tangentially related to what God does in the world, but are the very heartbeat of what he does, and this because, when they are joined together in the practice of church planting, they reflect the very being of God himself. God is constantly reaching out to the world (mission), grounded in the revelation and salvation won by Jesus Christ in his historical incarnation, crucifixion, resurrection and ascension; and he is constantly summoning men and women into the kind of community which is most perfectly seen in his own trinitarian life (church). Both church and mission can be seen as aspects of who God is and what he does. And so, on the one hand, it is small wonder that the story of the Bible, the work of Jesus and the life of the church are seen in the establishing of missional communities to show his love and glory in the world and to be centres of human flourishing and prophetic signs of the peace and justice of his kingdom; and, on the other hand, it is also small wonder that there is something profoundly mysterious about all this, something which defies definition and feels more dynamic and living than steady state. Church planting is simultaneously pragmatic, effective, simply the best way of doing mission by building community around the gospel of Christ, and also mysterious, multivariant, dependent upon context, existing in as many forms as there are church plants and church planters. We approach church planting with some of the reverence and sense of handling something holy and beyond us that we feel when we reflect on the being of the Trinity itself. And so, we gladly affirm church planting as something godly, holy, theologically vital; and, simultaneously, we resist trying to tie it down into any particular form or pattern or mode, for to do so is

---

[1] Bevans and Schroeder 2004: 287.

reductionist, and risks actually deforming, even denying, the very thing we are attempting to describe. 'God's temple is holy, and you are that temple' (1 Cor. 3:17).

So, with both confidence and humility, may we think together about the Holy Trinity and church planting, beginning with the Holy Spirit?

Church planting and the Holy Spirit

We have seen the central role of the Spirit in church planting throughout this book. Indeed, this section heading and its variants have come up more than once! The life of the church and that of mission, let alone the two married together in the theology and practice of church planting, are unthinkable without the Holy Spirit. Stephen Bevans writes boldly on this, but without overstepping the mark:

> I propose that the church will live out its mission worthily only to the extent that it allies itself with and is transformed by the Spirit's power. If the Spirit is the first way that God sends and is sent, the Spirit's activity becomes the foundation of the church's own missionary nature. If the church is to express its nature, therefore, it needs first to look at the Spirit's activity. Its task is, like Jesus, both to follow the Spirit's lead and to be the concrete 'face' of the Spirit in the world.[2]

What Bevans argues for mission in general is equally true of church planting, perhaps doubly so; if mission is predicated on the power of the Spirit, so too is church. Ecclesiology and missiology alike are, in a sense, built on a theology of the Spirit.

The Spirit brings an immediate sense of the presence of God in Christ

Bevans' point is that, in terms of actual human experience, it is the Spirit who leads us into encounter with Christ and the Father. Through Christ we have 'access in one Spirit to the Father' (Eph. 2:18). It is the Spirit who

---

[2] Bevans 1998: 102, quoted in Bevans and Schroeder 2004: 293.

convicts and convinces us, who gives us faith, who makes Jesus real and who makes prayer possible. Calvin puts it with striking force:

> We must understand that as long as Christ remains outside of us, and we are separated from him, all that he has suffered and done for the salvation of the human race remains useless and of no value to us.[3]

This happens through 'the secret energy of the Spirit'.[4] Gordon Fee, in his magisterial survey of the Spirit in Paul,[5] writes of how 'Paul's sociological *experience* of God is the starting point for understanding his inherent Trinitarianism'.[6] 'The Spirit is God's own personal presence in our lives and in our midst',[7] the Spirit is *'the absolutely essential constituent of the whole of Christian life*, from beginning to end',[8] and

> this means that our theologizing must stop paying lip service to the Spirit and recognise his crucial role in ... theology; and it means that the church must risk freeing the Spirit from being boxed into the creed and getting him back into the experienced life of the believer and the believing community.[9]

It is in and through the Spirit that Christian life begins and that church life happens. Church planting, then, is dependent on the Spirit of God in more than token ways.

This is the experience of every church planter, of course. This is why we pray. We are asking God to go ahead of us, to make happen what only he can make happen, to do what only he can do. Individuals come to faith only through the ministry of the Spirit in revelation and regeneration, and churches spring into being only through his power and grace. Nearly every church plant will have Holy Spirit stories, unaccountable and

---

[3] Calvin 1960: 537.
[4] Ibid.
[5] Fee 1994.
[6] Ibid. 843.
[7] Ibid. 845.
[8] Ibid. 898; emphasis original.
[9] Ibid. 902.

awe-inspiring instances of his sovereign activity in getting churches off the ground. There are few things, especially in the early days, more encouraging than signs that the Spirit is with us.

This means that any theology and practice of church planting must unashamedly give a leading place to the person and work of the Holy Spirit, not least as he makes Jesus, the gospel and the church real and meaningful and *felt* in the experience of those involved in the planting of churches. This is not an argument for any particular theological position, for surely every church tradition gives honour to God in this way. Maybe the language is different, but all church plants recognize a sense of priority to the Spirit, to grace, to the action of God going before us. What we are involved in is miraculous, the bringing into being of a community around Jesus to advance his kingdom in a particular context. We are utterly dependent on the Spirit's power to resurrect the dead and to constitute the church. Church planting is a Holy Spirit business, from beginning to end.

The Holy Spirit brings people together in Jesus

Michael Moynagh makes an imaginative and helpful suggestion when we come to think about the nature of church as community-in-mission:

> How can mission and community both be seen as being the essence of the church? One possibility might be to think more closely about the relationships that constitute the church. The church is comprised of four sets of relationships centred on Jesus – to the Godhead, between members of the local church, to the world and between each part and the whole body. In believers' experience, these relationships are what church is. Take any one set of these relationships away, and church would be less than fully church. These four sets of relationships are essential to the being of church.[10]

Moynagh's emphasis on relationships as being what church actually is, not least as it is experienced, gives us a way of bringing mission and church together, and a freedom to think creatively about what kind of new

---

[10] Moynagh with Harrold 2012: 106.

churches God might be bringing into being around the world and in our own local contexts. And, of course, when it comes to relationships, it is the Holy Spirit who is taking the lead. Rowan Williams writes of how church is what happens when people are drawn into relationship with Jesus and so into relationship with one another.[11] This is the constitution of the church by the Spirit: 'For in the one Spirit we were all baptized into one body – Jews or Greeks, slaves or free – and we were all made to drink of one Spirit' (1 Cor. 12:13).

There is one body because there is one Spirit, and it is he who brings diverse people from diverse backgrounds into the one body of Christ. This is at once a missionary and an ecclesial text; this is the nature of the church by virtue of its missionary origins. The beginnings and nature of the church, alike, are down to the power of the Spirit to draw people together in Jesus. Holy Spirit relationality is both with regard to Jesus (mission) and to fellow believers (church) at one and the same time; the Spirit's work of bringing faith and building the church is indivisible, anchored in his capacity to bring about relationship. Moynagh's four interlocking relationships that comprise church are born of a profoundly theological insight into what the Holy Spirit does.

Tom Smail, in his classic book on the Holy Spirit, *The Giving Gift*,[12] says that 'the Holy Spirit is the Spirit of relationship'.[13] Commenting on 1 John 1:3 ('we declare to you what we have seen and heard so that you also may have fellowship with us; and truly our fellowship is with the Father and with his Son Jesus Christ'), he writes:

> These two occurrences of the word clearly indicate the two dimensions of the [fellowship] which the gospel creates. On the one hand it is a *horizontal* sharing of life among believers; on the other it is a *vertical* sharing of life between believers on the one side and the Father and the Son on the other. One could hardly think of a more theologically succinct and practically challenging description of the Church. The Christian Church is, in the purpose and intention of God, that community of people who, as a result of their hearing and

---

11 Williams 2008–9, quoted in Moynagh with Harrold 2012: 107.
12 Smail 1988.
13 Ibid. 184.

believing the gospel, have been enabled to share through Christ in God's own life, and who, as a result, have begun to share their lives with one another on every level.[14]

The church is summed up in Christ who is the head, but also in the relationships in him that his people have. 'In other words, the Spirit who comes from the Father through the Son is himself the mystery at the heart of the Church.'[15] We may also add, 'And in mission.'

Smail lays down a theological foundation as to how and why this might be so. He alludes to how Augustine referred to the Holy Spirit as the 'bond of love' between the Father and the Son within the Trinity. He helpfully draws out that this has often led to confusion, at least in the Western church, as to whether or not we can properly speak of the Holy Spirit as a person, rather than just a force, or as merely an extension of the Father or the Son.[16] He goes on to put the matter more carefully:

The Holy Spirit is not the one to whom we relate but rather the one who makes the relating [to the Father and the Son] possible. It is Christ, and the Father through him, who relates himself to me and to whom I relate; it is the Holy Spirit who enables me to receive Christ and to give myself to him. The Holy Spirit is the bond of our union with Christ, the one who comes from his side of the relationship over to ours and enables us to receive and to respond.[17]

This is helpful, both missionally and ecclesially. It is the Spirit, in mission, who enables a response of faith to the gospel; but it is also the Spirit who enables us to draw near to one another by virtue of that response to Christ. Once again we see that, in the work of the Spirit, mission and church cannot be thought of separately. The one Spirit brings people to Christ and together in him: there is no other Spirit (so there cannot logically or theologically be unallied communities of faith), and his essence and ministry is to bring about oneness in Christ.

---

[14] Ibid. 182–183.
[15] Ibid. 189.
[16] Ibid. 43.
[17] Ibid. 61.

This explains why there is exceptional closeness in church plants, especially as they launch together. The emphasis on mission, and the methodology of community life as mission, both lean strongly into the territory of the Holy Spirit. The Spirit, thus, is the one generating a church which is one, holy, catholic and apostolic; it is united and universal by virtue of the life of God present in its mission and shared community.

Michael Moynagh alludes to the practice in some evangelical churches of thinking of church life in terms of 'up' (worship), 'in' (fellowship) and 'out' (mission), and argues for another dimension – 'of' ('being part *of* the whole body of Christ').[18] He is helping us see that the Spirit, by virtue of his work of bringing us together in relationship, is concerned not just with relationships *within* churches but also with relationships *between* churches. He argues that this element of unity is the one most likely to be missing in church plants, being focused as they are on local mission, but he laments this and points it out as a lack in the church-planting movement. There are encouraging signs that, even since Moynagh wrote his groundbreaking work (2012), this is changing. It is often church plants that are acting as catalysts for church unity across regions and in cities. This is particularly true of resource churches, planted with a particular remit of helping mission widely within a city or diocese and especially to be themselves planting multiple church plants. These churches, and their leaders, seem to have a particular passion for church unity – a clear reflection of this aspect of the Holy Spirit. It is no theological accident that these churches at the forefront of bold and creative mission should also be taking a lead in unity between churches.

The main point of this subsection is that a theology of the Holy Spirit as the great relator, the one who acts in relationship, is of a piece with a theology of church planting, where the gospel draws people not just to Christ but to one another in him, thanks to the Spirit's ministry. Coming to faith is part and parcel of coming into Christian community, and Christian community is the setting for individual conversion. Once again community and mission belong together, and it is the Spirit's work that means we must not separate them in either theology or practice. It is in planting churches that we see the Spirit acting in great power, because it

---

18 Moynagh with Harrold 2012: 113.

is in church planting that he has scope to bring about relationship, with Christ within the Trinity, and with fellow believers within the fellowship of the church.

The Holy Spirit anticipates the end

Christian mission, in one sense, is a working with God towards the perfection that he envisages for his creation. The middle section of Romans 8 speaks of the creation waiting 'with eager longing' to be 'set free from its bondage to decay' and to share 'the freedom of the glory of the children of God' (Rom. 8:18–25). The coming of God's kingdom in all its fullness is the time when 'the earth will be full of the knowledge of the LORD as the waters cover the sea' (Isa. 11:9; Hab. 2:14). This is the time when death and pain and suffering cease, evil is for ever vanquished, righteousness fills the whole earth and there is joy for ever in the presence of God (Rev. 21:3–4; 2 Pet. 3:13; Ps. 16:11). Christian mission is a working towards that time, and an anticipation of it. The Holy Spirit has a particular role in bringing about that future. He has been described as 'the perfecting cause': 'The Spirit's action is a renewing action, and therefore makes perfect that which enters the process marked by the accumulated corruption of the ages. The recreation of the world is begun.'[19]

Colin Gunton, whom I have just quoted, is at pains to locate the work of the Spirit as being *over against and toward* the order of [God's] creation',[20] in other words taking issue with the corruption and decay of the creation in line with God's promise that all shall one day be renewed and set free to be most truly itself. Gunton describes the action of God in raising Jesus from the dead by the Spirit as representative of all that the Spirit does.[21] Key to this process of revitalizing and healing the creation is none other than the church. This is why the creation longs for the 'revealing of the children of God' (Rom. 8:19), for they will be the ones through whom God brings the whole creation into freedom and wholeness.

The Spirit's first function is to realize in the life of particular human beings and groups of human beings the reality of what God in Christ

---

[19] Gunton 2002: 102.
[20] Ibid. 111; emphasis original.
[21] Ibid.

achieved on the cross ... The Spirit gathers around the risen Jesus a people whose *sole* calling is to praise the one who made them. That 'sole' should not be understood in any way narrowly. It involves both the praise of conscious and explicit worship and that worship carried over into forms of communal life and individual action.[22]

Gunton goes on to emphasize the social or communal nature of this calling, before making a clear declaration of the trajectory of the Spirit's work: '[These] principles [of the life and work of the Spirit] are all eschatological in force. The Spirit's work is to make real, from time to time ... anticipations of the true community of the last days.'[23] The Spirit anticipates God's future for the earth, as it is concentrated in the life of the church. It is as if the Holy Spirit comes from the future into our present to draw out of us what, by God's grace, one day we and the world shall be.

Gordon Fee explains how the vision of the future through the Spirit was so central in Paul's own theology:

On the one hand, the coming of the Spirit fulfilled the [Old Testament] eschatological promises, and was the sure *evidence* that the future had *already* been set in motion; on the other hand, since the final expression of [God's future] had *not yet* taken place, the Spirit also served as the sure *guarantee* of the final glory. It is impossible to understand Paul's emphasis on the experienced life of the Spirit apart from this thoroughgoing eschatological perspective that dominated his thinking.[24]

What we have, in the work of Gunton and Fee, is the location of the work of the Spirit towards (or, better, *from*) the future, in regard to both mission and the church. We see this double emphasis on the day of Pentecost. The coming of the Spirit anticipates that day when God's plan to 'gather up all things in [Christ], things in heaven and things on earth' (Eph. 1:10) will be fulfilled. So, in the speaking of the languages of every nation under heaven in Acts 2, we have not just the reversal of Babel, but

---

[22] Ibid. 121; emphasis original.
[23] Ibid. 122.
[24] Fee 1994: 897.

the anticipation of the heavenly worship of God seated on the throne and the Lamb by 'a great multitude that no one could count, from every nation, from all tribes and peoples and languages' (Rev. 7:9). This is why Lesslie Newbigin is so helpful in describing the church as on the move towards the ends of the earth and the end of time:

> The Church is the pilgrim people of God. It is on the move – hastening to the ends of the earth to beseech all [people] to be reconciled to God, and hastening to the end of time to meet its Lord who will gather all into one. Therefore the nature of the Church is never to be defined in static terms, but only in terms of that to which it is going. It cannot be understood rightly except in a perspective which is at once missionary and eschatological.[25]

Mission and church are once again inextricably intertwined, with the Spirit being the nexus of all their connection. If we locate this insight into a theology of church planting, we see a kind of authentication for it. *This is what God is doing in the world.* When the great day comes for the whole world to stand before the one seated on the throne and the Lamb of God, we will all be able to recognize what we see because this is what church planting was always about – the pilgrim people of God, not only as the way in which God was bringing his rule and reign to bear in love upon the world, but also as an anticipation of everything good and glorious that the last day will reveal.

The work of the Spirit thus helps us underscore the place of church planting in the purposes of God. The Holy Spirit has a central place in any theology of church planting, because it is he who inspires God's future: a church so infused by the love of God in Christ that it is impelled to live out and share that love with all those in its context and ambit.

Church planting and the kingdom of the Son

We have already considered the paradigmatic frame that Jesus gives to church-planting mission by virtue of his incarnation, and reflected on

---

[25] Newbigin 1953: 25.

what it means for the church to be known as the body of Christ. In this section, we will focus our attention on the relationship between the church and the kingdom of God, and Jesus as the king of this kingdom.

Theologies of church and kingdom in the twentieth century

There was a marked change in thinking on this relationship in the middle of the twentieth century, which is worth tracing. Beforehand, the kingdom of God was thought of as being, for all intents and purposes, identical with the church. Indeed, until the 1930s the kingdom of God was not mentioned in connection with mission at all.[26] The predominant relationship was that between the 'church', on the one hand, where God was, and the 'world', on the other, where he was not. Mission was therefore seen in terms of bringing the 'world' into the 'church'.

> For centuries a static conception of the church had prevailed; the world outside the church was perceived as a hostile power. Reading theological treatises from earlier centuries, one gets the impression that there was only church, no world. Put differently, the church was a world on its own ... The church filled the whole horizon. Those outside were, at most, 'prospects' to be won. Mission was a process of reproducing churches, and once these had been reproduced, all energy was spent on maintenance.[27]

Michael Moynagh helpfully sees this approach as that of a 'church-shaped kingdom'.[28] He quotes J. C. Hoekendijk, who, as we shall see, was to play a pivotal role in the development of church–kingdom thinking in the mid-twentieth century:

> The world has almost ceased to be the *world* and is now conceived of as a sort of ecclesiastical training-ground. The kingdom is either confirmed within the bounds of the Church or else it has become something like an eschatological lightning on the far horizon.[29]

---

[26] Moynagh with Harrold 2012: 100.
[27] Bosch 1997: 376.
[28] Moynagh with Harrold 2012: 100–101.
[29] Hoekendijk 1952: 324, quoted in Moynagh with Harrold 2012: 100.

Moynagh summarizes this when he states that, in this view, 'church and kingdom are virtually collapsed into one'.[30]

Things began to change, however. In the Roman Catholic world, the Second Vatican Council (1962–5) redefined the church by virtue of its relationship to the world. The church was seen as 'missionary by its very nature'. New language is used of the church as 'a kind of sacrament – a sign and instrument, that is, of communion with God and unity among all people'. Significantly, the church was not the same as the kingdom of God, but something that, at its best, pointed to this greater reality. The Council drew links between the life of the church and that of the rest of humanity: 'The joy and hope, the grief and anguish of the people of our time, especially of those who are poor or afflicted in any way, are the joy and hope, the grief and anguish of the followers of Christ as well.' Later Catholic thinking, building on the foundations of the Council, drew out the implications that 'if the church cannot be viewed as the *ground* of mission, it cannot be considered the *goal* of mission either – certainly not the *only* goal. The church should continually be aware of its *provisional* character.'[31]

The church was no longer the aim of mission, but was now seen as a part of it, working towards a greater goal than the church in itself. Johannes Küng wrote:

> The meaning of the Church does not reside in itself, in what it is, but in what it is moving towards. It is the reign of God which the Church hopes for, bears witness to, proclaims ... The Church is devoted entirely to its service.[32]

In the Protestant world, the World Council of Churches (WCC) was formed in 1948. An International Missionary Council already existed, and the two bodies were integrated in 1961. The worlds of church and mission were no longer seen as separate. The WCC adopted the language of sign and sacrament and instrument of the kingdom of God. A key pronouncement was made at the conference held in Uppsala in 1968: 'The

---

[30] Moynagh with Harrold 2012: 100.
[31] Bosch 1997: 377; emphases original.
[32] Küng 1968, 2001: 96, quoted in Bevans and Schroeder 2004: 311.

Church is bold in speaking of itself as the sign of the coming unity of mankind (*sic*).'[33]

In 1969, the theologian Wolfhart Pannenberg published a book of essays entitled *Theology and the Kingdom of God*, in which he drew a distinction between the church and the kingdom, and lamented how previous identifications of church and kingdom had led to 'the distorted notion that the Christian community is concerned with itself and with the piety and salvation of its members' and to 'privatized notions of religious communion'.[34] Jürgen Moltmann was to write in 1977 that 'the church's final word is not "church" but the glory of the Father and the Son in the Spirit of liberty'.[35]

What we have, in both Catholic and Protestant worlds, is the separation of church and kingdom, and an emerging view of the church in service to the agenda of the kingdom of God. David Bosch draws out the potential conflict inherent in this development:

> The new paradigm has led to an abiding tension between two views of the church which appear to be fundamentally irreconcilable. At one end of the spectrum, the church perceives itself to be the sole bearer of a message of salvation on which it has a monopoly; at the other end, the church views itself, at most, as an illustration – in word and deed – of God's involvement with the world. Where one chooses the first model, the church is seen as a partial realization of God's reign on earth, and mission as that activity through which individual converts are transferred from eternal death to life. Where one opts for the alternative perception, the church is, at best, only a pointer to the way God acts in respect of the world, and mission is viewed as a contribution toward the humanization of society – a process in which the church may perhaps be involved in the role of consciousness-raiser.[36]

Matters were to become even more polarized in the 1960s and early 1970s, not least through the influence of Johannes Hoekendijk.

---

[33] Quoted in Bosch 1997: 374.
[34] Pannenberg 1969: 75, 76, quoted in Bevans and Schroeder 2004: 314.
[35] Moltmann 1977: 19, quoted in Bosch 1997: 377.
[36] Bosch 1997: 381.

It should be remembered that this period in history saw extraordinary political events and massive sociocultural change, and against that background the church seemed complacent, bourgeois and irrelevant. Nonetheless, the theological swing was extreme: 'What else can the churches do than recognize and proclaim what God is doing in the world? . . . It is the world that must be allowed to provide the agenda for the churches.'[37]

The enormity of the theological change is set out without nuance or apology in a report that went to the WCC 1968 conference in Uppsala:

> We have lifted up humanization as the goal of mission because we believe that more than others it communicates in our period of history the meaning of the messianic goal. In another time the goal of God's redemptive work might best have been described in terms of [humanity] turning towards God . . . The fundamental question was that of the true God, and the church responding to that question by pointing to him. It was assuming that the purpose of mission was Christianization, bringing [humanity] to God through Christ and his church. Today the fundamental question is much more that of *true* [humanity], and the dominant concern of the missionary congregation must therefore be to point to the humanity in Christ as the goal of mission.[38]

Bosch summarizes by pointing out that 'the distinction between church and world has, for all intents and purposes, been dropped completely'.[39] This led to a disillusionment with the church, seen as powerless to play a part in bringing about change in the world, and even its rejection. Hoekendijk came to regard the church as having 'little more than the character of an "intermezzo" between God and the world'.[40]

This approach, in Moynagh's terminology, is a 'world-shaped kingdom':[41]

---

[37] World Council of Churches 1968: 15, quoted in Bosch 1997: 383.
[38] Ibid. 78, quoted in Bosch 1997: 383.
[39] Bosch 1997: 383.
[40] Ibid. 384.
[41] Moynagh with Harrold 2012: 101–102.

Instead of being narrowed to the church, the kingdom is expanded to the world. Theologians holding this view focus on the kingdom's presence outside the church. God's mission is about the Spirit growing the kingdom in society and in creation. The church's task is to recognize signs of this growth, help other people to see it too and work with it. Conversion and the church are means therefore not of entering the kingdom, but of recognizing the kingdom's silhouette in the world.[42]

Inevitably, there was a reaction to this approach, not least to the marginalization of the church and the conflation of the church and the world as the kingdom of God. Bosch wrote of this being 'a view that leads to absurdity'.[43] Rowan Williams, in another context, wrote of how '[t]he gospels make it harshly clear that belonging with Jesus upsets other kinds of belonging – of family, of status, even of membership of the children of Abraham'.[44]

For all its faults – and for all the benefits that hindsight gives us – this period of reflection on the relationship between church and world and kingdom raises profound questions. On the one hand, there are limitations to the 'church-shaped kingdom' paradigm, which need to be addressed without falling into the shortcomings of aspects of the 'world-shaped kingdom' (to adopt Moynagh's nomenclature). And, on the other hand, it raises the question of what a 'kingdom-shaped church' might look like.

Church and kingdom today

There is much that is good to come out of this theological history, and much that is still 'live' for church planters to have in their minds.

The first thing to draw out is that church and the kingdom of God are not the same thing. This insight leads to a humility for church planters, and to a pertinent theology of mission for the church plant.

Humility in church planting

The humility, first of all. Acknowledging that God's kingdom is not coterminous with the church allows us – and compels us – to recognize

---

[42] Ibid. 102
[43] Bosch 1997: 385.
[44] Williams 2000: 229, quoted in Moynagh with Harrold 2012: 102.

the frailty and failures of our churches. The 'church-shaped kingdom' paradigm made it hard for churches of previous ages to do this, because of the close identification of church and kingdom. Theologies of church as eschatological came to the fore to deal with the manifest absurdities of claiming a kingdom perfection for the church. Our age does not need to do this.

Bosch can write, at the very end of his long book on the history of the church in mission, about how '[t]hroughout most of the church's history its empirical state has been deplorable. This was already true of Jesus' first circle of disciples and has not really changed since.'[45] In contrast to previous ages, '[w]e now recognise that the church is both a theological and a soteriological entity, an inseparable union of the divine and the dusty'.[46]

John Baker points out the missionary dangers of not acknowledging this reality:

> The more we emphasize, in our description of the essential nature of the church, the divine sacramental and sanctifying life within the community, the more legitimate it becomes for the world to demand discernible results ... It is no use composing in-house descriptions of the church, however faithful they may be to scripture and tradition, if within the church they have the fatal effect of giving believers a warm illusion that all is well, and when read by humankind outside the church they seem to have parted company with reality.[47]

We do no-one any favours, and we dishonour God, when we falsify or cover up or pretend to a version of church which bears no relation to the ugliness of some of church life and history. This is true on the large scale, with the horrors of the abuse of children and vulnerable adults by the clergy and the subsequent cover-ups by those in power in the church; and it is also, lamentably, true of the racism and prejudice of the church at institutional and individual levels. It is also true when it comes to some

---

[45] Bosch 1997: 519.
[46] Ibid. 389.
[47] Baker 1986: 155, 158, quoted in Bosch 1997: 376.

of the rhetoric of church planting. Occasionally, church planting is portrayed and trumpeted as the great success story of the church in recent years. Doubtless, there are many instances where church plants have gone spectacularly well, but there are also many instances of failure. We must be careful to be scrupulously honest in our reporting of church planting, and wise and measured in our projections of the future. It is to be applauded that we have been seeing much more objective measures of growth in recent years.

This perspective has another application for church planters in the area of expectations and culture. A cultural narrative is springing up that church planting is succeeding where the rest of the church is failing. There are exceptions to both aspects of that tale. What is particularly germane for church planters is the expectation that everything in a church plant is exemplary and flourishing. Unless we are careful, this will make humble self-criticism all but impossible, and will replicate a culture within our church plants where critique and whistle-blowing are difficult. By distinguishing between the kingdom of God and the church, we allow ourselves the freedom not to expect perfection in our church plants, and to relate to one another as all-too-imperfect church leaders, teams and Christians.

Mission

This discussion prompts us to ask: 'What is the end of mission?' It may seem self-evident, but that may well be a sign to us that we are not thinking in sufficiently kingdom terms. Lesslie Newbigin writes: 'If we answer the question, "Why should I become a Christian?" simply by saying "In order to make others Christians," we are involved in an infinite regress. The question, "To what end?", cannot be simply postponed to the *eschaton*.'[48] Mission cannot be an end in itself. Michael Moynagh puts the point starkly:

> The risk with the 'church-shaped kingdom' is that horizons shrink away from the kingdom to the church . . . Though the view is right to emphasize the world's need of salvation, the danger is that not

---

[48] Newbigin 1953: 148.

enough attention is paid to what the church is for. Mission degenerates into a rather dispiriting attempt to bring more people into the church so that they can bring more people into the church ... Mission fails to connect with God's vision for the whole of creation.[49]

Mention should be made of the massive impact of the various liberation theologies arising in the church since the 1970s. In 1968, a conference of Latin American Catholic bishops met to think through how Vatican II affected their contexts. It led to the sense that 'mission was ... not only ... the proclamation of the gospel but ... a commitment to justice, genuine development and liberation'.[50] Evangelism and the pursuit of justice were seen as complementary aspects of the gospel – the liberation, especially of the poor, from all oppressive structures and powers. Gustavo Gutiérrez, in his seminal *A Theology of Liberation*, adopted the methodology of seeing the church as sacrament, and wrote: '[The church can be understood] only in relation to the reality it announces ... Its existence is not "for itself," but rather "for others." Its center is outside itself; it is in the work of Christ and his Spirit.'[51] Gutiérrez sees this as being an orientation of the church to the realities found in the kingdom of God. The church stands with the poor and the victims of injustice, announces the good news of the kingdom, and denounces the systems and structures that oppress others.

Liberation theology has developed substantially since then. Some polemics had argued that its origins were far too close to Marxist ideology,[52] which discredited it in the eyes of some. It is a good example, though, of how church and mission can find a common vision in service to the kingdom of God. The church is not the centre of things, but finds its essence in the kingdom of God. Similarly, although the world is clearly in view, it is not the world which sets the agenda, but rather the concerns of God's kingdom.

This finds practical application for church planters in the outworking of their theology of the kingdom of God. The *Mission-Shaped Church*

---

[49] Moynagh with Harrold 2012: 101.
[50] Bevans and Schroeder 2004: 312.
[51] Gutiérrez 1973: 260, quoted in Bevans and Schroeder 2004: 313.
[52] Although this is to oversimplify a complex matter. I am grateful to Mike Higton for this observation (in private correspondence).

report[53] was explicit that 'church planting should not ... be church centred'.[54] The object of planting a church should not find its terminus in having planted a church; rather, that should be the beginning, with kingdom mission flourishing in and from that church plant, and other churches being planted from it. Some, though, felt that the report remained far too church-focused. One articulate example was John Hull, the distinguished Methodist theologian. He felt that the report did not adequately distinguish between church and mission in their relation to the kingdom of God:

> The church is not the fulfilment or the flowering of mission. The flowering of mission is the Kingdom; church is merely an agent. Therefore, the mission cannot be attained merely by creating churches . . . Church is [not] the actualization of mission.[55]

Hull felt that the *Mission-Shaped Church* report, in spite of its best intentions, had ended up too focused on the church as an end in itself. 'We looked for a mission-shaped church but what we found was a church-shaped mission.'[56]

So, what might mission-shaped church look like for a church plant? Or, in Moynagh's terminology, what is 'kingdom-shaped church'?

Once again, we come back to the need to hold church and mission together, seeing both as equal partners in the service of something beyond both of them, in this case the kingdom of God.

David Bosch draws the same conclusion from his own analysis of the mid-twentieth-century debates on the relationship of church, mission and kingdom:

> One may . . . perceive the church as an elipse with two foci. In and around the first it acknowledges and enjoys the source of its life; this is where worship and prayer are emphasized. From and through the second focus the church engages and challenges the world. This

---

53 Archbishops' Council of the Church of England 2004.
54 Ibid. 85.
55 Hull 2006: 2.
56 Ibid. 36.

is a forth-going and self-sending focus, where service, mission and evangelism are stressed. Neither focus should be at the expense of the other; rather, they stand in each other's service.[57]

Moynagh draws out why this should be. If the church defines itself solely in terms of mission, then it ends up in the cul-de-sac of having no reason for existence beyond itself: 'The church is not . . . simply a means or agent of the kingdom, which would make the church dispensable once its job was done.'[58] The church has a real essential being for itself as part of God's purposes of the kingdom, as well as an integral role in his kingdom mission to the world. As Newbigin explains:

> The Church is both a means and an end, because it is a foretaste. It is the community of the Holy Spirit who is the earnest of our inheritance. The Church can only witness to that inheritance because her life is a *real* foretaste of it, a real participation in the life of God Himself.[59]

Sometimes, in general discourse, the 'kingdom' is used as a kind of shorthand for what God is doing in the world, which is distinguished from what he is doing in the church. Not infrequently, this last is mentioned in a way that implies the work of God in the church is secondary or inferior to what he is doing in the world. Moynagh's and Newbigin's point is that God is working in both the church and the world, and both are the work of the kingdom.

> This relationship between kingdom and church warns against prioritizing the kingdom at the expense of the church – as if we were to say, 'our call to serve the kingdom is too important to worry much about the sort of church our fresh expression [or church plant] becomes'.[60]

---

[57] Bosch 1997: 385.
[58] Moynagh with Harrold 2012: 103.
[59] Newbigin 1953: 147.
[60] Moynagh with Harrold 2012: 103.

Equally, we cannot identify our church plant as the sole arena, means or ultimate aim of God's kingdom: 'Nor is the church alone the goal of the kingdom, as if the kingdom's presence outside the church did not count.'[61] And so, the church is right to respond to society's rising call for urgent ecological measures or the end of racial injustice, and to hear these calls as the voice of the Holy Spirit.[62] Similarly, church plants may well take the agenda for their kingdom mission from listening closely to the needs and opinions of people in their neighbourhoods and networks.

And so we see that neither church nor mission is an end in itself, but both derive a mutually energizing life by refusing to prioritize one over the other, rather seeing this mutual life in terms of the wider canvas of God's kingdom.

Church planting and the king of the kingdom

What does all this have to do with the Trinity? The Trinity is at the centre of this discussion, because the kingdom is not an abstraction but is rather the term we use to describe the activity of God in the world. I know it is the convenience of shorthand, but it is striking how often we talk about 'the kingdom' and leave out 'of God'. This tendency can be extended so that 'the kingdom' becomes synonymous with further abstractions, such as 'justice' or 'working with the poor' or 'saving the planet', or even 'mission' and 'evangelism'. This obscures the human focus of these activities, but it also severs the connection between God and his kingdom. The 'kingdom of God' is not, as is often remarked, to be understood in geographical terms, as if it was like earthly kingdoms. Equally, it is not to be thought of in abstractions, but rather in dynamic terms, worked out in the realities of human affairs. God's kingdom is the arena, in space and time, of his action. Granted that God is Trinity, this means that we should expect to see each person of the Trinity involved in the world. This will be true of all aspects of mission and the life of God's people, including church planting.

---

61 Ibid.

62 This is not to say that there have not been voices calling for these things from within the church over the years. This point, though, does help us see how part of the work of the Holy Spirit in the church is to bring about a receptivity to what God is doing in the world, to recognize his action and to embrace it. My thanks for this insight go to Mike Higton (in private correspondence), who cites the work of Ben Quash in Quash 2013.

Further than that, God's kingdom is his rule or reign. It is the sphere of the king, an extension of his authority over all the powers ranged against him and the good of his creation. In Scripture, this rule is most clearly demonstrated and ultimately accomplished in the life and ministry of Jesus. It is in him that the long history of Israel, as God's people, is fulfilled. It is in him that the powers of sin, sickness, suffering and Satan are overcome. And, supremely, it is in him that the kingdom of darkness gives way to the kingdom of God through his death on the cross and his conquest of the grave. Put simply, Jesus is the king in the kingdom of God. Accordingly, when we talk about the kingdom of God being that over-arching theme to which both church and mission act as subthemes in church planting, we are describing the kingly action of Jesus Christ in the world, through both church and mission (and church-in-mission). We are back to our conclusion in the previous chapter of this theology section: it is in reference to Christology that both missiology and ecclesiology are to be understood. And, in trinitarian terms, the kingdom of God in church planting finds particular focus around the activity of Jesus, although all three persons of the Trinity can be discerned.

The kingdom of God is fully trinitarian. It is precisely that, the kingdom of *God*, made manifest through the person and ministry of Jesus in the power of the Spirit. Here are a few (of what could have been a great many) examples:

- We see the activity of the Spirit in the conception and birth of Jesus. When the angel Gabriel announces the birth of Jesus to Mary, he uses kingdom language ('the throne of his ancestor David', 'he will reign over the house of Jacob for ever, and of his kingdom there will be no end' [Luke 1:32, 33]). He is the Son – he will be 'called the Son of the Most High', 'he will be called Son of God' (Luke 1:32, 35). His conception will be because 'the Holy Spirit will come upon you, and the power of the Most High will overshadow you' (Luke 1:35).
- At his resurrection, again we see all three persons of the Trinity involved. Peter ascribes the resurrection to both the power of God and the intrinsic vitality of Jesus' nature: 'God raised him up, having freed him from death, because it was impossible for him to be held in its power' (Acts 2:24). Hebrews speaks of 'the power of an

426

indestructible life' in Jesus (Heb. 7:16). Paul writes of how God raised Jesus ('Christ was raised from the dead by the glory of the Father' [Rom. 6:4]) and also how it was through the Holy Spirit that the resurrection happened ('If the Spirit of him who raised Jesus from the dead dwells in you . . .' [Rom. 8:11]).

- In his kingdom ministry, Jesus speaks of the power of God ('If it is by the finger of God that I cast out the demons, then the kingdom of God has come to you' [Luke 11:20]), which is reported in Matthew as: 'If it is by the Spirit of God that I cast out demons . . .' (Matt. 12:28).
- At the cross itself, although it is Jesus who dies, the New Testament gives us glimpses of how the whole Trinity was involved: Paul tells us that 'in Christ God was reconciling the world to himself' (2 Cor. 5:19) and Luke writes of how God purchased the church of God 'with his own blood' (Acts 20:28, margin), while the author of Hebrews states that it was 'through the eternal Spirit' that Christ 'offered himself . . . to God' (Heb. 9:14) and John hints to us that the Spirit was given up at the death of Jesus, poured out into the world (John 19:30, 34).

We should not eisegete these scriptures, seeing the fully developed under-standing of the Trinity of the later church, but, nonetheless, it is clear that the whole Trinity was closely involved in the kingdom life and ministry of Jesus.

Tom Wright lays this out for us helpfully. He writes (in a book on the Gospels, hence his particular focus here):

All four gospels are telling the story of *how God became king* in and through [the] story of Jesus of Nazareth. This central theme is stated in a thoroughly integrated way, again in all four gospels . . . This integrated theme, with the kingdom and cross as the main co-ordinates, flanked by the question of Jesus' divine identity, on the one hand, and the resurrection and Ascension, on the other, is one that most Christians, right across the Western tradition, have failed even to glimpse, let alone preach. The story Matthew, Mark, Luke and John tell is the story of *how God became king – in and through Jesus both in his public career and in his death.*[63]

---

[63] T. Wright 2012: 175; emphases original.

427

Wright is not claiming, of course, that theologically there has ever been a time when God was not sovereign over all his creation. Rather he is focusing on the way in which different theological positions have sometimes struggled to integrate what we might call 'the two halves' of the Gospels. In the first half, Jesus carries all before him, healing the sick, raising the dead, building a community among the world's most marginalized people, demonstrating God's justice and kindness, repudiating the claims of the scribes and Pharisees to be the true guardians of Israel's identity as the people of God, and challenging alternative narratives. And, in the second, the verbs move from being active to passive, and Jesus is betrayed, arrested, tried in a kangaroo court, falsely convicted, beaten, humiliated and crucified, the seeming victim in death of all the powers, secular and spiritual, with which he has been in battle in the first half. It is only in the resurrection that the seemingly irreconcilable contradiction between these two halves is overcome, and Jesus is seen as Lord of all, vindicated by God as the one through whom sins are forgiven, evil is overcome and death is defeated. Wright argues for a more unified understanding of what is happening in the Gospels, that, in both 'halves', Jesus is inaugurating God's kingdom on earth, fulfilling the story of Israel and triumphing over everything that stands in opposition to God and the good of humanity. In typically provocative fashion, Wright encourages us to read the Gospels in this way, as being 'about new reality, the new reality of Jesus and his launching of God's kingdom'.[64]

What of Paul, in whose writings the phrase 'kingdom of God' occurs comparatively rarely? Elsewhere, Wright explains:

> It is not merely a miscellaneous 'theologoumenon', an arm-waving slogan that simply means 'this thing that we followers of the Messiah are on about', 'this new religious experience we all enjoy'. As several of the related passages show, Paul has reflected carefully on what it means that God will reign, that the Messiah is presently reigning, that the Messiah's people will reign in the future and that they can, somehow, start to do so here and now. The phrase appears to denote for Paul a state of affairs of which he sometimes can speak in terms

---

[64] Ibid. 276.

of present reality ... and at other times as a future state ... The important thing, the place where Paul's implicit plot comes to full expression, is that the creator is seen to be ruling the whole creation. This, in other words, is how God is reclaiming his sovereign rule over the world.[65]

In any theology of the kingdom of God, a key question is the extent to which that kingdom is present or yet to come in all its fullness. Jesus and Paul both spoke of the kingdom of God from both perspectives. The consensus of New Testament theology is to declare both to be true, and to hold this tension together in and through the person of Jesus. However we are to understand this, what is clear is that it is in Jesus, especially through his cross and resurrection, that the decisive advance for God's kingdom and the world's future has occurred. Although, in an important sense, God's sovereignty over the world has never wavered, there is a glorious sense that, in Jesus, his good purposes for the world take a decisive shift; this is the heart of the gospel message. It is in the life, death and resurrection of Jesus that God's kingdom is fully and irreversibly inaugurated. God's triumph in Jesus is achieved. The rest of human history is the outworking and application of that victory. This is what we mean when we talk about the kingdom of God. It is fully trinitarian, focused on Jesus, who he is and what he came to do in his earthly life, culminating at the cross.

The life of the kingdom of God continues in the life of church and mission. I will assume here the conclusions of our earlier textual work, showing how the life of the kingdom of God takes shape in the ecclesial missionary life of the early church. 'The Christian mission', writes David Bosch, 'is always Christological and pneumatological, but the New Testament knows of no Christology or pneumatology which is not ecclesial.'[66] God's kingdom continues in the work of the Son and the Holy Spirit, and this ties it inevitably to both mission and church. Church planting, with its privileged place of intersection between ecclesiology and missiology, lives at the centre of the trinitarian life of God as he interacts with his world, focused most clearly in the life and ministry of the Son.

---

[65] N. T. Wright 2013: 480–481.
[66] Bosch 1997: 385.

Church plants and the kingdom of God

What does it mean in practice, then, for church plants to be aware of themselves as expressions of the fully trinitarian life of God, most clearly expressed in the kingdom of his Son? I think this takes us back to the four perspectives we outlined in the previous chapter.

1 Church plants read the Gospels Christologically to set the agenda for kingdom life in both church and mission (and, indeed, for churches-in-mission). The Gospels are our ultimate source in so many ways. Granted their special value for training church plants and their leaders, as we have seen, they repay special study and meditation. Again, given that church plants will, in all likelihood, have many seekers and new Christians in their services, courses and projects, the Gospels will have special value in exposing them to Jesus, as he walked the earth, taught, healed, suffered and died. It is no coincidence that many church plants have sermon series around topics such as 'Conversations with Jesus', or 'Stories Jesus Told', or 'Jesus' Training in Mission', taken from the Gospels. The wider church is recapturing the value of reading the Gospels as a whole, most markedly in the Easter liturgies. Many church plants look at substantial sections of the Gospels, such as the Sermon on the Mount or the miracles in Matthew that follow it, or John 14 – 17, or the passion and resurrection narratives (as do many other churches, of course).

How might church plants take this a stage further? What might church-in-mission training look like for church-plant teams based on Matthew 10 or Luke 10, for instance? How might Matthew's purpose as a kind of training manual for church plants be fully utilized in our day? How could church plants help their people, especially new Christians, get to grips with the Gospels? And how might church-plant leaders make sure they are never far away from the Gospels in their own Bible reading and devotional lives?

2 Church plants take their cue from the whole Christ. We remember Tom Wright's call to read both 'halves' of the Gospels as an unbroken exposition of the kingdom of God, and Moynagh's admonition to see the resurrection and ascension as equally aspects of the incarnation. When we read Acts, we hear preaching and see community living and mission that springs from the enormity of the impact of the resurrection of Jesus. This is all of a piece with the recognition that it is in Jesus that we encounter the king of God's kingdom, and that his life, crucifixion and resurrection were total triumphs over the powers of sin, suffering, evil and death in this world.

Again in this book, we come across a call for faith at the heart of church planting. In the gospel of Jesus, in the life of his church, we find a core message which is a proclamation of triumph and hope. We are in touch with the kind of power in the kingdom of God which has overcome death itself, which tramples Satan under our feet, which is sufficient to see the whole cosmos remade. Too often we are timid or cowed by the powers opposed to God and his kingdom; we listen too carefully to those voices, in and around us, which tell us what cannot be done and what is impossible. When we realize that, in our church plants, we are inhabiting the centre of the Trinity as it touches earth through the cross of Christ, we are given a perspective that means a confidence and joy, and an ability to do things greatly beyond our own resources.

3 Church plants learn from the whole church about the whole Christ. There is so much to learn from God's universal church. We have already considered some aspects of how the Western church might learn from our sisters and brothers in the Majority World.

The church of Christ extends through history, as well as around the globe. Church planters have much to learn from church history. Many are studying church-planting movements in history and around the world. There are excellent books and resources on world mission available.[67] These histories and theologies can inspire and inform us in equal measure, and lend theological depth to our church planting.

4 Church plants put the cross at the centre, both as message and method. The cross is the subject of the church's central act of worship. It is the focal point of its message to the world. We believe that it is the cross through which salvation comes, on which churches are built, and which

---

[67] E.g. Irwin and Sunquist 2012; 2017; Sunquist 2015.

launches mission to the world. For all this, it is surprisingly easy for the church to build its life on something else. This can take theological expression in sophisticated ways, or it can play out in the shallowness of a kind of self-help religion. For church plants, the temptation is, I believe, towards triumphalism or exceptionalism: 'We are different from the rest of the church, special, the chosen ones, the successful ones where others have failed.' For obvious reasons, this does not sit well with the wider church, but it also rings hollow to the world around us.

- For one thing, the world can sometimes seem to put out a cacophony of claims to be successful in dealing with life's problems, most of which are palpably and demonstrably false. The church diminishes itself and its Lord by coming across as yet another charlatan, hawking fraudulent wares and positioning itself as just one among many other competing secular agencies, rather than the creation and agent of the risen Lord of all the earth and its future.
- For another thing, the church's hollow triumphalism bears little relation to the social realities of the end of Christendom and the diminished role of the church in society, at least in the West. The twentieth century was declared by the church in 1900 to be 'the Christian century',[68] but instead was the century of Western history which came to be defined by global, bloody conflict between 'Christian' powers, and ended with catastrophic decline in church attendance and with real question marks over the future existence of the church in the West in the twenty-first century. More than that, the church's reputation has taken massive body blows from the appalling horrors of the sex abuse scandals. Church life in the West appears dull, irrelevant or even toxic. Triumphalism provokes incredulity against such a backcloth.
- Perhaps even more importantly, our world is characterized by horrendous suffering. Global migration has never been so high. Wars, terrorism, famines, pandemics, ecological disaster – all make the future for many uncertain or alarming. And, along with this, mental health issues, identity confusion, financial uncertainty,

---

[68] Sunquist 2015: xvi.

economic disparity and political polarization are generating
enormous anxiety, unrest and distress in Western societies. For the
church to turn up announcing triumph, it can sound like fairy tales
to those listening to such pronouncements, and feel unsympathetic
and unwelcome. As Douglas John Hall writes: 'One thing may be said
with certainty: Whatever survives into the near and distant future
as Christian faith will have to achieve greater depths of wisdom
and courage than most of what has transpired . . . throughout the
fifteen-hundred-odd years of Christendom.'[69] Hall quotes Luther
at the head of his book: '*Theologia crucis* [the theology of the cross]
is not a single chapter in theology, but the key signature for all
Christian theology.'[70]

What this says to us in our church planting is that we have a message
which resonates profoundly with the poor and suffering of the world, of
a God who gave his life in crucifixion, and who continues to be present
in and to the sufferings of his creation. And it also challenges us to reflect
the cross in how we communicate our faith, just as Paul did: having
announced that he has resolved to know nothing 'except Jesus Christ, and
him crucified', he goes on: 'And I came to you in weakness and in fear and
in much trembling' (1 Cor. 2:2–3). It is worth reflecting closely on how
our lives, our speech and witness can best be aligned with the message of
the cross, in solidarity with the poor and weak and suffering, and not
come across as superior or triumphalistic. Triumph, yes, through the
cross, but triumphalist, no.

If church planting is to be truly and biblically trinitarian, it must
embody God's kingdom as it is sharply focused in the life and work of
Jesus. As Paul wrote: '[God] has rescued us from the power of darkness
and transferred us into the kingdom of his beloved Son' (Col. 1:13). It is
in relation to Jesus, and his inaugurated but yet-to-be-consummated
kingdom, that church planting (as the intersection of church and mission)
finds its identity and clarity of purpose.

---

[69] Hall 2003: 10.
[70] Ibid. 1; no reference is given for the Luther quote.

Church planting and the mission of God

A key concept, developed in the global church in the twentieth century, is that of the *missio Dei*, or 'mission of God'. In a 1932 missionary conference, Karl Barth spoke of mission as an activity of God himself. His friend Karl Hartenstein wrote similarly, coining the term *missio Dei* in 1934. Their thinking emerged clearly in the International Missionary Conference in Willingen in 1952. David Bosch summarizes:

> Mission was understood as being derived from the very nature of God. It was thus put in the context of the doctrine of the Trinity, not of ecclesiology or soteriology. The classical doctrine of the *missio Dei* as God the Father sending the Son, and God the Father and the Son sending the Spirit was expanded to include yet another 'movement': Father, Son, and Holy Spirit sending the church into the world. As far as missionary thinking was concerned, this linking with the doctrine of the Trinity constituted an important innovation. Willingen's image of mission was mission as participating in the sending of God. Our mission has no life of its own: only in the hands of the sending God can it truly be called mission, not least since the missionary initiative comes from God alone.[71]

This meant at least two things:

1 Mission ceased to be the property of the church. Theologically, it was no longer the church which sent people on mission. Rather, the church was itself the product of God's 'sending' into the world. 'It is not the church that has a mission of salvation to fulfil in the world; it is the mission of the Son and the Spirit through the Father that includes the church.'[72] As David Bosch concisely expresses it: 'There is church because there is mission, not vice versa.'[73]
2 God's mission was to be seen as something wider than the life and work of the church. The work of the churches in mission could no

---

[71] Bosch 1997: 390.
[72] Moltmann 1977: 64, quoted in Bosch 1997: 390.
[73] Bosch 1997: 390.

longer be understood as identical with the mission and work of God; the *missio Dei* was bigger than that. The task of the church in mission was to align itself as much as possible with God's mission, and to discern what God was doing in the world and to point others to it. It can be seen that, from this perspective, the *missio Dei* is close to what we were discussing in our previous section as the kingdom of God. 'The *missio Dei* is God's activity, which embraces both the church and the world, and in which the church may be privileged to participate.'[74]

This theological understanding of the *missio Dei* was rapidly adopted by other sections of the church. In the Catholic world, it was taken up into the Second Vatican Council; it was also embraced by Eastern Orthodoxy and by many evangelicals. David Bosch, famously, draws the conclusion of this thinking: 'Mission has its origin in the heart of God. God is a fountain of sending love. This is the deepest source of mission. It is impossible to penetrate deeper still; there is mission because God loves people.'[75] Bevans and Schroeder conclude their book with the strong sentence: 'Christians today must recognize at a deep level that first and foremost they share *God's* mission.'[76]

The *missio Dei* opens up for us not just the *origins* of mission (in the overflowing sending love of God) but its *nature* too. What is sent is nothing less than the life of the Trinity; mission becomes an invitation to share in the life of the Father, the Son and the Holy Spirit. As we saw in our last section, there was a period in missionary history, associated with Johannes Hoekendijk, when the concept of the kingdom of God was pulled away from any definite linkage with the church. There has been a similar movement in regard to the *missio Dei*. In acknowledging that God's mission and activity in the world is larger than that of the church, a further step was taken to focus on God's work in the world apart from the church, to the extent that the viability and necessity of the church was called into question. It is by tying the *missio Dei* closely to its trinitarian origins that this danger is avoided. By seeing the communal nature of the

---

[74] Ibid. 391.
[75] Ibid. 392.
[76] Bevans and Schroeder 2004: 397.

life of God as integral to his missionary activity in the world, the communal nature of mission is underscored. Church and mission are once more held together.

Stephen Bevans and Roger Schroeder trace this theological movement. They describe the work of Orthodox theologians who see mission as 'the inclusion of all creation in God's overflowing, superabundant life of communion . . . The church's missionary nature derives from its participation in this overflowing trinitarian life.'[77] In the world of Roman Catholicism, they refer to Karl Rahner's influential 1967 essay on the Trinity, with its famous line: *The "economic" Trinity is the "immanent" Trinity and the "immanent" Trinity is the "economic" Trinity.*[78] He is referring to a longstanding distinction between God's interior (or 'immanent') life, and what we can know of him by his actions in the world (or 'economic' life). Rahner's breakthrough was to question the distinction, arguing that what we experience of God is the same as who he is in his interior trinitarian life, and how we know the immanent life of the Trinity is by way of the economic Trinity, in other words by way of the actions of God the Father, Son and Spirit in salvation history.[79] It is as we experience the life of the Son in the Spirit that we are taken up into the life of the Trinity. All three mainstreams of twentieth-century Christian theology – Protestant, Catholic and Orthodox – emphasize the *missio Dei*, seeing mission as the overflow of God's generous, loving, trinitarian life: we base 'the foundation of mission on the fact that Christians participate in the trinitarian life and mission of God'.[80] Bevans and Schroeder underline its importance:

> Such a trinitarian grounding is in tune with some of the most important theology being done today, and it acknowledges unabashedly the centrality of the trinitarian mystery in Christian life and theology . . . Mission is the basic and most urgent task of the church, not because without human action so many might not

---

[77] Bevans and Schroeder 2004: 288–289, discussing Orthodox Advisory Group to the WCC-CWME 1992.

[78] Rahner 1976: 22 (emphasis original), quoted by Bevans and Schroeder 2004: 291.

[79] Care should be taken, though. Rahner is arguing that the immanent Trinity may be known only by way of the economic Trinity. Very many thanks to Mike Higton for this clarification (in private correspondence).

[80] Bevans and Schroeder 2004: 303.

reach some kind of fulfilment, but because to be Christian is to become part of God's life and God's vision for the world.[81]

To draw this discussion more closely to church planting, it is at once clear that the *missio Dei*, in emphasizing both mission and community as having their origins in the very life of God, highlights the theological strength and practical effectiveness of church planting. If God is sending the church into the world to serve his mission, then it is the church which is at the centre of his missionary purposes. Even while acknowledging that God's mission is wider and deeper than that of the church, church planting retains the vital role of the church in God's mission in the world. It rejects any ultimate understanding of mission that relativizes the role of the church. As we have seen, it is a misstep to prioritize church or mission over each other; both belong equally together in the purposes of God. More than this, though, the *missio Dei*, in highlighting the nature of mission as the overflowing life of the trinitarian God, serves to put community at the heart of God's mission. And where else is community most centrally experienced but in the church? The *missio Dei* puts church into the frame as God's way of inviting his creation to experience the communal nature of his own life. Once again, but with even greater clarity than before, we have the necessity of both church and mission. And once again, rather than seeing these two competing, in some kind of zero-sum theological contest, we have them coming fruitfully together within a wider concept, this time that of the Trinity's sending love.

Concluding thoughts: confidence and creativity

Two thoughts with which to close.

First of all, let us carry on planting churches, doing so with humility but confidence. Yes, mistakes have been made; yes, there is an imperative to do so with mutual respect and with the widest possible collaboration. And there is also a massive missionary mandate of considerable urgency, namely that people in Western societies are not hearing or receiving the

---

[81] Ibid.

gospel or experiencing the life of God's kingdom; and there is a robust biblical and systematic theology which says that the planting of churches was and is near the heart of how God makes himself and his love known in the world.

So, if you are thinking of planting a church, or if you are a gatekeeper or permission-giver for church planting, biblical theology encourages you to make that happen. I hope this book has given you a humble but indomitable confidence for the theological rationale concerning the planting of churches. It has always been the way in the history of God's people on mission in the world. Think back to the calling of Abraham to lead a people of blessing in all the earth; to Moses, and Israel as the covenant people of God in the world. Think of Jesus, fulfilling the purpose of Israel as the means by which God's glory and grace should reach all nations, and making possible a whole new way of being God's people for the sake of all humanity. Think of Paul's phenomenal achievement in planting churches all around the eastern Mediterranean in just over a decade, and his theological vision that lay behind it. Think of how the New Testament envisages what it is to be truly church, and how authentic mission happens. And then bring to bear the wider theological vision of how church and mission may not be ends in themselves, but instead find a mutual fruitful priority in the perspective of the greatness of Jesus and his kingdom and the mission of the triune God. May these reflections inspire you, and give you confidence, and generate models of practice for you and your teams in your church plants.

Second, and lastly, may this confidence give rise to creativity for you in your church planting. There is no one way to plant a church. In fact, there are as many ways as there are church planters. Much is being learned at the moment, but there is also much still to learn. Remember how surprisingly flexible both ecclesiology and missiology are, and draw courage and imagination from Jesus to explore new and innovative ways to express what church-in-mission might look like in your context. David Bosch wrote: 'There is a constant need for mission itself to be transformed.'[82] May you and I be part of that transformation in our day.

---

[82] Bosch 1997: 511.

This does not mean that we throw away the past, nor that we play fast and loose with solid theologies of church and mission. Bosch again:

The thesis of this study is that, in the field of religion, a paradigm shift always means both continuity and change, both faithfulness to the past and boldness to engage the future, both constancy and contingency, both tradition and transformation.[83]

In a beautiful phrase, he speaks of the church as 'God's experimental garden on earth'.[84]

So, in our church planting, may we have confidence, a trust in God that what we are engaged in is central to his missionary purposes for the world. And may we have the kind of confidence that is not afraid to try new things, to be creative and innovative. John Drane has reflected on how our times require a new view of ecclesial maturity in our mission:

The nature of maturity is being redefined as a quality that will enable us to live in the future rather than the past. The old maturity was characterized by nostalgia; the new maturity is marked by innovation. The old maturity valued tradition and rationality; the new maturity centres around imagination and creativity. The old maturity found a home in religious performance; the new maturity prioritizes values and spirituality.[85]

We urgently need new expressions of church planting as we establish and inaugurate churches in the multiple contexts of our cities, towns, villages, regions and networks in our country, in Europe and in the Western world. As we reflect on the gospel, on the Scriptures, on the church, on our traditions, and on the kingdom and the mission of God, may God give us vision and insight to plant a new wave of churches through which we may have the joy and privilege of participating in his mission in the world.

---

[83] Ibid. 366.
[84] Ibid. 11.
[85] Drane 2008: 92–93, quoted in Moynagh with Harrold 2012: 115. Mike Higton (in private correspondence) makes the good point that, alongside creativity and innovation, we must recognize that the Holy Spirit is also at work in more stable structures.

Epilogue: Church planting a city

Previously, whenever I read Paul's letter to the Romans, in my mind's eye I would imagine essentially just one church to which Paul was writing. I suppose I transferred a mental image of my current church experience onto the biblical text. I am not quite sure what I imagined the situation to be; I suppose I had not thought about it very much. I do remember thinking on occasion that the Roman church must have been very small at that stage. I knew it was not exactly St Peter's! And I had some anachronistic thought of the church in the catacombs. Then I would put these things to the back of my mind, and concentrate on the doctrine of the letter.

Romans 16 comes as a shock to that way of thinking. The reality is much more complex and much more exciting than that. There were actually multiple churches meeting in Rome, which must have been connected in a myriad of informal ways. Paul names some of them in this final chapter of greetings. This approach shows us just how fundamental and integral church planting was to the life of the early church.

There is much that we do not know, but an imaginative reading of Romans 16:1–16 provides a suitable epilogue to our examination of a biblical theology of church planting. What follows is a biblical case study, revealing the naturalness with which Paul shows us the life of these early churches. He is not setting out to justify church planting – he assumes it, as does much of the New Testament. In this oblique way, though, he shows us the power of church planting in the origins of the New Testament church, and its potential for our day, not least in reaching cities for Christ.

Here is the passage of greetings in full. Try reading it with the sense to the fore of who these people were. These are among our earliest ancestors in the faith. The more of a feeling we get of them as real people,[1] the more

---

[1] There are a couple of imaginative reconstructions that I think are really helpful: Gooder 2018; Keesmaat and Walsh 2019: ch. 2.

this passage will leap to life for us, and suggest ways in which our church plants may live up to their vitality, courage and faith.

I commend to you our sister Phoebe, a deacon of the church at Cenchreae, so that you may welcome her in the Lord as is fitting for the saints, and help her in whatever she may require from you, for she has been a benefactor of many and of myself as well.

Greet Prisca and Aquila, who work with me in Christ Jesus, and who risked their necks for my life, to whom not only I give thanks, but also all the churches of the Gentiles. Greet also the church in their house. Greet my beloved Epaenetus, who was the first convert in Asia for Christ. Greet Mary, who has worked very hard among you. Greet Andronicus and Junia, my relatives [or 'compatriots'] who were in prison with me; they are prominent among the apostles, and they were in Christ before I was. Greet Ampliatus, my beloved in the Lord. Greet Urbanus, our co-worker in Christ, and my beloved Stachys. Greet Apelles, who is approved in Christ. Greet those who belong to the family of Aristobulus. Greet my relative [or 'compatriot'] Herodion. Greet those in the Lord who belong to the family of Narcissus. Greet those workers in the Lord, Tryphaena and Tryphosa. Greet the beloved Persis, who has worked hard in the Lord. Greet Rufus, chosen in the Lord; and greet his mother – a mother to me also. Greet Asyncritus, Phlegon, Hermes, Patrobas, Hermas, and the brothers and sisters who are with them. Greet Philologus, Julia, Nereus and his sister, and Olympas, and all the saints who are with them. Greet one another with a holy kiss. All the churches of Christ greet you.
(Rom. 16:1–16)

The people

Paul concludes his magnificent letter with greetings to twenty-six people, twenty-four of whom are named. Some readers find this a bit of an anticlimax, and nearly all find it surprising that Paul should have known quite so many people in a city he had never visited. The chapter, though, serves to ground theology in the lived experience of the Roman churches, and Paul's writing to these particular people illuminates for us not only the major theme of the letter as a whole, but also parenthetically the place church planting had in the Christian life of Rome.

Who were these people? Robert Jewett has written a magisterial commentary on Romans.[2] Drawing on the groundbreaking work of Peter Lampe,[3] he is able to hypothesize about where most of the churches Paul writes to in Romans 16 were located in the city, and to draw out the sociological implications of this geography. The main locations are likely to have been in the Trastevere region of Rome and along the Appian Way around the Porta Capena. Both areas were swampy, and it was here that the poorest sections of Roman society lived. Trastevere was a harbour quarter, dominated by work related to the harbour and by brickworks. Porta Capena was an area of heavy traffic in and out of the city, with a large proportion of haulage work. 'The lowest social strata lived in the two regions, Trastevere and Via Appia/Porta Capena, so that it is not difficult to infer the social status of the Christians who dwelled there.'[4] By contrast, there is evidence to suggest that Christians also lived on the Aventine and an area known as Marsfield. Both neighbourhoods were of a higher social status than Trastevere and Porta Capena, the Aventine in particular. 'The address list of the Aventine reads like a "Who's Who" in the Empire.'[5] It was likely here that Prisca and Aquila lived, and where the church that met in their house was located (Rom. 16:5).

It is quite possible that Prisca and Aquila's house was quite large, at any rate sufficiently roomy to accommodate a Christian gathering of up to about forty people. The churches meeting in the poorer locations would not have had such spacious accommodation. The dwellings here were in tenement blocks, or *insulae*, where 90% of Rome's population lived. These blocks would have been four or five storeys high, frequently with shops and businesses at ground level, and with dwellings that became smaller and smaller the higher they went, with rooms of no more than 100 to 115 square metres.[6] They were 'dismal buildings',[7] with

---

2 Jewett 2007.
3 Principally in Lampe 2003.
4 Lampe 2003: 65, quoted in Jewett 2007: 63.
5 Ibid. 59, quoted in Jewett 2007: 63.
6 Jewett 2007: 54, citing the work of Frier 1980.
7 Frier 1980: 5, quoted in Jewett 2007: 54.

shared latrines and washing facilities, and 'a warren of tiny, squalid rooms, most of them not directly lighted and served by long interior corridors'[8]. Whole families lived in these tiny rooms. The risk of fire and plague was high. The population density has been estimated at 300 per acre, which is 'almost two-and-a-half times higher than modern Calcutta and three times higher than Manhattan Island'.[9] Imperial Rome was a hyper-urban environment. The Christians among them 'were located among the poor with possible connections with some high-status individuals'.[10]

There is debate about just how many Christians Paul was writing to in Rome. In Romans 16, he is addressing at least five churches (although Jewett thinks there could be eight to ten[11]). Estimates of their sizes vary from a maximum of forty in Prisca and Aquila's house to much smaller numbers for those meeting in the tenement apartment blocks. Scot McKnight says that 'we can guess there were fewer than two hundred and probably closer to one hundred Jesus followers in Rome at the time of [Paul's] letter'.[12] This in a city of between 800,000 and 1.2 million people.[13] Of course, there may have been many other churches of which Paul was not aware or to whom he chose not to write, so the numbers may be higher. Robert Jewett argues for much higher numbers on the basis that, by AD 64, when Nero was emperor and blamed the Christians for a great fire in Rome, the Roman historian Tacitus writes of a 'huge crowd' or a 'tremendous crowd' of Christians being condemned, and the Christians as a whole being made a scapegoat by Nero:

These details point to a movement that had grown to several thousand adherents by the summer of 64 C.E.. With membership in early congregations ordinarily estimated between twenty and forty persons, there would have been dozens of groups at the time that Paul wrote his letter some seven years before the fateful fire.[14]

---

8 Frier 1980: 15; Jewett 2007: 54.
9 Jewett 2007: 54.
10 McKnight 2019: 8.
11 Jewett 2007: 62.
12 McKnight 2019: 12.
13 Gooder 2018: 240.
14 Jewett 2007: 62.

Whatever the actual numbers, these early Christians would have felt themselves to be a minority, probably misunderstood by the majority, and vulnerable to the brutality and occasionally capricious power of Rome.

What about the more specific status and ethnicity of these early Christians in Romans 16? This is hidden by the custom of translating names into English from their Latinized equivalents. When this obscurity is removed, we find Greek names, Latin names and Jewish names (sometimes Hellenized or Latinized). 'There are seven (probable) Jews named [in Rom. 16] with one's "mother" added . . . The others have Greek names.'[15] Lampe analyses the names in the chapter, and finds (in Jewett's words) that

> two-thirds of the names indicate Greek rather than Latin background, and hence confirm the immigrant status. After a careful and rather conservative estimate, [Lampe] also concludes that of the 13 persons about whom something definite can be said, at least 9 point with great certainty to slave origins. Here, as elsewhere in the early church, the bulk of the members consisted of slaves and former slaves, with the rest coming largely from lower-class handworkers.[16]

Scot McKnight draws out a fascinating and significant implication: 'We can guess that the most common language of the house churches [in Rome] was Greek, the second-most common Aramaic or Hebrew, and the third-most common Latin.'[17]

So, these churches addressed in Romans 16 would have been highly diverse and multi-ethnic, with substantial social and economic disparities between them. And into this situation came the challenge of the relationship between Jewish and Gentile Christians. This was, as we have seen throughout this book, a profound and constant issue for Paul and his church-planting mission among the Gentiles. It was particularly acute in Rome. The earliest beginnings of Christianity in Rome almost certainly sprang out of the Jewish synagogues. There were eleven of these in

---

[15] McKnight 2019: 12.
[16] Jewett 2007: 63, referring to Lampe 2003: 182–183.
[17] McKnight 2019: 12.

first-century Rome, all independent. As Jews found in Jesus their Messiah, there was trouble in the synagogues, agitation and unrest. By AD 41, the emperor Claudius felt it necessary to close the synagogues. So, we can see how astonishingly early Christianity was finding a foothold in Rome; there was enough of an impact in the AD 30s for the Roman emperor to take note. By AD 49 things had got worse, and the Jews (and the Jewish Christians) were expelled from Rome by Claudius. Presumably, the earliest Christian churches in Rome grew out of the synagogues, and so were dominated by Jewish culture and led by leaders from a Jewish background. In 49, these leaders were expelled, along with those Christians from a Jewish background. This had a massive impact on the churches that were left in Rome, because these were predominantly composed of Gentiles, led by Gentile Christians, and were largely non-Torah observant. They were much more closely aligned with Paul's vision of the church than, say, that of the Jerusalem church or the Judaizers with whom Paul argued at the Council of Jerusalem.

In AD 54, however, Claudius died, and the edict expelling Jews from Rome was allowed to lapse. This meant that the Christians from Jewish backgrounds were able to return. When they did so, they found that the Roman house churches were majority Gentiles, and led by Christians from Gentile cultures and backgrounds. It is quite possible that the Jewish Christians returned to the churches they had founded, and now discovered them to be led by Gentiles and without the flavour of Torah with which they had initially been founded. The Jewish Christians, while still substantial in numbers, now found themselves with less influence and power. This is the background to Paul's careful discussion of the relationship between the 'strong' and the 'weak' in Romans 14 and 15. We will find it only just beneath the surface of the greetings in chapter 16.

So, Paul is writing to a network of churches beset with complex and fraught social relations. 'He is preoccupied with fostering a community of welcome and unity precisely because that was not the reality in the house churches of Rome.'[18] We have churches in which people are working out their identity as followers of Jesus the Messiah right at the

---

18 Keesmaat and Walsh 2019: 10.

heart of the Roman Empire, the majority of them from impoverished and slave backgrounds.

For contemporary church planters, multiple bells of recognition are already ringing. Here are acute questions around urban mission (just how do we reach whole cities for Christ?), church planting among the poor and vulnerable and socially marginalized, unity across church-planting networks, and the relationship between emerging and more traditional churches. We may well be amazed at the sheer diversity of these Roman churches and their backgrounds. Here is a challenge to the homogeneity of most of our networks.

The individuals

Let's look at some of the individuals.

Phoebe

When Paul writes to 'commend' Phoebe to the Roman Christians, he is using a term which was 'typically associated with letters of recommendation'.[19] It is highly likely that Phoebe has been tasked by Paul with delivering the letter to the Roman house churches, and maybe even with explaining its contents. To judge from her name, she was a Gentile Christian, maybe a freed slave.[20] She was wealthy and of high social standing. We know that she was 'a deacon of the church at Cenchreae' and 'a benefactor of many', including Paul (16:1–2). We must not read anachronisms of orders of ministry into her being a deacon, but it is clear that Phoebe was in some form of church leadership and ministry that would be recognized in Rome, as well as in Cenchreae, the port to the east of Corinth, where she served. Her being a 'benefactor', and to many, shows her to be a woman of considerable means, someone from whom Paul and others had received substantial financial help and other resources over the years. Robert Jewett writes: 'I infer that Phoebe had agreed to underwrite a project of vital significance to Paul and the letter he is writing.'[21] However, when Paul asks the Roman Christians to 'help [Phoebe] in

---

[19] Jewett 2007: 942.
[20] Ibid. 943.
[21] Ibid. 947.

whatever she may require from you' (16:2), which could mean assistance with a lawsuit or some other business concern, Jewett must be right when he says that the impoverished Roman Christians would not have been much help to such a significant and wealthy woman in her affairs. What Paul must have in mind is the mission to Spain he has just mentioned in Romans (15:24). Phoebe has the delicate task of bringing Paul's letter of unity in God's gospel in Jesus to a group of churches that are anything but unified, and enlisting their help for Paul's current church-planting mission to the far end of the western Mediterranean.

What a task! Paula Gooder brings out very well in her novelistic treatment of Phoebe's mission just how taxing it must have been.[22] We get a sense too, however, that there was something formidable about Phoebe; she was more than capable of this mission, and others would have seen that. We sense just how canny Paul was in spotting potential in people, and how generous in giving away ministry. This was a hugely strategic moment; the Spanish mission we know to have been close to his heart, and his desire to visit Rome a long-standing hope (1:10, 13; 15:23). Yet he was happy to place such a sensitive and significant job in the hands of a businesswoman from the port of Corinth. There is something here for us to see in our leadership. There must have been a temptation for Paul to hang on to this visit for himself (he could easily have justified it in terms of his apostolic authority and how much was riding on it), but he chose to give it to Phoebe, with generous praise, trusting the Roman Christians to receive her and to work with her on the Spanish mission.

Prisca and Aquila, and Epaenetus

It is clear that Paul is close to Prisca and Aquila, a seasoned missionary couple. Acts 18:2 tells us that they had been based in Rome before Paul met them, but they had been expelled as part of Claudius's edict of AD 49. They had worked together in Corinth, both in their shared tentmaking business and in the gospel. It is in Corinth that Priscilla and Aquila take Apollos to one side to explain to him the way of God 'more accurately' (Acts 18:26). This was a critical time in Paul's rethinking of his church-planting strategy, as we have seen previously, and maybe Prisca and

---

22 Gooder 2018.

Aquila were a key influence on him.[23] At any rate, when Paul moves on from Corinth, he takes them with him (Acts 18:18). By the time Paul comes to write 1 Corinthians, he sends greetings from Ephesus, from 'Aquila and Prisca, together with the church in their house' (1 Cor. 16:19). And now, in Romans 16, we read of them again, and 'the church in their house' (16:5). They seem to have been serial church planters, moving around the Mediterranean, partners with Paul in the Gentile mission, often at great cost to themselves. Paul puts them at the head of the list of greetings, expecting them to be honoured by all, and maybe to give credibility to the Gentile mission among the Roman Christians from a Jewish background.

So, who were they, Prisca and Aquila? There may well be an extraordinary story behind their relationship, at which we can only guess. Prisca[24] was probably a freeborn woman from a noble Roman family. Her name is usually listed ahead of her husband's in the New Testament, which almost certainly implies that she came from a higher social background. She had money and status, which explains how they were able to travel so much and so freely, and get Paul out of the trouble to which he alludes in verse 4. It would also explain how they came to live on the Aventine in a house big enough to have a church in it.

Aquila was a Jew from the Roman province of Pontus (Acts 18:2). He was probably a freed slave. Extraordinarily, Aquila may not be his actual name, but might refer to the Roman Acilian family, which may well have been none other than Prisca's aristocratic Roman family of origin. Theirs was 'a mixed marriage between a Roman noblewoman and a Jewish Christian freedman'.[25] Their marriage and ministry were a living demonstration of Galatians 3:28: 'There is no longer Jew or Greek, there is no longer slave or free, there is no longer male and female; for all of you are one in Christ Jesus.'

Epaenetus may well have been converted through Prisca and Aquila's ministry. He was 'the first convert in Asia for Christ' (16:5), and we know that Prisca and Aquila were ministering in Ephesus, the main city of Asia, before Paul's arrival there (Acts 18:26). When Prisca and Aquila returned

---

[23] And was it at this point too that he first met Phoebe (Acts 18:18)?

[24] She is referred to as 'Priscilla' in Acts, which is the diminutive version of her name 'Prisca'.

[25] Jewett 2007: 956.

to Rome, Epaenetus may well have travelled with them, hence how he came to be in their house church in Rome.

I love the relational nature of this missionary network. Paul and Prisca and Aquila; Prisca and Aquila with Epaenetus. These men and women knew one another well, were devoted to one another, took big risks for one another, were prepared to up sticks and repeatedly uproot themselves for the sake of the gospel. And we see in them what church planting looks like. There is individual evangelism (Prisca and Aquila lead Epaenetus to Christ), there is leadership development (Prisca and Aquila with Apollos), and all this is against the background of churches in Corinth, Ephesus and Rome (wherever Prisca and Aquila go).

Our context is very different from theirs (and, thankfully, there have been no edicts expelling Christians from Western democracies, at least not yet), but one cannot help but be struck by a mobility that is dictated by personal relationship in the gospel. Small wonder Prisca and Aquila were serial church planters: their lives consistently demonstrated mission and relationship going hand in hand. They embodied church-in-mission in how they lived their lives.

This is quite a challenge for contemporary church planters, and there are aspects of institutional church leadership which militate against such a mobile and relational modus vivendi.

Mary, Andronicus and Junia

Here we meet long-standing missionaries and church planters, possibly well known to the early church, and fellow movement leaders with Paul. It is testimony to the depth and vitality of the early church that this reference in Romans 16 is all we know of them. I wonder if they might not have been household names to the Pauline church plants.

Mary is the Latinized version of 'Miriam', so, in all likelihood, Mary was Jewish. Jewett gives us the fascinating background that the Jewish community in Rome began mainly as prisoners of war from one of Pompey's campaigns in 62 BC. This implies that Miriam came from a Jewish slave background. Paul tells us that she had 'worked very hard among you' (16:6), which is his way of saying she was intimately involved in mission and church leadership. This shows us the Jewish origins of the original Roman church. It is likely that Paul would have met Miriam during the Jewish exile from Rome, following Claudius's edict, which would date their knowledge of each other to between AD 49 and 54. Since Paul speaks of just how hard Miriam worked in setting up the Roman churches, this may imply long-standing work, and may put her pioneering church planting much earlier than 49.

Andronicus and Junia date even earlier. They were probably a husband-and-wife team. Their names imply that they came from a slave background, and were now freed. As with Mary, they are Jews – Paul calls them 'relatives' or 'compatriots', a phrase he uses in Romans 9:3 to denote fellow Jews – so Paul's working with them may date from the days of the Jewish expulsion from Rome. During this time, they must have worked together, ending up in a shared prison (16:7). They evidently returned to Rome post-AD 54, maybe to the churches that they had originally founded. What is really fascinating is how Paul says that they were converted before he was, which means before AD 34. Paul describes them as apostles; if we take this in the usual sense, this means that Andronicus and Junia were eyewitnesses of Jesus after his resurrection. Maybe, too, they were among those 'visitors from Rome' (Acts 2:10) present in Jerusalem on the day of Pentecost, and perhaps they were members of the 'Hebrew' part of the early church in the initial disputes over the organization of the fledgling church (Acts 6:1–6). At any rate, Paul is at pains to show them great honour. Brendan Byrne wonders if 'the fulsomeness' of his praise 'has the ring of a studied attempt to be gracious, suggesting a more distant relationship with Paul'. Whether or not this was the case, it is clear that they were highly regarded by the Roman churches, and, along with Miriam, 'their venerable status . . . would make them important persons for Paul to win to his cause', not least in bringing unity between the Jewish and Gentile Christians in their joint support of the Spanish mission.[26]

We have a fascinating insight into just how much we do not know about the earliest days of the church after the resurrection and ascension of Jesus. We sense some of the energy of what happened, the explosion of missionary activity, the starting of many churches, and just how un-stoppable and irrepressible it all was; after all, how could a mere imperial edict stop the spread of the gospel! From the New Testament we know the

---

[26] Byrne 1996: 451.

big names, but just how many others would there have been, people about whom we know nothing? I always think of the church in Damascus that Saul went to stamp out in Acts 9, and the church in Syrian Antioch in Acts 11 and 13, which was to have such a missionary impact; who planted these churches? We just do not know. And Peter and Paul chose to stay on the northern side of the Mediterranean, so who founded the hugely significant churches in Alexandria and North Africa? There are countless church-planting heroes about whom we know nothing, and whose identity now only heaven will declare. They may be unknown to us, but it is clear from Romans 16 that the wider church knew many more of them than we are aware of. It is instructive just how careful Paul is to give honour to these people. He is mindful that he will be building on the labours of others who have gone before, some of whom might be sore about recent developments.

Here is much for us to learn as contemporary church planters. We are part of a movement. Andronicus and Junia and Miriam have gone before us, literally and metaphorically. Some of our co-workers we will know; others we will not. By the same token, some of us will be known widely, others of us only to the Lord and those among whom we work in the Lord. In our celebrity age and culture of self-publicity, how doubly important it is to push back against the need to be named and acknowledged. Some of the great names of the church served in churches and contexts of obscurity.

We can be intentional in following Paul's practice, shown here, of giving honour to others. This is particularly so when church plants are building on the work of previous generations. In church revitalization projects, it is all too easy for those who have gone before to feel ignored or even slighted. An important aspect of such scenarios is to honour the past, to acknowledge previous clergy and church leaders and their teams, to thank God for the good they have done, and humbly to acknowledge that the baton is being handed to us to play our part in our time.

A striking feature of Romans 16 is the part that women played in the planting of churches in Rome. Nine of the twenty-six people named or mentioned are women, and four of them (Mary/Miriam in v. 6; Tryphaena and Tryphosa, and Persis in v. 12) are described as those who worked hard in the Lord, which is a Pauline shorthand for church-planting and missionary work. The most striking is Junia, who is included as one of those 'prominent among the apostles' (16:7). Leaving aside the long-running debates about the nature of apostleship, it is clear that the early Christians and Paul hugely valued women in the leadership of these missionary church plants. As John Stott says: 'The prominent place occupied by women in Paul's entourage shows that he was not at all the male chauvinist of popular fantasy.'[27]

This is not a book about women in leadership, and it is written with the hope of unifying the wider church around the apostolic task of planting churches in our day, but, at the risk of alienating those who espouse a complementarian view of the role of women in the church, the place of women in leadership in Romans 16 seems too striking to ignore. We have a female apostle, and women playing a crucial role in the establishing of the earliest churches in Rome; they are among those who have kudos throughout the entire world of the early church; they are named and honoured by Paul for their role in the planting of churches; they are greeted by name as part of a concerted effort from Paul to unify the church around its common missionary task. It seems unavoidable to conclude that women played a full and equal part in the planting of the Roman churches. There may be wider theological and cultural questions to consider, but it would seem to be going against Paul's practice if we attempt to plant churches in our time without women taking a lead just as much as men. I have many friends (traditional Catholics and conservative evangelicals) for whom there are substantial questions, and I respect them. I also have had the privilege of working closely with some truly remarkable women, whose leadership I admire, not least in pioneering church-planting and movement leadership. I think Junia, Miriam and the others would be cheering them on.

The households of Aristobulus and Narcissus

Although the NRSV writes of the 'family of Aristobulus' (16:10) and 'the family of Narcissus' (16:11), what is meant is the Roman household of these men, rather than a modern Western family. 'The household was much broader than the family in modern Western societies, including not

---

[27] Stott 1994: 396.

only immediate relatives but also slaves, freedmen, hired workers, and sometimes tenants and partners in trade or craft.'[28] This would mean the homes of wealthy Roman citizens, which also doubled as places of business. Their families would have lived there, and their slaves, and even some of their business and trade clients.

These two households are particularly interesting. The fact that Paul does not greet either Aristobulus or Narcissus implies that they are dead, and it seems that neither man was a believer, but that there are those in their households who are. So, what we most probably have is two churches, each meeting in the large home of a wealthy household. They are almost certainly the slaves of the household, and their masters not Christians. It must have been a delicate and occasionally risky venture. Paula Gooder captures it brilliantly in her novel *Phoebe*, where the Christians gather in the kitchen of the household of Aristobulus to hear Paul's letter to the Romans read for the first time, after everyone else has gone to bed. Others imagine the churches meeting in the gardens of the bigger houses, or in the larger rooms, if the household was favourable to Christianity.[29]

We do not know for certain who Aristobulus and Narcissus were, but there is a likelihood that they were both powerful men. Aristobulus may well have been the grandson of Herod the Great and the brother of Herod Agrippa, and been educated with the future emperor Claudius.[30] We know that this Aristobulus made a protest in the courts against Caligula erecting his statue in the Jerusalem temple. He died in AD 45 and left his household in his will to his friend the emperor Claudius, who incorporated it into the imperial bureaucracy. So, here we have a church, probably made up of slaves, that was right at the very heart of the Roman administration.[31]

Narcissus is similarly interesting. 'Those of his household' again means that the church was in all probability made up of slaves. We know of a wealthy and influential freedman, called Narcissus, who worked in a powerful position in the administration of the emperor Claudius, being

---

[28] Meeks 2003: 75–76.

[29] Murphy-O'Connor 1996: 149, 169.

[30] The fact that Herodian is mentioned immediately after the household of Aristobulus strengthens the case that Aristobulus was indeed the man with connections to the Herodian family. Herodian may have been a member of the Aristobulus house church. See Jewett 2007: 967.

[31] See Jewett 2007: 966.

in charge of the emperor's correspondence. He amassed an enormous fortune, but was executed in AD 54, when his estates and administrators were confiscated and amalgamated into the emperor's possessions. So, once again, we have a house church that was centrally involved in the imperial bureaucracy. These slaves may well have been in a delicate, even perilous, position, having served a powerful official who fell out of the emperor's favour.

Slavery in the ancient world was different from the transatlantic slave trade.[32] Although all slaves were owned by others, and had no rights or possessions, and although some did menial and dangerous tasks, the slaves in the households of Aristobulus and Narcissus were 'imperial bureaucrats . . . well educated and comfortably maintained, with prospects of advancement and ultimately freedom after years of faithful service'.[33] Of course, all this is relative, and any slave's life was harsh and subject to constant indignity and suffering,[34] but these slaves were highly educated and capable people.[35] Here is the gospel influencing the highest levels of power, but from a position of weakness and great vulnerability.

When we think of our contemporary church-planting situation, these two household churches give us inspiration for how church plants can have an impact on workplaces, even quite hostile working environments. There is great scope for church planting among shops and businesses, not least because for many working in these sectors, the majority of their daily hours are spent in their work environments.

The 'brothers and sisters', and the 'saints'

Our last snapshot of these early church plants in Rome is of the two churches of verses 14 and 15: 'Greet Asyncritus, Phlegon, Hermes, Patrobas, Hermas, and the brothers and sisters with them. Greet Philologus, Julia, Nereus and his sister, and Olympas, and all the saints who are with them' (Rom. 16:14–15).

---

[32] See Rupprecht 1993: 881.

[33] Jewett 2007: 968.

[34] See Keesmaat and Walsh 2019 for an effective fictionalizing of some of the possible stories in Rom. 16 to helpful and powerful effect.

[35] Robert Harris's trilogy of the life of the orator Cicero, *Imperium* (Hutchinson, 2006), *Lustrum* (Hutchinson, 2009) and *Dictator* (Hutchinson, 2015), gives us an imagined example of such a slave in the fictional narrator, Tiro.

Robert Jewett helps us see that we have two house churches here.

1 There is the first list of five names, and then 'the brothers and sisters who are with them'. Jewett analyses the names, and discovers a mixed group, mainly Gentile, some slaves, some freedmen, some lower-class Greeks. The reference to the 'brothers and sisters with them' implies that the named five are the leaders, and the others are the members of this church. Maybe they even called themselves 'the brothers and sisters'.

2 The second group is similar, with five leaders, and those who are 'with them', implying the existence of a house church here. They may have called themselves 'the saints', 'indicating a possible affinity with the moral legacy of conservative Jewish Christianity'.[36]

It seems that Paul had not met the members of these churches, but he had heard of them, hence his not knowing the name of Nereus's sister. This church appears to have different origins and organizing principles from the other churches, which we will consider shortly.

One thing to notice here (and throughout the list of names in the entire chapter) is the prevalence of family connections among these early church plants. In the Greek of verse 15, Philologus is linked by an 'and' to Julia, which probably means that they were married. We have seen the same with Andronicus and Junia in verse 7, and Prisca and Aquila in verse 3. Many have suggested that Nereus and his unnamed sister are the children of Philologus and Julia, although we cannot know for sure. It does make us note, though, that Tryphaena and Tryphosa in verse 12 were almost certainly sisters, maybe even identical twin sisters,[37] and the reference to Rufus and his mother in verse 13 is also intriguing, as he may well have been the son of Simon of Cyrene.[38] The point is that close family relationships play a significant part in the make-up of these Roman church plants.

When it comes to the leadership of some of our contemporary church plants, there is a significant shift to leadership by married couples. The

---

[36] Jewett 2007: 971.
[37] Ibid. 968.
[38] See Mark 15:21, which speaks of 'Simon of Cyrene, the father of Alexander and Rufus'.

historic denominations struggle with this, still having a model of church leadership which is focused on one person. What we have in Romans 16 is evidence of a leadership and a partnership in ministry that is frequently shared not just by more than one person, but by couples, sisters or even families. There are potential issues in this model, as power can be unhelpfully accrued to families, but it is illuminating to think how pioneering church planting seems frequently to have been led by these family groups. What might contemporary church planting look like if we encouraged families to think of themselves as church-planting teams?

Thinking of the individuals

What a fascinating and revealing list of names this is, as Paul asks these individuals to be greeted in Romans 16! We meet familiar names, such as Prisca and Aquila, and discover fascinating histories that go right back to the time of Jesus (with Rufus and his mother, and with Andronicus and Junia) and to how churches were first planted in Rome (as with Mary).[39] We meet slaves and free people, some from positions of affluence and influence, some right at the heart of the machinery of empire, some right on the margins,[40] some who were probably hauliers, working shifts and nights, and others who were like modern-day civil servants. We come across those from Jewish backgrounds, planted into Jewish-Christian churches, and others in Gentile churches; we can feel the tensions behind the two groups, and wonder how they reacted when they first heard Romans 14 and 15 read out. In all probability, these were the leaders of the house churches that Paul knew of in Rome;[41] there may of course have been many other house churches, unknown to the apostle, and there would certainly have been other Christians that made up the congregations and networks of these churches. It is stirring to think of our ancestors in the faith as real people of flesh and blood, living their lives and living out their faith right at the heart of the Roman Empire.

---

[39] 'It is worth thinking that Andronicus and Junia, along with Prisca and Aquila as well as Mary, were the primary gospel agents in the city of Rome' (McKnight 2019: 13).
[40] It is shocking to find the name Phlegon, which used to be a dog's name in ancient Rome (Jewett 2007: 970).
[41] N. T. Wright 2002: 761.

What we … have is a small, vulnerable church, needing to know and trust one another across various boundaries; a church many of whose members were not native to Rome, living most likely in immigrant communities within particular areas; a church in which men and women alike took leadership roles; a church where families and households formed the basis of worshipping communities. There is something both attractive and frightening about this picture: enormous potential, huge risks, a community both lively and vulnerable. This is the community that will now be the first to hear one of the greatest letters in the history of the world.[42]

What is striking is how each individual matters. Paul evidently knew many of these people and had history with them, but many he did not, even though he had heard of them. Each, though, was an individual to him, with a role to play in God's global purposes, certainly in Rome and maybe in the ever-expanding mission. Some, one suspects, would have been deeply suspicious of Paul, and disagreed profoundly with him over his analysis of what he called the 'weak' and the 'strong'. Yet each is greeted by him with honour and with love.

The application to our church plants is obvious but critical. Not least when it comes to cooperation between church-planting networks, the individuality of each leader, each church plant, each ministry, is sacrosanct. The sense of the holiness of God in his work across a city is palpable in these greetings. The urgency and weightiness of sharing in God's mission is right to the fore: this is why Paul is writing the letter. Nonetheless, the affection for these leaders, the sense of the church as a whole, is what we meet on the surface. Yet again, both mission and church are inseparable – church planting is about churches on the move in the mission of God. We see and feel the deep purposes of God, his longing for the western Mediterranean to hear the gospel, and we also see and feel his love for the churches in Rome and the imperative of unity together in this mission. The mandate for church planting can be felt in the history of the churches planted in Rome and in the relationships between them and the continuing apostolic mission. The road map for missionary church planting

---

[42] Ibid. 763.

is clear, but so are the relational challenges that are part and parcel of this great work. It is the same in our churches today. May we share Paul's burden for global church planting, and his affection for the churches and commitment to their unity.

The churches

Lastly, let's think of what we may learn from the church plants themselves from Romans 16. Some of this is imaginative, but, regardless of the accuracy of the details of interpretation, we come away with an inspiring picture of what it might look like when the Holy Spirit inspires the planting of churches across an entire city.

The diversity of the church plants

As well as the mixed ethnic and social backgrounds of the churches, and their differing religious backgrounds (Jewish and Gentile), we can discern at least three different types of church plants.

First of all, there is 'the church' in the house of Prisca and Aquila (16:5). This is the only plant which Paul calls a church. It seems to have been the classic shape of an apostolic church plant. The church would have met in the houses of its more affluent members. Often, these people would have taken on the leadership of the churches meeting in their homes. Estimates of the size of these house churches vary, but they would probably have been around forty to fifty people.[43]

Then there are what we might call 'household churches'. These had the same model as the house church, but they met in households where the householder was not a Christian (as with the households of Aristobulus and Narcissus). To be a follower of Jesus in such a household was risky; most of the members of these household churches would have been slaves, and so totally at the mercy of those over them.

Both these types of church plants had patrons or the equivalent. The Priscas and Aquilas, or the Aristobuluses and Narcissuses, would likely have provided the food required for the Lord's Suppers and *agape* meals,

---

[43] Jewett 2007: 958–959. We read of these house churches here at Rom. 16:5, and also in 1 Cor. 16:19; Col. 4:15; Phlm. 2.

around which the early Christians based their common life and worship. The other category of church plants, however, had no such patron, and each member would contribute what he or she could to provide the food and drink for their shared meals and life together.[44] These churches did not have households in which to meet, so they probably met in the *insulae*, or tenement blocks, in which the slaves who made up the churches lived. Jewett calls these 'tenement churches'.[45] He postulates that these churches would have met in the ground-floor shops of their apartment blocks, which were a common feature of the tenement structure, or that they managed to merge adjoining apartments on the same floor of the blocks in which they lived.[46]

The first two categories of church plants would have operated on different leadership models from the third. The household churches would have met under the auspices of the patron, most probably the person or people who owned or rented the property. Wayne Meeks explains the implications:

> The head of the household, by normal expectations of the society, would exercise some authority over the group and would have some legal responsibility for it. The structure of the [household] was hierarchical, and contemporary political and moral thought regarded the structure of superior and inferior roles as basic to the well-being of the whole society.[47]

And so these church plants would have been multigenerational, have had both slaves and free people in them, and reflected the cosmopolitan make-up of the Roman households in which they met. Their leadership would also have reflected that of the social structures of the household, albeit exercised with the love and kindness the gospel brought.

By contrast, the tenement churches ('the brothers and sisters' and 'the saints') did not have any patronage. They each have five leaders listed, but with no indication that any one individual is overall leader. The fact that

---

[44] Ibid. 971.
[45] Ibid. 65.
[46] Ibid.
[47] Meeks 2003: 76, quoted in Jewett 2007: 65.

one of these tenement church plants may have called itself 'the brothers and sisters' implies a much flatter, more egalitarian leadership structure. Probably, the Christians in both tenement church plants felt that the Holy Spirit had anointed their five designated leaders. 'The leadership pattern appears to be collective rather than hierarchical.'[48] If the house and household churches reflected a more upper- and middle-class milieu and assumptions, these tenement churches 'consisted entirely of the urban underclass, primarily slaves and poor freedmen/women'.[49]

If the church plants were markedly different from each other in make-up and how they operated, maybe this came out of their origins. How a church is planted will have a powerful influence on the nature and practices of its common life and mission. We can only speculate on how the tenement churches came to be founded, but it seems highly likely that the gospel spread along social lines both in the imperial bureaucracy and in the tenement blocks themselves. By contrast, maybe the house and household churches were founded as the patron was converted and opened his or her home to the work of the gospel.

Paul seems to use distinctive, even stylized, vocabulary in how he addresses some of those being greeted in Romans 16. We may discern four different categories.

1 There are the 'apostles', Andronicus and Junia, with reference made, along with them, to the other apostles, including Paul himself (16:7).
2 Then there are those who 'work hard in the Lord'. This is how Paul addresses Mary (16:6), Urbanus (16:9), Tryphaena and Tryphosa (16:12) and Persis (16:12). This was, for Paul, almost a technical word for church planting. It is used by him twenty-three times as a verb and eighteen times as a noun,[50] and implies involvement in the Pauline mission and churches.
3 Next there are those whom Paul singles out for expressions of affection. There is 'my beloved Epaenetus' (16:5), Ampliatus 'my beloved in the Lord' (16:8), 'my beloved Stachys' (16:9) and 'the beloved Persis' (16:12).

---

[48] Jewett 2007: 65.
[49] Ibid. 66.
[50] See Jewett 2007: 961.

4 And finally there are those who are simply named, with no further description.

Some of these differences in appellation can be explained by whether or not Paul had met them before, but I wonder if there might not be something else going on here. Could there be hints as to how leadership training and deployment went on in the world of church planting in the earliest years after the resurrection of Jesus?

Categories 1 and 2 could go together. These are the pioneer planters. Both groups are apostolic in the sense that they are establishing church plants. Those specifically designated 'apostles' carried a greater authority from having seen the risen Lord, but both alike had the sense of being called and anointed to establish churches. This is what Paul means when he talks about people 'working hard in the Lord'. Category 4 comprises those who lead these church plants, such as the tenement churches of 'the brothers and sisters' and 'the saints', and others, such as Apelles (16:10), Herodion (16:11) and Rufus and his mother (16:13).

Category 3 (the beloveds) are particularly interesting. Often they are named as going along with an apostolic or church-planting (working-hard-in-the-Lord) person or team. So, Prisca and Aquila have 'my beloved Epaenetus' with them (16:5); 'my beloved Stachys' is with 'Urbanus, our co-worker in Christ' (16:9); and 'the beloved Persis' is with 'those workers in the Lord, Tryphaena and Tryphosa' (16:12). It is not universally and tightly true, but can we not discern a pattern in which church planters have someone alongside them, a person whom Paul is at pains to describe as 'beloved'? Might we be glimpsing here Paul's special heart to raise up the next generation of church planters? Are these the people he wants to encourage into church planting themselves? Persis actually spans both groups; she is both 'beloved' and 'has worked hard in the Lord' (16:12). Perhaps she is just crossing over and these are her first forays into pioneering church planting.

We cannot know for sure, but the repetitive nature of Paul's vocabulary and rhetoric suggests that something is going on, even though we do not have full access to its meaning. It would fit with our knowledge from elsewhere of how Paul was constantly raising up co-workers, those who in time could share in church planting with him.

This reinforces what we have seen throughout this study in terms of methodology: how church planters are *both* apostolic *and* focused on spotting and training up those who could in turn carry on and develop the momentum of church planting. Paul's vocabulary and his practice help us in this.

- Church planting is covered by two terms: 'apostolic' and 'hard work'. Church planters have a sense of having been commissioned by the Lord to do something new, to be pioneering, and they prove by experience that it is tough and demanding work.
- The training and nurturing of up-and-coming church planters is encapsulated in the word 'beloved'. These people may be apprentices, trainees, interns, ordinands, licensed workers and so on. But before any of that, they are 'beloved'. It is love which is the necessary soil and ambience in which potential planters can grow, develop and come to flourish.

What we see then, in Romans 16, is a diversity of stories, make-ups and ways of operating in these church plants. As we have discovered, some are of Jewish background, some Gentile; some slave, some free; some rich, some poor. Beyond that, they are different sorts of churches; some are house churches, some are household churches, some are tenement churches. Some operated within the social structures of the day, while others must have seemed a profound challenge to the powers and hierarchies of the time. And they will nearly all have had different founders, exerting a variety of apostolic and church-planting influences to shape their origins and developments.

What we come away with is a sense of the independent life of these church plants. They had the freedom, under God, to be founded and to develop in their own unique and authentic ways. No one pathway was the same as another. We are bewildered by the number of leaders, the variety of ways in which they operated, the distinct social patterns they lived within. It is striking that Paul does nothing to regularize or homogenize these varieties. Instead he honours each of them.

Just as we ended our review of the more systematic theology of church planting with a plea for innovation and imagination, so this section too makes us yearn for ecclesial and missional freedom and creativity in our contemporary church planting. Just as in Paul's day, so in ours: there is no one way to plant a church, and every church plant will be unique. Doubtless, there will be commonalities and shared principles; but each church plant must also have an inner freedom to find its own way. The more we can celebrate variety, delight in multiple leaders and rejoice in startlingly different ways of doing things, the more we will find whole cities and contexts being changed by the gospel. It is interesting to me that innovation and creativity are coming to the fore in the minds of many church planters and pioneers.[51] Could this freedom, imagination, experimentation be the Spirit's way of generating fresh church planting in multiple contexts in our time?

The unity of the church plants

If diversity is a major theme of the greetings in Romans 16, then unity is no less so. This has been the burden of chapters 13–15 in Romans, and it is grounded in these concluding personal communications.

We note Paul's relational priority. The language of family comes through again and again:

- Phoebe is 'our sister' (16:1);
- Andronicus and Junia (16:7) and Herodion (16:11) are Paul's 'relatives' or kin (probably through their shared Jewish roots);
- the language of 'households' has a familiar angle to it, hence NRSV's translation 'family' in 16:10 and 11;
- Rufus's mother was 'a mother to me also' (16:13);
- and there are 'the brothers and sisters' of one of the tenement churches (16:14).

All this goes beyond formality and tokenism, especially when we consider the Roman background, where the honour of one's family could be paramount. Paul's family of the church is of a very different order from the customary Roman model; there would not have seemed much honour in being a slave family to many in imperial Rome's power structures.

---

[51] E.g. Drane 2008; Male 2016; Moynagh 2017; Selvaratnam 2022; Winfield Bevins and Mark Dunwoody, *Missional Formation Coaching* (forthcoming).

Even more emphatic is the language of the church plants' relation to Jesus:

- Phoebe is to be welcomed 'in the Lord' (16:2);
- Prisca and Aquila worked with Paul 'in Christ Jesus' (16:3);
- Epaenetus was 'the first convert in Asia for Christ' (16:5), just as Andronicus and Junia were 'in Christ before I was' (16:7);
- Ampliatus is 'my beloved in the Lord' (16:8);
- Urbanus is 'our co-worker in Christ' (16:9);
- Apelles is 'approved in Christ' (16:10);
- those from the Narcissus household who are 'in the Lord' are to be greeted (16:11);
- Tryphaena and Tryphosa are 'workers in the Lord' (16:12);
- Persis has 'worked hard in the Lord' (16:12);
- Rufus was 'chosen in the Lord' (16:13).

The repetition is remarkable and striking. Scot McKnight comments:

> Every person in each of the house churches in Rome had formed an identity apart from Christ and then in Christ, and the emphasis on 'in Christ' or 'in the Lord' in the names is as emphatic as it is often unobserved. Life for the Christians in Rome is life in Christ, which they share with others throughout the Pauline mission churches. What they share now is sibling relationship.[52]

This 'sibling relationship' is all the more significant as there are real tensions within and between the house churches. Paul relentlessly reminds his readers of their primary shared identity in Christ as the basis of all their relationships. He is also insistent that the work of church planting is 'in the Lord'. To be 'in Christ' is to be committed to one another, and also to the mission.

Church planting can be controversial; it can be disruptive and lead to tensions. Paul would remind us to base all our discussions and disagreements firmly within the context of our shared life as Christians; we

---

[52] McKnight 2019: 13–14.

relate to one another first and foremost because of Jesus and in and through Jesus. I wonder, too, if Paul would not insist that church planting is something 'in the Lord' for us, just as it was for him; it is something that Jesus is doing. It is not something that can be written off, at least not without theological violence. Once more, we see that church planting holds church and mission together; both alike are 'in Christ', and it is by reference to Jesus that we find that both ecclesiology and missiology sit fruitfully together.

And, lastly, Paul appeals expressly to that which builds up a common life. At the conclusion of the roll call of the church plants he knows in Rome, Paul's climactic point is: 'Greet one another with a holy kiss' (16:16). This must have been part of the liturgical life of the earliest churches. Paul draws it out, and enjoins all the churches to deal with one another as churches just as they would do with the individuals within each church plant. Unity, he is telling them, is as crucial between churches as it is between Christians. That is why he concludes with reference to 'all the churches of Christ' which 'greet you' (16:16).

There is one other interesting footnote to this last point. Paul refers to 'the whole church' (16:23), a phrase he also uses in 1 Corinthians 14:23. Jerome Murphy-O'Connor picks up on this: 'If believers met only as a single group the adjective "whole" is unnecessary. Its use necessarily implies the existence of sub-groups, "the church in the house of X".'[53] Here is a fascinating glimpse into Paul's ecclesiology on the ground, and how he expected these Roman church plants to relate to one another. It is clear that the church plants met independently of one another; they had separate lives in Christ, their own leaders and cultures. Nonetheless, there was such a thing as 'the whole church'. It is this to which the church plants belonged. It is interesting that Paul conspicuously does not refer to the 'church in Rome' in his greetings, in the way in which he would normally start a letter. In fact, he refers only to the church plant in Prisca and Aquila's house as a 'church'. For him, it is obvious that this house church is not equivalent to the 'whole church' in Rome. If we compare it with 1 Corinthians, we read at the beginning of that letter of 'the church of God that is in Corinth' (1 Cor. 1:2), which presumably is 'the whole

---

[53] Murphy-O'Connor 1996: 149.

church' (1 Cor. 14:23) in a way that the 'household of Stephanos' (1 Cor. 16:15) is not.

Unity, then, is as essential to church planting, in the eyes of the apostle, as diversity in mission. Across all the tensions of the 'whole church' in Rome, he models a 'sibling relationship', reminds the Christians of how Jesus has relativized all other identities between them, and urges them to live out their liturgy in their inter-church as well as inner-church relating. This unity, though, is not a kind of self-justification for church *apart from* mission; it is, of course, a highly practical appeal for a unity *in* mission. Paul is hoping that *all* the church plants, the 'weak' and the 'strong', will get behind him for the Spanish mission (15:24). Yet again, we see unity and outreach, church and mission, ecclesiology and missiology held tightly and inextricably together. In neither theology nor practice will Paul allow us to think of church apart from mission, nor mission apart from church. For him, the two are unavoidably two sides of the same coin.

Mission and unity must go together, and our perspective of the love and glory of Jesus Christ makes that both obvious and electrifying. It is only in mission that the church is fully and authentically itself, and it is only in the context of church that mission really makes sense and is effective. It is in church planting that these two things hold together, and it is in the perspective of the glory of Jesus that church planting can become all it is meant to be in the purposes of God. Whatever the future of the practice of church planting in our Western contexts in the coming years, may it grow and develop with faith, imagination, effectiveness and, above all, love.

Bibliography

Abbott, W. M. (ed.) (1966), *The Documents of Vatican II*, New York: Guild Press, America Press, Association Press.

Addison, S. (2015), *Pioneering Movements: Leadership That Multiplies Disciples and Churches*, Downers Grove: InterVarsity Press.

Allen, R. (1962), *The Spontaneous Expansion of the Church*, Grand Rapids: Eerdmans.

____ (2011), *Missionary Methods: St Paul's or Ours?: A Study of the Church in the Four Provinces*, Mansfield Centre: Martino.

Anglican Consultative Council (2022), 'The Five Marks of Mission', <https://www.anglicancommunion.org/mission/marks-of-mission.aspx>, and Bonds of Affection-1984 ACC-6, 49; Mission in a Broken World-1990 ACC-8, 101.

Archbishops' Council of the Church of England (2004), *Mission-Shaped Church: Church Planting and Fresh Expressions of Church in a Changing Context*, London: Church House.

Baker, J. (1986), 'A Summary and Synthesis', in G. Limouris (ed.), *Church-Kingdom World: The Church as Mystery and Prophetic Sign*, Faith and Order Paper no. 130, Geneva: World Council of Churches, 152–162.

Banks, R. J. (2020), *Paul's Idea of Community: Spirit and Culture in Early House Churches*, Grand Rapids: Baker Academic.

Barrett, C. K. (1971), *The First Epistle to the Corinthians*, BNTC, London: A & C Black.

____ (1978), *The Gospel According to St John: An Introduction with Commentary and Notes on the Greek Text*, London: SPCK.

Bartholomew, C., and M. Goheen (2014), *The Drama of Scripture: Finding our Place in the Biblical Story*, London: SPCK.

Bauckham, R. (2003), *Bible and Mission: Christian Witness in a Postmodern World*, Grand Rapids: Baker Academic.

Bauer, W. (1979), *A Greek-English Lexicon of the New Testament and Other Early Christian Literature*, tr. and ed. W. F. Arndt and F. W. Gingrich, rev. F. W. Danker, Chicago and London: University of Chicago Press.

Beasley-Murray, G. R. (1993), 'Baptism', in G. F. Hawthorne, R. P. Martin and D. G. Reid (eds.), *Dictionary of Paul and His Letters*, Leicester: Inter-Varsity Press; Downers Grove: InterVarsity Press, 60–66.

Beitzel, B. J. (2013), *The SPCK Bible Atlas: The Events, People and Places of the Bible from Genesis to Revelation*, London: SPCK.

Bevans, S. B. (1998), 'God Inside Out: Toward a Missionary Theology of the Holy Spirit', *International Bulletin of Missionary Research* 22.3: 102–105.

―――― (2002), *Models of Contextual Theology*, Maryknoll: Orbis.

Bevans, S. B., and R. P. Schroeder (2004), *Constants in Context: A Theology of Mission for Today*, Maryknoll: Orbis.

Bevins, W. (2017), *Church Planting Revolution: A Handbook for Explorers, Planters and Their Teams*, Franklin: Seedbed.

Blackburn, B. L. (1992), 'Miracles and Miracle Stories', in J. B. Green and S. McKnight (eds.), *Dictionary of Jesus and the Gospels*, Downers Grove: InterVarsity Press, 549–559.

Blocher, H. (2016), 'Let Us Make Mankind: Church Planting and the Story of Mankind', in S. Timmis (ed.), *Multiplying Churches: Exploring God's Mission Strategy*, Fearn: Christian Focus, 43–61.

Bock, D. L. (1992), 'Luke, Gospel of', in J. B. Green and S. McKnight (eds.), *Dictionary of Jesus and the Gospels*, Downers Grove: InterVarsity Press, 495–510.

Boer, H. (1961), *Pentecost and Missions*, Nashville: Lutterworth.

Bosch, D. J. (1997), *Transforming Mission: Paradigm Shifts in Theology of Mission*, Maryknoll: Orbis.

Bridges, J. (2006), *The Discipline of Grace: God's Role and Our Role in the Pursuit of Holiness*, Colorado Springs: NavPress.

Brown, R. E. (1970), *The Gospel According to John XIII–XXI*, The Anchor Bible, New Haven: Yale University Press.

Byrne, B. (1996), *Romans*, Sacra Pagina, Collegeville: Liturgical Press.

―――― (2004), *Lifting the Burden: Reading Matthew's Gospel in the Church Today*, Collegeville: Liturgical Press.

_____ (2008), *A Costly Freedom: A Theological Reading of Mark's Gospel*, Collegeville: Liturgical Press.

_____ (2014), *Life Abounding: A Reading of John's Gospel*, Collegeville: Liturgical Press.

_____ (2015), *The Hospitality of God: A Reading of Luke's Gospel*, Collegeville: Liturgical Press.

Cadbury, H. J. (1920–33), 'The Summaries in Acts', in J. Foakes-Jackson and K. Lake (eds.), *The Beginnings of Christianity, Part 1: The Acts of the Apostles*, London: Macmillan, 392–402.

Calvin, J. (1960), *Institutes of the Christian Religion*, ed. J. T. McNeill, LCC 21, London: SCM Press.

Caragounis, C. C. (1992), 'Kingdom of God / Kingdom of Heaven', in J. B. Green and S. McKnight (eds.), *Dictionary of Jesus and the Gospels*, Downers Grove: InterVarsity Press, 417–430.

Childs, B. S. (1974), *Exodus*, London: SCM Press.

Cole, N. (2011), *Journeys to Significance: Charting a Leadership Course from the Life of Paul*, San Francisco: Jossey-Bass.

Collins, H. (2020), *Reordering Theological Reflection: Starting with Scripture*, London: SCM Press.

Corbett S., and B. Fikkert (2014), *When Helping Hurts: How to Alleviate Poverty without Hurting the Poor . . . and Yourself*, Chicago: Moody.

Croft, S. (ed.) (2006), *The Future of the Parish System: Shaping the Church of England for the 21st Century*, London: Church House.

_____ (2008), 'Formation for Ministry in a Mixed Economy Church: The Impact of Fresh Expressions of Church on Patterns of Training', in L. Nelstrop and M. Percy (eds.), *Evaluating Fresh Expressions: Explorations in Emerging Church*, Norwich: Canterbury, 40–54.

_____ (ed.) (2009a), *Mission-Shaped Questions: Defining Issues for Today's Church*, London: Church House.

_____ (2009b), 'Fresh Expressions in a Mixed Economy Church: A Perspective', in S. Croft (ed.), *Mission-Shaped Questions: Defining Issues for Today's Church*, London: Church House, 1–15.

Crouch, A. (2008), *Culture Making: Recovering Our Creative Calling*, Downers Grove: InterVarsity Press.

Davies, W. D., and D. C. Allison (1988), *The Gospel According to Saint Matthew: Volume 1*, ICC, London: T&T Clark.

_____ (1997), *The Gospel According to Saint Matthew: Volume 3*, ICC, London: T&T Clark.

Davison A., and A. Milbank (2010), *For the Parish: A Critique of Fresh Expressions*, London: SCM Press.

Dearborn T. (1988), *Beyond Duty: A Passion for Christ, A Heart for Mission*, Monrovia: MARC.

Dockery, D. S. (1992), 'Baptism', in J. B. Green and S. McKnight (eds.), *Dictionary of Jesus and the Gospels*, Downers Grove: InterVarsity Press, 55–58.

Dodd, C. H. (1968), *The Interpretation of the Fourth Gospel*, Cambridge: Cambridge University Press.

Drane, J. (2008), 'What Does Maturity in the Emerging Church Look Like?', in S. Croft (ed.), *Mission-Shaped Questions: Defining Issues for Today's Church*, London: Church House, 90–101.

Dulles, A. (1974), *Models of the Church*, New York: Image.

Dumbrell, W. J. (1998), 'The Prospect of Unconditionality in the Sinaitic Covenant', in A. Gileadi (ed.), *Israel's Apostasy and Restoration: Essays in Honour of Roland K. Harrison*, Grand Rapids: Baker, 141–155.

Dunn, J. D. G. (2003), *Christianity in the Making: Jesus Remembered*, Grand Rapids: Eerdmans.

Ellis, E. E. (1993), 'Paul and His Coworkers', in G. F. Hawthorne, R. P. Martin and D. G. Reid (eds.), *Dictionary of Paul and His Letters*, Leicester: Inter-Varsity Press; Downers Grove: InterVarsity Press, 183–189.

Eswine, Z. (2015), *The Imperfect Pastor: Discovering Joy in Our Limitations through a Daily Apprenticeship with Jesus*, Wheaton: Crossway.

Fee, G. D. (1987), *The First Epistle to the Corinthians*, NICNT, Grand Rapids: Eerdmans.

_____ (1988), *1 and 2 Timothy and Titus*, NIBC, Peabody: Hendrickson.

_____ (1994), *God's Empowering Presence: The Holy Spirit in the Letters of Paul*, Peabody: Hendrickson.

Fee, G. D., and D. Stuart (2002), *How to Read the Bible Book by Book: A Guided Tour*, Grand Rapids: Zondervan.

Flett, J. G. (2016), *Apostolicity: The Ecumenical Question in World Christian Perspective*, Downers Grove: IVP Academic.

Flew, R. N. (1943), *Jesus and His Church: A Study in the Idea of the Ecclesia in the New Testament*, 2nd edn, Peterborough: Epworth.

France, R. T. (1990), *Divine Government: God's Kingship in the Gospel of Mark*, London: SPCK.

_____ (2007), *The Gospel of Matthew*, NICNT, Grand Rapids: Eerdmans.

Frier, B. W. (1980), *Landlords and Tenants in Imperial Rome*, Guildford: Princeton University Press.

Frost, M., and A. Hirsch (2009), *ReJesus: A Wild Messiah for a Missional Church*, Grand Rapids: Baker.

Gaventa, B. R. (1986), 'To Speak the Word with All Boldness, Acts 4.23–31', *Faith and Mission* 3: 76–82.

_____ (2003), *The Acts of the Apostles*, ANTC, Nashville: Abingdon.

General Synod of the Church of England (2018), GS 2098, *Report from the Evangelism Task Group and the Evangelism and Discipleship Team*, London: Church House.

_____ (2019), GS 2142, *A Mission-Shaped Church and Fresh Expressions 15 Years On*, London: Church House.

Gladding, S. (2010), *The Story of God, the Story of Us: Getting Lost and Found in the Bible*, Downers Grove: InterVarsity Press.

Gooder, P. (2018), *Phoebe: A Story*, London: Hodder & Stoughton.

Goodhew, D. (ed.) (2012), *Church Growth in Britain: 1980 to the Present*, Farnham: Ashgate.

Green, J. B. (1997), *The Gospel of Luke*, NICNT, Grand Rapids: Eerdmans.

Green, M. (1993), *Evangelism through the Local Church*, London: Hodder & Stoughton.

_____ (2009), *Thirty Years That Changed the World: The Book of Acts for Today*, Grand Rapids: Eerdmans.

Grudem, W. (1994), *Systematic Theology: An Introduction to Biblical Doctrine*, Grand Rapids: Zondervan.

Gunton, C. E. (2002), *The Christian Faith: An Introduction to Christian Faith*, Oxford: Blackwell.

Guthrie, D. (1990), *The Pastoral Epistles: An Introduction and Commentary*, TNTC, Downers Grove: InterVarsity Press.

Gutiérrez, G. (1973), *A Theology of Liberation: History, Politics, and Salvation*, Maryknoll: Orbis.

Haacker, K. (1988), 'Urchristliche Mission und kulturelle Identität: Beobachtungen zu Strategie und Homiletik des Apostels Paulus', *Theologische Beiträge* 19: 61–72.

Hall, D. J. (2003), *The Cross in Our Context: Jesus and the Suffering of the World*, Minneapolis: Fortress.

Hanson, A. T. (1961), *The Pioneer Ministry*, London: SCM Press.

Hardy, D. W. (2001), *Finding the Church: The Dynamic Truth of Anglicanism*, London: SCM Press.

Hirsch, A. (2006), *The Forgotten Ways: Reactivating the Missional Church*, Grand Rapids: Brazos.

Hoekendijk, J. C. (1952), 'The Church in Missionary Thinking', *International Review of Missions* 41.3: 324–336.

_____ (1967), *Kirche und Volk in der deutschen Missionswissenschaft*, Munich: Chr. Kaiser.

Hooker, M. (1991), *The Gospel According to St Mark*, BNTC, London: A & C Black.

House of Bishops (2018), 'Church Planting and the Mission of the Church', <https://www.churchofengland.org/sites/default/files/2018-06/CHURCH%20PLANTING%20AND%20THE%20MISSION%20OF%20THE%20CHURCH%20-%20June%202018_0.pdf>.

Hull, J. M. (2006), *Mission-Shaped Church: A Theological Response*, London: SCM Press.

Hunsberger, G. R. (1996), 'The Newbigin Gauntlet: Developing a Domestic Missiology for North America', in G. R. Hunsberger and C. Van Elder (eds.), *The Church between Gospel and Culture: The Emerging Mission in North America*, Grand Rapids: Eerdmans, 3–25.

Irwin, D. T., and S. W. Sunquist (2001), *History of the World Christian Movement, Volume 1: Earliest Christianity to 1453*, Maryknoll: Orbis.

_____ (2012), *History of the World Christian Movement, Volume 2: Modern Christianity from 1453–1800*, Maryknoll: Orbis.

Jenkins, P. (2011), *The Next Christendom: The Coming of Global Christianity*, Oxford: Oxford University Press.

Jeremias, J. (1958), *Jesus' Promise to the Nations*, tr. S. H. Hook, London: SCM Press.

_____ (1972), *The Parables of Jesus*, tr. S. H. Hook, New York: Scribner's.

Jewett, R. (2007), *Romans: A Commentary*, Hermenia, Minneapolis: Fortress.

Johnson, L. T. (1992), *The Acts of the Apostles*, Sacra Pagina, Collegeville: Liturgical Press.

Jolley A., and I. Jones (2016), 'Formation for Mission in Urban Britain: The Birmingham Mission Apprentice Scheme', *Journal of Adult Theological Education* 13.1: 33–47.

Käsemann, E. (1974), 'Zur ekklesiologischen Verwendung der Stichworte "Sakrament" und "Zeichen", in R. Groscurth (ed.), *Wandernde Horizonte auf dem Weg zu kirchlicher Einheit*, Frankfurt: Otto Lembeck, 119–136.

Keesmaat S. C., and B. Walsh (2019), *Romans Disarmed: Resisting Empire / Demanding Justice*, Grand Rapids: Brazos Press.

Keller, T. (2010), 'Leadership and Church Size Dynamics: How Strategy Changes with Growth', New York: Redeemer City to City, <https://seniorpastorcentral.com/wp-content/uploads/2016/11/Tim-Keller-Size-Dynamics.pdf>.

_____ (2012), *Center Church: Doing Balanced, Gospel-Centered Ministry in Your City*, Grand Rapids: Zondervan.

Kirk, J. A. (1999), *What Is Mission? Theological Explorations*, London: Darton, Longman & Todd.

Knight III, G. W. (1992), *The Pastoral Epistles: A Commentary on the Greek Text*, NIGTC, Grand Rapids: Eerdmans.

Knox, J. (1964), 'Romans 15:14–33 and Paul's Conception of His Apostolic Mission', *JBL* 83.1: 1–11.

Köstenberger, A. J., and P. J. O'Brien (2001), *Salvation to the Ends of the Earth: A Biblical Theology of Mission*, Downers Grove: InterVarsity Press.

Kraus, C. N. (1978), *The Authentic Witness: Credibility and Authority*, Grand Rapids: Eerdmans.

Küng, H. (1968, 2001), *The Church*, London: Burns & Oates.

_____ (1984), 'Was meint Paradigmenwechsel?', in Hans Küng and David Tracy (eds.), *Theologie – wohin? Auf dem Weg zu einem neuen Paradigma*, Zürich and Cologne: Benzinger, 19–26; ET 1989, *Paradigm Change in Theology: A Symposium for the Future*, New York: Crossroad.

_____ (1987), *Theologie im Aufbruch: Eine ökumenische Grundlegung*, Munich: Piper.

Lampe, P. (2003), *From Paul to Valentinus: Christians at Rome in the First Two Centuries*, tr. M. Steinhauser, Minneapolis: Fortress.

Legrand, L. (1990), *Unity and Plurality: Mission in the Bible*, tr. R. R. Barr, Maryknoll: Orbis.

Leithart, P. J. (2018), *The Gospel of Matthew through New Eyes, Volume 2: Jesus as Israel*, West Monroe: Athanasius Press.

Limouris, G. (ed.) (1986), *Church-Kingdom World: The Church as Mystery and Prophetic Sign*, Faith and Order Paper no. 130, Geneva: World Council of Churches.

Lings, G. (2012), 'A History of Fresh Expressions and Church Planting in the Church of England', in D. Goodhew (ed.), *Church Growth in Britain 1980 to the Present*, Farnham: Ashgate, 161–178.

Lings, G., and S. Murray (2012), *Church Planting in the UK since 2000: Reviewing the First Decade*, Cambridge: Grove Booklets.

Longenecker, R. N. (1981), *The Acts of the Apostles: Introduction, Text and Exposition*, in F. Gabelein (ed.), *The Expositor's Bible Commentary*, vol. 9, Grand Rapids: Zondervan.

Luz, U. (2001), *Matthew 8–20: A Commentary*, Hermeneia, Minneapolis: Fortress.

McGavran, D. A. (1990), *Understanding Church Growth*, Grand Rapids: Eerdmans.

McKnight, S. (2019), *Reading Romans Backwards: A Gospel in Search of Peace in the Midst of the Empire*, London: SCM Press.

Male, D. (2013), *Pioneering Leadership: Disturbing the Status Quo?*, Cambridge: Grove Booklets.

_____ (2016), *How to Pioneer (Even If You Haven't a Clue)*, London: Church House.

Maloney, F. J. (1998), *The Gospel of John*, Sacra Pagina, Collegeville: Liturgical Press.

Marcus, J. (2000), *Mark 1–8*, Anchor Yale Bible, New Haven: Yale University Press.

_____ (2009), *Mark 8–16*, Anchor Yale Bible, New Haven: Yale University Press.

Marshall, I. H. (1992), 'Church', in J. B. Green and S. McKnight (eds.), *Dictionary of Jesus and the Gospels*, Downers Grove: InterVarsity Press, 122–125.

_____ (1993), 'Lord's Supper', in G. F. Hawthorne, R. P. Martin and D. G. Reid (eds.), *Dictionary of Paul and His Letters*, Leicester: Inter-Varsity Press; Downers Grove: InterVarsity Press, 569–575.

Martin, R. P. (1993), 'Worship', in G. F. Hawthorne, R. P. Martin and D. G. Reid (eds.), *Dictionary of Paul and His Letters*, Leicester: Inter-Varsity Press; Downers Grove: InterVarsity Press, 982–991.

Meeks, W. (2003), *The First Urban Christians: The Social World of the Apostle Paul*, 2nd edn, New Haven: Yale University Press.

Meyer, B. F. (2002), *The Aims of Jesus*, Eugene: Pickwick.

Miller, C. J. (1986), *Outgrowing the Ingrown Church*, Grand Rapids: Zondervan.

Minear, P. S. (1960), *Images of the Church in the New Testament*, Louisville: Westminster John Knox.

Moltmann, J. (1977), *The Church in the Power of the Holy Spirit: A Contribution to Messianic Ecclesiology*, tr. M. Kohl, London: SCM Press.

Moo, D. (1996), *The Epistle to the Romans*, NICNT, Grand Rapids: Eerdmans.

Motyer, A. (2005), *The Message of Exodus: The Days of Our Pilgrimage*, Downers Grove: InterVarsity Press.

Moynagh, M. (2017), *Church in Life: Innovation, Mission and Ecclesiology*, London: SCM Press.

Moynagh, M., with P. Harrold (2012), *Church for Every Context: An Introduction to Theology and Practice*, London: SCM Press.

Murphy-O'Connor, J. (1996), *Paul: A Critical Life*, Oxford: Oxford University Press.

Murray, S. (1998), *Church Planting: Laying Foundations*, Carlisle: Paternoster.

_____ (2010), *Planting Churches in the 21st Century: A Guide for Those Who Want Fresh Perspectives and New Ideas for Creating Congregations*, Independence: Herald Press.

Musasiwa, R. (2007), 'Contextualization', in J. Corrie (ed.), *Dictionary of Mission Theology: Evangelical Foundations*, Downers Grove: InterVarsity Press, 66–71.

Myers, C. (2015), *Binding the Strong Man: A Political Reading of Mark's Story of Jesus*, Maryknoll: Orbis.

Neill, S. (1959), *Creative Tension*, New York: Morrison & Gibb.

Newbigin, L. (1953), *The Household of God: Lectures on the Nature of the Church*, London: SCM Press.

_____ (1989), *The Gospel in a Pluralist Society*, London: SPCK.

O'Brien, P. T. (1993), 'Church', in G. F. Hawthorne, R. P. Martin and D. G. Reid (eds.), *Dictionary of Paul and His Letters*, Leicester: Inter-Varsity Press; Downers Grove: InterVarsity Press, 123–131.

O'Donovan, O. (2007), 'What Kind of Community Is the Church? The Richard Hooker Lectures 2005', *Ecclesiology* 3.2: 171–193.

Orthodox Advisory Group to the WCC-CWME (1992), 'Go Forth in Peace: Orthodox Perspectives on Mission', in James A. Scherer and Stephen B. Bevans (eds.), *New Directions in Mission and Evangelization 1: Basic Statements 1974–1991*, Maryknoll: Orbis, 203–231.

Ott, C., S. J. Strauss, with T. C. Tennent (2010), *Encountering Theology of Mission: Biblical Foundations, Historical Developments, and Contemporary Issues*, Grand Rapids: Baker Academic.

Ott, C., and G. Wilson (2011), *Global Church Planting: Biblical Principles and Best Practices for Multiplication*, Grand Rapids: Baker Academic.

Paas, S. (2016), *Church Planting in the Secular West: Learning from the European Experience*, Grand Rapids: Eerdmans.

_____ (2019), *Pilgrims and Priests: Christian Mission in a Post-Christian Society*, London: SCM Press.

Pannenberg, W. (1969), 'The Kingdom of God and the Church', in *Theology and the Kingdom of God*, Louisville: Westminster.

Parkinson, I. (2020), *Understanding Christian Leadership*, London: SCM Press.

Payne, J. D. (2009), *Discovering Church Planting: An Introduction to the Whats, Whys, and Hows of Global Church Planting*, Downers Grove: InterVarsity Press.

Pelikan, J. (2005), *Acts*, Brazos Theological Commentary on the Bible, Grand Rapids: Brazos Press.

Pesch, R. (1986), *Die Apostelgeschichte (1–12)*, Zürich: Benziger.

Piper, J. (2003), *Let the Nations Be Glad: The Supremacy of God in Missions*, Downers Grove: InterVarsity Press.

Quash, B. (2013), *Found Theology: History, Imagination and the Holy Spirit*, London: Bloomsbury.

Rahner, K. (1976), *The Trinity*, Freiburg: Herder & Herder.

Ramsay, W. (1900), *St Paul the Traveller and the Roman City*, London: Hodder.

Richardson, A. (1958), *Introduction to the Theology of the New Testament*, London: SCM Press.

Richter P., and L. J. Francis (1998), *Gone But Not Forgotten: Church Leaving and Returning*, London: Darton, Longman & Todd.

Ridley, C. R. (1988), *How to Select Church Planters: A Self-Study Manual for Recruiting, Screening, Interviewing and Evaluating Qualified Church Planters*, Pasadena: Fuller Evangelistic Association.

Roberts, V. (2009), *God's Big Picture: A Bible Overview*, Downers Grove: InterVarsity Press.

Rowe, C. K. (2010), *World Upside Down: Reading Acts in the Graeco-Roman Age*, Oxford: Oxford University Press.

Rupprecht, A. A. (1993), 'Slave, Slavery', in G. F. Hawthorne, R. P. Martin and D. G. Reid (eds.), *Dictionary of Paul and His Letters*, Leicester: Inter-Varsity Press; Downers Grove: InterVarsity Press, 881–883.

Rütti, L. (1972), *Zur Theologie der Mission: Kritische Analysen und neue Orientierungen*, Munich: Chr. Kaiser.

Sarna, N. M. (1996), *Exploring Exodus: The Origins of Biblical Israel*, New York: Schocken.

Schnabel, E. J. (2008), *Paul the Missionary: Realities, Strategies and Methods*, Downers Grove: InterVarsity Press.

Schreiner, P. (2019), *Matthew, Disciple and Scribe: The First Gospel and Its Portrait of Jesus*, Grand Rapids: Baker Academic.

Schweizer, E. (1975), *The Good News According to Matthew*, Louisville: John Knox.

Selvaratnam, C. (2022), *The Craft of Church Planting: Exploring the Lost Wisdom of Apprenticeship*, London: SCM Press.

Senior, D., and C. Stuhlmueller (1983), *The Biblical Foundations for Mission*, London: SCM Press.

Shenk, D. W., and E. R. Stutzman (1998), *Creating Communities of the Kingdom: New Testament Models of Church Planting*, Independence: Herald Press.

Smail, T. (1988), *The Giving Gift: The Holy Spirit in Person*, London: Darton, Longman & Todd.

Stein, R. H. (1992), 'Last Supper', in J. B. Green and S. McKnight (eds.), *Dictionary of Jesus and the Gospels*, Downers Grove: InterVarsity Press, 440–450.

Stetzer, E. (2006), *Planting Missional Churches: Planting a Church That's Biblically Sound and Reaching People in Culture*, Nashville: B&H Academic.

Stibbe, M. W. G. (1996), *John*, Sheffield: Sheffield Academic Press.

Stott, J. R. W. (1975), *Christian Mission in the Modern World*, Saint Neots: Falcon.

_____ (1979), *The Message of Ephesians: God's New Society*, BST, Downers Grove, InterVarsity Press.

_____ (1990), *The Message of Acts: To the Ends of the Earth*, BST, Downers Grove: InterVarsity Press.

_____ (1992), *The Contemporary Christian: An Urgent Plea for Double Listening*, Downers Grove: InterVarsity Press.

_____ (1994), *The Message of Romans: God's Good News for the World*, BST, Downers Grove: InterVarsity Press.

_____ (1996), *The Message of 1 Timothy and Titus: The Life of the Local Church*, BST, Downers Grove: InterVarsity Press.

Sunquist, S. W. (2015), *The Unexpected Christian Century: The Reversal and Transformation of Global Christianity, 1900–2000*, Grand Rapids: Baker Academic.

Tennent, T. C. (2010), *Invitation to World Missions: A Trinitarian Missiology for the Twenty-First Century*, Grand Rapids: Kregel.

Thiselton, A. C. (2000), *The First Epistle to the Corinthians*, NIGTC, Grand Rapids: Eerdmans.

Thompson, J., with S. Pattison and R. Thompson (2008), *Theological Reflection*, London: SCM Press.

Thompson, J. A. (1995), 'Church Planter Competencies as Perceived by Church Planters and Assessment Center Leaders: A Protestant North American Study', PhD dissertation, Trinity Evangelical Divinity School.

_____ (2007), *Church Leader Inventory: A PCA Qualitative and Quantitative Study*, Lawrenceville: Presbyterian Church of America.

Thompson, M. M. (2015), *John: A Commentary*, NTL, Louisville: Westminster John Knox.

Thorpe, R. (2021), *Resource Churches: A Story of Church Planting and Revitalisation Across the Nation*, London: Gregory Centre for Church Multiplication.

Tidball, D. J. (1993), 'Social Setting of Mission Churches', in G. F. Hawthorne, R. P. Martin and D. G. Reid (eds.), *Dictionary of Paul and His Letters*, Leicester: Inter-Varsity Press; Downers Grove: InterVarsity Press, 883–892.

Tilby, A. (2008), 'What Questions Does Catholic Ecclesiology Pose for Contemporary Mission and Fresh Expressions?', in S. Croft (ed.), *Mission-Shaped Questions: Defining Issues for Today's Church*, London: Church House, 78–89.

Timmis, S. (ed.) (2016), *Multiplying Churches: Exploring God's Mission Strategy*, Fearn: Christian Focus.

Tomlin, G. (2014), *The Widening Circle: Priesthood as God's Way of Blessing the World*, London: SPCK.

Turner, M. M. B. (1992), 'Holy Spirit', in J. B. Green and S. McKnight (eds.), *Dictionary of Jesus and the Gospels*, Downers Grove: InterVarsity Press, 341–351.

Valentine, J. H. (2020), '"Theology That Actually Works": An Analysis of Those Aspects of Theological Formation Which Best Equip Church Planters for Their Work', unpublished dissertation, Asbury Seminary.

Van de Poll, E., and J. Appleton (eds.) (2015), *Church Planting in Europe: Connecting to Society, Learning from Experience*, Eugene: Wipf & Stock.

Van den Berg, J. (1956), *Constrained by Jesus' Love: An Inquiry into the Motives of the Missionary*, Reading: Koch.

Wagner, M. (2000), 'Signs and Wonders', in A. S. Moreau (ed.), *Evangelical Dictionary of World Missions*, Grand Rapids: Baker, 875–876.

Walls, A. F. (1996), 'The Gospel as Prisoner and Liberator of Culture', in *The Missionary Movement in Christian History: Studies in the Transmission of Faith*, Maryknoll: Orbis, 3–15.

Waltke, B. K. (2001), *Genesis: A Commentary*, Grand Rapids: Zondervan.

Walton, S. (2008), 'Primitive Communism in Acts? Does Acts Present the Community of Goods (2:44–45; 4:32–35) as Mistaken?', *EvQ* 80: 99–111.

Ward, P. (2017), *Introducing Practical Theology: Mission, Ministry and the Life of the Church*, Grand Rapids: Baker Academic.

Wells, S. (2015), *A Nazareth Manifesto: Being with God*, Chichester: Wiley Blackwell.

Williams, R. (1995), 'Doing the Works of God', in R. Williams, *A Ray of Darkness: Sermons and Reflections*, Cambridge: Cowley, 221–232.

–––––– (2000), *On Christian Theology*, Oxford: Blackwell.

–––––– (2008–9), 'The "Strength" of the Church Is Never Anything Other Than the Strength of the Presence of the Risen Jesus', *Mixed Economy: The Journal of Fresh Expressions*, Autumn/Winter: 12–13.

–––––– (2014), *Meeting God in Mark*, London: SPCK.

–––––– (2020), *The Way of St Benedict*, London: Bloomsbury.

Williamson, P. R. (2003), 'Covenant', in T. D. Alexander and D. W. Baker (eds.), *Dictionary of the Old Testament: Pentateuch*, Downers Grove: InterVarsity Press, 139–155.

Wimber, J., and K. Springer (1985), *Power Evangelism*, London: Hodder & Stoughton.

Winter, R. D., and B. A. Koch (2002), 'Finishing the Task: The Unreached Peoples Challenge', *International Journal of Frontier Missions* 19.4: 15–25.

Witherington III, B. (1995), *John's Wisdom: A Commentary on the Fourth Gospel*, Cambridge: Lutterworth.

–––––– (1998), *The Acts of the Apostles: A Socio-Rhetorical Commentary*, Grand Rapids: Eerdmans.

World Council of Churches (1968), *Church for Others, and the Church for the World: A Quest for Structures for Missionary Congregations*, Geneva: World Council of Churches.

Wright, N. T. (1992), *The New Testament and the People of God*, London: SPCK.

_____ (1996), *Jesus and the Victory of God*, London: SPCK.

_____ (2000), *The Challenge of Jesus*, London: SPCK.

_____ (2002), 'The Letter to the Romans', in L. E. Keck (ed.), *The New Interpreter's Bible*, vol. 10, Nashville: Abingdon, 393–770.

_____ (2003), *The Resurrection of the Son of God*, London: SPCK.

_____ (2013), *Paul and the Faithfulness of God*, Parts I and II, London: SPCK.

Wright, T. (2002), *John for Everyone, Part 2: Chapters 11–21*, London: SPCK.

_____ (2003a), *Paul for Everyone: 1 Corinthians*, London: SPCK.

_____ (2003b), *Paul for Everyone: 2 Corinthians*, London: SPCK.

_____ (2003c), *Paul for Everyone: The Pastoral Letters 1 and 2 Timothy, and Titus*, London: SPCK.

_____ (2006), *Paul for Everyone: Romans Part 1: Chapters 1–8*, London: SPCK.

_____ (2007), *Paul for Everyone: Romans Part 2: Chapters 9–16*, London: SPCK.

_____ (2012), *How God Became King: Getting to the Heart of the Gospels*, London: SPCK.

_____ (2018), *Paul: A Biography*, London: SPCK.

Yamauchi, E. (1992), 'Synagogue', in J. B. Green and S. McKnight (eds.), *Dictionary of Jesus and the Gospels*, Downers Grove: InterVarsity Press, 781–784.

Ziesler, J. (1989), *Paul's Letter to the Romans*, TPI New Testament Commentaries, London: SCM Press.

Zizioulas, J. (1985), *Being as Communion: Studies in Personhood and the Church*, Crestwood: St Vladimir's Press.

Index of Scripture references